Animal Faith and Spiritual Life

Century Philosophy Sourcebooks

JUSTUS BUCHLER *and* STERLING P. LAMPRECHT, *Editors*

George Santayana

Animal Faith and Spiritual Life

PREVIOUSLY UNPUBLISHED AND UNCOLLECTED
WRITINGS BY GEORGE SANTAYANA WITH
CRITICAL ESSAYS ON HIS THOUGHT

Edited by

John Lachs

College of William and Mary

Appleton-Century-Crofts / New York

Division of Meredith Publishing Company

667-1

Library of Congress Card Number: 67-20665

PRINTED IN THE UNITED STATES OF AMERICA

E 77600

PREFACE

In preparing and publishing this volume I have incurred more debts than I can acknowledge. Yet the help I have received from some persons was so generous and effective that it should not go without my public thanks.

I am grateful, first of all, to Mr. Daniel Cory for his kindness in permitting me to print the manuscripts and to reprint those previously published articles which come under his jurisdiction as literary executor of Santayana. I should like to express my thanks also to the authors and publishers of the critical articles included in the book: without their generous cooperation this volume would have been immeasurably weaker.

Mr. Corliss Lamont and Mr. Clifford W. Barrett should be commended for their foresight and beneficence in donating important collections of Santayana manuscripts to the Columbia University and the University of Virginia libraries. Had Professor Justus Buchler and Mr. Jack K. Burton not taken an active and informed interest in stimulating renewed discussion of the work of Santayana, however, the manuscripts here printed would still be in the dark vaults of these libraries. I am grateful to them for the help and encouragement they gave at every stage of the preparation of this book.

It is appropriate to express my gratitude to the American Philosophical Society for a grant from the Penrose Fund and another from the Johnson Fund for the purpose of working on the manuscripts of George Santayana in a number of libraries in this country.

Miss Shirley Mellow, who has since changed her name to mine, has my warmest thanks for her invaluable work in deciphering virtually unreadable manuscripts and in patiently typing a long succession of drafts. I am grateful to Mr. Douglas M. MacDonald for ideas concerning the organization of the book, and to Mr. C. Michael Smith for preparing the index.

Finally, all my thanks go to my mother and father who helped me not just to do but to be.

J.L.

Contents

III. Essence, substance, and existence

IV. Perception, knowledge, and animal faith

V. The impotent mind

VI. THE SPIRITUAL LIFE

VII. REASON, MORALITY, AND THE GOOD LIFE

VIII. ART AND BEAUTY

POSTSCRIPTUM

Introduction

PURPOSE

In the seventy-three years since his first book was published, George Santayana received more routine praise and less serious attention than any other major contemporary thinker. Each year sees the appearance of new books on Whitehead, Bergson, and Wittgenstein, but there has never been a full-scale critical study of the philosophy of Santayana. The relatively few important articles on his thought are lost in old issues of periodicals. Some of his own papers have suffered the same fate; others became unavailable when the books in which they appeared went out of print. A number of his essays have never been published: they lie virtually forgotten in the manuscript collections of libraries.

Although the time is ripe for a thorough critical examination of Santayana's philosophy, this is not the task I have set for myself here. Acting on the assumption that the most effective way to stimulate interest in the work of Santayana is to make it readily available, I have collected a group of his more significant philosophical essays. Some of the papers are reprinted from periodicals, others appear here for the first time. Proceeding on the assump-

1

tion that the most effective way to stimulate a philosophically constructive interest in Santayana is to make the work of his critics readily available, I have added to the collection a group of critical and expository essays. I have attempted to forge a unified whole out of these diverse elements by mating Santayana's work with critical articles in a series of chapters which are designed to cover the entire scope of his systematic philosophy.

The primary purpose of this book, therefore, is to present a set of dialogues on the central topics of Santayana's thought. It is hoped that the expositions, objections, and replies will prove no less relevant to the independent study of the philosophical problems raised by Santayana than to the understanding and evaluation of his system as a whole. Important subsidiary purposes of the volume include the reprinting of unavailable essays by and about Santayana, and the presentation of a collection of his hitherto unpublished manuscripts. Although some of the articles included are of an advanced character, the book as a whole could be used as an introduction to Santayana's thought. Individual chapters are suitable as introductory readings on such philosophical theories as critical realism, epiphenomenalism, and ethical relativism.

PRINCIPLES OF SELECTION

In choosing previously published Santayana articles for inclusion, I was guided by two considerations. First, I wished to include only those articles that seemed to have direct philosophical significance. Secondly, I wished to avoid the republication of works readily available in book form. I have specifically excluded all of the articles collected in *Obiter Scripta,* which will, hopefully, soon have a second edition; but I have decided to include the important "Three Proofs of Realism" which, even though it was included in *Essays in Critical Realism,* has never had the attention and distribution it deserves.

Among critical articles I selected those that appeared to me the most successful from the standpoint of Santayana's systematic thought. It may be thought that the quality of these essays is somewhat uneven. To the extent that this judgment is not the result of personal preference on the reader's part, it may be due to my regard for covering the entire field of Santayana's philosophy. I considered it important to present here a variety of views and assessments of Santayana: the informed reader should have no difficulty in detecting those of them that may be weak, biased, or incorrect.

It is extremely difficult to make a correct estimate of how many Santayana essays and fragments there may still be which are both unpublished and worthy of publication. What I have included here is only a portion of what is publishable in the manuscript collections of Columbia University and the University of Virginia. The University of Texas has recently acquired a large body of Santayana manuscripts: it is reasonable to believe that a portion of that collection is both unpublished and philosophically important. After several volumes of posthumous essays, therefore, there does not appear to be an early end to the manuscripts still to be brought out. It is to be hoped that with the help and encouragement of Mr. Daniel Cory, Santayana's literary executor, the process of bringing to light the rest of Santayana's literary work will continue, and that eventually all his writings will find their way into an authoritative Collected Works. In the current volume I have included only those essays and fragments that seemed to be of particular philosophical interest. These range from the early and relatively well-polished "The Photograph and the Mental Image" through "Materialism of Idealists," meant probably as an alternative version of Chapter X of *The Realm of Matter,* to "Elements of the Realm of Spirit," a stylistically unembellished entry in one of Santayana's philosophical notebooks. Here again, I tried to achieve as wide a scope in the topics covered as was compatible with the literary quality and philosophical content of the selections.

THE PREPARATION OF MANUSCRIPTS

In preparing the manuscripts for publication my first aim was to provide a text as close to Santayana's original as grammar and good sense would allow. I have retained, throughout the manuscripts, Santayana's preference for the English spelling of words, and I have not made any attempt to change or indicate awkward grammatical constructions. The only changes I felt justified in making were the correction of obvious spelling errors, the provision, in brackets, of occasional missing words which were clearly implied by the context, and the addition or alteration of punctuation where without it the sentence would have made no sense. Such minor slips would have been caught and corrected by Santayana in preparing the essays for press: their presence in the manuscripts is the clearest indication that these essays never reached the stage of final literary polish. There are a few places, in fact, where whole sentences appear to be in need of rewriting. Since it would have been inappropriate for me to take the liberty of such revisions, I have contented myself with indicating the scrambled sentences by the addition of the sign "[*sic*]."

Some of the Columbia manuscripts appear to have been hastily pencilled and then extensively corrected in notebooks small enough to fit into a jacket pocket. These manuscripts are exceptionally difficult to decipher. I have spent a considerable amount of time with them, and have taken every reasonable precaution to provide as accurate a reading of them as possible. My greatest difficulty has been with isolated words: this, luckily, has meant that the possibility of alternative readings of sentences was virtually excluded. And I am confident that, in the light of Santayana's thought and style, the specific context of the doubtful words provided ample grounds for reasonable conjectures.

ORGANIZATION OF THE BOOK

The essays are arranged by topic in a series of chapters. Except for the first chapter, devoted to general assessments of Santayana, each is designed to cover a major area of Santayana's philosophy. Within each chapter I have endeavored to create the sense of dialogue by juxtaposing articles critically relevant to each other. Some of these articles, such as Santayana's "The Efficacy of Thought," were meant as direct rejoinders to the critical essay with which they are printed. Others, such as Lachs' "The Proofs of Realism," are particularly apposite to the essay with which they are mated, without having been meant as a response to it originally. If this dialogue format is successful, it should open some new and profitable avenues of thought for the reader. But even if nature made it impossible for him to appreciate the creative chaos of discordant views, he should be able to enjoy the pure and unsullied notes of Santayana.

I

THE PHILOSOPHY OF
GEORGE SANTAYANA

George Santayana—Naturalizing the Imagination

JOHN HERMAN RANDALL, JR.

George Santayana is surely one of the most impersonal of think-ers. He tried—so at least he would have us believe—to see himself as a free and pure spirit, and to look upon those life brought near him as timeless essences. His pages abound in insights of universal validity, classically expressed, whose truth strikes home to any candid and reflective mind, whatever its complexion.

Yet, taken as a whole—and it is a whole—Santayana's vision is a peculiarly personal vision—so personal, that it is hard to con-ceive of anyone save Santayana himself dwelling without chafing within the world it beheld. That world, like the world of his sonnets, is a complete world, coherent, well-articulated, seen stead-ily and whole by a mind that knows what it intends and can dis-criminate what it loves. But the world of Santayana's vision is a limited world; and it is almost impossible for any American—or indeed any non-Latin—to remain within it without straying be-yond its boundaries. It is no accident that Santayana's closest

John Herman Randall, Jr., "George Santayana—Naturalizing the Imagina-tion," *The Journal of Philosophy*, 51 (1954), pp. 50-52. Reprinted by permission.

analogues are French—Renan, and, to a lesser extent, Anatole France.

Nevertheless, Santayana was a major influence on many of the most original philosophic minds in America during the last generation, minds of very diverse convictions; and through his impact on their teachings he has remained a continuing influence on their students. Why was this so? None of these thinkers shared his vision completely. Certainly none dwelt wholly within his world. All of them supplemented what they derived from Santayana with ideas drawn from very different sources. What did Santayana do for them that makes him the key figure in transforming nineteenth-century materialism into twentieth-century "naturalism" (the very term and the christening are his)?

Woodbridge used to say that Santayana was a "natural idealist." That is, he combined the two positions, Idealism and Naturalism. His "Idealism" was a fundamental concern with the "realm of the imagination," with the ideal products of human vision, with the commentary of the spirit of man on its encounters with nature—"spirit, the ever renewed witness and judge of existence." His "Naturalism" was a sober recognition of Idealism's natural conditions and limitations, of the natural basis of those ideal fulfillments, disclosed not so much to science—for the details of which he always had little interest—as to common sense.

In the time and place in which Santayana reached intellectual maturity, the major philosophical problem was to find a way to naturalize the idealistic traditions, a way to construe them in terms that would not be at variance with "scientific knowledge." Idealism clearly had all the insights, all the sensitivity to values, all the careful discrimination, all the devotion to the great ideal enterprises of art, religion, and philosophy. But in its immediate German form, philosophic Idealism was wild and wayward, the expression of Romantic egotism; and even in the garb of the classic tradition, Idealism was tied to an incredible cosmology, in which spirit was held to have created matter and existence.

Yet the "science" that was claiming to have discovered at last the ways of the world, was represented in those days and parts by—John Stuart Mill and Herbert Spencer! Could the winged spirit of man ever rest content within the straightjacket of a

Utilitarianism, however inconsistently enlarged, or dwell without fretting within the narrow confines of a Brighton boarding-house?

Most of the thinkers troubled by the problem were then asking, How much of the idealistic tradition can be saved, and somehow fitted in with "scientific" knowledge? Santayana gave a fresh answer: all of it, provided we recognize it for what it really is. Science gives knowledge, Idealism gives not knowledge but vision. The fullest acknowledgment of the mechanisms nature displays, whatever they may turn out to be—and Santayana never much cared what—need not preclude an equal acknowledgment of the profusion of ends and fulfillments those mechanisms effect, through the imagination of men. Human experience of nature's ways reveals an extraordinary economy of means to the generation of a spendthrift extravagance of ends.

In those days of the first flush of the evolutionary faith, others were working eagerly to naturalize the Mind of man, his cognitive experience. Santayana, to be sure, tried his hand at this job also. But he was too little interested in science to contribute much to what has turned out to be a very technical and laborious enterprise. A still larger number were working to naturalize man's Will —to turn the task of reason in creating the world into the labor of intelligence in reconstructing it. Santayana smiled at the bustling business of the reconstructors, like Dewey, and came to feel more and more that the nature that has generated spirit will in the end crucify its own offspring—a disillusionment much in the temper of the present moment.

It is Santayana's crown—the crown of oak, not of olive—to have naturalized the human Imagination, to have given a natural status and function to the wealth and variety of man's imaginative experience. Among the many evolutionary philosophers of the turn of the century, Santayana almost single-handed made central the imaginative vision, as found in the poets and the prophets and the philosophers of the past—the sweetness and glory of man the imaginative animal. This is what the American philosophers of the last generation learned from Santayana. The "scientific" philosophies of the nineteenth century had taken a negative or even a hostile attitude toward the imaginative aspect of human experience and of man's ideal enterprises. They had

seen that aspect as leading either to uncontrolled speculation—
that is, to a seductive rival of sober science—or else to an exclusive
allegiance—that is, to a fanatical rival of common sense.

But Santayana was able to show that imaginative vision need
be neither waywardly speculative, nor fanatically exclusive. He
made clear that it must indeed play a central rôle in the Life of
Reason. And a large part of what sets off the "naturalistic" philosophers of today from their earlier nineteenth-century predecessors, like poor Spencer, is that Santayana has thoroughly taught
men that the imagination is a natural inhabitant of the realm of
being.

In our present preoccupation with analysis and criticism, with
the close scrutiny of the pronouns and punctuation, in which we
so often seem to be redoubling our effort when we have forgotten
our goal—which is Santayana's definition of fanaticism—when
among philosophers, charitably so-called, the methodists are many
and the men of vision very few—it is a lesson we can still do well
to learn from Santayana.

The Wind and the Spirit

GEORGE SANTAYANA

Philosophy in old men tends to coalesce into a few convictions
by which their other sentiments are coloured. In my case most of
these convictions are ancient or even primitive. Absolutely primitive is the one on which all living beings act by the force of impulse and which I call animal faith: I mean the assumption that
if you see anything you might touch it and perhaps eat it; that
things remain where they are put, unless carried away by the

George Santayana, "The Wind and the Spirit," *What I Believe,* Selected and
arranged by Sir James Marchant, K.B.E., published by Odhams Books Limited,
London (1953), pp. 30-36.

wind, a burglar, or some other material agency; or the assumption that there was a yesterday and that there will be a tomorrow. These convictions are not infallible and sceptics or idealists will give us clever reasons for regarding them as illusions; but they themselves continue to trust that refuted faith in action, because action assumes its truth. Life as a whole might very well be a dream or perhaps an existentialist nightmare; and yet in that dream we should be compelled to trust the assumptions involved in action, even if the action itself was an illusion.

This most primitive belief being thus questionable, I am forced to complete and to control it by introducing another, namely, the distinction between appearance and reality: a distinction, not a separation; because appearances, if not sustained and connected by something more substantial, would be volatile little realities in themselves. That in fact they are the only realities was the assumption of the philosophy which I first had to study and even to expound, adding as brief and modest comments as possible: but my own views took shape precisely in revolt against that position. Not that I had any distaste for appearances; on the contrary, being a lover of form, it was appearances that held my attention and seemed to me the more decent and beautiful side of the real world. For in themselves no matter how evanescent and unsubstantial, appearances are not intrinsically false; intrinsically, if we fix our attention upon them, they are much purer and clearer than material objects or than any dynamic reality; they are the flower of life in our senses and intellect, in music, poetry, mathematics and religion.

But although these products of imagination might well be the best things I found in the world or in myself, they were also the last, the most highly conditioned, and therefore, in an existential sense, the most superficial. If we want safety, if we want power, if we want truth, we must transcend appearance. It is not in appearances that appearance itself is grounded; it is from dust and from blood within our bodies that appearances draw their magic and their beauty. Never out of appearances could the spirit have come to which they appear. For it is not a part of the scene surveyed that surveys it, but something on a deeper plane that watches it pass, and can remember it. Only a drop of blood from the very heart of reality could have this sensibility to the bounty and cruelty of the unexplored realities that surround it.

Of the many names given to reality in contrast with appearance I find none quite satisfactory. Although intended to designate an objective self-existent agent, such as animal faith posits or flees from or pursues, these names are almost always identified with the feeling or image which that agent excites in the mind. Aristotle observes satirically concerning the Ionian philosophers (who were intent on discovering the genuine reality behind appearance) that one said that in reality all things were water, another that they were air, and a third that they were fire; but no one said that they were all earth, which is what the vulgar believe. Yet those naturalists were great observers, as Aristotle himself was; and some of them seem to me to have shown much greater penetration than he into the secrets of Nature. For instance, when Heraclitus gave to the substance of the universe the name of fire, I like to think he did so not guided by appearance, although the aspect of the starry firmament might have excused such an inference, but because he felt how volatile that element was, which, when violent, devoured everything, including itself, but when hidden, and concentrating in the dark all its generative powers, bred every appearance and every passion.

Still, as a name for reality, the word fire seems to me too redolent of brilliance, passion and torment to express the profound darkness and silence that, in contrast to our accidental and very special experience, we must suppose to brood in the womb of Nature; and I should rather choose the name of another element, as familiar as earth and as much neglected by fastidious philosophers: I mean the wind.

Wind is an uncontrollable reality that assaults and may destroy us: it bloweth where it listeth; it is obviously powerful and present, yet invisible. In all these respects it resembles the reality at work in the world at large and in our own bodies and minds. Certainly we know now what are the general causes of the wind's blowing or not, though its exact force or direction is not yet predictable; but this seems to me an added claim on its part to be taken as the type of reality. For the effect of the wind when it buffets us or pushes us along against our will is not, like the usual effects of physical agencies, to evoke in us a sensation wholly foreign to the active power and invented by our human sensibility. This would be the case if the wind, instead of vapulating and ventilating us, caused us to hear sweet music or to sniff some intoxicating scent. As it is, given the radical simple substratum, air, the whole essence of wind is spontaneous motion; and this simple essence, motion, which, for a philosophy that works with appearances and mathematical ideals, remains a mystery, is easily transmitted by contact or attraction to the human person. The wind, therefore, in transmitting motion to us together with its propulsive power, reveals it to us in its reality; not merely, though this may come by the way, through a picture or an equation in scientific symbols. Nor is spontaneous motion, due to inequalities of pressure or temperature, at all foreign to our nature; for though it is possible for us, if not very young, to sit still, the propensity to move, and to push along anything that is movable, is innate in the race.

I am encouraged in my respect for the wind as a good symbol for reality by the ancient and constant assimilation of wind with breath and of breath with life and with divine action. The circle of these affinities or identifications is complete in the first verses of the Book of Genesis.

Here is a document acceptable to Jewish orthodoxy and to the theology of the Christian Church. The Creation is the work of a personal God, Who thinks, plans, speaks, and commands. He anticipates the genera and species of Aristotle, after which He models the flora and fauna of the earth. We may even infer with Leibniz that the Creator has in mind the infinity of possible worlds, chooses the one He prefers, and, like a human artist, loves it afterwards the more for seeing it realized. The critics, however, find traces in this account of earlier and more naturalistic conceptions. In the second verse things seem to begin with chaos. The earth was without form and void, and darkness was on the face of the deep. And the spirit of God moved upon the face of the waters.

But what is it, I cannot help asking, that really moves upon the face of the waters except the wind? And we know that the word "spirit" originally meant breath, the warm air exhaled by all living creatures who with their last breath die. And has not this last exhalation been identified popularly with the soul slipping out of the mouth and becoming a spectre in the night air or a sort of angel in heaven? The echo of life in death is taken for the source of life in the beginning. And this use of the word Spirit for the opposite poles of existence, motion and potentiality in chaos at the bottom and intelligence and love at the top, has not disappeared with time, but remains an equivocation in civilized language.

In German, the word *Geist* is not attached to the "I think" of Descartes or the "transcendental ego" of Kant, but to any romantic drift in opinion or in institutions, such as Montesquieu imagined in his *L'Esprit des Lois,* and the word *geistig* does not mean spiritual but intellectual or theoretical. In America, where language bends to popular taste rather than to literary fashions, spirit means zest, initiative and "push"; precisely what I have been calling wind. And I gather that in speculative physics everywhere the word "energy," which Aristotle applied to perfection of function or ultimate realization of potentiality, is now the discrete name given to matter. Yet the opposite term in Aristotle's theory, *dunamis,* might have been juster and fitted better the contemporary taste for the "dynamic"; but doubtless the public thinks less of any good that the dynamic process might end in than of the movement for its own sake: the joy of exercising power, as in sport, for itself and not for any end. Both energy and dynamism thus revert to a divine wind blowing over the waters of chaos.

Respect for Power has always been fundamental in human religion and society. The fear of the Lord is the principle of wisdom, prudence and morality. But this comes about because there is a human impulse or interest to go on living, and to prosper, which demands adaptation to circumstances. Now when this is done, or in peaceful interludes while it is being pursued, the human psyche develops its free faculties, music and language, for instance, and all sorts of games. Imagination begins to be organized and perhaps to interfere with the instinctive automatic adjustment of action to the objects and opportunities really at hand. The free life of the mind is fascinating, and not insignificant, because, however wild its inventions may be (and all men-tality is invention), it is rooted in reality and must keep step with it, or become a vital waste and perhaps that fatal disease which we call madness. Wisdom and piety therefore exert a certain degree of repression upon imagination and spirituality. Spirit, as the Indians, Descartes and Kant, conceive it, whom I follow at this point, is indeed present in all conscious processes; it is a spark that life strikes at certain points or phases in its synthetic growth; but ordinarily spirit is subject to slave labour: I mean it works, and it may even play a little, but on vain and often painful themes, as in a nightmare. The liberation of spirit from this captivity is often fallacious, when it mistakes its dreams for realities inaptly; for normal illusions, like colours in things, are true signs and do not mislead in action.

Spirit is freed from these normal illusions when it learns to take fictions for fictions. Music and poetry are so freed for clear minds, and religion might be if the abuse of it had not provoked in coarse minds a hostility not to its defeats but to its mysterious powers. Although I value imagination in itself even more than its utility in supplying mental signs for things familiar but unintelligible, I am an enemy of all dominations, even that of spirit. The human psyche is not made for a diet of light only.

Let me turn again to the text of Genesis; for in the midst of my naturalistic version of it I find a touch that admirably evokes the character of pure spirit. This is the famous phrase: "Let there be light, and there was light." Not that the fiat creating light manifests a more miraculous power than the creation of animals: much less, surely, since physically light is far simpler and more primitive. The singular thrill, the sudden sense of sublimity, comes to us not from the power of the fiat but from the wonder of the sight revealed. What a joy is this illumination! And yet this joy-giving light is a mere appearance; without the eye, without vision, light would be a universal tremor or radiation, like the electricity that runs up a wire when we turn on the light; something curious and mysterious, no doubt, but not sublime or entrancing. It is illumination flooding the visible scene, revealing to us a thousand objects at once and their relations, with all manner of perspectives, gloriously expending for us what was a narrow focus of attention in the fog of a crawling existence. We pass into a world not ours, and this intellectual self-transcendence, disinterested and potentially boundless, is the essential characteristic of spirit.

Yet this life of spirit, with everything imaginable for its possible theme, has in each case a little knot of reality, a whirl in the wind, for its source and its test. It depends on an animal psyche for its station in time and space, and for the range of appearances that entertain it. As the eye blesses it with light, so other organs and passions of its psyche bless or curse it with their obsessions. That which the spirit, in proportion to the energy and the perfection of its organ, imposes on the general economy of life, is like what the portrait painter imposes on human faces or the dramatist on human passions: precision, self-identity, ideality. It arrests and immortalizes a life that hardly knew itself as it passed. In so far as spirit fails, as it always does partly, in realizing this transformation, it has been carried away, gently or violently, by the wind. In other words, what I call spirit is mind in so far as it takes the divine point of view, comprehending all partial interests but attaching itself to none. In each object it prizes the inner virtue of it, not its convenience for other objects; and it sees all times as parts of eternity.

I should say that all intelligence aspires to the condition of spirit in the sense in which all the arts aspire to the condition of music. Spirit does not render minds similar; it only renders each mind pure. There can be no spirit without wind to impel it; but wind may also blow spirit out. It is each time a new song of the wind, joyful while it blows free, and unreturning.

Some Notes on the Deliberate
Philosophy of Santayana

DANIEL CORY

The later and more deliberate philosophy of George Santayana, as systematized in his *Realms of Being*,[1] is less familiar to the general public than the earlier expression of his position in the celebrated series of books, *The Life of Reason*. Perhaps the very title of his more technical work is somewhat alarming to the prospective reader, who may well feel that he is primarily interested in *achieving* if possible a life of reason, rather than in merely *clarifying* in his own mind the various dimensions of being. Both of these efforts are important, however, and in an ideally civilized person there ought to be not only a firm organization of impulse and reason in the interests of a balanced life, but a supplementary attempt to settle the ontological status of the open foreground and the natural background of experience itself. If we allow that this second business is deserving of at least some consideration, and is not wholly unnecessary or nonsensical, I propose to set down some random notes, or possible clues, that may embolden the hesitant reader who is secretly tempted to plunge into the deep waters of Santayana's deliberate system of philosophy. It is a fact of experience that deep water may become wonderfully clear to an ambitious open-eyed diver. And these clues or notes that I offer have not been derived solely from an assiduous perusal of the written word, but also from many years of conversation with Santayana in Europe.

Daniel Cory, "Some Notes on the Deliberate Philosophy of Santayana," *The Journal of Philosophy*, 47 (1950), pp. 113-124. Reprinted by permission.

1 See the new One-Volume Edition of *Realms of Being*, Scribner's, 1942.

I. ESSENCE

Let us turn, first of all, to the central notion of *essence*, and I think it might be helpful and somewhat novel to approach it from the standpoint of the cognitive claims of memory. It is the Santayana that I knew in Rome or Paris before the War that I now "summon up" in the quiet of my room in Bexhill. And I find him in the green setting of the Pincio in April, or sitting in a café on the Champs-Élysées in June, with the sun slipping behind the Arc de Triomphe. Memory is a curious and wonderful gift of the gods. The past is dead, materially speaking: only the present occasion is actual. Yet man, by virtue of this strange gift of memory, can in a way be said to *recapture* the past. But in what way?

I have always thought it extravagant in Bergson to maintain that the past is literally preserved in existence—is somehow still *there* and never lost. Although I can remember vividly a dinner I enjoyed last Christmas, the memory of a devoured turkey does not nourish me now. Santayana, on the other hand, has told us that we can recover the *essence* or *form* of a past occasion, but not its substance or pulse of existence. And his Platonic distinction between the eternal and the transient is not difficult to grasp if we consider, for example, the history of a flower. This crimson rose in a vase on the mantlepiece has a brief material life: it is here today and gone tomorrow. But its peculiar shade of crimson, or its ravishing scent, are intrinsically immune to the perishing ways of existence. *Another* rose can exemplify the *same* shade of crimson—can shed the *same* perfume in the stillness of *another* evening. The forms or essences of things are eternal: their substance or matter is change itself. If we grant Santayana's distinction between a realm of essence and a realm of matter, it solves quite neatly the riddle of the way in which the past can be re-captured in memory.

This insight into the nature of essences, and especially their rôle in memory, has been enjoyed by Marcel Proust. In reading Proust some years ago with Santayana, I remember how delighted he was to discover in the last volume of *À la Recherche du Temps Perdu* an unexpected and striking confirmation of his doctrine. We went over the relevant passages together and discussed whether or not Proust had really grasped the ontological status of essences. And since that time I have come across several passages in the earlier volumes of Proust's great work which indicate quite clearly that he had realized the nature of essences. Take the following sentence, for example, from *La Prisonnière,* when Proust writes of "—a certain philosopher who is happy only when he has discovered in two works of art, in two sensations, a common element." That "common element" in two different sensations, or works of art, can be nothing but some timeless essence: like the peculiar shade of red that can be found in many roses. This same fundamental insight is a leading feature of Whitehead's system:

> Every scheme for the analysis of nature has to face these two facts, *change* and *endurance.* There is yet a third fact to be placed by it, *eternality* I will call it. The mountain endures. But when after ages it has been worn away, it has gone. If a replica arises it is yet a new mountain. A colour is eternal. It haunts time like a spirit. It comes and it goes. But when it comes, it is the same colour. It neither survives nor does it live. It appears when it is wanted. The mountain has to time and space a different relation from that which colour has.[2]

In the illustration I gave of the shade and perfume of a rose, we were considering the nature of *simple* essences, but there is no difference in principle involved if we take a *complex* essence like the eternal pattern of a musical composition—or even the total complex essence of the world at any moment. And I find Whitehead and Santayana again in agreement on this point, except that the former would speak of a complex "eternal object" and the latter of a "complex essence." Essences, whether simple or complex, are indifferent to their embodiment in the world of events. Their intrinsic ontological capacity for realization in the network of existence is not troubled or flattered by the intermittent emphasis of some local space-time setting.

The realm of essence is the home of infinite possibilities for the moral essences of consciousness and the formal essences embodied in the external world. It is not, however, in the words of Dewey,

2 *Science and the Modern World,* p. 121.

to be conceived as "a kind of absolute perduring existence or Being." An essence, or eternal object, as Whitehead has put it, "—neither survives nor does it live. It appears when it is wanted." And this is precisely what I mean when I speak of the ontological capacity of any essence, whether simple or complex, for embodiment in the world of events. The infinite possibilities contained in the realm of essence are not difficult to conceive if we consider another homely example. The other day I was watching the final match of a billiard contest between two champions, and I was struck very forcibly by the manner in which the two contestants studied the various alternatives to every stroke they elected to play. If we remember the infinite number of possible strokes that might be executed on a billiard-table, the vastness of the realm of essence is not hard to imagine.

The relations obtaining between all essences are internal, while the relations between physical events are external. Santayana looks at this matter in a very simple way (he once told me he had never read a book on formal logic). When I reminded him of the fiery discussions that ensued soon after the turn of the century over this knotty issue of "internal" and "external" relations, he said to me:

I am not a learned man, but it seems perfectly obvious to me that the relation between two shades of color, or two ideas in the mind, must be an esthetic, logical, or internal relation. On the other hand, if I move the chair in my sitting-room into the bedroom, it seems equally obvious to me that the chair now stands in different natural or external relations.

In the light of this simple illustration, I must confess that the dust of much argument was blown permanently away from my own mind.

Many of the traditional puzzles concerning the nature and extent of our knowledge of the external world are overcome if we can accept the doctrine of essence. For we can then maintain that although the causal conditions of perception may hinder us from enjoying an immediate face-to-face acquaintance with physical objects, there is good ground for suspecting that at least the mathematical skeleton of nature is revealed to the human mind through an identity of structure mediated by certain mathematical forms. The essence of four is not only given to intuition, but is also formally embodied in the four legs of a chair.

II. MATTER

A reader who is acquainted with popular books on current science is apt to be wary of the very title, the *Realm of Matter*. Have we not been informed that the old "impenetrability" of matter has gone, and that any causal "pushiness"—to use Whitehead's word—in nature is an illusion? The specialists now talk of spasms of energy that radiate from mysterious centers, rather than bits of matter in an absolute framework of space and time. The world is composed only of spasmodic events that get clotted together in stubborn bundles to form so-called "material things" like stars and rocks and chairs. Under certain circumstances these ultimate spasms of energy dart off in myriad directions and somehow succeed each other to constitute "causal chains." All is uncertain, loose, and exciting, and the "pointer-readings" on scientific dials and clocks may not after all refer to anything that we can either conceive or picture truly in human terms. Perhaps the "pointer-readings" only point to other "pointer-readings," and the mathematical calculations involved are ultimately tautologies.

If we turn to the fashionable schools of philosophy for instruction our uneasiness in speaking of a realm of *matter* is only intensified. A material thing like a piano is dissolved by the phenomenalists into a logical collection of given and hypothetically obtainable sense-data. The trunk which I can not help assuming is still stored in the basement is only a more or less "permanent possibility for sensation." If we demur against this intellectual emasculation of our vulgar notions—this sophisticated uprooting of our robust "animal faith" in the power and permanence of matter, we are informed by the semanticists that we have been misled by *language,* that the idea of substance or matter is an unfortunate complication of certain grammatical tricks that we picked up in childhood. It would seem that some malicious demon is active in a more insidious form than was imagined by Descartes.

Let us see if Santayana can restore our intellectual balance. I remember raising this question of substance several times in his presence.

Not only contemporary philosophy [he would explain patiently], but all modern English and German philosophy has been an attack on the notion of substance. But the substance I believe in and presuppose at every turn in life has nothing to do with a list of categories, a subject-predicate form of statement, or some purely logical "possibility for sensation." If Mill had said "potentiality" instead of "possibility" he would have been wiser if less English in his outlook. A "possibility" can hardly be said to *exiṣt,* which is just what material things do independently of sense-experience. No, for the most part the critics have entirely missed the mark, and like some professorial Sancho Panza, spent their time tilting at figments of logic and grammar. You must take examples from the arts if you wish to understand what I—or any normal person—mean by substance.

With these words, or words very like them, Santayana taught me to suspect profoundly the sophisticated manipulation of isolated sense-data and meanings that is so characteristic of modern philosophy. And if we turn to the domestic art of cooking for an illustration, it is easier to see what he has in mind. We all know that recent science has flouted the old-fashioned law of the conservation of energy, but nevertheless a competent cook will insist that from a bushel of apples only just so much applesauce can be made. It is hardly the roundness or the redness or the hardness of the apples that has been transformed into applesauce. These immediate qualities are only certain essences that pop into experience and guide the cook in his material operation. It is the substance of the apples that has undergone a real transformation and acquired new forms in experience—the forms or essences that are given when we eat applesauce. As Santayana says:

Undoubtedly the word substance suggests permanence rather than change, because the substances best known to man (like the milk and wet sand of the young architect) evidently pass from place to place and from form to form while retaining their continuity and quantity. Such permanence is not contrary to flux, but a condition of flux. The degree of permanence which substance may have in any particular process, and the name which should be given to this permanent factor, are questions for scientific discussion. They may not, and need not, receive any ultimate answer. But that *some* permanence, not the casual persistence of this or that image, is interwoven with the flux of things, follows from the reality of this flux itself. If change were total at any point, there transformation and existence would come to an end. The next, completely new, fact would not be next; it would be the centre, or the beginning, of a separate world. In other words, events, if they are to be successive or contiguous, must be pervaded by a common medium, in which they may assume relations external to their respective essences; for the internal or logical relations between these essences will never establish any succession or continuity between them, nor transport them at all into the sphere of existence.[3]

We have seen that it is fashionable for contemporary philosophers to analyze a physical thing, say, a chair, into a "logical construction" of given and obtainable sense-data, and then to supplement their analysis by maintaining that the "meaning" of a physical thing can be resolved into an indefinite set of experiential "if-then propositions." Now I should agree that a *part* of what I mean when I make the statement, for example, that "there is a trunk in the basement," can be explained by saying that "*if* I undertake this or that action, *then* I shall probably have this or that experience." But the core of my meaning is rather the radical belief, or latent assumption of "animal faith," that the trunk will remain in existence whether or not I or anyone else troubles to investigate the matter. And it is here we find the ineluctable notion of substance operating in the human mind. It is not the immediate qualities of experience that we believe in and assume in action: these intermittent essences are only signals reporting to us the distribution and operation of material things (or constant systems of events) in a natural background of experience. The notion of substance has flowered in the human mind under the fire of an antecedent external world: there is no need to relapse into Kant, but only to acknowledge frankly the natural categories that we find operating in experience.

It is the same story with the sister notion of causation. We are informed on high authority that there is no such thing in the world as physical compulsion or causation: there are only certain stubborn sequences in experience that the vulgar mistake for

3 *The Realms of Being*, pp. 207-208.

"causes and effects." It would seem that nothing at all goes on beneath and beyond the superficial phenomenal veil that philosophers find so absorbing. If I have a headache and swallow two aspirin tablets, and then a little later experience a sense of relief, there is nothing to be taken into account except a sensation of swallowing that is usually followed (after a strange hiatus) by a feeling of relief. To assume with the vulgar that many hidden causal processes have occurred in my body during that mysterious gap is quite unnecessary. Let us be more sophisticated and either maintain with Berkeley: (1) the entire so-called "external world" is sustained and ordered in the mind of God, and He alone has introduced the "relief-feeling" into my finite center of experience (or yours, as the case may be) at just the appointed moment; or (2) say with the phenomenalists that the sensation of swallowing the aspirin tablets was really followed by a relevant series of "unsensed sensibilia" that for some reason I did not bother to experience.

Is it not obvious, however, that any philosophy which attempts to construct a world out of sense-data and feelings is bound to appear superficial and insincere in the long run. We are all constrained to assume in practice that the world is infinitely wider than the fragmentary data of consciousness, and to insist on clothing the realm of matter in the domestic items of human perception is a symptom of extreme provincialism in philosophy. Santayana put his fingers on the nerve of the problem when he said to me one day—"the trouble with being a phenomenalist is that you're trying to get on with less than you assume."

If we distinguish carefully a realm of essence from a realm of matter (the terminology is not important if the distinction is granted), so many of our pet philosophical puzzles are seen in a fresh light. No minute inspection of the size, shape, or weight of a bit of grain can determine logically why a rose should grow from a particular seed rather than a radish. The qualities of experience (essences) are intrinsically indifferent to the contingent material objects and processes they may signify. A reasonable gardener, however, does not demand an epistemological guarantee of the continued fulfilment of his expectations; he looks to the heavens for signs of rain and is untroubled by the "problem of induction."

Our irresistible assumption of the constancy of familiar causal operations is a result of certain "habits of expectation" that have been furrowed in the nervous system under the fire of an external world. As long as nature is disposed to run in these settled grooves our "animal faith" that the future will conform to the past will doubtless be rewarded. The basis of induction is physiological.

The purpose of the *Realm of Matter,* then, is to clarify once and for all the fundamental assumptions of common sense that underlie every passing fashion in physics, and are taken for granted in all art, experiment, and daily life. Unless we remain loyal to these assumptions, our philosophy becomes lost in high abstraction, and loses hold of the very world it originally sought to understand.

III. TRUTH

The *Realm of Truth* is a difficult book to appraise without fanning the flames of current prejudice. For during the present century there has been a persistent tendency in official quarters to disparage the category of Truth, and the specialists are inclined to sneer if we spell the word with a capital T. As Santayana has an intuitive rather than an analytical mind, the period of gestation had been somewhat trying in the case of this volume—perhaps his most technical work. When the manuscript was finally completed, I remember writing to him: "The architecture of the argument is admirable. Your key definitions have been faithfully adhered to throughout, so there is nothing inconsistent in your conclusions."

I don't think Santayana was impressed by my comment. To speak as if a man's philosophy were merely a matter of formulating a few tight definitions, and then being wary to take any false logical steps, is not very flattering, and hardly true of the *Realms of Being.* Language is important, but so is intuition, and there appears to be a dearth of the latter commodity at the moment.

At the risk of being both technical and unfashionable, then, let us turn to one or two recurrent themes in the *Realm of Truth.*

Suppose I make the statement, for example, that an Indian swam across the Hudson River, at a point where the George

Washington Bridge now spans the water, on July 10, 1400, at 6:30 A.M. I think that an enlightened layman would agree that such a statement expresses a proposition that is either true or false; that is to say, that an Indian either did or did not swim across the Hudson at that date and at that time. But a fashionable school of contemporary philosophers are inclined to object that unless the meaning of my statement can somehow be *tested,* it is nonsensical to speak of the truth or falsehood of a proposition. But if no other human being had been present to observe whether or not our hypothetical Indian swam across the Hudson on the morning of July 10, 1400, or had ever since expressed an opinion on the matter, the absence of such psychological testimony can not affect the status of the Truth concerning this alleged event in the past. Our most careful scientific methods of verification do not *create* the Truth about any matter of fact: we simply *discover* what has been enacted in the external world and prefigured in the realm of truth.

That public verification is a woefully inadequate criterion for the truth or falsity of many propositions is quite evident in the case of dreams. Even in regard to the few dreams that I can remember, there is no possibility of confirming more solidly the bare fact that I claim that I have experienced them. And what about the myriad dreams that I have forgotten? It is still true or false, as the individual case may be, that certain dreams have or have not been experiences of mine. The psychological fact that I am unable to remember them, or the fact that the rest of mankind knows nothing about them, has nothing to do with their truth or falsehood. And the same is true to a large extent of the total experience of any individual life.

The other theme in the *Realm of Truth* that I should like to call attention to is the strict disavowal of any teleological compensations that many philosophers are inclined to read into the formal pattern of history. Now for Santayana the realm of truth is simply "that segment of the realm of essence which happens to be illustrated in existence." This is not the best of all possible worlds, it is rather a contingent "chapter of accidents, a medley improvised here and now for no reason, to the exclusion of the myriad other farces which, *so far as their ideal structure is con-*

cerned, might have been performed just as well." But what happens when a philosopher of Dr. Whitehead's persuasions makes a similar distinction between a realm of infinite possibilities and the actual course of history?

The order of the world is no accident. There is nothing actual which could be actual without some measure of order. The religious insight is the grasp of this truth: That the order of the world, the depth of reality of the world, the value of the world in its whole and in its parts, the beauty of the world, the zest of life, the peace of life, and the mastery of evil, are all bound together—not accidentally, but by reason of this truth: that the universe exhibits a creativity with infinite freedom, and a realm of forms with infinite possibilities; but that this creativity and these forms are together impotent to achieve actuality apart from the completed ideal harmony which is God.[4]

This last quotation makes quite clear the close similarity in ontological structure between the full-blooded philosophical systems of Whitehead and Santayana. But the consequent temperamental differences in interpretation are interesting. The actual order to be found in this world and formally exemplified in the realm of truth is for Santayana a "chapter of accidents" when considered against the infinite background of the realm of essence: for Whitehead, on the other hand, the order of this world is symptomatic of a divine "conceptual envisagement" and kind of logical control of the otherwise dangerous unlimited freedom of "pure creativity." When I called Santayana's attention to this remarkable divergence in interpretation, and added that it was probably a matter of "temperament," he was not slow in defending his philosophy:

What does Whitehead mean by a "conceptual envisagement" of the realm of essence? In order to "envisage," that is to *face* anything, there must first be the psyche—an animal body which by its reactions in a natural medium gives birth to spirit and a perspective of the world.

Unless we assume that God has a *body* (a monstrous suggestion), it is extremely difficult to understand how there could be even a *"conceptual* envisagement" of the entire realm of essence. Concepts are complications of sense-experience, and Whitehead's

4 *The Making of Religion,* p. 90.

rehabilitation of Aristotle's aloof God (in a more tender form) leaves us with all our old difficulties. So on this issue I am inclined to side with Santayana. The actual order that I find in this world strikes me as being rather local and superficial: I detect little evidence of a divine "conceptual envisagement" in the present state of affairs. It might be prudent to recall the sober words of John Dewey: ". . . to call existence arbitrary, or by any moral name, whether disparaging or honorific, is to patronize nature."[5]

IV. SPIRIT

The last volume of Santayana's tetralogy is perhaps his most *personal* book. This may sound like a paradox when we discover that its central theme (I almost said *message*) is an examination of the spiritual possibility of overcoming the entanglements of the self, or biased human psyche, in a precarious material world. But if the single desire of certain men at certain periods of history has always been to transcend the limitations of the self and live—as we put it in religious phraseology—"in the Presence of God," it would be true to say that this desire, this pure flame, was the most characteristic, the most personal thing about them. The longest and, perhaps, most important chapter in the *Realm of Spirit* (Chapter VII on "Distraction") might be summarized as follows: What are the conditions that hinder or prevent the spirit from the realization of its proper goal; namely, an impartial enjoyment of the innocent forms of all things? One might answer immediately by saying "Existence itself, with its thwarting and often incalculable ways." But if existence, organized in a human psyche, is the culpable source of distraction to spirit, we must not forget that it is this same primordial flux of events that has given birth to spirit, and by its blind rhythms suggested to her *the possibility of happiness.* Spirit must somehow become reconciled to her precarious place in this world, and the first step in her interior education is an understanding of the fatality of all interludes of light, and a consequent acceptance of her material conditions. As Santayana writes in a beautiful passage:

[5] *Experience and Nature,* p. 76.

The freedom and glory of spirit comes from its impotence; by its impotence it is guiltless, by its impotence it is universal, by its impotence it is invulnerably supreme. Its essence is to be light, not to be power; and it can never be pure light until it is satisfied with an ideal dominion, not striving to possess or to change the world, but identifying itself only with the truth and beauty that rise unbidden from the world into the realm of spirit.[6]

The kind of esthetic salvation advocated with such authority in this volume is to a great extent an inevitable outcome of Santayana's theory of the relation between spirit and body, and it is *this theory* (a form of epiphenomenalism) that is the proper object of discussion. It is not only an occasion for questioning an unresisting reception of all influences for the sake of their possible forms. The suggestion that Santayana is indifferent to the urgencies of conventional moral issues, or the inner voice of duty, is slightly out of focus if the critics in question are prepared to accept, on other grounds, the causal inefficacy of consciousness in nature. If we decide that Santayana is correct on this latter point, then we must all grant that the *Realm of Spirit* is a book of utmost importance for the life of the inner man.

Epiphenomenalism is the theory that causation occurs only in the physical world. There is no causal relation between one conscious state and another, or between a state of consciousness and a succeeding physical event. In both cases the only causation involved is some series of physiological events in the body. In other words, as Dr. Stapledon has put it, "all experiencing is a sort of by-product of physical machinery, like the noise of a factory." Spirit, or consciousness, is only an intermittent light that plays over but does not intervene in the material processes of nature.

Santayana has little use for any philosophy that attempts to avoid the distinction between mind and body by some ingenious "serial view" of the self as a "construction" out of organic feelings, memory images, and other phenomenalistic data. States of consciousness can not be fitted into the causal machinery of a human brain. Spirit arises when the appropriate movement of physiological events, instigated (usually) by some external impinge-

[6] *Realms of Being*, p. 643.

ment on the senses, occurs in a responding human body. What is *given* to consciousness in any instance of spirit is some pure appearance. These pure appearances or essences are normally signals to an active being of "the influences, of whatever nature, to which the mind is subject from whatever is without and independent of itself."[7] But when the body is operating smoothly, nature seems to conspire to turn the whole machinery of life into a conscious triumph of esthetic value, and a man may well be duped into believing that he is the master of the forces of nature that silently support his buoyant spirit. Now there are many arguments for and against this explanation of the "mind-body" problem, but here I wish only to remind the reader again that it is the truth or falsehood of this proposed solution that is at stake in appraising the last volume of the *Realms of Being*.

It is a fact that Santayana's *official* philosophy, both in conception and expression, is not fashionable in the academic climate of today. His key terms ("matter," "essence," "truth," "spirit") are looked upon with suspicion, and the very calmness of his tone and general attitude is sometimes taken as a symptom of indifference to that anxiety of analysis that possesses the logical positivists, or the tumult about social reform that excites the moralist. As for the dissatisfaction that has been voiced over the employment of a rather traditional terminology, it is necessary to remember that when old verbal terms are used in their simple elementary senses, they often escape a technical criticism that only attaches to some special meaning of these words associated with the recent history of philosophy. When the current tempest in a teapot over the meanings of words has subsided, it may be possible to recover our linguistic innocence.

The charge that Santayana has been indifferent in his later works to what Dean Inge has called "the current valuations of the worldling," is only justified if a philosopher is supposed to "take sides" on every issue of contemporary interest, be it moral, social, or political. It is true that Santayana is by nature a spectator of the manners of this world, rather than a reformer. But that is hardly a sufficient reason for equating his absolute impartiality with indifference. Intellectual charity is not a conscious approval

[7] I. A. Richards, *Coleridge on Imagination*, p. 157.

of existing conditions: it is a way, a spiritual way, of meeting those conditions and overcoming them through direct *insight*.

There is something so timeless, so above a local planetary disturbance, about Santayana's philosophy, that it is difficult for most of us to attain the composure necessary for a just appreciation of his work. But from time to time there will always be men who will discover in the *Realms of Being* a permanent expression of that latent wisdom that lies buried in their hearts.

Santayana's Defiant Eclecticism

CHARLES HARTSHORNE

Santayana's philosophy is, perhaps most of all, a sharp reaction to modern idealism in that form which argues that knowing is creative of its objects. Santayana sees that if the thing known depends upon the knowing, then not even one's own past can be known, since in knowing it one would in part at least create it. And a past event created in the present would not be past. Also, if in knowing I create what I know, then the neighbor's mind that I try to know must turn out to be my own mind, my own idea, not my neighbor's. Thus the logical result of such an idealism is solipsism of the present moment—one knows at most one's present mental state.

With this *reductio ad absurdum*, Santayana dismisses idealism. He entirely overlooks the more sensible form of idealism that Peirce represented, according to which the thing known in a particular case is not in the least created by *that* act of knowing, but rather constitutes an independent First to which the knowing is a Second; however, the independence or Firstness of the known is relative only, since the thing known itself (memory is the most

Charles Hartshorne, "Santayana's Defiant Eclecticism," *The Journal of Philosophy*, 61 (1964), pp. 35-44. Reprinted by permission.

obvious example) was also a Reactive feeling or experience, presupposing a still earlier one as *its* First. (In the foregoing I have
somewhat stylized Peirce's doctrine and have given it a Whiteheadian twist.) The argument for idealism is not that knowing
constitutes its objects, but that it constitutes *itself* as a new object
available for being known and that this self-constitution or self-
creation of a potential object is the only model we have for the
coming to be of reality in general. No such idea ever dawned on
Santayana, for reasons which have as much to do with the errors
of idealists as with any blunders of his own. Prior to Whitehead
the primacy of self-creation had scarcely been put clearly into the
center of discussion.

Memory cannot create the past; it remains to ask whether the
past can in a fashion create memory, that is, be present in it as
its cause. Unfortunately, Santayana is not content to safeguard
the independence of the earlier from the later; he also asserts the
absolute logical independence of the later from the earlier. Memory is a self-contained present state, not intrinsically related or
relative to the past at all. Thus Hume, in his extremest statements, is reincarnate: events are mutually independent in their
logical being. How then do we know that the remembered ever
happened? We have "animal faith" that, in general, this is so.
Strictly we do not know it, even as probable. Given a memory, the
past logically could have been anything you please. What grounds
has Santayana for this view? Apparently only one, the well-known
occurrence of "mistakes" of memory. If memory were intrinsically
related to the earlier events themselves, how could it ever be mistaken? We do not—Santayana concludes—intuit the past, but only
an "essence," which as such is timeless. We intuit a quality, which
may have qualified the past, but also may not have.

I venture to think this a rather crude analysis. There are
"memories" and "memories" and all degrees of possible confusion
between those referring to what is past by a fraction of a second
and those referring to experiences that occurred many years earlier. Above all, there is danger of confusion between memory intuitions and judgments as to what the intuitions mean. A memory
going back millions of seconds will skip over countless intervening experiences, in many at least of which the earlier event in

question will have already been recalled; therefore, one is in danger of confusing memories of previous memories of the event with direct memory of the event itself. Not only previous memories, but also previous interpretations of previous memories, intervene between the given memory and the event. Thus George III "remembered" being at the battle of Waterloo. What did he really do? Did he merely have a present image which he interpreted as a memory of his own presence at Waterloo? Of course the matter was much more complicated. Near the time of the battle he may have thought about the possibility of having been there; his mind became filled with images of experiences he then would or might have had. Later he forgot that these were only imaginings of such experiences, but he did not forget the imaginings themselves. Imagined experiences, if sufficiently vivid, being much like real ones, it was easy enough eventually to interpret them as having in fact been real. But this was a *judgment* based on memory in a complex manner, not a simple memory. Without the distinction between direct experience and its interpretation, there is no clear meaning to "direct experience"; and hence the question: Is the past directly experienced? ceases to constitute a definite question.

Only by ignoring the two confusions, that between immediate and remote memory, and that between interpreted memory and simple memory, can one prove the lack of intrinsic connection between present and past experience. Santayana is one of legions who have based a philosophy upon precisely these mistakes.

Present experience, he holds, is self-contained, so far as memory is concerned; the reference to the past associated with memory is only a claim, a postulate, or a faith. What of perception of the world around us, is that too only a postulate or faith? Santayana replies in the affirmative. The mistakes of perception, like those of memory, exclude the possibility of direct awareness of the surrounding world. The qualities we intuit in perception are given only in their own qualitative nature; but whether or not they characterize anything except our perceptions themselves we cannot know. All experience is but a series of dreams plus the animal faith that there is a real world corresponding to the dreams.

We have here the same two mistakes that were committed with

regard to memory: failure to distinguish (a) between the more and the less immediate objects of perception, and (b) between sheer givenness and interpretation. In a dream we do not experience real things outside the body as they really are. But then, even in waking experience, there is no good reason to regard the extra-bodily object as the *most* immediate datum. If we start with some obviously remote object of perception, such as a stellar explosion that took place a light year away, it is strange indeed to suppose that the most direct object of this experience is separated from the experience by a year in time and six trillion miles in space. But there is only a difference of degree between such an event and any perceived event outside the body. In all cases it takes time for the stimulus to reach the sense organ and initiate there the activity with which the experience is, in temporal terms, most closely associated. Thus, as Russell (also Whitehead) has cogently argued, the only nonarbitrary choice for the most direct object of the experience is the physiological process. Anything else is by comparison less direct. Attempts to refute this conclusion seem to turn upon some degree of confusion between experience and judgment. We instantly *interpret* the experience as perception of the external object, but this is quite compatible with the assumption that the physiological process is more directly given, provided we give due heed to the facts of genetic psychology concerning the vast amount of learning that has gone on since birth, or even before, as to how to correlate data from one sense with those of another (including kinaesthetic sensations) so as to get on in a world full of dangers and rewards, which can be avoided or won only if, much of the time, we attend to inner-bodily states, not as such, but as comprehended signs of extra-bodily events. Not a single known characteristic of sight or hearing is contradictory of this explanation. The dream theory of experience then takes on the following harmless form: in all experiences, awake or asleep, we experience most directly inner-bodily states (which are always really there), but only in waking experiences do the functions of interpretive correlation, or reading of these sensory cues as signs of external events, operate correctly. In sleep and in certain abnormal states interpretation breaks down. But the locus of the most direct physical data is in all cases inner-bodily. This theory

has not been refuted. It has been smiled at or ignored. I have yet
to see an argument against it worthy of the name. (The so-called
"sense-datum" theory, or the "causal theory" of perception, as these
are commonly defined and criticized, are not the theory just set
forth, and the difficulties with which they are rightly charged are
irrelevant to our theory.)

Having cut off the present experience wholly from its past,
Santayana can then triumphantly turn upon the idealist and say,
your "mind" is wholly incapable of furnishing the link between
successive events. Only the despised "matter" can do this. The
enduring substance and causal connectedness of the world is in
matter only, not in mind. But how does "matter" explain identity
through change and causal interconnection? That is what the concept is invented for; so of course it must be able to render this
service. Look as you may in Santayana's writings, you will not
find more than this by way of argument on this point. I submit
that the explanation is pure verbiage and absolutely nothing
more. We experience no intrinsic relatedness of the present of a
piece of matter to its past or future, and no causal reference from
one piece of matter to another. We verbally postulate that since
we could find no such linkages in mind they must reside in something else, which we call matter. But the situation then is just
this: in memory we have at least a claim on the part of mind to
relate itself to the past and a similar claim on the part of sense
perception to relate itself to other things in space (which need
not, in the most direct cases, be outside our skins). The claims are
examined by Santayana, hastily and with every mark of bias in
the mode of examination, and found wanting. So it is triumphantly concluded that the unity of the world must be found in
"matter," although we have not even an illusory notion, comparable to memory, as to how states of a body influence their successors, nor even an illusory notion, comparable to perception, as
to how events in one body causally imply changes in another
body.

I maintain that Santayana's procedure has no logical force, and
that only immense anti-idealistic bias could account for his supposing it had. This bias was real and strong, as I think any
reader of Santayana will concede. To take memory and perception

as illusions plus animal faith is the most suspect epistemology conceivable. To base an ontology upon it is inadmissible, since all that could really follow is that we know nothing.

If we do not literally experience anything past, or contemporary, relative to experience, we must experience either that very experience itself only or something not in time at all. Santayana sees the absurdity of saying that an experience is merely of itself, and chooses the other horn of the dilemma: we experience "essences," which in themselves are timeless. This leads to three puzzles. One is: how do we even have the idea of events or experiences, if we do not experience either, but only a mere essence? Actual existence is never a datum, Santayana says; only essence, a form of being which is neutral to the distinction between existence and nonexistence, can be given. It is all very well to say that we posit existence by instinctive faith; how do we know what is meant by an "existence" we have never experienced? Our experiences have occurred, but as occurrences they are not data of any possible experience. Apparently we intuit the essence, "existence," but not as embodied in any example.

The second puzzle is: how can we know that an essence is independent of all existence? This is just the old thesis, attacked by Aristotle, of "separable forms." When an essence is known, it at least qualifies an actual experience; by what mode of experience could we find out what an essence or quality would be if it qualified nothing, not even an experience?

The third puzzle is: suppose (which the doctrine implies to be conceivable) nothing existed and there were only the realm of essence. In that case, either this realm could of itself produce a world, could function as a creator (or a world could spring into being without a cause, other than the realm of essence, which comes to the same thing) or else not only would there be no existing world but there would not even be a "possibility" of such a world, and it would be impossible.

The conclusion seems to be that a simply independent realm of essence explains nothing, and is itself unintelligible.

Let us now consider Santayana's treatment of the religious problem. He holds that the medieval idea of God was "eclectic," in that it claimed to combine in a single concept what are really several concepts. There is, first, the concept of essence or pure being, the presupposition of all existence, itself presupposing no existence whatever. This was God as wholly independent of the world, which, however, is dependent upon Him. There is also, second, the concept of real power, "omnipotence," capable of producing all sorts of things and actually producing whatever does come to exist. Santayana suggests that it is matter which has this omni-capacity. All things manifest the power of matter. Finally, third, there is the notion of Truth, the total character of existence. Theism identified this with the content of omniscience, but since, Santayana holds, a truth is not made by the consciousness of it, this identification is illegitimate. Truth, for Santayana, is merely the immeasurably complex essence that sums up the cosmic development throughout all time.

Thus for God, Santayana substitutes (a) timeless essence, (b) matter to whose fertility in producing new forms we can set no final limit, and (c) a certain segment of the realm of essence. This is surely very ingenious. Moreover, there is some validity in it. For it is quite correct that God as infinite power, for instance, cannot be simply identical with God as omniscient. For God to know what his Power has actually produced out of all that it could produce is for him to be in a determinate state, exclusive of some of the otherwise possible actualizations. It is to be somehow finite, and not simply infinite. As simply infinite, God would at most know only what he could produce; but to register in his consciousness the particular actual productions is to take on their determinateness, and to be no longer merely infinite. The segment of essence that is actualized is not all essence, and knowing that this is the actualized segment is not all possible knowledge; for it excludes knowledge that some other segment has been actualized instead. Yet this segment too was possible.

The same duality is involved in the notion of divine will. God could will to create all sorts of worlds; but he does will to produce just this one. Hence his actual volition is not infinite in the sense in which his possible volition is infinite. As Santayana cleverly and rightly says: a God creating a certain world is already himself a certain world, that is, a certain determinate existing divine state among the possible ones. I find this strictly correct and a devastating criticism of traditional theism. But it is not so devastating against a theism which admits real distinctions between actual and possible in God.

There is a flaw in Santayana's theory of truth: an essence can tell no tales about existence, and so the segment of essence that is embodied in events is, as essence, no different from unembodied essence. Only existence can mark the distinction. Now existence does not occur all at once; it is progressively actualized, and only the present is fully real. What then constitutes truth as a time-less whole? That it is timeless, we are told. But neither in exist-ence nor in essence does there seem any place for such a whole. The segment in question is there, all right, among essences, but nothing marks it as *the* segment; only certain bits of it are marked off by what is going on at a given time in the world as *then* true of the world. But what marks the entire sum of such bits as the comprehensive Truth? Apparently nothing. Existence never is summed up as a whole; not in the world, for the past is gone and the future not yet realized; not in essence, for it is innocent of the difference between exemplified and unexemplified essences; not in divine knowledge, for this is not admitted.

What light does Santayana throw upon traditional philosophi-cal problems? Let us consider, for instance, the question of free-dom. He began as a determinist, but eventually decided that this was an arbitrary doctrine. Because of the independence of essence from existence, it is merely contingent that anything exists at all, and it seems unreasonable to suppose that this fundamental con-tingency is combined with an absolute conditional necessity of everything within the world. (Here there might possibly be an influence of Peirce, who had argued similarly: why suppose that the arbitrariness of matters of fact came in a single primordial dose, instead of seeping into the world bit by bit? Determinism, taken absolutely, implies this single-dose theory of contingency.) So far, so good. But not having the idea of divine freedom, San-tayana has no clear universal principle for the distribution of freedom in reality.

Concerning substances and events, Santayana adds nothing sig-nificant to the historical debates on the logic of genetic identity. He does, in one fine passage, imply a wiser view than he ever actually utilizes systematically. He attacks the self-interest theory of motivation on the ground that self-identity is not such an absolute thing as the theory assumes. Here he is close to the Buddhistic insight which most of the rest of the world has so signally missed, in both Orient and Occident.

This passage is too fine to be left unquoted:

When we apply reason to life we immediately demand that life be consistent, complete, and satisfactory when reflected upon and viewed as a whole. This view, as it presents each moment in its relations, extends to all moments affected by the action or maxim under discussion; it has no more grounds for stopping at the limits of what is called a single life than at the limits of a single adventure. To stop at selfishness is not particularly rational. The same principle that creates the ideal of a self creates the ideal of a family or an institution.

The conflict between selfishness and altruism is like that between any two ideal passions that in some particular may chance to be opposed; but such a conflict has no obstinate existence for reason. For reason the person itself has no obstinate existence. The *character* which a man achieves at the best moments of his life is indeed something ideal and significant; it justifies and consecrates all his coherent actions and preferences. But the *man's life,* the circle drawn by biographers around the career of a particular body, from the womb to the charnel house, and around the mental flux that accompanies that career, is no significant unity. All the substances and efficient processes that figure within it come from elsewhere and continue beyond; while all the rational objects and interests to which it refers have a transpersonal status. Self-love itself is concerned with public opinion; and if a man concentrates his view on private pleasures, these may qualify the fleeting moments of his life with an intrinsic value, but they leave the life itself shapeless and infinite, as if sparks should play over a piece of burnt paper.[1]

How rich this passage is! It is in such reflections upon values that Santayana shows us his noblest side and his most authentic wisdom. Note the implied rejection of the view that to be simply "infinite" is to be ideally good and great. On the contrary, Santayana has the Greek insight that form means definiteness, and hence limitation, being this and therefore *not* that. (To worship infinity as though it were identical with deity is, some of us think, a species of idolatry.) Note also that the human individual is

[1] *The Life of Reason,* Vol. V (one-volume edition, 1953), ch. 8, p. 462.

taken not as a substance but as a temporary assemblage of substances, implying that substance is for ethics not a primitive concept but something further analyzable and derivative. But now I ask: what has all this to do with Santayana's metaphysics? No use is made of independent essence, and for ethics at least one does not need "substance"; nay more, one must subordinate the substance concept (as equivalent to individuality) in order to express the way in which rational motivation sees the distinction between one man's good and another's as beside the main point. And what quiet penetration in terming selfishness an "ideal passion"! So far from being the intuitive or rational absolute of motivation, self-interest is a theory, an intellectual construct, which arbitrarily inflates a relative tendency of the subrational life into an ultimate. This is what Buddhism means by calling the selfish attitude "writhing in delusion."

But now, with all my admiration for this passage, and some others like it, I wish to suggest that the metaphysics that most effortlessly fits the ethical point of view therein expressed is not Santayana's but the Buddhist or Whiteheadian systems in which the real primitives are states or events, not substances. Did Santayana have any distinct knowledge of such systems? I doubt it. His references to Oriental thought seem to have Orthodox Hinduism in mind, not Buddhism, least of all Northern Buddhism.

Is Santayana a rationalist or an empiricist? His metaphysical doctrines are clearly not empirical. Existence, essence, and truth are defined, and so is experience in relation to these, not on the basis of an inductive inquiry, with the admitted possibility of factual falsification, but on the basis of a priori intuitions or pronouncements. In any world, it would be matter, not mind, which existed; and as for essence, it is even independent of there being any facts at all. I think Santayana is, in metaphysics, a rationalist, and the better for that; but unfortunately, he is one who has failed to find rational solutions for the metaphysical or a priori problems. He has indeed written very instructively about these problems, showing us what results from taking an extreme (which means, unempirical) Humeanism seriously, also how this almost forces us to accept also an extreme Hobbesian materialism and an extreme Platonism of essence, and how none of these by itself, nor the three together, gives us much understanding of life or the world.

The fault was not mainly with Santayana. He had studied, of imaginative systems, chiefly Greek metaphysics, medieval theology, and German idealism, and in his rejection of all these I at least can only salute his good judgment. If he was not a sufficiently creative genius to find a viable alternative, that is chiefly his and our bad luck. His chances might, however, have been better had he been less easily satisfied with the defiant pose of saying the opposite of his teachers or masters. He defended Hume and Hobbes against Royce, Bradley, Hegel, and Lotze; false or extreme Platonism against genuine Platonism; and all three unpopular extremes against medieval theism and James's pragmatism and Will to Believe. Thus he defied everybody who had irritated him. At the same time he made a fine show of housing his world and his values in the various *Realms* that he so scintillatingly described. It was a somewhat morose tour de force—in literary elegance and intellectual agility reminiscent of Schopenhauer. There is perhaps no one element in Santayana quite so concentrated in its effect as Schopenhauer's proof that life is evil, or the Schopenhauerian theory of art; still the great range of ideas in Santayana (and his gifts as novelist and poet) perhaps evens the scales. He has certainly enriched English literature to the benefit of all of us.

Ultimate Disillusion and Philosophic Truth

WILLARD E. ARNETT

I

George Santayana's right to the title 'philosopher' is perhaps now more frequently challenged than honored. Many of the current analysts have concluded that he was essentially a poet, and that poetry and philosophy (though not altogether incompatible or mutually exclusive) have nothing in common. In a similar vein others declare that philosophy is by its very nature concerned with ontological problems and the absurdity of man's existence, while Santayana was preoccupied exclusively with essence, with the delight of imaginative and aesthetic landscapes, and therefore unable to articulate the concrete and distinctive attributes of man's anguished being in the world. Still others, less explicit in their charges, betray the conviction that because of first principles that are patently false or inadequate, he cannot be taken seriously as a philosopher.

In spite of the fact that much relevant and penetrating insight has often accompanied such claims, they all unequivocally fail to substantiate the charge that Santayana was not a philosopher, or that he should no longer be taken seriously in the philosophical arena. In regard to the claim that he was essentially a poet and consequently not a philosopher, it seems sufficient here to point out that historically philosophers have attempted to judge the world in terms that are just to both the formal, or structural, elements of being and to the qualitative and dynamic dimensions

Willard E. Arnett, "Ultimate Disillusion and Philosophic Truth," *Revue Internationale de Philosophie*, 17 (1963), pp. 5-17. Reprinted by permission.

of experience. Thus philosophy (if one means by this term the body of literature commonly called philosophy) has never been essentially less poetic than conceptual, or logical, in form, and philosophers have obviously assumed that there are genuine and irreducible features of experience and being which can be articulated and communicated only in poetic terms.

Concerning the second claim, it is of course true that Santayana was preoccupied with essence, or at least by modes of thought in which both the possible and the purely ideal were regarded as no less relevant to experience and being, and therefore to philosophy, than the existential. Anyone who claims to take the existential situation more seriously than Santayana, however, is apt to be only estimating the situation differently. Santayana was convinced, in the first place, that knowledge of the ultimately real—matter—can never be literal, or that there can never be a one to one correspondence between the "facts" and "knowledge of the facts." In the second place, therefore, "You may stop at what stage you will, according to your sense of what is real and important; for what one man calls higher another man calls unreal."[1] In other words, all that can be known is essence, and every man must interpret, or find existential import in, the essences he encounters. This, according to Santayana, *is* the existential condition of man.

The third claim, that his first principles are false or inadequate, begs all the issues that are presumably in question wherever philosophical inquiry is taken seriously as an open arena in which every person may demonstrate his skill in defending the principles and convictions which seem to him fundamental. And until all the evidence is in, and the philosophical truth is spread before us in all its conceptual accuracy and qualitative fullness, disagreement with any system so fully articulated as Santayana's must be an equally defensible and serious exploration of the structure of existence and the quality of experience, and not simply a categorical denial of the basic principles of the system. It may in fact be the case that Santayana's fundamental principles are false but that much that he claims about particular matters of importance is nonetheless relevant and revealing. Philosophies, or sciences, must be judged not so much by the empirical truth of their basic

[1] Santayana, *Three Philosophical Poets*, p. 206.

premises as by their fruitfulness on the on-going philosophic, or scientific, enterprises.

Santayana was deeply concerned, like all serious-minded men, not to be deceived, or to judge the world in the terms and accents in which it may be truly judged. And if philosophy may be said to seek conceptual truth while also attempting to promote (or provoke) the pursuit and achievement of particular qualities of thought and life which are presumably implied (if not required) by the conceptual envisagement, then Santayana was a philosopher par excellence, even though his metaphysics may be false, his epistemology self-contradictory, and his moral theory simply a statement of preference. For surely Santayana had a generalized conception of the irreducible features of existence, or a metaphysics, and was convinced that both his epistemology and his moral judgments flowed from and substantiated his metaphysical concepts.

II

In the most general terms Santayana's philosophy may be characterized as *the philosophy of ultimate disillusion*. In science and philosophy as well as in religion, he thought, both the way and the substance of truth is disillusion. And he took altogether seriously the task of indicating in philosophic terms the perennial perplexity of a creature that escapes from credulity only by way of disillusion.

In *Scepticism and Animal Faith*[2] he describes the three ways by which the honest mind may escape, not illusion itself, which is inescapable, but the fear of illusion. The first way is death. But death, since it destroys and does not explain or redeem, is no genuine escape. The second way is to correct the errors of judgment which constitute the illusion, or to substitute different beliefs for the misleading ones. This, according to Santayana, would be the most satisfying method, and is the method that men generally seek to adopt. But critically regarded, he continues, no belief is justified except by "custom, comfort, and the accidental

[2] Santayana, *Scepticism and Animal Faith*, pp. 72-73.

absence of doubt."[3] This escape, then, is no genuine haven for the scrupulously honest mind seeking wholeheartedly not to be deceived. The third, and the only critically defensible escape, is, consequently, "to entertain the illusion without succumbing to it, accepting it openly as an illusion, and forbidding it to claim any sort of being but that which it obviously has; and then, whether it profits me or not, it will not deceive me."[4]

This philosophy of ultimate disillusion was implicit (and sometimes explicit) in *The Life of Reason;* it was the chief theme of *Scepticism and Animal Faith,* and the unifying element in *The Realms of Being.* In the last, essence is, above all, only appearance; matter never appears at all; spirit is the recipient of (but can never justify or explain) the passing parade of essence; and the truth (except the conventional and homespun varieties by which men live their animal lives) is only an ideal in the pursuit of knowledge which no one approaches and few entertain. The problem, then, is not whether Santayana was a philosopher. He most certainly was. The important question, instead, is whether this philosophy of ultimate disillusion has important—at least partially, if not wholly, true—things to say about man's ways of passing judgment on existence. Does Santayana have anything of importance to say about the arts, religion, science, and philosophy itself?

III

Santayana's disillusion was probably most complete, and most notorious, in regard to religion. "Religion and art," he wrote, "have had their day; indeed, a part of the faith they usually inspire is to believe that they have long ago revealed their secret."[5] Yet had his disillusion extended to no other disciplines and areas of experience, or had he carried this aspect of his disillusion with more equanimity and less regret, his repute as a philosopher might have suffered less, except within the circle of religious

---

3 *Ibid.,* p. 72.
4 Santayana, *Scepticism and Animal Faith,* pp. 72-73.
5 Santayana, *Reason in Science,* p. 3.

philosophers. For after all, the disillusion of Santayana differed from that of other contemporary philosophers and scientists only in scope and degree. Many of his contemporaries (and ours) have shared his disillusion in regard to established religious traditions. But most of these have retained their faith in the methods, if not also in the content, of science and philosophy. And so almost paradoxically (since religion and the arts have always been closely related), the most recent decades have witnessed an amazing re-surgence and re-formulation of the idea that although neither religion nor science, nor philosophical reason, can discover and articulate the truth, the arts (particularly the novel and the literary-philosophical essay) may enable man to articulate and to see more clearly his existential predicaments.

Santayana, unlike many of his contemporaries, was obviously not pleased with the conclusion that he must regard religions as so many fictions mistaken for genuine accounts of existence. Unlike many whose spiritual vision is less developed, or developed in different directions, Santayana was unable to share the view that the ascendancy of science has removed at all the mystery that per-vades the world and man's existence in it. The conclusion that religion "has absolutely no standing ground in fact" did not mean to Santayana (as it did to many of his contemporaries) that the world is ultimately more intelligible, or more amenable to the understanding and control of men, than the religious approach has always seemed to suppose. The conclusion that religions are products of fancy and desperate hope meant primarily to Santa-yana that "the best things" belong only to the imagination, and that their appearance is secondary, or derivative, ephemeral, and altogether irrelevant to the causal order of nature.

The great difference between Santayana and other distin-guished philosophers and scientists who have reached similar con-clusions about the status of religious visions and claims is, then, that the latter have, by and large, been able to maintain or sub-stitute faith in science or philosophy or the arts, or even social reform, for their discarded religious faith. Many of course have never really been tempted by religious doctrines, and so have re-garded the "illusion of religion" as simply a fact accepted without struggle or regret, though partly perhaps because they have not seen as deeply and thoroughly as Santayana did into the sources and functions of religious teachings and practices. For although he professed to believe that the collocations and convolutions of matter are the ultimate sources of all phenomena, including ideas, his account of the origin and nature of religion is nonetheless an illuminating inquiry into the conditions and needs of the human spirit. Thus, disillusioned as he was, Santayana could by no means have agreed with A. J. Ayer, for example, that religious and theological claims, philosophically considered, are nonsense, though he would perhaps have been equally critical of recent efforts to find ontological, if symbolic, truth in religious and poetic claims. The primacy of matter, and the imaginative character of the arts and religions, implied precisely that nothing real—nothing with executive power or influence—can be discovered in or through the religious and artistic enterprises.

But since, according to Santayana, life is not possible without illusion or a judicious life without disillusion, life must be evaluated in terms of the ideals that occur to the imagination rather than in terms of the material powers and relations that make life possible. Religion and the arts are meaningful—the most *meaningful* of all man's activities and achievements, since without them all else would be ashes in the mouth. So those who dismiss religion as irrelevant to the judicious life of man are wrong, even though they are right in the claim that religion has no ontological basis or implications. Religious visions and claims cannot be trusted in the pursuit of truth, though they are the sources of the greatest values when seen as the delightful illusions which they are.

IV

Observed from one direction Santayana apparently had great confidence in science while from another direction it is clear that he trusted the sciences even less than he trusted the arts and religions. Certainly he was not averse to appealing to the authority of science in the defense of his materialism. Yet his materialism, unlike that of many nineteenth century thinkers, was not inspired (though it was supposedly warranted) primarily by science; and consequently he was justified when, in his last years and in response to critics, he insisted that mechanism was never a central or crucial aspect of his system, and revised *The Life of Reason* accordingly.

More than most men, Santayana apparently had a profound sense of being carried along by the current of events without in any measure affecting those events. His view of science, and all knowledge, as well as his religious and moral philosophy, were profoundly related to this sense of being in the grip of "some alien and inscrutable" power—of living, thinking, and dying without the power to live, or think, or die. In a different age he might have agreed with Saint Augustine that the power by which one lives and thinks is the power of the Holy, the Truth, or God. Yet there is little evidence, though his sense of both beauty and tragedy was in some respects deep and extraordinary, that he ever actually experienced the world as the Holy, or even as an "awful and wonderful excellence."

Santayana's materialism, then, though he thought modern physics supported it, was essentially that of Lucretius: unscientific, aesthetic, and moral, a sense that dark impersonal and indifferent powers determine every event. The view that matter is omnipotent apparently neither generates nor is generated by profound love or fear. The logic of materialism requires only that one "hold the lofty and serene positions well fortified by the learning of the wise, from which [he] may look down upon others and see them wandering all abroad and going astray in their search for the path of life. . . ."[6] Materialism, as conceived by Santayana since matter itself is never known, claims (as did the phenomenology of Husserl) that, in the analysis of knowledge, "Nothing is ultimately left except the passing appearance or the appearance of something passing."[7] Santayana might have said with Wittgenstein, then, that "At the basis of the whole modern view of the world lies the illusion that the so-called laws of nature are the explanations of

6 Lucretius, *On the Nature of Things*, Book II.
7 Santayana, *Realms of Being*, p. 200.

natural phenomena."[8] What he did in fact say was that science is "tentative, genial, practical, and humane, full of ideality and pathos, like every great human undertaking."[9] For Santayana, then, as for Wittgenstein also, science is by no means rendered futile by the illusions it generates and represents. For Santayana, science was "useful and delightful," though its view of existence is "essentially fallible," and, like all knowledge, "only a claim put forth, a part of that unfathomable compulsion by force of which we live and hold our painted world together for a moment."[10] But he could never have said with Wittgenstein that "The proposition is a picture of reality" and "The logical propositions describe the scaffolding, or rather they present it."[11] The "painted world" of Santayana is purely imaginative, or fictional through and through, even though it may be pragmatically and experimentally justified. Both views regard science as an important achievement. But the one rests on the assumption that disillusion is the only wisdom in an opaque and intractable world while the other still reflects faith in the ideal of possible logical coherence and clarity in which illusion will give way to reality, not to disillusion.

"To live by science," Santayana said in *The Life of Reason,* "requires intelligence and faith, but not to live by it is folly."[12] Yet he also thought that apart from the illusion that accompanies every experience of the world, there is no reason to think that the needs and hopes of man can or will ever be satisfied by science. "Knowledge of the world and of what is possible in it, though it may discourage some vice, will not solve for us the question of what is our true good. For what the world can offer, when tried, may seem to us vanity."[13] Ultimately, then, science neither discovers the truth about the world nor guides man to a fulfillment of his own hopes and destiny. The claims and promises of science are no less illusory—and no less in need of purification by disillusion—than the claims of the various religions.

---

8 Wittgenstein, *Tractatus Logico-Philosophicus,* 6.371.
9 Santayana, *Reason in Science,* p. 309.
10 *Ibid.,* p. 318.
11 Wittgenstein, *op. cit.,* 4.01 and 6.371.
12 Santayana, *op. cit.,* p. 319.
13 Santayana, *Dominations and Powers,* p. 464.

V

What about philosophy? There is no doubt that Santayana regarded most, if not all, philosophy as tentative, imaginative, "a
painted world," and no less illusory than religion or science. "At
heart," he wrote, "these finer philosophers [Bergson and Hegel],
like Plato, are not seeking to describe the world of our daily
plodding and commerce, but to supply a visionary interpretation
of it, a refuge from it in some contrasted spiritual assurance,
where the sharp facts vanish into a clarified drama or a pleasant
trance." Yet he also added: "Far be it from me to deride the imagination, poetic or dialectical; but after all it is a great advantage
for a system of philosophy to be substantially true."[14]

Substantially true? What can this mean in the context of a
philosophy which also claims that "If the scientific world be a
product of human faculties, the metaphysical world must be
doubly so; for the material there given to human understanding is
here worked over *again* by human art"?[15] Santayana had no doubt
that the world has (as C. S. Peirce put it) a real character (the
truth) which is independent of what anyone thinks or believes
about it, and that every appearance presented, and every model
constructed, misrepresents to a greater or lesser degree the totality
of facts, and its own relation to them. "Every part of experience,
as it comes, is illusion; and the source of this illusion is my animal
nature, blindly labouring in a blind world."[16] If this is so, the
only "substantially true" philosophy must be one that recognizes
the "inevitable illusion" which infects every version of experience
and knowledge. Experience, and the claims and systems based on
it, may provide relatively reliable guides to conduct, or to the
future course of events. To that extent they may be trusted—or,
indeed, must be trusted. But that they are more than this, or that
they may not be succeeded by utterly different yet equally or more

[14] Santayana, "The Unknowable," in *Obiter Scripta* (ed. Buchler and
Schwartz), p. 163.
[15] Santayana, *Reason in Common Sense*, p. 275.
[16] Santayana, *Scepticism and Animal Faith*, p. 52.

reliable systems and claims, is always unjustified in regard to either a philosophy or a science. One illusion cannot be more illusory than another, and every recognition of the inescapable illusion at the heart of experience is equal to every other as a method of avoiding deception.

Thus Santayana did not claim that his own philosophy was true, except to the extent that it re-expressed the "conventional truths" adopted by those, in the West, who have sought to live in the spirit, and at the same time recognized the arbitrary and illusory character of this choice and the claims that have flowed from it. The possession of absolute truth is beyond the range of human apprehension. "The function of mind is rather to increase the wealth of the universe in the spiritual dimension, by adding appearance to substance and passion to necessity, and by creating . . . private perspectives, and . . . emotions of wonder, adventure, curiosity, and laughter. . . ."[17] The philosopher, like the poet and the scientist, does not discover the world as it is but creates models and perspectives. And he can know the truth only in so far as he recognizes that these are imaginative and illusory although they may coherently interpret and reliably predict all the important and complex events of the world and man's life in it.

VI

It was perhaps the chief wisdom of Santayana that he granted a kind of equality to all the forms of experience and judgment. If he disparaged one of man's cultural and judicial forms, he disparaged all. He established no hierarchy of method and judgment, and perceived that all the ways in which man orients himself to the world, whether common sense, art, religion, or science, though certainly illusory, may be both functional and splendid. Few men have loved the arts and religions more than he did, and few have been more willing to leave "the last word" about the "real" to the scientists without thereby abdicating his own intellect or becoming credulous in the face of problems and methods

17 Santayana, *Realms of Being*, p. xiii.

which he did not pretend to understand. And if he thought that the ultimate result of every method of inquiry and judgment is illusion, there is a similarity to the humble words of Socrates who says in *The Phaedo* that "A man of sense will not insist that these things are exactly as I have described them. But I think that he will believe that something of this kind is true . . . and that it is worth his while to stake everything on this belief."

Taking matter (or blind impersonal and indifferent stuff) to be the basic existential fact to which all other facts and appearances are reducible, Santayana had no choice but to regard religion, the arts, science, and philosophy as essentially symbolic—or more accurately, as symptomatic—of the dark and impenetrable origin of life and light. "The light of the spirit which shines in the darkness cannot see the primeval darkness which begat it and which it dispels."[18] But just what absolute, or non-symbolic, truth would be, Santayana never seriously discussed. Yet this is not clearly either a crucial or avoidable fault. The import of his claim is clear: man's knowledge of himself and the world is at best superficial, only provisionally validated, and extremely limited. No one can logically claim to be certain of the truth about anything. Dogmatism is out. Yet the world is appropriately judged religiously and artistically as well as scientifically and philosophically, if in all instances one guards against illusion by reminding oneself that all is appearance, and that the dark fertility of nature is ultimately unaffected by the visions and revisions which are stimulated in the minds of men.

That experience and judgment are endemically illusory—in spite of its paradoxical nature—is not a claim that the candid mind can easily dismiss. There is too much evidence which supports it. Dogmatists by predilection, most men come only slowly (and often too late) if at all to question the reliability of their claims, or to admit the possible relevance of the contrary claims of others. Yet apart from the question of the kind of world that would result from widespread adoption of the view that all modes of judgment are essentially illusory, there are apparently utterly sane and logical reasons for describing science and philosophy, and in some respects the arts and religions, as systems of reason-

18 *Ibid.*, p. 249.

able belief and veridical judgment rather than as modes of animal faith or illusory symbols and appearances.

Nothing seems more certain, of course, than that scientific innovation and discovery will continue, or that the arts, religions, and philosophy will continually undergo revolutions, as long as man's intellect remains viable. It was nonetheless only by oversimplifying the primal existential fact—by accepting too literally the conclusions of an immature physics—that Santayana was unable to see that man's judgments of the world need not be wholly illusory, even though they are partial and inconclusive. After all, the world that man knows best is in many respects a product of his own judgments, and is surely the most substantial sort of illusion if illusion at all.

Indeed Santayana's own works are part of that world, a part which, contrary to his own view, apparently enters into the causal order of nature, or at least becomes for a time one of the factors that influence the decisions of other men. And it is not necessary to claim either that man is "a nothingness," or "an openness to the world," or "the unconditioned," or that his logical propositions mirror the structure of the world in order to defend the veridical and non-illusory character of judgment. Man is in the world, a part of it. So long as his experience and decisions maintain the direction of life and inquiry, even though man is himself something specific and limited and the world in many respects irrational, there is at least as little reason to doubt the veracity of his judgments as to trust them. If reason requires that we trust our logic in order to remain reasonable, then surely it may also be said that morality, science, religion and art must be trusted for similar, if somewhat less obvious, reasons. For by judging the world morally, the world may be kept moral; by judging it scientifically, science itself may become a more pervasive, and perhaps beneficent, part of the world; and the judgments of religion and art may, respectively and together, keep the world holy and aesthetically profound and pleasing.

If it is for some such reasons as these that the various forms of judgment must be trusted—if each form of experience and each discipline *in some measure* creates and sustains, and not only reflects, the conditions of its own truth—then surely Santayana himself did much, not to increase illusions which must be discounted, but to keep the world both philosophical and beautiful. For the disillusion he encouraged was not the disillusion of ignorance forbidden to eat the fruit of the tree of knowledge but the disillusion of wisdom provoked because wisdom does not altogether rule the world.

A Free Thinker's Catechism

GEORGE SANTAYANA

First Lesson: On the Order of Knowledge

1. *The Doctor:* Did you ever discover that you were wrong in anything?

The Student: Only too often.

2. *The Doctor:* Why "too" often? Would you rather have lived happy in your errors? That would not have been happiness; for error defeats intelligence and endangers other human goods.

The Student: No: such happiness could not be human, but I wish I might have been always right in the beginning.

3. *The Doctor:* Would it have been possible, in that case, *to know* that you were right?

The Student: No: I should have been carried along by a prosperous faith, as little able to defend as to question it.

4. *The Doctor:* Now, after experience has tossed you about and thrown you into your present posture of belief, is your resulting confidence less irrational?

The Student: No: it is as egregious as any other instinctive persuasion, and while reflection has given me grounds for sus-

George Santayana, "A Free Thinker's Catechism," *Columbia Manuscript Collection,* XIV:5:c. © 1967 by Daniel Cory.

pecting that, as usual, I may now be mistaken, practice compels me to assume that this time, at last, I am right.

5. *The Doctor:* Is it impossible, then, to progress in wisdom? No: an opinion, if experience of the world has revised it, is learned in a better school than one constituted in the a priori darkness of the womb. New impulses, when they prompt new ideas, are probably the ground of new errors and (if they do not arise in all men at once) of new estrangements: but opinions shaped by experience grow more true, and (if men live under the same external influences) more communicable. Does not the wider experience yield the more communicable belief?

The Student: Undoubtedly.

6. *The Doctor:* If you now found that all men agreed with you would you have more assurance of knowing the truth than . . . [had you] never disagreed with yourself?

The Student: I should have less: for that all the world agreed with me as I did, would be only my opinion, and that what the world believes is true, would hardly be even that.

7. *The Doctor:* Why, then, did you ever change your mind, and how comes it that you feel any force or authority in criticism?

The Student: Because the landscape changes. Fresh impressions come, and old thoughts lose their importunity. My last opinion judges all the others. It thrusts them back at first, perhaps, only a little, and without letting them go; but in time they somehow cease to figure in the play; they have stiffened into scenery. What I thought yesterday is like a dead king; what I shall think tomorrow is his unborn heir, quite possibly illegitimate; and meantime what I think today holds the regency.

8. *The Doctor:* Has any actual opinion any rational authority?

The Student: None whatever, and if my present opinion were not my present opinion, I should never dream of crediting it.

9. *The Doctor:* Can nothing corroborate opinions, and so rationalise them?

The Student: Yes: but that occurs with a given opinion,

not corroborated itself, but opining that its parts or its objects corroborate one another.

10. *The Doctor:* You have then no serious conviction?

The Student: Yes, I have: conviction, I should say, is a product of life, not of reasoning. Reasoning is but an explication of what the given conviction implies.

11. *The Doctor:* Can opinions differ in weight and value?

The Student: They can. I have at present certain interests at heart which would be outraged by absurdities, chilled by scepticism, furthered by discovery. What touches these interests is serious and respectable in my eyes; the rest is vexatious fooling. I will not listen to people who say that two and two are seven, not caring for what they mean; or that men begin by dying of old age and end by becoming children in the womb, not caring for observable reality. I will not make the least concession to those who urge that whatever happens is equally good, or that I shall be eternally tortured in hell unless I presently turn three somersaults in the air. There are points I will not stoop to argue, as there are things I will not stoop to do. Those opinions are contemptible which are altogether at cross purposes with what I mean, with what I find, and with what I want. By their relevance to life I test all opinions, and this relevance I call reason.

12. *The Doctor:* That is a brave answer. You do well to summon all things in heaven and earth to the bar of your free conscience and bid them justify themselves there. Indeed, unless you do so once in your life your philosophy will never be more than a party doctrine, picked up by chance in the world, and no honest expression of a liberal nature. But seeing that you make yourself for the nonce the very fulcrum of the universe, and that nothing merits consideration save as it touches you, perhaps you will tell me what you understand by yourself. We all use the word "I" too often, and too inconsiderately: but in your case what it stands for, if not less obscure than usual, would seem to be unusually important.

The Student: By myself I do not, of course, mean my body, nor even my life-long dream, in distinction from the organs that sustain it; for my inner dream passes before me and is one of the things I take note of and judge. By myself I mean the wakefulness that observes that vision; and this wakefulness has a scope and intensity which, as I can easily discover, correspond exactly to the fortunes of my body in the world of matter; so that I am my body's soul, I am the impulses of a mortal organism awaking to their satisfaction or discomfiture, and partly apprehending the surrounding opportunities and dangers.

13. *The Doctor:* Another brave answer, and one which might possibly turn out to be right, which would be better than bravery. Yet, in your sceptical mood, you might easily call in question at least the historical part of what you have just affirmed. You might doubt that your visions "passed before you," that is, that they existed elsewhere first and, after appearing to you, retired again beyond your ken. You might doubt that you had a body, or that the supposed stationary spectator of your passing dreams was in any way seated in that body, or dependent on it. Are these things more than traditional commonplaces or instinctive fancies? And to come at once to a fundamental point, how do you know that anything is in flux at all, and that this flux is observed by something comparatively stable?

The Student: What is the use of challenging a conception, if we have no other to put in its place?

14. *The Doctor:* No doubt things seem to change: we have a feeling of what we call transition. But this feeling of change might well be a single fact, either eternally existent or arisen all at once; and the distinction we make between successive experiences and a person that gathers them might be a second illusion, founded on the first, I mean, on the false notion that the experiences themselves had been many. All existence might be only an instant picture, and the recession in it might be but painted; yet, being painted in perspective, it might suggest the verbal fiction of a traveller that had moved forward from the background and brought with him a report of what that background had been. Time and change may be unreal, and *a fortiori* that contemplative and enduring spirit would be unreal whose function was to neutralise change and time by observing them.

The Student: I see that if change did not exist, a spiritual principle to bridge change over would be needless; if the first was illusory the second could be but nominal. What I cannot conceive is that change should not exist. Even if I succeeded in conceiving it, by passing myself to so new a thought, I should be creating that variation which I was denying.

15. *The Doctor:* Of course the notion that you had changed your mind would, in that case, be itself the illusion. Either the former opinion had never existed, or He that had it once would have it still. But these are mysteries which it takes solitude and discipline to fathom; and they may prove hollow in the end. You seem as yet not to walk in step with the philosophers, along this road; for many of them have believed, or said they believed, that reality was immutable; but usually, at least in modern times, they have not ceased on that account to assume a spirit that should bear witness to eternal truth. Were they not justified in this assumption?

The Student: Certainly not; for if mind and its objects moved at the same rate, or were both stationary, any distinction between them would be impossible.

16. *The Doctor:* Then the very notion of a pure or universal mind is, according to you, illegitimate?

The Student: It is not illegitimate in poetry; but it is absurd in science. The notion is mythical, since the whole force of it comes from conceiving the Absolute on the analogy of an impressionable precarious being, addressed to what is occurring without him or to what occurred to him at other times, or to what might occur to him in future.

17. *The Doctor:* You are not sure, then, in your own case, that you are saying anything serious when you speak of a "wakefulness" to which visions appear?

The Student: The seriousness of that distinction, as of every other, would lie in its designating things actually divisible in the world; but when the world itself, and all alteration in it, have been called in question, words have lost their function and yield nothing but a mocking echo of what they once signified.

18. *The Doctor:* You are, then, nothing assignable apart from the place you fill in the world; and the world itself must be taken

for granted on the strength of a certain practical habit, or cognitive art, which draws you into conventional thinking?

The Student: Quite so: when I try to recede behind convention, or to get under it, I find that I am rejecting the substance of convention only by abusing its moulds. I am like a fop who, to be absolutely in fashion, should go shivering in the paper patterns of his own clothes.

19. *The Doctor:* Let us then leave "you" aside, not that you are altogether negligible, but that we cannot for the present make out what you are. Perhaps we may discover eventually, if we begin by inquiring more accurately what you mean by the things that seem to be present to you. What, for instance, do you understand by body?

The Student: By body I understand what keeps its form and position, or changes them in a traceable and continuous manner. Body is recognisable matter.

20. *The Doctor:* Dear me! But what is matter, or recognition, or continuity, or change, or form, or position? To answer one question is often to raise a thousand.

The Student: I thought that was just the beauty and the use of philosophy. Yet I suspect this flood of questions might be reduced to one or two. Position illustrates forms, since it is relative to points and distances deployed in a field which they define. Continuity also is an instance of form; and form in turn leads back to recognition, to the art of identifying ideally things distinct in act and in existence. But distinction in act and in existence is a condition of change; and both distinction and change depend on matter, since forms could not come and go, they could not be given or be recognised, if they were forms merely. Existing forms occur, that is, they are embodied or exemplified: and this is what I meant in the beginning by saying that things "passed before me." I did not really fancy, as you maliciously made out, that they came and went out of a veiled world, where at other times they disported themselves unobserved: I meant that in their instant and casual being they *illustrated an idea,* after which I named them. When the same idea was illustrated by a fresh existence, I said the thing had re-

curred; not that the existence had come out of a hiding-place
and was the same existence, but that the flux had resumed an old
shape and was performing a known function. Now, that ideas
occur here and now, with particular modifications, and in a particular alien context, is a fact worth noting. In noting it we
frame the conception of what, in good English, is called matter;
matter being the right name for that quantitative existential
principle which is responsible for the occurrence of forms.—My
definition of body, then, comes down to this: that what I seem
to find before me has recurrent and recognisable shapes. These
shapes, though in their nature eternally distinct and at peace
with one another, are, in their embodiment, imperfectly expressed, flowing, and competitive. Whatever parcel of substance
each of these shapes holds for a moment against its rivals, and
enables me to identify and to name, I call a body.

21. *The Doctor:* When you scrutinise body, if I understand
you, all you come upon is an ideal nature, a term in discourse?

The Student: Yes; but I come at the same time upon the
fact that this ideal nature exists, being illustrated sensibly now
and here, and coming in a sequence of forms, lapsing but consecutive, and ideally irrelevant to one another. Hence what I find is
not an idea but a thing. The essence of it clothes for the moment
some portion of an existential flux.

22. *The Doctor:* But is the ideal illustrated in nothing except
things and bodies? Do not mental images exist as well, and do
they not likewise portray certain essences?

The Student: You broach a subject about which all I have
read in modern books seems to me singularly oblique and confusing. They speak as if what we knew [were] mental images, and
as if things were consequently either unknowable (in which case
they would be irrelevant to the images) or else mere propositions
about the order in which images may be expected to flow (in
which case the things would not *exist* at all). Now what is obscured by such a sophistical posing of the question is that *images,
in so far as they have any cognitive value, are themselves propositions;* and that what they assert the existence of is not themselves, the propositions, but an object having the qualities posited

by the terms of that proposition. Thus the image of a green tree says "A green tree is there, in space" not "The image of a green tree is here, in consciousness." What is true concerning the tree, as that it grew from an acorn, is false concerning the image; and the observed qualities, like greenness, are possible predicates of a tree, but impossible predicates of the observation of it. An image picturing itself, a knowledge possessing the qualities it assigns, is an unthinkable entity; it is a spiritual existence with physical attributes. What helps, however, to fashion this idol of the den is the fact that images, besides being propositions, are also feelings. The qualities which, as propositions, they find in their object may accordingly, by a fallacy of transposition, by an insincere interpretation of intent, be turned into qualities of the feeling that they exist. But feeling is never green, nor loud, or round, nor near; it is a feeling that these are qualities of what is present. The proper qualities of feeling lie in other dimensions altogether, in the intensive dimension of pain and pleasure, in the transitive dimension of tendency or yearning, in the indescribable material dimension of existence itself. Such are the attributes which images truly possess, the others are the qualities they attribute. Thus your word "portray" seems to me equivocal, since it might designate either exemplification or knowledge, or neither, or both.

23. *The Doctor:* Are not existence, tendency, and value, which you admit to be properties of images, illustrations of ideal essences, much as are the properties you discover in things?

The Student: No. It is obviously repugnant that existence or tendency should be an ideal nature. "Ideal nature" means determinate form, *goal* of possible tendency, *kind* of possible existence: existence and tendency in general are not themselves kinds or ideals. The same thing may be said of value; although a certain mystification may be easy to fall into here, owing to the degraded Platonism that has long prevailed in the schools. The good is in one sense the most ideal of ideal natures, since it is what all ideals have in common, namely, their authority in respect to what they define the perfection of. But the good is no specific good, and in that sense it is no ideal; so that the intensive dimension of feeling, by which feeling may become an illustration and seat of the good, is not itself the illustration of any ideal essence. It is merely the initiation of that movement of preference which makes it possible for any form to possess a value.

24. *The Doctor:* What relation do you conceive to subsist between the intensive and the cognitive aspects of images? I suppose there must be relation: thus, for instance, the intensive character is a condition of the cognitive; for if images had no intensity they would not exist, and not existing they would hardly exercise the cognitive function, or any other. On the other hand, if cognitive functions were wholly suppressed, what would an image be? Would it retain any intrinsic relation to anything? And if not, how could it be dated, related, or known to exist at all?

The Student: Nohow: from the outside a feeling that knows nothing is quite unknowable; and from the inside it is not worth having. Yet out of such blind and pathetic feeling, I suppose all our vibrating and discursive consciousness has grown; grown by becoming the vision and drama of that real world of which at first it was nothing but the conscious friction. Feeling at first, and while it is nothing but feeling, is ignorant of its context, and hardly implies a context at all. Its association with that particular state of body, which as a matter of fact is its basis, then seems quite arbitrary; the feeling of green might, for all we see, have been attached to the stimulus which actually yields the feeling of blue. Relevance between the mental and bodily states emerges later, as the feeling begins to have a subject-matter and, through this subject-matter, a specific place in the world. Thus we begin to perceive some inner congruity between feeling and its occasion when the feeling is a pleasure or a pain; for a fulfilled tendency or instinct in the body is *expressed* by conscious preference or satisfaction as it would not be by conscious revulsion or unrest. Much more does an irreversible congruity appear between feeling and its causes, when the feeling is a perception, and tries to describe something; for what it tries to describe is evidently some part of its actual causes, of its actual environment, sadly as it may at first fail in describing it correctly. We may accordingly establish a hierarchy among feelings according to their degree of inward relevance to the situation in which they arise. At the bottom would be blind feeling, with no such relevance; at the top pure knowledge, where relevance is all.

25. *The Doctor:* Such a series of feelings would be ideally attached to the material world; it would, in its perfection, represent that world and give it a value, a *raison d'être;* but would consciousness on that account be at all explicable materially, or understood in its origin?

The Student: No. Perhaps it is a mistake to try to explain spirit in that way: being superfluous materially it may well be materially inexplicable. That things should have an ideal co-efficient might remain as groundless a peculiarity of them as that they should be in space, or in flux. At any rate, the genesis of feeling is not what I am trying to justify. We are investigating now the first assumptions of knowledge—the reasons I may have for believing that anything has a genesis or history at all.

26. *The Doctor:* Yet you acknowledge that mental images are themselves existences; and I wished to know if the analysis you gave of existences in general—that they were ideal forms exemplified in the flux of matter—could be true of mental existences in particular. It would seem either that consciousness itself would become a second kind of matter, or that mental facts would be forms without matter at all.

The Student: That forms reappear, and that there is a matter that takes on those forms, are two truths *discovered:* they are not necessary truths. Such an analysis would not fit a universe consisting wholly of feeling—which is perhaps the reason why modern sensualism, which makes feeling the only substance, neglects this Aristotelian distinction. A universe consisting wholly of feelings might contain no recurrences, and therefore no forms worth discriminating; and it might have no quantitative continuity, no local derivations, and therefore no intelligible matter. And even if feeling constituted, not the whole, but an independent province, of being, the distinction between matter and form, not being important in that province, would become much less important on the whole, since it would not be of universal application. What tempts me, nevertheless, to look for it even in the region of feeling is that feeling is an existence of a secondary and ineffectual sort; the form and the matter of it are the form and matter of something else first, and, since feeling borrows them, it can seem to live with no matter or form of its own. It borrows the matter of its *basis;* it borrows the form of its *object;* and these two principles, though extraneous to feeling in its abstraction, while it remains blind feeling, are the only principles by which it is knit to the world, either when it comes to understanding or when it comes to be understood. Thus the toothache, a volatile demon, contains no matter because there is matter enough to sustain it in the tooth; and it hardly envisages a form, because its true theme, if it could perceive it, would be the decay setting in in that member. It suffices, therefore, to understand the toothache, either medically from without, or experimentally from within, to reach the world in which its matter and its ideal are given; nor could the toothache be understood otherwise. The obscuring of matter and form in feeling is therefore due to its being inherently inchoate, essentially an echo and an index. To find what it indicates, to complete what it implies, is to pass to an articulate world of formed matter, to which feeling opens an avenue for the soul.

One Santayana or Two?

JUSTUS BUCHLER

Santayana said of Kant that the contradictions in his system were not simply of the type inevitable in all original work but were fundamental and inexcusable. If such an extreme verdict was never brought against Santayana himself, it was only because the circumstances of his life suggested a different avenue of evaluation. The academic man in America had given way to the clois-

Justus Buchler, "One Santayana or Two?" *The Journal of Philosophy,* 51 (1954), pp. 52-57. Reprinted by permission.

tered student of existence and essence in the Eternal City, and this seemed to be paralleled by a transition from one mode of philosophizing to another. It was contended, and primarily by admirers of Santayana, that the later philosophy was incompatible with the earlier, his own protestations to the contrary notwithstanding. The critics' reasons were compelling, and everyone remembers the time when the whole problem, peculiarly challenging and self-clarifying to the interpreter, imposed a certain urgency of decision. Eventually, in the consensus of the witnesses, the two Santayanas emerged, with similar virtues and graces but with irreconcilable commitments. The earlier was a humanistic naturalist, the later an Olympian mystic. The earlier was dedicated to the ideal of rational sociality, the later to spectatorial disinterestedness and the contemplation of essences. To the earlier, knowledge was a fact; to the later, it was a miracle.

Is this portrait with two faces just? It is not possible in so brief a space adequately to re-think the question. But piety to the philosopher requires us at least to re-open it. My own feeling is that the "earlier-later" approach is a misleading one, beguilingly fostered by the patterns of Santayana's career. Santayana was emotionally a hermit before he got to Rome and unremittingly a naturalist after he got there. There *are* two strains in his philosophy. But they are not sequential. They cohabit in *each* of his major works. He did not grow a second face in the course of time; from the beginning he had a divided soul. In a moment I shall try to define the character of this division. What has bothered most people is the apparent abyss between *Realms of Being* and *The Life of Reason,* and the unquestionable difference in texture. But do such considerations prove anything? If the two works are surprisingly unlike in flavor, it is not because of a difference between earlier and later thinking. For there is a basic *likeness* in flavor between *Dominations and Powers* (which is much later than *Realms of Being*) and *The Sense of Beauty* (which is much earlier than *The Life of Reason*). A philosopher has the right to alter his themes or to magnify them. When Santayana chose in 1923 to concentrate on matters epistemic, he produced unfamiliar notes; but when he chose in 1950 to resume his analysis of the human animal, seeing it politically as in 1896 he had seen it esthetically, he appeared to be rounding out a re-markably homogeneous viewpoint.

An examination of *Reason in Common Sense*--a key work in the understanding of Santayana's persistent intent, his philoso-phic aspirations, and his methods—shows the presence in it of much that later disturbed his readers in *Scepticism and Animal Faith*. Each of these two books, whatever else it may be, is a nat-ural history of "consciousness." In the earlier one, the movement of investigation is from "The Birth of Reason" to "The Discovery of Natural Objects" to "Nature Unified and Mind Discerned" to "Discovery of Fellow Minds." In the later one, it is from "Noth-ing Given Exists" to "The Discovery of Essence" to "Belief in Experience" to "Belief in Substance." The parallelism is unmis-takable. Even the manner and the terms of the later book are to be found in the earlier. For instance (in *Reason in Common Sense*): "We attribute independence to things in order to normal-ise their recurrence. We attribute essences to them in order to normalise their manifestations or constitution." Or: "The several repetitions of one essence given in consciousness will tend at once to be neglected, and only the essence itself—the character shared by sundry perceptions—will stand and become a term in mental discourse." Or: "A thing . . . is discovered only when the order and grouping of . . . recurring essences can be observed, and when various themes and strains of experience are woven together into elaborate progressive harmonies."

When I was a graduate student, much concerned with the in-fluences at work among recent thinkers, I inquired of Santayana concerning the sources of some of his ideas. A letter of October 15, 1937 reads in part:

. . . I heard one of [Peirce's] Harvard lectures. He had been dining at the James's and his evening shirt kept coming out of his evening waist-coat. He looked red-nosed and dishevelled, and a part of his lecture seemed to be *ex-tempore* and whimsical. But I remember and have often used in my own thought, if not in actual writing, a classification he made that evening of signs into indexes and symbols and images: pos-sibly there was still another distinct category which I don't remember. The index changes with its object but does not resemble it; the symbol resembles the object loosely and by analogy. . . .

Whether 'firstness' has any relation to my idea of essence, you can judge better than I, as I have not read Pierce [sic] on that subject, or know what he said. My idea came, apart from Plato, from Russell and Moore in their early phase, when they were writing their [sic] *Principia Ethica* [sic]; and perhaps they got it from Brentano, whom I have never read. I also got a vivid glimpse of the realm of essence as a whole, and as the inevitable background of all reality, out of a Persian or Arabian philosopher—I forget his name—mentioned in a French *Life of Avicenna* by Baron Cara de Veaux (or Vaux)—an old book that I have never been able to lay my hands on again.

One could never tell whether Santayana's innocent factual lapses contained seeds of irony. His sharp observations, on Peirce for example, reveal how much went on in his reflection that failed to appear either in his theoretical work or his autobiography.

The notion of essence, as the foregoing remarks indicate, brewed early in Santayana, though only at a relatively late date did it begin to assume a position of centrality in his writing. The profound similarities between *Reason in Common Sense* and *Scepticism and Animal Faith* escape attention only because in the former the metaphysical allegiance is announced beforehand and colors the procedure, whereas in the latter it is deferred with the expectation that it will be warranted as a conclusion. Recall that in the earlier book it was "the English psychologists . . . whose traces we have in general followed in the above account." The very same statement, of course, could have been made in the later book. In both books, and in almost all of his books, Santayana declared the purposes of the English psychologists to be "malicious." But their method he was powerless to evade; and when it was not the older empiricists who tyrannized over him, it was "Russell and Moore," in one form or another, and more covertly than he suspected.

Anyone who thinks that Santayana's sense of eternality and spirit of detachment is characteristic only of his later ethical writing must not have read the chapter on "Charity" in *Reason in Religion,* nor indeed the whole book, which stands to *The Realm of Spirit* as *Reason in Common Sense* does to *Scepticism and Animal Faith*. In this case the parallelism is even more evident. Suffice it here to say that from first to last Santayana affirmed the natural basis of value, appropriated Christian symbols to dramatize ideals, damned the literalists and fundamentalists as worse than the nihilists, and articulated the sense of tragedy. A letter of July 1, 1936, complied with a request I had made of him to comment on the "earlier-later" issue in his ethics. It happens to be an important statement.

. . . What people . . . dislike is not so much the materialism or ontology slipped under the life of reason, as the "spiritual life" supposed to be substituted for it in my estimation.

That is a complete misconception. No doubt when I wrote *The Life of Reason* I was taken up with rational ethics and interested (as I still am) in the theory of government and the pro's and con's of religious institutions. But I never thought of life in society, or of moral economy, as the obligatory or only worthy life. I am not a dogmatist in ethics. In so far as we legislate, and arrange things for mankind at large, of course we must do so rationally, with as fair a regard as possible for all the interests concerned. But these interests change and fade into infinity, and the art of government or education must, in practice, be rather empirical and haphazard. The best results, like the worst, will be unforeseen. Meantime actual life in each creature has its exquisite or terrible immediate reality. It is a spiritual life. It is spiritual in children as easily as in anchorites. This is not a substitute for the life of reason, but the cream or concomitant ultimate actuality of what the organized life of reason produces in consciousness. Of course, in so far as a man's thoughts are absorbed in instrumentalities, in business or politics or war or jollification, we do not call his experience spiritual: but those very actions might be food for a spiritual life if a recollected and mystical man performed them: so that the rationality of his life and its spirituality might be called two concomitant dimensions of it, the one lateral and the other vertical. The vertical or spiritual dimension is what inward religion has always added to life in the world, or in the cloister, which is a part of the world: that element may be more or less emphatic or genuine, according to a man's temperament or experience, but it is always an element, optional, private, like the love of music or like love at large. The legislator may salute it, he cannot contract to produce it.

What were the strains that divided Santayana and that made each of his major works an adventure in equilibrium? His real problem was a methodological one. He oscillated precariously all his life between two orientations that have never been harmonized in the history of philosophy. On the one hand, he had the impulse to make "human orthodoxy" or "common sense" the basis of speculation, the material that guides the philosopher in the discrimination of pervasive traits. But on the other hand, he had an equally strong impulse to eschew such a basis, as the insidious enemy of philosophy. On the one hand, he wished to accept the universe "as a going concern"; on the other, he felt compelled to construct the universe out of the data of sensuous immediacy. On the one hand, his concept of nature prescribed the direction of his epistemology; on the other, the impetus of his epistemology loosened the moorings of his concept of nature. On the one hand, he stressed the inevitability of natural assumptions; and on the other, he could not resist the urge to "start from scratch," to wipe the slate clean, as so many philosophers he distrusted had tried to do. His heart was with the Greeks, his mind with the British empiricists. He always fancied that his own variety of methodological scepticism was uniquely and safely worked out, that it was purgative and normal and desirable. He thought of it as an auxiliary device, and remained unaware of the fact that it threatened to devour his naturalism. He came fully as close to disaster in *The Life of Reason* as in *Realms of Being*. During his brief controversy with Dewey in the '20s, when each sought to disparage the other's version of naturalism, he accused Dewey of being dominated by "the foreground," oblivious of his own perennial entanglement in the foreground.

Santayana's limitations were as great as those of every other great philosopher. His contribution to the philosophic heritage and to the idiom of the human imagination is enormous. He revolutionized naturalism by giving it a new freedom of expression and a new vocabulary, by widening the scope of its inventiveness. Sometimes when he fatted it he poisoned it; but since it was older than he was, it could only profit ultimately from the plenitude of his inquiries. He was a true systematizer, yet he avoided extravagance. Perhaps no other modern has so successfully blended sobriety and poetry. He was a powerful analyst—and not merely because he could make other philosophers change their minds, or because he could show how many senses one term had. All of that he could do, eminently. He was primarily an analyst of structures, as philosophers perforce are; and of grand and intricate structures, as Hegel was. And in helping naturalism out of its starkness and rigidity he showed what it was in other traditions that was available to liberal understanding. If, then, when all is said and done, there are two Santayanas, if with the one substance we must associate two essences, so much the better.

II

MATERIALISM AND IDEALISM

Materialism of Idealists

GEORGE SANTAYANA

Proud one-sided systems deservedly remain famous, like the
Brutuses and the Catos, because of the moral force which they
express, even in their perversity: for there is a gallant virtue in
vice, when it is uncompromising. More blessed in the end, however, are those philosophers who are teachable, observant, em-
barrassed, never defying the nature of things: things carry them
on their shoulders and like Caesar they inherit the earth. It is true
that for the most part the prudent are inconspicuous in their
minds and persons, and are forgotten: but their very modesty
should reconcile them to this fate, if by the complex operation of
things their caution is vindicated; and they triumph anony-
mously when mankind, without knowing why, is compelled to
adopt their opinions. Even personal systems of philosophy or religion, when they take root, lose their sharpness, sometimes entirely
forget their first inspiration; because, if people are to live under
a system, they must stretch it so as to cover somehow all the facts
of life. All prevalent systems thereby neutralise their sectarian
colour and become windows—no doubt each is of a special archi-

George Santayana, "Materialism of Idealists," *Columbia Manuscript Collection*, XIV:1. © 1967 by Daniel Cory.

tecture and glazing—through which the varied champaign of nature is somehow visible. So it is conspicuously with all the religions; they must all reckon with their host, which is unregenerate human nature, indomitably young; and so, in a smaller field, it is with all idealisms: nature takes her revenge on those who deny her. Idealists are the advocates of mind, love it, defend its prerogatives, and are themselves (I am free to confess it) more richly endowed with mind than other mortals, and more muffled in it. Mind in nature is something very special, singular, and local: a good station, indeed the only possible station, for surveying nature, but a narrow, a punctiform, field if mind be reduced to surveying itself. This the idealists set about doing when they aver that everything is mind: because matter, and essence, and truth, they say, can be nothing but objects of mind, verbal, conceptual, and visionary; so many themes with which mind concerns itself and which it devises for its entertainment; because evidently the great danger which mind would run if mind were absolute is that it should have nothing to do and nothing to think about. Let us give rein to this reflective impulse, and see what happens. There shall be no matter or truth or essence considered, save the *ideas* of essence or matter or truth which the mind has so far framed: there shall be no objects but only descriptions of objects, no world but only discourse about a world. When reflection retreats in this way into the spirit it puts on the cap of Gyges and becomes invisible: nature cannot attack or even discover such a transcendental sanctuary. But when idealists cease to manipulate ideas and begin to believe, when they attribute existence to the discourse to which they reduce nature, then nature triumphs not so much over them as in them: because without suspecting it they have abandoned the sanctuary of spirit, and posited mind in relations with mind which are external, and not merely visioned and imputed in some act of thinking: and thereby they have made mind itself material. For the great difference between mind and matter does not lie in the provinces of essence which they respectively realise: geometrical essences, for instance, may be realised in matter, by being embodied there, like the pyramid in the Pyramids; and the same essences may be realised by mind, by being inspected, as the triangle by Pythagoras or the Pyramids by the tourist. The great difference lies in the manner in which these essences touch existence in the two realms: for in the realm of matter they touch existence by becoming the essences of things, and in that embodiment possessing external and variable relations in physical space and time: whereas in the realm of spirit they touch existence only by being thought of or contemplated in their own sphere, so that only the intuition, and not the essence inspected, exists at all, or has any home (and this by adoption only) in nature. Hence it suffices that essences present to thought should be asserted to lie in external relations to one another in physical time or space for these essences to be regarded as substantial things: and the only question that remains is whether such substances are those which actually compose nature, or whether nature is composed of other substances. The idealists descend, if they attribute existence to their minds or to their ideas, into the arena of physics: their hypotheses become scientific hypotheses; and their idealism is no longer a withdrawal into the inexpugnable citadel of spirit, but is one dogma among so many dogmas regarding the constitution of the natural world.

Let me give some historical illustrations of idealism becoming in this way, against its will, a form—but a warped and fantastic form—of naturalism.

Plato, lest we should be inclined to regard intelligence as the privilege of mortals, or as an exigency of life in the midst of dangers, compares it with fire: as the fire in the hearth is but a spark of the celestial fire brought down from the stars by Prometheus, so our troubled intelligence is but a drop of that clear intellect which keeps the heavens in orderly motion. This simile is too noble not to be treacherous. It may perhaps be true that fire—or in modern parlance, electricity—is the substance of the universe, or inseparable from its substance, so that the crusts of planets and the bodies of animals are but shells in which parcels of it are still burning, and are soon dissipated or crumble without its inward heat. The human soul might thus, on its physical side, be a parcel of the soul universal, or the original cosmic principle which has shaped the stars. But the soul, so conceived, is not actual thinking, and this cosmic fire is not a light seen. Seen light is intermittent; it comes and goes with the opening and closing of the eyes. So does actual thought with the occasions in which adaptation and harmony are established between plastic animals and their surroundings. If mind is made a cosmic principle it ceases to be mind, in the intensive and discursive sense: it ceases to be feeling or thought. It has become a mythological name for the principle of motion and order; we have substituted a fable —no doubt a good fable—for a sober analysis of the facts. Actual mind is like fire in being a flame, a light: it is not like fire in being a radiation of material energy, equable, mathematical, infinitely diffused; a force measured and defined by its effects elsewhere rather than, as actual mind is, by its intrinsic energy, or light. To make a substance of the immaterial is to make it matter.

The propriety of assimilating mind with light comes from the fact that seen light is not a substance but a flash given out by the motion or shock of substances. The mind has that sort of relation to its conditions: it bursts from them like a flame, dies in being born, and endures only if perpetually renewed. It is contagious, because the metabolism which supports it is so; and it exists in as great quantities and in as many places as its fuel: but as a flame cannot spread in a vacuum, where no combustible train has been laid to conduct it, so mind at each point expresses the movement of its organs, and never spreads where no grosser instrument has been fitted and trained to sustain it. What tendency has the intellect of my wiser neighbours to flow into mine? None, if we happen to belong to different races, religions, classes, or traditions of speech. I should first have to lead their lives and learn their languages: then, indeed thoughts like theirs would spring up in me also: possibly I might anticipate their feelings and be hailed by them as a prophet. But between thoughts and thoughts there is no nearness in space, no pressure, not even, intrinsically, any common date: the character of each is what its instant birth and natural ground have made it, and its proper relations to other thoughts are only ideal relations.

I neglect the ambiguities in the term $νοῦς$ or reason, when used for a physical or metaphysical principle, because whether $νοῦς$ means a special substance or means an actual order in nature favourable to good in general or to thought in particular, my observations hold of it equally. If suffices that at one point either of these unconscious principles of reason should culminate in actual thinking for nature to be proved to be, to that extent, intelligent or fruitful in mind; but such a culmination might occur once without ever recurring, and the fact that such a disposition, favourable to thought, exists in nature at that point is no argument to prove that it exists elsewhere, much less that it is ubiquitous.

To skip from the earliest to the latest philosophy, William James and many other writers in arguing of interaction between mind and body invoke the Darwinian principle that useless organs tend to be atrophied; so that unless consciousness had helped to adapt animals to their circumstances it would long ago have died out. This is a very materialistic argument, because it assumes that unless consciousness has material functions it can have no hold on existence. That it should have moral functions would not, on Darwinian principles (which are unwittingly but thoroughly materialistic), be any ground for persistence in the world: the world, it is assumed, is governed by matter only. If mind exists, then, it must be coordinate with matter; its modes must alternate with the modes of matter: in effect and in substance, therefore, mind must be a material thing, and its apparent spirituality must be an illusion, or an epiphenomenon. It was therefore consonant with the inner logic of this position that the same persons who advocated the efficacy of consciousness, should soon afterwards maintain its non-existence: for that spiritual actuality which made consciousness consciousness was precisely the mode of being which could not possibly be aligned with material events, not having any spatial, qualitative, quantitative, or even temporal frontiers in common with them: in other words, not being observable or traceable in the material world. The spiritual life of nature has to be *read into* her material movement by a mythologizing spirit: this reading proves indeed that a mythologizing spirit exists; and if we assume that it is the spirit of a part of nature (the thinker's body) there may be analogies justifying a reflective philosopher in assuming spirit of a like sort in similar animals: but this ulterior and indirect argument for the existence of diffused consciousness, does not imply that it is an observable link in natural processes: on the contrary, being the *moral mean-*

ing of those observable events it *cannot* be a material part of them, as the meaning of a phrase *cannot* be one of the syllables in it.

Moreover, the argument in question begs the question, since it supposes that consciousness absorbs energy and is a drain on the system, so that if it were useless it would be a material handicap to those who possessed it. It would be a bad habit, deranging or weakening the organism, like masturbation. So too dreaming, worrying, nagging, and arguing—in a word, philosophy itself—are terribly fatiguing and make people unfit for steady work. The nervous habit concerned does this: and as actual bodily economy at this depth is not known or picturable, we let the moral appearances involved, as discourse unrolls them, stand for those biological complications. So when the nervous habit is useful, the moral appearances it generates are omens of utility, and pass for useful in their own persons. But of course the reflection which recognizes the spirituality of consciousness, thereby removes it from the physical plane altogether: so that it *cannot* be a waste or even a use of material energy: therefore neither a help nor a hindrance in evolution.

The theory of interaction between mind and body is a combination of psychologism and materialism: and as even pure psychologism, against its will, turns mind into matter, so a world alternately material and psychological would be everywhere materialistic: the patches of psychological existence being only a dramatic and moral transcript of the same material series of events which elsewhere were described in sensuous or scientific terms. We are transported to that graphic but crude method of observation which identifies mind in others with their gestures, words, and actions, and in oneself with the immediate objects of attention—often words, and actions of one's own, i.e., motions of one's body, sometimes pictures or thoughts, sensuous or intelligible essences, probably taken for things or for the essences of things. We say that a man's head is bowed down with grief, or with the weight of thought, or that his step is made slow by his solemn feelings. If we *mean* by grief whatsoever bows down his head, then certainly grief is a material agent, in that it does ma-

terial work; but just in the same measure, grief becomes an observable thing and the emotion itself is left out of account; so that
the mental factor to which we mean to ascribe efficacy has disappeared. It turns out, on our own showing, that consciousness, after
all, is inefficacious, since it is non-existent. The theory of interaction between mind and body thus dies in the arms of behaviourism. The only factors recognized are observable factors, and nothing immaterial, moral, intensive, and invisible, governs them from
behind the scenes.

But behaviourism is ambiguous, and the false sort of materialism in it may be corrected by pointing out that the immediate
objects of observation are not things but essences, so that the theory may still be interpreted idealistically, in that the bodies observed to behave in these animated ways, may not be bodies, but
only images or ideas of bodies. We shall then be brought back to
psychologism, the theory which conceives nature to be composed
exclusively of various strands of feelings, and thoughts. Psychologism is one of the modern forms of idealism, transcendentalism
being the other: and since transcendentalism can escape materialism if it remains a romantic attitude, without any dogmatic cosmology, dogmatic history, dogmatic psychology, or dogmatic
memory, so too psychologism may escape materialism if it remains purely literary, like the world of a novel, and when pressed
to specify where the existential elements of its literary landscapes
are to be found, retires into the citadel of transcendentalism, and
says they are found by being feigned, or by being actually experienced. But if transcendentalists find it impossible, in constructing
a system, to avoid some dogmatic beliefs, say as to the course of
events, the psychologists do not even attempt such rigour; and
they take for granted that perfectly well-known experiences fall
to everybody's share: that these persons communicate their feelings, know of one another's existence, and receive the same hard
knocks at assignable times, without there existing any common
environment, any spacial relations, or any connecting medium
between their various experiences. Such, at least, would be their
doctrine, if they had one: but I suspect that, even when criticising
conventional beliefs, they continue to share them, and that they

always conceive experience as going on in animal bodies in a common material habitat. Even the experiences recounted in a novel must be imagined to go on in a material world of some kind: and the moment this material world is retracted, and reduced to an image in the mind, the whole experience described in the book retreats into the same sanctuary, and it becomes impossible to believe that, except in the mind of the author and his readers, who belonged to the material world, any such experience ever occurred.

Suppose mind (which is to be the only sort of existence admitted by psychologism) is composed of *ideas,* which are at once instances or moments of life and objects of attention: both active feelings and given essences. How is this thinkable, and what sort of a world can be made of such stuff?

To maintain that there are no such things as ideas would be paradoxical. We say at every turn, "I haven't the least idea," and are convinced that we might have one and, on most subjects, we have many true ones. These ideas known to common speech are bits of knowledge or imagination, the observations, conclusions, and fancies which life has put at our command. Their quality in a man determines his intellectual calibre and the moral tone of his conversation. There can be no doubt that there are ideas in this popular sense: but what, exactly, are they? Essences, sensuous, logical, or intelligible? Acts or modes of thinking? Existing objects of thought? Portions of the mind itself?

The common man believes that he has ideas when the objects which he is thinking about are not in the same space and time with his body; when the objects are present he would, if questioned, agree with the Scottish philosophers that no *idea* is involved in his perceptions, but that on the one hand there is his mind, seated in his body, and on the other hand the thing, affecting his senses. But this account is not adequate, if the thing present is material, because then it will be easy, by recovering the innocence of the eye, or of any other organ of sense, to discover an image or feeling differing in many ways from a material object, and discoverably dependent (as the material object is not) upon the organs of sense and their condition at the moment. This image or feeling seems to be an intermediate factor between the mind and the material thing; and since it is very like the images and feelings which, in dreams or thought, visit the mind in the absence of all relevant material agents, this intermediate factor may be called an *idea*. It is the sort of thing which the arts play with: a presentment of things in their absence, or a perspective view or mimic reproduction of them even in their presence. These ideas are not material things; they are purely visionary; yet they are not mere essences, since they grow and fade, tingle with life, and are obviously continuous with the unconscious processes of growth (for instance in the maturation of passion or of eloquence) by which they are saturated, like a sponge half out of water: the essences discerned at any moment are only arrested phases of this sensible flux. The inner life can be only caught in glimpses, by quick turns of attention much less continuous than its own voluminous motion; in this respect sensibility or psychic life is like a material thing: indeed, it is a material thing of a certain sort, like a telephone system or a phonograph; a dynamic unit embedded in an organism which it only partially controls, and within which it operates. The psyche is, when noticed at all, an external object to the attentive mind, though a part of the body which that mind animates, and a whole, of which the organ of that mind is a part. The psyche contains the traces and generates the revival of past experiences; she generates the form of experiences which are original: she sketches the external things which attract her notice. The movement in the organs of sense or in the brain, which brings ideas before the mind is of course not *similar* to these ideas: that is, if that movement were studied microscopically it would not present a picture like that which it evokes in the living mind. The living mind is like a landscape painter; the physiologist studying the organs of living mind is like a geologist enumerating the constituents of the country-side which the painter, with one eye closed and his head aslant, is trying to compose into a magic pattern. In both cases a swarm of minute material processes is caught and transmuted, with extraordinary haste and freedom, into a summary unit of an original quality. This specious unit is the *idea*.

The Latent Idealism of a Materialist

JOHN HERMAN RANDALL, JR.

"In a world that in extent and complexity so far outruns human energies," wrote Mr. Santayana some twenty-five years ago, "physical knowledge ought to be largely virtual; that is, nature ought to be represented by a suitable attitude toward it, by the attitude which reason would dictate were knowledge complete, and not by explicit ideas."[1] Although in the intervening quarter-century the ideas by which natural philosophers represent nature have been tumbled about in a kaleidoscopic whirl, and although Mr. Santayana himself has insisted that in his thought nature has come forward to push the life of reason into the background,[2] the passage of time has not altered this essential conviction. In *The Realm of Matter*[3] he is not concerned with the current winds of doctrine so briskly blowing among the physicists, and so confusedly fluttering the pages of our philosophic journals. He does not deign to enter the lists with Einstein, Whitehead, and their ilk; he hardly condescends, even by implication, to look down upon the jousting and hurl a transfixing metaphor into the midst of their sallies. No longer is it his crown to mock the runner's heat; he has more serious business afoot. Let others quarrel about explicit ideas; for him the prize is still a reasonable attitude toward nature, and that prize is his before the tourney begins.

John Herman Randall, Jr., "The Latent Idealism of a Materialist," *The Journal of Philosophy*, 28 (1931), pp. 645-660; reprinted by permission. A review of George Santayana, *The Realm of Matter*.

[1] *Reason in Science,* p. 169.
[2] *Reason in Common Sense,* Preface to 2nd ed.
[3] George Santayana, *The Realm of Matter.* New York: Scribner, 1930. Pp. xvi + 209.

In his comments upon the second of the realms of being Mr. Santayana resists all temptation to forsake his character. He remains the sceptic and the moralist, and does not seek the mantle of the natural philosopher. Since he first transcribed the drama of the life of reason, the years have brought a mellower scepticism, perhaps, and some enlightenment on the means whereby spirit can win its deliverance. Yet the reader who noted that Mr. Santayana had smelt out news in the realm of essence will find that little has disturbed the even tenor of the realm of matter. The theme of mechanism, recurrent in those older days, is not heard so loudly now. Perhaps he had outgrown the awe felt for his earlier teachers; perhaps, now that pedagogues have waxed so disputatious, he is content to leave them to their idle strife. Be that as it may, there is a singularly timeless quality about the comments of this observant and intelligent spirit upon the flux of matter and its dark complexities; and herein lies their chief moral value. How could it be otherwise? How could the discovery of new and intricate patterns in the flux alter the immemorial conditions of human life, when once the spirit has attained a clear perception of its essential dependence and glory? For matter is matter, by whatsoever name it be called; it remains the principle of existence and movement, implied in the very denials of foolish philosophers. This is the burden of the book, and its climax is fittingly reached in the brilliant demonstration that this fundamental materialism of all human wisdom lies latent even in the thought of those who shudder at the name. The proudest eagle must take his flight from solid earth, and to it he must return. If Mr. Santayana prefers to make his point with his eye upon truly noble soarings, it holds equally of those lesser birds of the moment who think to have escaped matter by transmuting it into pure light. When physicists vie to disclaim materialism because, forsooth, matter will not be bound by the guesses of Newton, it is good to have materialism as a moral faith so clearly disentangled from its adventitious scientific trappings.

For it must be repeated that the materialism of Mr. Santayana is no hypothesis of the physicist; it is the materialism of a moralist anxious to inculcate respect for the flux of nature that perception, enjoyment, and wisdom may flourish more freely. One might suggest, indeed, that materialism as an historic doctrine seems ever to have been the insight of the moralist seeking to guide human life, and not, save accidentally, the vision of the scientist trying to explain nature. By and large, the men of understanding have been impressed rather with the intelligibility of nature—an all-too-human credulity, comments Mr. Santayana—and have been prone to read the pattern of their knowledge as nature's core. Such a skeleton of logical structure Mr. Santayana's world conspicuously lacks. It is for him enough that the life of the spirit recognize its essential dependence on that enveloping world which sustains it and of which it is the commenting voice, that world which is matter just because it is neither spirit nor its vision. "The recognition of the material world and of the conditions of existence in it," he has pointed out, "merely enlightens the spirit concerning the source of its troubles and the means to its happiness and deliverance." [4]

For Mr. Santayana, despite his materialism in physics—because of it, he would maintain—is an idealist, an idealist in that happy sense in which a just appreciation of the machinery of living liberates the spirit from preoccupation with such vain concerns to exercise its originality in the sphere of poetry and feeling. All idealists, he insists, have been materialists in secret; and his own open avowal but renders his loyalty to spirit the more complete. The pantheism in which modern idealism culminates "is more materialistic than materialism, since it assigns to matter a dignity which no profane materialist would assign it, that of having *moral* authority over the hearts of men,"[5] whereas a true idealism must distinguish sharply between the things of God and the things of Caesar, between the devotion due to essence and the respect owed to matter. And nowhere is Mr. Santayana's thought and love more firmly fixed upon essence than when his eye surveys the realm of matter. "Even a materialist," runs his confession of faith, "might be a true idealist, if he preferred the study of essence to that of matter or events; but his natural philosophy

<hr />

[4] *Contemporary American Philosophy*, Vol. II, pp. 248-249.

[5] *Realm of Matter*, p. 205. Subsequent page references are to this book unless otherwise designated.

would keep his poetic ecstacies in their proper place."[6] This, then, is the function of natural philosophy, the end at which all understanding of the realm of matter should rightly aim: to keep the life of the spirit in its proper place, to render its conduct sane and sober, its philosophy secure, and its ambitions truly spiritual.

Nay more: the study of existence has for its goal the liberation of spirit from all the earthy contamination inflicted by the exaggerated piety of practical souls, who in their preoccupation with the flux of matter and its vain redistribution spend all their labor in tending the mother from whom they have sprung, and seek to drag spirit herself from her high estate to aid in that menial service. Is it amiss to suspect that Mr. Santayana's chief concern with matter lies precisely in the protest against such desecration of spirit? Matter disregarded can make its claim heard; the insistence of the flux is for mortals inescapable. But to confuse it with spirit is high treason, "treason to spirit, to truth, to essence, to those trembling immaterial lights and that infinite immutable background which, unless sharply contrasted with the matter which they surround, may be transposed in confused apprehension to the plane of matter, and saddled with material functions. Have not both truth and spirit, not to speak of essence, been represented in our day as things physical, temporal, instrumental, and practical?"[7] Such theories are ignobly and crassly materialistic, since they ignore or deny the existence of spirit that can transcend the remorseless flux, look upon the eternal world, and redeem the labors of life by bringing joy into it.

That spirit may live free and untrammeled, taking no thought for the morrow, matter must do the dusty work of the world; just as the grace and charm of some fair king's daughter can cast their light only against the background of the sweat and toil of countless slaves. That spirit, having once found its way to the fresh sunlight of the realm of essence, need never return blinded to the material cave, the inhabitants of that dark region must be fully competent to conduct all their affairs themselves. Mr. Santayana jealously guards spirit and essence against the lightest burden of

[6] P. 190.
[7] P. vi.

labor; their sole function is to be, and in their being to enrich the scene of life. All the tasks which less aristocratic philosophies have from time to time saddled upon them must for him be assumed by that tireless Caliban, the flux of matter. The living of life, the intelligent manipulation of matter, all that man does and thinks and is—these functions belong to that complication of restless matter that is the psyche. Not even the immemorial duty imposed upon essence to hold the world together, to serve as the architecture of heaven and earth, is here permitted. Dialectic is a habit imposed by matter, not the eternal scaffolding of the world. Every existential relation must be grounded in matter—a fact that overwhelms the phenomenalist. A materialism that lightly performs all that the most abandoned idealism has ever demanded, that laughs at hard round atoms and inexorable law, as the baubles of children playing—such a materialism has surely lost its sting. Indeed, the barbarous democrat, blind to the glories of a court and hardened of heart against the graces of a shining aristocracy, might well complain that Mr. Santayana's world would manage beautifully with the entire realm of essence banished to a Platonic past. Loyalty to such a *fainéant* dynasty, incomprehensible enough while Mr. Santayana was explaining that it did nothing for good or ill, must seem to his crudity a touch of madness now that the competence and ability of matter are so boldly extolled. Yet Mr. Santayana insists that essence and spirit are secure only so long as, like the British Crown, they refrain from taking part in the politics of earth. And who knows but that in morals as in politics such an apologetic may not be impregnable? Give all power to Caesar, and the most fanatical Roman need not grudge a prayer to God.

But if Mr. Santayana's chief concern in discoursing of matter is to guard against treason to spirit, what is this matter in its own right, this substance, this flux of existence? That, alas, man can never know. Matter does not lie open to intuition like essence; its ways are dark and hidden, its powers germinate underground, and only its foliage and flowers emerge into clear light. "It is in terms of essence that any possible physics is condemned to describe nature."[8] Yet "the intrinsic essence of matter being unknown, it may be figured almost indifferently by any image of sense or thought,

[8] P. 83.

as by 'the gods' or 'the devil,' provided that expectation and action are not misled by that symbol."[9] This dilemma is not without its difficulties for the philosophic mind: it condemns all investigation of matter to the realm of expectation and action.[10] The very existence of matter, as Mr. Santayana was so careful to explain in his prefatory volume, is an hypothesis of animal faith, forced on the psyche by her manifold pursuits. "The postulate of substance —the assumption that there are things and events prior to the discovery of them and independent of this discovery—underlies all natural knowledge. . . . It is not the task of natural philosophy to justify this assumption, which indeed can never be justified. Its task, after making that assumption, is to carry it out consistently and honestly, so as to arrive, if possible, at a conception of nature by which the faith involved in action may be enlightened and guided."[11]

Since all knowledge of nature must bear the stamp of its instrumental function, Mr. Santayana has no special reverence for science, and, truth to tell, shows little interest in its bulletins. Of course all human notions of matter, even if not positively fabulous, must be wholly inadequate.[12] "I am not concerned with repeating, correcting, or forecasting the descriptions which men of science may give of the world. I accept gladly any picture of nature honestly drawn by them, as I accept gladly any picture drawn by my own senses. Different circumstances or different faculties would certainly have produced different pictures. From Genesis to Thales, to Ptolemy, to Copernicus, to Newton, and to Einstein the landscape has pleasantly varied; and it may yet open other vistas. These variations and prospects show the plasticity of human thought, for it is not the facts that have much varied, nor the material station of man, nor his senses and destiny. The incubus of existence remains exactly the same."[13]

The scientist swears by his calculus; for him matter is that in nature which his human instruments have so far been able to

9 P. vi.
10 "The realm of matter is the field of action; it is essentially dynamic and not pictorial," *Realm of Matter*, p. xi.
11 Pp. viii, 2.
12 P. viii.
13 P. 7.

measure.[14] But science is at best conscientious fiction;[15] its terms, like those of sense, are essences describing in human discourse the objects encountered in action.[16] The deeper it goes the thinner it gets, and it cheats us altogether if we mistake its symbols for the reality of nature.[17] Mathematical views are impartial, but wretchedly abstract; number is a just category to apply to the field of action, but a miserable essence to substitute for it. "Accurate science has this defect, that it seems to describe the distribution of units of nothing and to record averages in movements that elude sense, and yet are conceived and posited only in reference to pictorial objects."[18] In mathematics we fancy we have grasped the very essence of substance; yet in this our darling "we find ourselves in possession of a perfect method of notation from which everything to be noted has disappeared; and the only truth of our most accurate science turns out to be practical and utterly blind. We must revert, in order to recover our sanity and the subject-matter of our natural science, to crude experience and to the common arts."[19]

The poet, the moralist, the humble man, equally with the scientist, have hit upon symbols of value to describe nature. "All these partialities in the conception of matter are honest and inevitable. Each view, in stretching its special language as far as possible, may serve to disclose some side of the true order of nature. But this order is that of actual generation and existential flux, something that happens and is not conceived; so that no sensuous or graphic or mathematical transcript of it should be so pressed as to be substituted for it."[20] It may even be true that nature forms a universal mechanism, which human discourse may at length trace in symbol. "Yet however perfectly such a system

[14] "In scientific speech, at each stage of it, the word matter comes to denote such aspects of natural things as have become calculable at that stage," *Realm of Matter,* p. viii.

[15] "There are presumably no atoms and no laws separable from the concrete strains and movements of the flux, by which its substance is intimately modified," *Realm of Matter,* p. 82.

[16] P. 49.
[17] P. 41.
[18] P. 88.
[19] P. 82.
[20] P. xi.

might transcribe the flux of existence, it would not *be* that flux in person, or in its lapsing life; and science can not well be truer of it, though true at a deeper level, than are all the vulgar essences which visibly give it character."[21] Mr. Santayana does not spare the superstitions of contemporary learning. "Finally, in our own times, when physics speculates chiefly on bodies so remote or minute as to be known only through variations in light, matter seems to evaporate into these visible variations, as if light had no source, or as if man had no contact with nature except through the eye."[22] The proudest inventions of modern physicists appear in Mr. Santayana's pages only as the incidental illustrations of persistent fallacies.

No, useful as the attempt may be for practice, matter can not be forced into a definition. Matter is no human idea; it is rather the unintelligible alloy added to whatever essences may be assigned to it.[23] Matter is properly a name for the actual substance of the natural world, whatever that substance may be.[24] "Substance is always more and other than the essence which it exemplifies at any point. Its residual being, or not-being, is antithetical to essence altogether, and irrational. We may enjoy it, we may enact it, but we can not conceive it; not because our intellect by accident is inadequate, but because existence, which substance makes continuous, is intrinsically a surd, a flux, and a contradiction. What we may discover of it is not its essence, but its place, its motion, its aspects, its effects."[25]

Hence the folly of those who protest that materialism is absurd and exploded. By matter they understand some pictorial or mathematical idol substituted for the pregnant and unfathomable substance of things.[26] "To say that matter, as it truly exists, is inert or incapable of spontaneous motion, organization, life, or thought, would be flatly to contradict the facts: because the real matter, posited in action, and active in our bodies and in all other instruments of action, evidently possesses and involves all those

21 P. 98.
22 P. x.
23 P. 82.
24 P. 140.
25 Pp. 26, 18.
26 P. 200.

vital properties. . . . It must evidently have been perfectly fitted to produce everything which it actually produces; and it may therefore be decorated retrospectively, by a Chinese piety, with all the titles won by its children; indeed, these its eventual manifestations are the sole index which we possess to its intrinsic nature."[27] Since matter is the principle of genesis and the true arbiter of fortune, it has often been what men have symbolized under the name of God.[28]

Such a materialism amounts to saying there is a world, and human life is part of it. One need not long wonder that every thinker is brilliantly and triumphantly convicted of it. For the moralist this is the beginning and the end of natural wisdom. Yet the natural philosopher—and Mr. Santayana is content to travel a little way with him—is driven to ask a deeper question: How much can sense or science reveal concerning the dark engine of nature? Within what limits does any description of nature, picturesque or scientific, retain its relevance to animal faith and its validity as knowledge of fact, and at what point does it become pure speculation and metaphor?[29] Our moralist could remain on essentially Aristotelian ground; but once he turns naturalist he finds himself enmeshed in the toils of the critical philosophy. From the transcendental point of view he must criticise the claims of experience and science to be true knowledge. Bravely he sets forth as an empiricist. "By transcendental reflection I understand reversion, in the presence of any object or affirmation, to the immediate experience which discloses that object or prompts that affirmation. Transcendental reflection is a challenge to all dogmatism, a demand for radical evidence."[30] But since immediate experience can only be of essences, the toils of Locke seem closing about him. The only escape is into the arms of transcendental faith, which demands a world to be posited and described. *Im Anfang war die That!* And if action be not an illusion, several properties *must* belong to substances and the world they compose.[31] The hunt grows exceedingly dialectical, and Mr. Santayana proceeds

27 Pp. 137, 187.
28 P. 205.
29 P. 7.
30 P. 8.
31 P. 9.

to a transcendental deduction of nature. The pages which follow might have been penned in Jena a century ago; and one is hardly surprised, once one has grown accustomed to Mr. Santayana speaking from a German *Katheder,* to come upon romantic arguments. "We may therefore confidently attribute the forward tension proper to our life to all the rest of nature, down to its primary elements, without attributing to those elements, or to that total, any specifically human quality. . . . We may therefore appeal to our experience of action on the human scale to suggest to us the nature of action even in the heart of matter, which a mere diminution of mathematical scale or use of the microscope may never reach."[32] And thus nature, for Mr. Santayana too, turns out, at least metaphorically, to have free will.[33] Is this but the latent idealism of materialists, or has our moralist turned natural philosopher been drinking too deep of the heady draught of modern physics? Dubious of recording what nature is, he follows the more cautious course of prescribing what she must be. And once again, what she transcendentally must be, it turns out, is just what experience reveals her as being. "A world in which action is to occur," runs the summary of the dialectic, "must be external, spatial, and temporal, possessing variety and unity. Action, when rational, presupposes that the transformations of substance are continuous, quantitatively constant, and regular in method; and that the spirit, without being a part of that material world, is the consciousness proper to one of the agents there."[34]

Above all, in positing substance as the dark principle of existence, the practical intellect imposes upon it an essential contingency and instability. "Its secret flux involves at least as many contrasts and variations as the course of nature shows on the surface. Otherwise the ultimate core of existence would not exist, and the causes of variation would not vary. But how shall that which puts on this specious essence here and not there, be in the same inner condition in both places? Or how shall that which explodes now, have been equally active before? Substance, if it is

[32] P. 91.
[33] P. 195.
[34] Pp. 10, 42.

to fulfil the function in virtue of which it is recognized and posited, must accordingly be for ever changing its own inner condition. It must be in flux.''[35]

This flux of matter imposes movement and change on a spirit addressed by its own genius rather to the eternal. It is characteristic of Mr. Santayana's world that in it change and existence should present a major problem. Why are not all essences eternally present to the unclouded intuition of spirit? Why do some possess that peculiar urgency for practice we call embodied existence? He feels it necessary to argue at length that change is real, that there must be a principle of change to account for the instability of spirit's observations. And matter all but dissolves into a name for the fact of change itself. "Matter is the invisible wind which, sweeping for no reason over the field of essences, raises some of them into a cloud of dust: and that whirlwind we call existence.''[36]

Matter thus not only possesses a life of its own, it is the very life of nature. As such, it needs no external time in which to work its wonders, physical time being indeed but another name for its native instability.[37] The terms of its change are natural moments, events exemplifying a single essence. Possessed of a forward tension, each natural moment leads to another; as if ashamed at the irrationality of having one form rather than another, matter hastens to the exchange; and this haste is its whole reality. Such moments are involved in a web of lateral tensions from companion moments; all nature seems to be a mechanism of circumstances. That the world is in truth such a universal mechanism Mr. Santayana no longer confidently affirms; such an hypothesis he now treats as mere speculation. He is far more concerned to insist on the spontaneity and groundlessness of the flux, its primeval plastic stress, its sole creativity.[38] To drag essence from its happy heaven to regulate with inexorable law the dull course of existence were a violence from which his loyalty shrinks.

It is at this point that the argument, like the flux of nature,

[35] P. 15.
[36] P. 94.
[37] P. 84.
[38] Pp. 99, 109.

deserts one essence for another. When the forms of events are envisaged, transcendentalism gives way to empiricism. It is after all for experiment and science, not for logic, to discover what sort of matter matter is.[39] To the essence of an event, the order of its moments, Mr. Santayana gives the name of *trope*; and the moralist's examples are, characteristically, dramatic events like the life of a man or a battle. Some tropes like birth and death are habitual and ingrained in nature. It is this regular repetition which alone saves the flux from chaos, by embodying a universal mechanical trope which makes knowledge and science possible. Nature is full of coiled springs and predestined rhythms; of mechanisms so wound up that, as soon as circumstances permit, they unroll themselves through a definite series of phases. Yet even such tropes, constantly repeated and therefore mechanical, remain contingent and arbitrary: they might have easily been otherwise, and each occurrence is spontaneous and original. In so far as the laws of nature are considered more rigid than habits of the flux, they are but human artifices of notation.[40] "Belief in law when hasty is called superstition or when more cautious empiricism: but the principle in both cases is the same. Both take expectation for probability; and what probability can there be that an expectation, arising at one point, should define a law for the whole universe? Expectation is an animal attitude resting not at all on induction and probability, but on the fact that animals are wound up to do certain things and vaguely but confidently posit a world in which their readiness may become action."[41] The uniformity of nature is only a postulate of action and reason, which contingent, substantial, and original facts may at any point disallow.[42] There is hence no necessity in the relation between cause and effect, and no assurance that law is constant.[43] "It follows that whenever a trope of any sort has been distinguished and found to prevail in nature, as far as our knowledge extends, it need by no means prevail beyond the limits of this domesticated region, nor above or below the level of our human sensibility. It need not even ex-

[39] P. 196.
[40] P. 110.
[41] P. 111.
[42] P. 110.
[43] P. 111.

clude anomalies and outbreaks of chaos in the interstices of the prevalent tropes."[44]

Moreover, these mechanical laws, even when reasonably stable, are but human measures of events, habits of nature selected to serve action. A mathematical skeleton may indeed be traced within the body of nature; "but it is no skeleton in its operative function, like that of an animal; it is no rigid substance within the soft substance of events; it is only a trope, which the thrifty mind selects from the tangle of relations which hold those facts in the mesh of existence."[45] Hence no trope can be exclusive or fundamental. Mathematical tropes may pervade the realm of matter, supporting occasional moral and esthetic tropes without interrupting them.[46] Nor can the discovery of a rhythmic repetition, a natural law, explain why or how a thing happens. The tropes which mark the obvious metres of nature tell nothing of the inspiration, the secret labor, or the mechanism which brings them forth.[47] For like his predecessors in the empirical tradition, Bacon and Locke, Mr. Santayana has no doubt that nature has her latent processes and real essences, inscrutable to man. "Did we really wish to understand, we should inquire into the inner elements of a mutation in any one of its instances: because a thing must happen each time by a concourse of motions there, and not because the same thing happens also in other places."[48]

Thus at the last Mr. Santayana does not escape the legacy left by Locke: the spectrum of sense and the categories of thought are not imposed upon man by the world, but are original creations of the psyche. "Surely pleasure and pain, hunger, lust, and fear, do not first reside in external objects and pass from them into the mind; and these are the primary, typical data of intuition. All the rest—colors, sounds, shapes, specious spaces and times and sensations of motion—is hatched in the same nest; it all has a similar psychic seat and dramatic occasion. . . . The psyche is a poet, a creator of language; and there is no presumption that she will perceive material things, including her own substance and

[44] P. 114.
[45] P. 112.
[46] P. 112.
[47] P. 125.
[48] P. 118.

movement, at all in the terms or in the order and scale in which they exist materially. On the contrary, only the reactions of her organism are represented in her feelings. The whole of life is a predicament, complex and prolonged; and the whole of mind is the cry, prolonged and variously modulated, which that predicament wrings from the psyche."[49]

When the setting of human life in the life of nature is considered, however, Mr. Santayana returns from transcendental and empirical excursions to a sober Aristotelianism. Here the concern of the moralist is to render unto the psyche those things that are the psyche's, and unto spirit those things that are of the spirit. "I will beg the reader to distinguish sharply two levels of life in the human body, one of which I call *the spirit* and the other *the psyche.* By spirit I understand the actual light of consciousness falling upon anything—the ultimate invisible emotional fruition of life in feeling and thought. On the other hand, by the psyche I understand a system of tropes, inherited or acquired, displayed by living bodies in their growth and behavior."[50] The psyche is thus a habit in matter, and for a scientific psychology behavior is the only conceivable seat of mind.[51] "The whole life of the psyche, even if hidden by chance from human observation, is essentially observable: it is the object of biology. Such is the only scientific psychology, as conceived by the ancients, including Aristotle, and now renewed in behaviorism and psycho-analysis."[52]

Yet the psyche has also an inner invisible experience, a thin flux of consciousness, which is the life of spirit, a commentary on events in the language of essence.[53] The existence of this commentary makes possible a second kind of psychology, literary psychology, more congenial to the moralist than the scientific variety, and much beloved of Mr. Santayana. Consciousness is the most highly conditioned of existences, an overtone of psychic

[49] Pp. 159-160. Cf. "Mind comes to enrich the essence of the world, not to reproduce it. . . . The essences given to spirit are forms of imagination and thought: they never were and never will be the essences of things; and it is only by poetic licence and conventional symbolism that we are compelled to clothe things in the garb of our sensations," *Realm of Essence,* pp. 132, 136.

[50] P. 139.

[51] P. 123.

[52] P. 140.

[53] P. 158.

strains, mutations, and harmonies.[54] All action, all struggle, desire and intelligence, even reason itself,[55] are the complex tensions of matter, the life of the psyche; conscious spirit is the chorus celebrating in appropriate measures that bodily life. "Existence and movement, even in spirit, are therefore the work of matter; while the perception, the enjoyment, the understanding of both matter and spirit are the life of spirit itself. . . . It is the body that speaks, and the spirit that listens."[56] As Mr. Santayana has put it in one of his unforgettable metaphors, "there are not two parallel streams, but one stream which, in slipping over certain rocks or dropping into certain pools, begins to babble a wanton music; not thereby losing any part of its substance or changing its course, but unawares enriching the world with a new beauty."[57]

But, alas, a great part of human thought has been unable to discriminate the rôles of matter and spirit. Matter in its waywardness has repelled the moralist, while its dark unfathomable nature has held little lure for the metaphysician. Men have sought to honor spirit by clothing it with matter's authority; and the issue has been tragic. The heirs of the saints have assumed the pomp and circumstance of power; worldliness has at length corrupted the fabric of the church. Forgetting its true glory, these false devotees of spirit have transformed it into but another name for matter. Such treason to spirit is the worst of philosophic crimes; and Mr. Santayana rapidly sketches in the outlines of this degradation. As Plato, having delineated the true state, proceeds to depict its corruption, so he narrates the decline and fall of materialistic wisdom. And the end is reached in that objective idealism which, having completed the identification of spirit and existence, exhausts all its loyalty upon existence and has no devotion left for essence. To liberate spirit from such a dungeon, to cast off the materialistic shackles which professed idealists have rudely laid upon her, was the stern duty which led the moralist into the realm of matter. To matter belong the kingdoms and the glory of this world; but spirit's kingdom is not of this world. Born in the flesh, and ineluctably linked to the flesh, she yet in

54 P. 155.

55 P. 147: "Reason is not a force contrary to the passions, but a harmony possible among them."

56 P. 146.

57 *Realm of Essence*, p. 134.

the flesh shall see God. Woe unto those who seek to tempt her from her true vocation!

What shall be said of this discourse on matter that is a paean to spirit, of this materialism that seeks to conserve all the insights of supernaturalism? Had not Mr. Santayana so disarmingly forestalled the impeachment,[58] it would be easy to wonder at its eclecticism, and to marvel at the ease with which the lions and the lambs of philosophic history are made to lie down with one another. It has been recorded that Mr. Santayana's essences were sired by John Locke out of Plato; the bearings of his matter seem more richly quartered. The observant eye can there discern the arms of Aristotle, Fichte, and Schopenhauer as well as of Locke and Hume. So generous a heredity may be welcomed in one who takes truth where he finds it; but narrower partisans must needs grow restive, and pride of family may raise the cry of the bar sinister. To the Aristotelian it will ever seem a pity that Mr. Santayana has quaffed so deeply of modern empiricism, and escapes the penalty of utter psychologism only by the seductive transcendental path. Indeed, it is patent, to all but Mr. Santayana, that he has not escaped, but is now deeply mired in that bog of paradox, confusion, and ultimate inexplicability through which trickles the thin stream of British empiricism; that the flaw which marred the first volume of the *Life of Reason* stands revealed, in the *Realms of Being*, as a progressive malady; and that today he must needs fight shoulder to shoulder with, say, Mr. Bertrand Russell against a common sea of troubles. The less tender-minded naturalist will not cease to mourn the gulf that is digged between matter and essence, and to find compromising and half-hearted the nostalgic longing for Platonic eternity in an alien world. To him Mr. Santayana will be only what he so pre-eminently is, a moralist and a poet, victorious in self-knowledge and self-expression; and his hypostatization of a realm of essence but another instance of that incurable egotism that writes large upon the firmament the heart's desire. To such a whole-hearted naturalist, it can not cease to be a marvel that Mr. Santayana, so deeply sceptical of all else, should still in this day preserve so touching and unclouded a faith in the incredible psychology of John Locke; that, wisely banishing it from the life of

[58] *Realm of Essence*, p. xviii.

the psyche, for which Aristotle and our experimentalists suffice, he should yet suffer it to reign unchecked in his metaphysics, parcelling out the realms of being and ruling the communion of spirit and essence with unquestioned authority. However, but little good may come of charges and counter-charges of "mere failure in discernment"; we should rather give thanks that the world has been enriched with another perspective, and if the lines seem a little awry the colors are all the richer.

It is not after all as an idolatrous metaphysician that Mr. Santayana would wish to be judged, but as a moralist; and in truth his metaphysical dualism between matter and essence is at bottom moral, the expression of a whole-hearted allegiance to spirit. It is in such human and dramatic terms that the essential problem posed by his insight must be couched. Mr. Santayana has of late confused his friends and confounded his critics by seemingly forsaking the life of reason to dally with the spiritual life. What would he have? Is it the part of wisdom to be a rational animal, or is it rather our true destiny to be as pure spirits? His own explicit preference lies still with the Greeks;[59] but the spiritual life has certainly become the major theme of his discourse, and the life of reason now plays but a faint obligato. Is this because of the seductive appeal of the spiritual life as a topic for literary exploitation and jeweled language, or does it represent a surrender to an undoubted native bent? Like Aristotle, Mr. Santayana seems unable quite to decide between the life of practice and the life of *theoria,* the life of the psyche immersed in matter and bent on action and the life of the spirit bathed in essence and given to contemplation; and, also like Aristotle, he has not told us how the same body is to live the two lives. Here is a problem for the moralist to elucidate, if he will and can. Is it too much to hope that in the remaining realms of being these two levels of living will be somewhat more nicely adjusted to each other? Further illumination as to Mr. Santayana's metaphysics patently awaits the harmony of his loyalties.

The main lines of such a harmony are perhaps indicated in the trinity of essays called forth by Mr. Babbitt's late irruption.[60] Be-

[59] *Realm of Essence,* p. 65.

[60] *The Genteel Tradition at Bay.* George Santayana. New York: Scribner, 1931. P. 74.

neath the gentle mockery and ironic advice there runs a deeper current: the balance of the claims of spirit against a wise and rational acceptance of the materials which the accidents of modernity present for moral integration. It is true that the gist of modern history, the many-sided insurrection of the natural man with all his physical powers against the regimen of Christendom, has been a great surrender of the spirit to the flesh, of the essence for the miscellany of human power. It is true that in gaining creature comforts, a respectable exterior, and intellectual liberty, we have reduced spirit to an instrument, and so lost its genuine fruits. But why be dissatisfied? Virtue and happiness are still possible; the particular elements which shall enter into the harmony of the life of reason are nowhere prescribed, and to reason itself are indifferent. To exchange one's native religion and morality for a foreign one is merely to blight in oneself the only life that is really possible. Then, too, understanding relieves a truly intelligent man from fussiness about social institutions and conventions; they are absurd, yet absurdity is not incompatible with their natural function, which may be indispensable. "But in philosophy, when ultimately the spirit comes face to face with the truth, convention and absurdity are out of place; so is humanism and so is the genteel tradition; so is morality itself."[61]

Morality is the principle of all choices in taste, faith, and allegiance. It is the life of the psyche, illuminated by reason and guided by intelligence. It is that aspect of experience which perceives and pursues ideals. But spirit does not choose, neither does it pursue: it sees. To it is given vision, *theoria*. It beholds life and nature and the vast realms of essence spread out before it as in a spectacle. For the spiritual life is now for Mr. Santayana—it was not ever thus, as readers of *Reason in Religion* will recall—the purely intellectual life, and spirituality but the esthetic contemplation of the intellect.[62]

If then it be asked how morality and spirit, how choice and not choosing comport, Mr. Santayana would seem to answer, as prac-

[61] *Genteel Tradition,* p. 71.

[62] "Spirituality is only a sort of return to innocence, birdlike and childlike. Experience of the world may have complicated the picture without clouding the vision. In looking before and after, and learning to take another man's point of view, ordinary intelligence has already transcended a brutal animality; it has learned to conceive things as they are, disinterestedly, contemplatively.

tice and vision. Like the true patriot, the philosopher must plant his feet firmly in the native soil of his own preferences and allegiances, and from that vantage-point survey the world. "Such a free mind might really have understood the ancients, and might have passed grandly with them into a complete naturalism, universal and impartial on its intellectual side (since the intellect is by right all-seeing) but in politics and morals fiercely determinate, with an animal and patriotic intensity of will, like Carthage and Sparta, and like the Soviets and the Fascists of to-day."[63]

What he earlier celebrated as the life of reason Mr. Santayana now calls morality; religion, art, and science are alike comprised within the practice of the psyche. The burden of his present writings, addressed to empiricists and idealists, to humanists and Christians, to Plato himself, is that morality is not enough. One must live by rational choice, one must understand by knowledge, but to live harmoniously and even to know are not enough. One must also *see;* and in that vision life finds its consummation and reason its crown.

Bishop Berkeley

GEORGE SANTAYANA

Youth and genius, piety and radicalism conspired to make of Berkeley the most amiable of philosophers. Even if he was not

George Santayana, "Bishop Berkeley," in Bonamy Dobrée, ed., *From Anne to Victoria: Essays by Various Hands* (London: Cassell, 1937), pp. 75-88. Reprinted by permission of Cassell and Company, Ltd., and Philosophical Library, Publishers.

Although intellect arises quite naturally, in the animal act of dominating events in the interests of survival, yet essentially intellect disengages itself from that servile office (which is that of its organ only) and from the beginning is speculative and impartial in its own outlook, and thinks it not robbery to take the point of view of God, of the truth, and of eternity. . . . The fruition of happiness is intellectual, or as perhaps we should now call it, esthetic." *Genteel Tradition*, pp. 65-66.

[63] *Genteel Tradition*, p. 8.

always young or always radical—for he became a bishop—the genius of youth and of radicalism never forsook him. His intuition remained ardent and simple, even when his piety was clothed in ampler and more learned robes. His maturest projects were chimerical: to found a college at Bermuda from which to christianize North America, and to cure all minor human ills by the virtues of tar-water. It was in youth that his philosophy had come to him, as if by inspiration: and whilst he recognized afterwards its affinity to Platonic speculations, he never explored or analysed its affinity with any technical diligence. It sufficed him to have shattered the illusion that we are living in an obdurate material world, and to feel instead that this world was nothing but a beautiful picture-book, a book of fables, in which God was teaching our childish minds his admirable ways.

It is usual to regard Berkeley, in the history of philosophy, as a stepping-stone between Locke and Hume; but this seems to me a grave injustice, convenient for compiling text-books, but born of the mania for seeing evolution everywhere and, what is worse, evolution in single file. Undoubtedly Hume had read Berkeley, and Berkeley had read Locke: and there are points in which each carried the arguments of his predecessor one step further, or applied them to a further problem; but Berkeley had speculative genius; his thought was radical, single and complete; whereas Locke had only miscellaneous intelligence and Hume analytic malice. These two critics of human opinion really carried on the same work, and progressively dissolved traditional philosophy into something else, they knew not what; for they hardly asked themselves whether it was logic passing for psychology, or psychology becoming metaphysics. But Berkeley, like Descartes, though more simply, saw suddenly what seemed to him a new and safer way of defining Christian philosophy and purifying it, as well as all human science, of useless accretions. To call Berkeley a stepping-stone between Locke and Hume is like calling an upright obelisk a stepping-stone between two sphinxes that may be crouching to the right and to the left of it. No doubt the three are in perfect alignment along one particular path, and this may be the most interesting fact about them to a person hurrying by them towards something else. Yet even that subjective analysis of ideas which was begun by Locke and completed in Hume, figured in Berkeley only as a cathartic, or an argument *ad hominem,* calcu-

lated to clear the mind of proud scientific illusions and bring it
in all humility face to face with God. His intuition pointed stead-
ily, like an obelisk, to the zenith; whilst his more contorted and
pregnant neighbours, like sphinxes, digested their inward contradictions.

Youthful genius is essentially lyrical rather than cognitive: in
Berkeley, as afterwards in Shelley, it was blinded by too much
light. Like Shelley, Berkeley felt how horribly unnecessary everything was that contradicted the convictions that came to him
irresistibly when he first looked upon and challenged the world.
Such assurance is not always immature; it may be radical and
ultimate in one direction. In Berkeley it brought a fresh intuition
of the nature of experience, a true, if partial, intuition never to be
cancelled; had it been otherwise, there would be no occasion to
speak of genius, but only of one more academic extravagance.
Young courage may embrace any illusion; but only young genius,
justifying courage, can clear away vast accumulations of prejudice
and convention, and discover the obvious. Berkeley gloriously detached the "idea," the pure phenomenon, from the irrelevant
strains of presumption and idolatry with which animal life originally encumbers it. The stupid world calls this an act of abstraction; but Berkeley, who hated abstractions, knew it to be an act
of realization. Realization, indeed, simply of the obvious, and of
the ideality and unsubstantiality of the obvious. He rose at once
to a radical insight which it had taken all the experience and discipline of Indian gymnosophists to reach, the insight that perception, if taken for truth, is illusion: the very insight that the aged
Malebranche was then propounding critically, basing it on the
lamentable incapacity and deceptiveness of the human senses. But
this discovery, in the ear of youth, may have a pleasant sound; it
may bring not so much renunciation as enfranchisement. The instinct to look for the sake of looking, to play for the sake of playing, to enjoy making-believe, and to find the highest vitality in
enacting a great show known not to be real, is no incapacity in a
child; and for a poet the power of imagination is not deceptive,
but on the contrary the one free, beautiful, appointed way of
celebrating the truth. When Berkeley denied the existence of matter, he felt not the unreality but the intense reality of experience,
enjoying it as a vast web of heavenly music, perfectly composed

and performed, with its recurrent phrases coming in at the right places: and he felt no base craving to hug the words or hold on to the notes, but passed over everything buoyantly at the due pace, as it was meant to be passed over. This exercise, which we call life, is difficult enough, and we get sadly out of time and tune; yet it is essentially a festive ritual and a rare spectacle for the eye, the very tragedy of it being a fable. This world would have been horrible, had it been more real than that. The gladness of it came of its vividness as an experience and its unreality as a power.

Nevertheless such an intuition, by its lyrical truth and sufficiency, cuts off the young enthusiast from the complexity of mundane things, and even from other forms of intuition. His inspiration seems to him adequate only because it monopolizes his attention, and arrests him, as it were, at a sort of spiritual adolescence. The mark of his genius may remain in the world indelibly, but only like the portrait of a noble child, consecrating an innocence that we are both glad and sorry he never should have lost.

For anyone with a speculative turn of mind this simplicity and depth in Berkeley render him an approachable and exciting writer. He stimulates attention at once by a tremendous paradox, telling us that we are bodiless spirits, and that material things are nothing but images in our minds. At the same time he partly reassures us, in what might seem our sudden visionary solitude, by a religious revelation. These images—including that image of our own bodies to which we seem so mercilessly tied—though unsubstantial in themselves are full of significance. They are visible or tangible words, in which God is continually speaking to us with an overwhelming eloquence, marshalling them in irresistible cohorts, in order to manifest his power, guide our affections, and prove his love.

Piety thus steps in opportunely to correct the bottomless scepticism that might otherwise have invaded us. I am a bodiless spirit, certainly; but I am a *created* spirit. This second perception, or this reversion to an underlying unquestioned belief, if less intuitive than the first perception, is far wiser. It might be justified by the cumulative evidence of all history and practical art; yet the intuitive first principle of Berkeley, or of Descartes, if it had stood alone, could never have justified this correction. A conventional unchallenged piety was requisite to convince the idealist that the ideas visiting him had their source beyond his own spirit. It was religion, not critical acumen or worldly wisdom, that introduced this element of sanity into Berkeley's system. He felt from the beginning to the end that he was dependent on a sustaining power at work behind the scenes, a divine musician that kept the variegated notes of this sensuous symphony in their due places and order. No substance or power whatever lay *within* our "inert ideas" to lend them an efficacious existence on their own account; yet a power and a substance did most emphatically lie *behind* the fact of their occurrence, lending the most precise moral and practical import to their quality and sequence, as to the metrical words of an oracle. The plot of life retained all its seriousness and dangers, although it was only the plot of a poetic drama.

Youth, genius, and piety could thus accept with alacrity a view of the world which might easily have proved morose and paralysing or, as afterwards in Schopenhauer, mephistophelian. Were we not wisps of consciousness floating in vacancy? Who could tell what would become of us next? So a heathen poet might have cried, overcome by the visionary self-dissolving mockery of life; but Berkeley felt religiously so secure, that he rejoiced rather that his limpid direct intuitions should have no substance and no inside. It became absurd to burrow into them or to fear them. He was happy to connect surface with surface. Was not the glory of God visible in the Bay of Naples? Why prowl about the unsavoury town or hurl oneself into the crater of Vesuvius? Empedocles had been doubly a madman, first in his mechanical philosophy and then in his blasphemous suicide. Berkeley hated "minute philosophers" even more than "scholastic triflers." Not that he despised argument when carried on with the courtly elegance of that age. A part of his perennial youthfulness was to be keen and brilliant in controversy, composing capital debating dialogues and noble sermons; but in theology as in metaphysics he kept to large edifying views and ignored difficulties.

Moreover, this idealist was no hermit. His ardent temperament and staunch Protestantism drew him into the vortex of contemporary society, then most confident of its lights and superior powers. Even his piety was not too secret or mystical, but public and sober, like that of a good Churchman; and he was always a diligent student, a man of many projects, a controversialist, and as a recent commentator has said, "a fighting Irishman; and when he saw a head to hit, he hit it."* His metaphysics never disturbed his moral sanity and heartiness, never induced in him any reversal of values or radical challenge to Church or State. Unworldly he was eminently, as an unspoiled child is unworldly; yet he was a man of the world; and this conjunction in him of convention with intuition and of culture with fervour lent a singular felicity and charm to his words. A golden light suffused all things in his mind, without distorting them; and in his philosophizing he avoided both too much analysis and too much elaboration. There was no construction in his science, as there was no criticism in his theology; a good Englishman in race and type of allegiance, even if Irish by birth and somewhat Irish in imagination. He knew how a gentleman should live and feel; and this moral sureness removed all undue urgency from the speculative radicalism of his views. There was, unfortunately, the mystery of evil; but this mystery could only quicken one's missionary zeal in the cure of souls. A hopeful cure, since the most degraded of spirits was still by nature an angel and a native of heaven.

Living as Berkeley did in this atmosphere of convention electrified by intuition, it is intelligible that the technical developments of his philosophy should not have been thorough or solid. His first impetuous desire was to denounce occult entities and abstractions, of which matter was the worst. Yet wasn't the idea of spirit at least as abstract and unimaginable as that of matter? To this objection Berkeley replied that we had indeed no *idea* of spirit, but we had a *notion* of it; we knew what it meant. This notion, in his case, could not have been any primitive animistic semi-material notion of spirit, but was doubtless that of Descartes, who had said that the essence of the soul was to think: so that if it ceased to think it would cease to be. From this Descartes had drawn the inference that the soul, being immortal, can never stop thinking. But an opposite and less edifying inference could have been drawn just as well: namely, that since thought as a matter of fact is often interrupted, the soul too only exists intermittently; or rather that no soul or spirit exists at all, but only discrete and scattered perceptions, each thinking or feeling itself. This was the conclusion

* A. B. Luce: *Berkeley and Malebranche,* p. 131.

adopted by Hume and by all later British empiricists; and it
might seem only inadvertence or prejudice in Berkeley that kept
him from anticipating it. Or perhaps we should rather say that if
his genius had been as patient as it was brilliant and as subtle as
it was clear, he might have discerned the nature of spirit in almost
any intuition. For in surveying any complex image we are aware
of contrasting and comparing its parts, thereby distinguishing
apprehension from its subject-matter; so that evidence of thinking, or of the presence of spirit, is continually at hand. Attention,
inspection, analysis, and synthesis, not to speak of expectation and
memory, are spiritual lights flooding ideas, which but for this
intellectual dominion over them would compose no cumulative
experience and would appear to nobody. Even a dream includes
a witness that is engrossed in the dream.

It was another consideration, however, less intuitive and more
traditional, that probably would have had most weight with
Berkeley in confirming the reality of spirit. Spirit, he took for
granted, was a power; and matter being removed, and ideas being
passive and merely spectacular, there remained no other power
except spirit to carry on the world. Unfortunately the will, or
spirit exerting power, was open to the same dissolving psychological analysis as spirit merely thinking. Dissected retrospectively,
wishing, deciding, and commanding are sheer phenomena. They
may be conjoined with other phenomena, if there is a synthetic
memory to conjoin them. But phenomena cannot be derived from
one another inwardly by a material generation, since by definition
there is no substance in them and no power. The alleged regular-
ity or law of their sequence is a scientific fiction, based on a few
recorded instances roughly similar, with no insight into any real
continuity or necessity in the original events.

This psychological analysis, reducing power to a superstition,
was instantly obvious to Hume: why did it escape Berkeley? Because his piety and simplicity transported him initially into a
moral world; and in a moral sense there is more than juxtaposition between the will to do a thing and the performance, between
the desire for a thing and the possession of it, or between a prayer
and the answer to that prayer. Nor are these things connected by
a scientific law. They go together, when they do (which is not

always) because it is fit and beautiful that they should do so. The only power morally perspicuous is the power of God, or of the good; for as the Scholastics said the will acts always *sub specie boni*, attracted by something that seems a good. Love of the good moves the spirit which moves the world.

Moral sentiment carried Berkeley smoothly over these serious difficulties; and, strange as it may seem, intellectual prejudice carried him no less smoothly over others. His early confident radicalism and nominalism were not based on intuition, but rather on verbal arguments, reinforced by sympathy with the spirit of the times and a semi-political hostility to scholastic tradition. Loving warmth and immediacy as he did, and hating the chill of distance, he was not content with the lightning vivacity that sensuous images actually have—since every landscape shows, at each instant, precisely the degree of clearness or confusion which it shows—but he impetuously ascribed to these treacherous images a kind of precision only to be found in conceptual objects or material things. Yet as any impressionist painter will tell us, our conventional physical and mathematical standards of reality are irrelevant to the proper lucidity of vision. The vaguest thing intellectually may be æsthetically the most obvious. That a three-cornered hat has three corners, or triangularity, may be perceived as directly as its precise shade of colour; and this mere three-corneredness is far more easily ascertained and remembered and may be more expressively indicated in a bold sketch, than the total image cast upon the retina, or the total shape and exact size of the material hat. Evidently Berkeley, when he argued about ideas, was thinking and not looking. He supposed them to be definite physically, and sometimes called them things. The idea of the triangular hat had to be equilateral or non-equilateral; and every image had to choose between conceptual alternatives which in actual intuition are not broached at all.

Even in the religious or spiritual direction Berkeley hardly reached the heights or the depths to which his primary intuition seemed to open the way. This intuition was mystical, in the sense of vaulting over and discarding all intermediaries between spirit and spirit, between the heart and God. The world was nothing and could be nothing but the language in which God, for the moment, was speaking to the soul. In this intercourse we might be dull and sullen, like a dog disobeying his master, or we might be quick to follow or even to anticipate the thought that conducted us. Evidently a most difficult and heroic spiritual discipline lay before any human being really possessed by such an inspiration: for how should the least wilfulness, the least impurity, subsist in us, when there exists no machinery at all for our ingenuity or our strength to work upon, and no source for our own darkness or suffering except our perverse wishes, or the beneficent chastening of a fatherly hand? All care, all concern about the future, should instantly vanish; and an indomitable faith, accepting all things with equal thanks, should fill the dark night of our worst trials with an unearthly joy. This joy would be that of a perpetual martyrdom, since every natural preference or hope, for another life no less than for this life, would first have to be extirpated. All our interests must have ceased to be ours, before we can unfeignedly accept every turn of fortune. No labours or dangers would any longer seem terrible to us. The greatest mystics may be prodigious fighters or missionaries or controversialists: not for a moment that these tasks represent any ambition or hope of their own—for they have renounced all hope and ambition—but because, the tasks being imposed or inspired by the manifest will of God, to labour at them becomes as easy and as indifferent as to suffer martyrdom in any other form. Yet it is always martyrdom: because these saints are men living in the body; and a complete exaltation above all human instincts and affections can be obtained only by continually fresh self-abdication: above which the rapture of spiritual freedom and divine love floats like a sunset cloud over the silent earth.

Was this the spirit of Berkeley's life? Was he a martyr? Where are the tears, the fasts in the desert, the Job-like trials, the heart-searchings and temptations, the agonized soul abandoning all things that have betrayed it, and dying, happy to die, upon the cross?

Berkeley was a Low-Church bishop of the eighteenth century. He could be blameless, he could be benevolent: it would have been unseemly in him to be a saint. Neither his heart nor his station called him to austerity of life. Experience was indeed to him

a conversation with God, but not with God alone. There were
other well-known spirits, like Dean Swift and Dr. Johnson, taking
part on equal terms in the dialogue. No sane man, no hearty
kindly Christian could doubt it. Yet how did this matter stand on
Berkeley's principles? In each of us the notion of human society
is evidently a dramatic reading of men's actions and speech. But
if men's bodies are only ideas in my mind, the notion of their
minds, suggested by those ideas, must be doubly native to my
fancy. The case is like that of the characters in a novel. The only
actual spirit concerned, beyond that of the reader, is that of the
author. Certainly the divine Poet who is speaking to me in all my
perceptions may be speaking also to countless other spirits: but
that is not my affair. The persons that laugh and suffer in my
painted world are figures in a fable that God is inventing for my
instruction. They come, as does the rest of my experience, to test
and develop my character and to enlarge my knowledge of God's
mind, as do these lovely vistas of earth and sky, and this menag-
erie of curious animals, which are also theophanies. Morally the
most decisive and transforming part of my fate is precisely the
character of the people I live with and love, and who perhaps love
or do not love me. If this part of experience be subtracted from
my contact with God, the importance of that contact will be singularly diminished. Life would be a conversation with God only for
an hour on Sundays, or when I walked expressly alone among the
mountains, hoping to be inspired, or perhaps in the presence of
death or of an earthquake. But that is the religion of the worldling: nature and society might get on, he thinks, perfectly well by
themselves, and the divine presence and power in all things seems
to him an empty word. The whole spiritual elevation of Berkeley's philosophy comes with the opposite intuition, that sees God
in all things and all things in God. People will be masks and
voices in a divine revelation, as they are in Dante's *Divine Comedy*. If they become powers collateral with God's power, and
spirits collateral with the spirit in us that finds or imagines them,
then we have lapsed altogether from our idealistic insight and
reverted to the assumptions of common sense and of vulgar
naturalism.

Perhaps Berkeley should be congratulated on having halted

half-way in his idealism, assigning only material phenomena to God, and social phenomena to the dubious devices of the human heart. In this he may have been true to a certain positivistic and moral instinct latent in his blood. Where trade prevails over agriculture, debate over handicrafts, politics over war, and morality over religion, it is intelligible that society and social intercourse should seem the first and surest of realities. Philosophers may then be prone to intercept their criticism of knowledge, and to reason as if men's moral personalities could exist in a physical vacuum, like so many angels, remaining distinct and communicating magically, without any bodies or any books. Society, which is a development of animal life, may then seem to subsist undisturbed, after we have spirited away, in theory, the animal life that supported it. Berkeley lived under the spell of this social convention, as we see also in his philanthropic endeavours. A Buddha or a Saint Francis would have been more impartial in scepticism or in faith; and charity in either of them would have been all the more religious and tender for being without political illusions.

Even in politics, however, the immaterialism of Berkeley might have suggested utopias more visionary than any that he actually entertained. When meditating on the future of America he composed some verses, of which the last stanza is well known:

> Westward the course of empire takes its way:
>   The first four acts already past,
> A fifth shall close the drama with the day;
>   Time's noblest offspring is the last.

Here, if there be any illusion, it is the illusion of simplicity. We have Ockham's razor applied to history, leaving it shorn of all sad tangles and gross hybrid endless extensions. Only Babylon, Greece, Rome, and England, with America to follow; and then nothing. The five clear episodes of a classical tragedy would end with a pleasant hush of exaltation, like an eloquent sermon: an enthralling composition, and not too long. America, flatteringly expected to be the noblest of empires, was also to be the last: the force of nature, or of divine intervention, could no further go either in time or in sublimity; and just as physical objects had no inside, and as events had no causes save the moral fitness that they should come as they do, so when once the general edifying function of existence had been fulfilled, any further events would have lost their excuse for being.

In fine, Berkeley never transferred his life to the world revealed by his philosophy. Like other idealists, he had been bred in the atmosphere of homely materialism and traditional religion, and he loved them both: it was only scientific materialism, incompatible with religion, that he hated. His mystical paradox, if taken to heart, would have dissolved these conventions; but he used it only argumentatively, as a technical device for defending them. The simplification, when once familiar, made all things easy. It was a private product of critical wit, like the answer to a riddle; a happy thought that seemed suddenly to clarify and to explain everything. It was a *trouvaille*. And Berkeley kept it, certainly not hidden, yet lovingly held somewhat in reserve, as many an Englishman, half humorously, half proudly keeps his dearest hobby, to be bravely defended in public when occasion demands, but not to be suffered in the meantime to derange at home the rational course of his existence. Yet neither the homely materialism nor the historical Christianity by which Berkeley lived could ever have arisen if mankind had been possessed from the beginning by his new intuition of a universal miraculous intercourse between disembodied spirits. This intuition had to remain somewhat intermittent and esoteric.

Perhaps a humorous logician, convinced by the same arguments, might have allowed his common sense and his traditional religion to subsist in an ironical form; and having become secretly aware that life is a dream, he might have continued talking to his friends, eating, and travelling: all with a not unpleasant sense of acting a harmless comedy and fooling himself to the top of his bent. But this was not at all the mood in which Berkeley took his philosophy. He was not humorous. His logic had made a scenic illusion of the world, but he was not by nature histrionic. If ever he mocked fashionable infidels or cast ridicule on glib philosophers, he did so in profound earnest, and for the triumph of truth. He was all noble charity, luminous conviction, and untroubled faith. If his thought never rose into devout ecstasy, as his speculative system seemed to demand, it was never narrowed to

the logical dilemmas which that system presented. His manhood
kept the balance. He remained a humanist, with religious faith
strained through the triple sieve of good breeding, simpleness,
and high speculation: a Quixote of the Schools, conventional at
heart, in spite of his mysticism, and tenderly loving mankind,
whilst demonstrating, with proofs strong as Holy Writ, that they
had all been arrant fools from the first dawn of creation.

Some Developments of Materialism

GEORGE SANTAYANA

The materialism of Karl Marx and his followers debouches into
history through two channels: one is economics, the other dialectic. That materialists should explain history through the natural operation of economic forces requires little comment. Do not
all animals migrate and foregather in search of food? Do they not
multiply, and do they not "liquidate" their rivals, where they find
food in abundance? That is fundamental. And if wars, international and civil, sometimes cut across the vegetative fortunes of
mankind, need they blind the shrewd naturalist to the radical
causes of such strife, and of success in it? Feeding brings breeding,
and breeding brings fighting, and the best fed and most numerous
win the battles. A materialist, on these lines, may readily recom-
pose legendary history so as to illustrate his principles.

An impartial critic, however, considering materialism merely
as a possible hypothesis, might observe that the materialist draws
his inspiration and chooses his models from the largest and most
obvious fields of science, such as the stellar universe or the solar
system or the romance of biological evolution. So perhaps the dependence of history on economics may seem obvious when we

George Santayana, "Some Developments of Materialism," *The American
Scholar*, 18 (1949), pp. 271-281. Reprinted by permission of Daniel Cory.

consider very large units, such as mankind and the earth's surface. But when we come to the closer texture of history, to particular wars or particular forms of government or religion, the obvious considerations are psychological and moral, and the historian becomes more plausibly a moralist, a poet, perhaps a theologian. The economists that Marx himself studied operated chiefly with human psychological forces: and the "economic man," which for them was the measure of all things, was a pure ideal. How, then, shall the materialist conceive materialistically those economic causes to which he would attribute the march of history?

Psychology is a crucial subject for the naturalist. If the solar system arose according to the nebular hypothesis, all life on earth, and the whole spiritual development of man, must have lain dormant in that nebula, and presumably lies still potential in the substance of the sun, as unforeseen explosions lay in the substance of the atomic bomb. The internal causes of human action (and all causes, according to the materialist, must be fundamentally material), are therefore never to be found by tracing the movements of units on the scale of the human senses—that is, by tracing phenomena—much less by tracing ideas and passions in men's minds, which are all evoked from moment to moment by the secret life of the psyche. This secret life, which, according to the materialist, lies on the same plane as the surrounding movement of nature and society, is indeed publicly revealed in part, in purely dramatic, emotional and verbal terms, by his visible actions; and the same hidden life is revealed privately to himself by his thoughts, although what a man thinks is the most superficial part of his total being. And if the materialist is to be consistent, he must recognize this merely conventional symbolic significance of all literary psychology. It can represent the dynamism of nature only at a great remove, in the conventional terms of the human senses and of human grammar.

How then did it happen that the classical British economists, whom Marx followed, showed so realistic a sense for the movement of social institutions? Their psychology was phenomenalistic and conventional, when it was not abstractly ideal: how came it that their wisdom was so close to hard facts? They were immersed in the study of actual trade, of actual industry, of the actual transformations of national life; and the thin psychological language that they used deceived them only in their speculative conclusions. It rendered their philosophy narrow and transient; it did not prevent it from being truly descriptive and full of local sap. And this, I think, may be the case also with this element in the Marxian theory. Psychology is crucial for systematic materialism: but Marx followed Hegel and all the German idealists except Schopenhauer in neglecting psychology. To ignore psychology was perhaps a prerequisite to idealism; and to master psychology would be a prerequisite to an adequate materialism.

But let us suspend for a moment the discussion of economics, and turn to dialectic, the other Marxian avenue from materialism to history. Dialectic is a mode of argument, a use of logic to clarify purposes and opinions. How should material processes become dialectical? Stalin* gives a brief answer to this question. Materialism becomes dialectical on ceasing to be metaphysical. It was metaphysical, according to Stalin, when it conceived nature as a casual collection of changeless atoms, or a circular repetition of ideal types; it becomes dialectical when it learns to conceive nature as an unreturning flow of concrete but inwardly unstable formations, mutually conditioned. This philosophy is therefore dialectical in its method of tracing relations between the phenomena of nature, but materialistic in its theory of their status and substance.

Stalin is no professional philosopher—nor was Lenin, or even Marx—and it would not be fair to their honest intentions to cloud their words with a swarm of dialectical variations and distortions. Before asking whether materialism was ever really metaphysical, or can ever become either dialectical or historical, let me therefore say this: that in my opinion the philosophy of Marx and Lenin, as interpreted by the Russian Communist party (and this is the only interpretation politically important), is really materialistic, but not really either dialectical or historical in any speculative sense. If it were so, the metaphysics driven by Marx out of the door would have come back again through the window, and his materialism would not only have become metaphysical; it

---

* In his essay on "Dialectical and Historical Materialism," included in *Questioni del Leninismo*, traduzione di Palmiro Togliatti, Roma, Società Editrice *L'Unità*, 1945, Vol. II, pp. 271-301.

would have become idealistic. Such traditional terms, however, are vague and equivocal: and we may well be not only tolerant but relieved if, in using them, political reformers have their eyes fixed not on ideal concepts, but on concrete earthly facts, and on positive moral transformations to be prepared. It is then as applied to these living undertakings, not as technically definable, that their words should be understood.

There is one technical point, however, in which this philosophy seems to me to have penetrated the fog of controversy and to have said the simple truth. Materialism is not properly metaphysical. The sweeping systems of the Ionians, who were the first and purest materialists, were all clearly physical, not metaphysical; cosmological, not ideological or moralistic. Each of them lighted on a common element, water, air or fire, to which he sought to reduce everything else; and ultimately Greek physics adopted these three, with the judicious addition of earth, to be the materials of nature. These materials were judged to be dynamic in themselves and to fall spontaneously into a natural order and life: an assumption which is essential to an adequate materialism. It is true that Democritus adopted from the Pythagoreans those perfect geometrical shapes which he attributed to his atoms; and from the Eleatics he borrowed that void, identified with Non-Being, which is the most metaphysical idea conceivable. Democritus had an irrepressible imagination. To posit atoms was a stroke of genius. This symbol marks the granular many-centered distribution of things in nature, from the dust to the stars, from the individual soul to the seed from which it develops. Leibnitz, who was also a genius, perceived the same affinities; but to have too much genius is dangerous, if you wish to see the truth. Democritus, as we learn today, should not have supposed atoms to have exact geometrical shapes or to be indestructible or pellucid and structureless, as a jewel looks to the eye, or a glass of wine traversed by the light. These are idealizations foreign to natural science. In nature atoms are such only functionally, as soldiers are in an army: you must never take from matter, if it is to be the substance of this world, the relativity of its dimensions and motions and the fertility of its hidden depths. Of this the Ionians had a healthy intuition; and Democritus himself, though betrayed by the very clearness of his thought into a sort of ideolatry, yet in the main was faithful to his evidently materialistic intentions. For he felt the reality, the authority, the unfailing order of the world in which we move and act, amid objects collateral with our own bodies, and amid forces continuous with our own physical force; in contrast to which, he mocked that evanescent world of images, passions and words which drifts before us as in a waking dream.

In Marx, this spirit of materialism seemed to blow also, insofar as he chose material agencies, like the equipment of industry and the crowding of population, to explain political movements conventionally attributed to the might of ideas. Had he been a laughing philosopher, like Democritus, he might have traced the domination of matter satirically through the romantic revolutions of modern politics and philosophy: his residence in England and labors at the British Museum would not have left him without details to adduce the evidence. But Marx was not a satirist; he was an ardent Hebrew prophet, and the great prophet Hegel, also essentially eschatological, had been his master. It was impossible for him not to see the handwriting on the wall. Things were moving toward a great deliverance. Matter, as always, would prove the instrument of destiny.

"My dialectical method," Marx himself tells us, "not only differs from the Hegelian method in its foundations, but is diametrically opposed to it. For Hegel, the process of thought (which he actually transformed, under the name of Idea, into a separate thinking mind) is the Demiurgos or Artisan of the cosmos, which cosmos is merely an incidental exemplification of that (divine) Idea. For me, on the contrary, the ideal factor is nothing but the material factor transferred and transmuted in the brain of man."*

This sounds categorical, and we might infer that Marx meant his dialectic to be only an intellectual perspective or dramatic formula imposed upon events by the bias of human apprehension. Yet he speaks of *self-contradiction* driving each phase of economic history to turn into the next. Hegel could use such language because for him "history" did not signify a series of actual events, but rather the secret magic or meaning of such a series of events revealed to the genius of the historian. In such a dialectical

* *Ibid.*, pp. 271-2.

idea there might well be contradiction, as for instance in Protestant theology, if the absolute inspiration of Scripture and the absolute inspiration of the private heart were articles of the same creed. An evolution in that faith was then compulsory logically, although it need not occur historically in every Protestant community. But Hegel, who in his dialectic was intent on the dynamics of change—really a physical problem—thought only of the real contradiction that might lie in the *inspiration* of each stage in the movement, not deigning to consider the instability of its physical equilibrium, which for the materialists was the ground of all those inspirations and of their contradictions. It was therefore this instability that deserved the name of dialectic, by which Hegel had always meant the dynamics of change.

But then Marx should never have called the instability of events a *contradiction*. In the ruin of private enterprise overwhelmed by monopolies there was never any contradiction. There was only underselling. Yet this incapacity to survive in private business is not a logical predicament. No divided will troubles the monopolist, but a socialist revolution confiscates his millions, or he is annexed by a shrewd dictator, to be Secretary to the People's Treasury. So when a private picture-gallery is turned into a public museum. Probably the passion to collect has not yielded in the amateur to a sense of civic duty; but none of his heirs will have the desire or the means to preserve the collection, which must be bequeathed to the State or else dispersed. The solvent of human achievements is not dialectic but misfortune.

And what, properly speaking, is dialectic? Only, I think, a play of variations in meaning. It was invented by the Sophists, as a method of confusing and discrediting all received opinions. It was rescued and turned against its inventors by Socrates, without making it into pure logic: for dialectic had, and has always retained, an element of foresight and malicious intent, which in Socrates became benevolent irony. He employed dialectic in the pursuit of self-knowledge, in the effort to discover, beneath current language and prejudice, what at bottom a man really thought, or loved. When, for instance, one of his sons complained of Xantippe, Socrates asked him whether he thought his mother wished him ill. No: the boy, abashed, said he didn't think that.

But then, Socrates continued, why not be content with knowing that she loves her son, and disregard her words as of no consequence? Thus a little dialectic, showing up hasty anger in a new light, could modify that anger in the interests of reason and peace.

To transfer dialectic from its moral and quizzical sphere to the realms of matter and history was, then, possible to Hegel only because he regarded the true being of nature and history not as a procession of actual events, but as perspective chosen and distinguished by the dramatic intuition of the philosopher, perhaps only poetically or religiously, but more often in some special political or moral interest. Such history or science is evidently not the full truth of things as they have occurred, but speculative romance, where almost everything is omitted, the parts retained are transfigured, and a moral is superposed.

I think we may safely say that if Marx retained this dialectic, without its theological fulfillment, in his view of history, the reason was that he had a moral and dramatic future much more at heart than any speculative rigor or consistency. For any materialist, the automatism of nature is generative: I mean events there grow out of one another in a wasteful meandering multitude of local derivations and conjunctions, not according to any assignable plan or dramatic unity. Yet throughout nature automatism, in its foundations, is self-repeating, so that recognizable cycles of change are established, as in the reproduction of plants and animals, graphic historical units being thus forced on our attention. In astronomy and mechanics these cycles are so precise and unchanging that we may predict them with confidence. Where reproduction is by fusion of two different automatisms, as when it is sexual, each new individual is novel and unique; yet none comes to satisfy any intention or idea operating without physical means. The same is true in politics: everything there is planned and replanned by dozens of hotheads: but what ensues materially is the product of mutually checking and deviating influences, so that nothing happens as anybody wished. This, however, is not an observation agreeable to prophets; and we can understand that Marx, feeling justly that a profound social transformation was brewing in the industrial melting-pot of the nineteenth century, could not refrain from adapting to his ends the extremely graphic

and tempting dialectic of Hegel, and seeing in it, in spite of his
own materialism, a predestined "phenomenology of the spirit."

We must remember that Marx was at once a tireless student and
an irrepressible reformer, offended by contrary evils and errors in
the world, and agitated by diverse inspirations. Like the Hebrews
of old, he was deeply moved by the undeserved misery of the
laboring poor; it was a physical misery and a physical injustice;
and it should be by a revolution in the physical conditions of life
for the masses that honest relief should be found. Here the prophetic vein intervenes and inconsistently dominates: this relief
must not be partial or temporary: it must be total, final and already in sight. The eschatology of Hegel could lend a specious
speculative sanction to this visionary demand: there, too, the
world of nature and history was brought violently round to a
glorious millennium. Yet both the method and the final good to
be achieved were for Marx material, and such as a shrewd observer of the contemporary world might see to be possible or even
inevitable in the near future; so that materialism could be en-
thusiastically retained and felt to be the predestined herald of a
miraculous redemption.

Leaving, however, the interpretation of Marx to his followers,
as it is but fair to do, we may put a more speculative question.
Would a materialism free from all admixture of idealism or militancy involve any particular code of politics or morals? Essentially
and directly, it certainly would not. Materialism intends to be
scientific, and science is a description of nature as it is and as it
functions, not an ideology or a collection of precepts. Moreover,
materialism traces, and traces sympathetically, the whole generative movement of nature; it feels the equal right of every animal
to strive to live, and in that sense its sympathies might be called
democratic. A moral ideal in this system must be omnimodal or, if
you prefer, non-existent. But at the same time materialism records,
at every step, the ruin of everything that is inopportune, the
agony of crime, the ignominy of vice, the madness of passion.
Thus the picture it paints of existence is full of silent warnings
and monitions, yet also full of glorious and lovely models. In this
sense the tragic but stimulating lesson it teaches is aristocratic,
severe, hard-hearted, yet always leaving a tempting vista open to

the bold, to the artist, and to the thinker. It invites all nations and all arts to try their luck: but it discloses a past covered with ruins, and a future in which little that we can care for or understand may be expected to exist.

More subtly rendered, with no alloy of illusion, the personal morals and politics inspired by materialism may be found in the best known of Epicurean poets—I mean, in Lucretius and in Horace. They are diverse in dignity, as nature is; and each touches different notes of the moral gamut, as nature touches them in the unintimidated human heart. Lucretius begins with an enthusiastic invocation of Venus, identified for the moment with *natura naturans*. I would not assert that sympathy with omnimodal nature is imposed by materialism on the philosopher, or even on the poet: this miscellaneous abundance may bring on the vertigo. At any rate it brings on the most cruel conflicts between incompatible forms of life, each of which is alike a child of *natura naturans*, each bent on its particular faculty and occasions. Initially, all careers are open to the will; but eventually, in the world where they meet and cross one another, almost all careers are closed. And Lucretius, after his outburst of sympathy with everything growing and blooming, begs Venus to imprison her lover, Mars, in her arms, and compel him to grant peace not (it would be too much to ask) to the world, but to the Romans. The hymn to life ends at once with a prayer for peace, as a special favor.

Elsewhere Lucretius shows us (what he forgets here) that Venus herself is the source of war. All these natural passions that breed so much splendor and beauty are presupposed by the naturalist; yet he knows that they are not only dangerous in view of untoward circumstances, but are poisoned inwardly by their own lusts and reciprocal hatreds. Peace again seems the only true good; because pleasure, which Epicureans officially declare to be the good, is not wholly pleasant when actual, but pleasant only by definition; for *from the very fountain of its sweetness bubbles up something bitter that stings in the midst of the flowers.* Lucretius, in saying this, was thinking of love, of love so pursued in all its forms by anxiety and sorrow. But the contradiction is no less present in pride, wealth, power, ambition, reputation, enthusiasm and religious faith. Satisfaction cannot be complete so long as the soul is divided and the mind full of incidental things. To be pure, as Lucretius demands that pleasure should be, it must be enjoyed in tranquility—I had almost said in Nirvana. Human dispositions differ; Lucretius seems to have sought the highest good at last in a voluntary death. But to me unalloyed pleasure seems to come daily in two things, both disinterested in origin and both potentially all-comprehensive in scope—I mean, intelligence and laughter: the very things, according to tradition, that delighted Democritus, the patriarch of materialism.

By Horace, who was without any hearty passion, Venus and simple pleasures were habitually praised, somewhat ironically. They were a resource when there was nothing better; they were amiable, and they were cheap. Green young people would rave about them; they were innocent and human, and would be disillusioned in time. A court poet was also bound to sing artificially the praises of rustic religion and of successful campaigns; but Horace does not allow traditional piety to deceive him, nor does he deceive posterity by his flattery of Maecenas and of Augustus. Glory is like Venus. You may be dazzled by it, and may pursue it in your day; but *miseri quibus intemptata nites!* That is the lesson of the whole business. The jungle is open to the sportsman, but he must be strong and well equipped. Nature is by no means hostile to greatness, whether of mind or of fortune. It breeds and fosters the lion no less than the lamb, yet both conditionally, temporally, under strict inner and outer requirements. True, there are some princely souls that spontaneously know how to be masters of things and of their own passions; such a one Horace paints in the young Paulus Maximus, *centum puer artium,* fit to carry far and wide the banners of love, as well as of war. Yet the best fortune is clouded a little, and evaporates quickly. In the fifth act of the most brilliant tragedy the tone, though reconciled, must always be funereal. The spirit then, in the presence of the sum of things, passes into a twilight world, the sphere of reflection, the realm of eternal truth.

Thus materialism also, by its very hopelessness, opens the way to *metanoia*. For it, as for the Indian sages, the endless succession of catastrophes and paradises is an old story. Redemption is not to be sought horizontally, but vertically. Life would be a predicament in any paradise; the point is to make a fine art of it, whatever it may chance to be. Claim possession of nothing that you are not ready to surrender. Then you may live a reasonable life—free, as Lucretius says, from care and from fear, with judicious abstention here, with smiling participation there, with perhaps some small achievement on your own part, and above all with a little of that philosophy which the ancients preached and sometimes even practiced. Then, neither boastfully nor mournfully, you might say to yourself daily: I have lived. Nations and philosophies might learn to make the same reflection, if they had been noble and clear enough in their day to render that reflection satisfying.

Is this lesson of honest materialism that which inspires the government of communist Russia? It does not seem so on the surface; but I am not competent to judge either what is the fundamental spirit of the Russian people or what is the final aim of their leaders. If all that stirs were open-minded humanity in its motive, with universal justice toward the poor and enslaved of all nations for its goal, this immense movement would not be really entangled in any dialectical theory of history. It would be simply a recovery of unsophisticated human kindness and realistic good sense, made conscious and unified by the modern facilities for intercommunication. And a government concerned only with a rational universal economy, and controlling only material services, as the commissariat does in an army, might well bring the same advantages to all nations that medicine brings to all ailing individuals. Where nature has set down conditions for welfare, it is not tyranny but kindness for the expert to point them out to the unsuspecting layman; but he must speak by the authority of things, not by the inspiration of any fantastic ideology or of any racial or national ambition. Were government confined to regulating rationally the economic order of human society, spirit, relieved of all animal anxiety, might for the first time be free in its own sphere.

III

ESSENCE, SUBSTANCE, AND EXISTENCE

Of Essence and Existence
and Santayana

DONALD C. WILLIAMS

George Santayana was master of a solemn showmanship which
is to blame for his being taken for a more trivial and alien philosopher than he was, both by those who like the trivial and the alien
and by those who do not. There are an inimitable golden mean-
ness and flatness about his philosophy, which speaks of truth without curiosity, of good without hope or ambition, of the holy gods
without either credence or contempt. The nacre of his prose,
precious with a sanity so polished as to seem more morbid than
another man's madness, his skeptical reserve toward the contingencies of existence and his remote aristocratic gaze on the picture
gallery of essences—all these have endeared him to esthetes and
positivists and to various other fine urban breeds who read in
him their own gospel of disillusion and dissolution, while they
correspondingly have alienated us peasant souls who think life
is real and earnest and that things are more than what they
seem. It is customary to understand even his show of metaphysics

Donald C. Williams, "Of Essence and Existence and Santayana," *The Journal of Philosophy*, 51 (1954), pp. 31-42. Reprinted by permission.

as like the materialism of Epicurus or of Marx, an allegorical
backdrop for the morality play upon the stage.[1] He said himself
that his "materialism is not a system of metaphysics; it is a speculation in chemistry and physiology."[2] or indeed no more than common sense and conventional sanity.[3] The longer one peers, however, through the opalescent glass with which his style conceals
the man, the more one discovers of a more solid philosophical
citizen. That he fears the word "metaphysics" is because of its
association with "visionary insolence in the Germans"[4] and
with more traditional attempts to palm off "moral or psychological figments" for explanatory facts.[5] He deplored in modern
philosophy the "radically subjective and sophistical thing,"[6] the
semanticism for which "language is more real than its meaning,"[7]
and the "curious self-degradation" which he thought the common quality of positivism, pragmatism, and idealism.[8] For himself, he asserted, there is an ontology, a theory of being, latent
in his work "from the beginning" and giving support and substance, what he called "dramatic wholeness" and "orthodoxy,"
to everything else.[9] He would have thought it impudence to
prate of the Life of Reason with nothing to be reasonable about.
And in fact his *Realms of Being* and its prolegomenon in *Scepticism and Animal Faith* are among the world's few good treatises
in ontology. However long men may pay their respects to the
Santayana who is the elegant and perceptive essayist, it is in his
ontology that he proves himself a philosopher of the grand mold,
a philosopher, if I may borrow a flourish from Mr. Wyndham

[1] See, for example, Professor Blau, who in his *Men and Movements in
American Philosophy* (New York, 1952), generally a responsible enough book,
chapters Santayana not with realism, but as a vaguely agnostic "naturalist."
Cyril Bailey, on the other hand, exculpates Epicurus (*Lucretius*, p. 7).

[2] *Three Philosophical Poets,* Cambridge, 1935, p. 27.

[3] See *The Philosophy of George Santayana,* ed. by Schilpp, Evanston, 1940
(hereafter *"Santayana"*), pp. 12, 505.

[4] *Little Essays,* ed. by Smith, New York, 1920, p. 176.

[5] *Realms of Being,* New York, 1942 (hereafter *"Realms"*), p. 828. Compare
Santayana, p. 519, and *Scepticism and Animal Faith,* New York, 1923 (hereafter *"Scepticism"*), p. vii.

[6] *Santayana,* p. 500.

[7] *Santayana,* p. 522.

[8] *Realms,* p. 449.

[9] *Santayana,* pp. 25, 30, etc.

Lewis, "absolute, displayed, and regardant, in the Chief, the Pale, and the Quarter Fess."[10]

Even more firmly ingrained, however, than the error that Santayana was an esthete with a weakness for epistemology, is the belief that he was in America an alien bird who in season flew back to his ancestral shore. He, his teachers, and his students all underlined whatever separated him from our climate. He called himself "a man whose spiritual attachments lie in one quarter and his linguistic attachments in another."[11] Far from resenting it when William James expostulated, "You are a Scholastic!" he reiterated it, reminding us incidentally that James himself defined Scholasticism as "common sense made consistent."[12] When James commented on his "moribund Latinity" he retorted amicably with a remark about the philosophical limitations of mere berserk vigor,[13] and he proceeded to fancy himself a Spanish mystic, a "Don Quixote sane," a southern European, even a Greek.[14] He saw his philosophy as delayed and damaged by his having been miseducated by New England,[15] and it is well advertised that he turned his back on her to dwell with the ancient "dignity" of Rome—Swiss Guards, Black Shirts, and all.[16]

The most popular manner of treating such nice questions of tribal affinity in American intellectual circles today is to ignore or avoid them. It is an essential part of Santayana's philosophy, however, to be cognizant of them and their importance, and the only reply worth making to the theory which would assign him to Southern Europe is that it is not true. I do not mean merely that he could say when he was not far from eighty, "It is as an

10 *The Stuffed Owl, an Anthology of Bad Verse,* New York, 1930, p. 179. The editors, D. B. Wyndham Lewis and Charles Lee, were paying their respects to Longfellow as a poet.

11 *Realms,* p. 833.

12 *Santayana,* pp. 499, 591, 604; *Realms,* p. 93. What James wrote, if I recall aright, was that Scholasticism is common sense become *pedantic.*

13 James in R. B. Perry's *Thought and Caracter of William James,* Boston, 1935, Vol. II, p. 319; Santayana, ibid., p. 321.

14 *Santayana,* pp. 604 and 598; "Brief History of My Opinion," in *Contemporary American Philosophy,* ed. by Adams and Montague, New York, 1930, Vol. II, p. 249.

15 *Santayana,* p. 21.

16 See *Time,* March 9, 1953, p. 106; *Santayana,* p. 603.

American writer that I must be counted, if I am counted at all,"[17] nor that his message was always beamed to America, nor that what he found in Italy was not spiritual fellowship but the quiet of a philosophical desert.[18] It is not merely that his teachers and colleagues at Harvard remained the most real forces in his life, fascinating and fecundating, and that his own erudite waywardness was so much their lesson. It is rather that for better or for worse the very fiber of the metaphysics at the core of his thought is a product of the Anglo-American air, incapable of germinating and unlikely to be propagated elsewhere. To bring this home it is enough to compare him with that more precious expatriate Mr. T. S. Eliot, who with no boast of Latin blood contrives to make himself more foreign than Pharoah.

When Santayana went back of the teachings of his American contemporaries it was not, as he sometimes pretended, to recover a secret of the ancients or some subtlety of the Spanish schools, but to consummate better than the English and the Americans a principal theme in our own heritage. For in an important respect the nineteenth-century spokesmen catalogued as typically American, and so irksome in that capacity to Santayana, represented a freakish and foreign episode. James, Dewey, Royce, Thoreau, Whitman, even Emerson, native enough by birth and animus, drenched themselves to distraction in the imported liquors of German idealism, of French spiritualism, and even of Indian mysticism. Their transcendentalism and "egotism," as Santayana called it, mistaking their thoughts for the masters and makers of reality, taking, as he said, the turnips and cabbages of their own kitchen gardens for the signs of the zodiac,—these were academic borrowings from Europe and Asia. For two and a half centuries before them, our countrymen had been taught in a profoundly different philosophy of realism, that of dissenting Christianity and Cartesian science, the common sense of Locke, of the Scottish philosophy, and of the plain citizen who had to contend with Indians and the weather. What Santayana did, in effect, was to restore the older and deeper strain, disciplined and criticized with all the mordant

[17] *Santayana*, pp. 601, 603.

[18] Italian thought, it appeared, was as barbarously idealistic as German; *Santayana*, p. 507.

ingenuity which he inherited from the later British empiricists, and sweetened, perhaps, with a certain specious Iberian nostalgia. As Locke's philosophy was to its Scholastic prototype, reformed by a more scientific logic and plain speaking, so Santayana's is to Locke's. His lip service to Scholasticism is a manifesto of natural realism and a declaration of sympathy for the Scholastic concern for the nature of "being as such." But even his doctrine of essence, which he considered the most foreign and traditional part of his philosophy, he did not learn from Aquinas or Suarez but from Russell and Moore.[19]

The quality of the Santayanan reformation could be shown in any of his realms of being. For though he always insisted that he was "intellectually a convinced materialist,"[20] he was not a materialist in the strictest sense—not one who believes that there is nothing except the matter and events deployed in the space-time of physics. He thought of the realm of matter as only one of four realms of being—matter, essence, spirit, and truth—all but the first of them specifically *im*material. He is a materialist mainly in that he holds that only matter *does* anything;[21] and even then he often means by "matter" no more than whatever flux of existence engenders our lives and experience. Physics is appointed to discover it, but though it looks like electrons and protons now, it will doubtless turn out very different in the long run.[22]

With more leisure we might examine Santayana's tender and subtle account of spirit as an emergent emphasis, a "living light of discrimination,"[23] "a sort of invisible vegetation flourishing in some of the stars."[24] Or we could look at the realm of truth, better perhaps called the realm of fact—not a subjective affair of coherence or warranted assertibility, but outside and eternal, "the wake of the ship of time, a furrow which matter must plough upon the face of essence."[25] These are somewhat darker oracles, however, and their principles are derivative from those of essence

19 *Santayana*, p. 587.
20 *Realms*, p. 549. See *Scepticism*, p. vii.
21 *Santayana*, p. 509; *Realms*, pp. 828, 845, 851, etc.
22 *Santayana*, pp. 507-509; *Realms*, p. 829.
23 *Scepticism*, p. 273.
24 *Realms*, p. 826.
25 *Scepticism*, p. 227; quoted in *Realms*, p. 405.

and existence. They lack topically the poignancy which recent discussion has given the latter, and they are less close to Santayana's own heart. For "Josiah Royce," he tells us, "once said to me that the gist of my philosophy was the separation of essence from existence," and he is glad to confess to the soft impeachment.[26]

The primordial contrast of essence and existence was treated portentously by the ancients and the Scholastics, was handled very gingerly by Locke, and was despised by most of the positivists, but it lurks in the center of contemporary polemic over existentialism and is fundamental to any informed controversy of nominalism with realism. Santayana revived the categories with a sunny caustic sophistication and stripped them to their fighting weight.

To draw the line between essence and existence is no more than to notice the difference between *what* a thing is and *that* it is, between its character or kind and its occurrence as a case of the kind, between the rosiness of the rose and the fact that it is *there*. Language and logic as well as metaphysics have always found the contrast well nigh indispensable, from Socrates to Carnap, but for the scientific purposes of modern philosophy it has been spoiled and discredited by the metaphysical marvels which have been associated with it.

Plato, for example, taught that the essences are eternal prototypes, an ethereal aristocracy of ideals, laid up in heaven as patterns to be distantly imitated by the things that exist here below. Aristotle taught that the essence of a thing is its inner principle, its ontological soul which preserves and improves it, explains it, and makes it what it is, in contrast with the rest of its properties, which are merely accidental. Both of those philosophers, and most of their more official heirs for two thousand years, agreed that true essences are relatively few, that they are accessible only to reason, that they are good, that they are what things ought to be, that they act on things by luring or egging them forward, and that in so far as things fall short they not merely are wrongly constituted, they are *un*constituted, intrinsically deficient and vague. This is the metaphysics of the dog show: that there is a sublime essential Poodlehood, for example, to which every poodle

26 *Santayana*, p. 497.

aspires and deserves a blue ribbon if he achieves it better than other poodles. In human society it has been, too often, the metaphysics of natural aristocracy and natural slaves and natural law, for it suggests if it does not entail that ontological experts can discern our one true Nature and decree what is proper and what is improper to it, and allot each to his caste according as he conforms or not.

Though congenial to the human heart and endowed with that *prima facie* plausibility which is the one chief organ of Peripatetic thought, this "moralistic physics," as Santayana called it,[27] was worse than useless to the scientist and a millstone round the neck of the ethics it was supposed to salvage. Its effects in fantastic teleologies and the theory of fixed animal species leap immediately to our minds, but there are others which run deeper; to discredit the Aristotelian doctrine of falling bodies, for example, Galileo had not to make any experiment but only to point out the fallacy of the notion, derived from the theory of substantial essences, that a "thing" is an absolute unit in nature. In ethics, the theory caught men in that futile circle by which the proper good for any individual is what fulfills its "real" essence, the "real" essence is that whose fulfillment makes the individual truly happy, and true happiness is the achievement of the individual's proper good. It is no wonder that the hard-headed modernist has generally thrown out the whole notion, even though he thus fell into the counterpart puerilities of nominalism.

Santayana saw with rare exactitude that the logic and ontology of essences are independent of the moral load laid upon them, and can be kept all the better when the latter is removed. The main error of the old theory was that it required of analytic ontology a discrimination between "essential" properties and unessential ones which it could not provide. The cure, however, is not the nominalism which proclaims that there are no "real essences," but what Santayana calls the homeopathic one,[28] that *all* properties equally are "real essences" in the sense that they *are* and are essences but that none is so in the sense that it shines inherently with a metaphysical prerogative. Instead of denying

27 *Realms*, p. 503.
28 *Scepticism*, p. 77.

the choice Platonic natures, he drowns them in an ocean of logical realism. What the dog fancier regards as a perfect poodle has just the nature it has, but so does every other poodle, actual or possible, and so does everything else, real or imaginary. Every dog and every man, every planet or pebble, and every atom therein, takes the metaphysical first prize in its own proper class. For the realm of essence, Santayana writes, "is simply the unwritten catalogue, prosaic and infinite, of all the characters possessed by such things as happen to exist, together with the characters which all different things would possess if they existed."[29] It is infinitely more of a privilege to belong to the realm of existence which Plato despised than to the realm of essence which he adored, for there are infinitely more essences than there are existents. The realm of essence itself "is a perfect democracy," "not peopled by choice forms or magic powers," but "neutral in value."[30] We may like some more than others, but "in the realm of essence no emphasis falls on these favorite forms which does not fall equally on every other member of that infinite continuum. Every bad thing . . . illustrates an essence quite as accurately as if it had been good."[31] As essences are not moral models, neither are they principles of intelligibility, and they are as open to raw sensation as they are to *nous* itself. Since they are serene and timeless logical identities, finally, they can *do* nothing, either to push or to pull. To cure thus the confusion between the notion of essence or nature and the notion of an ideal power is to cure logic of a kind of idiocy and ethics of a kind of idolatry, for the very distillate of idolatry is to confound preëminence of value with preëminence of power or existence.

The notion now of existence, correlative to that of essence, has suffered even more from accretion and inflation than the latter has. What traditionally marked off the existent thing both from other existents and from the mere bundle of properties or essences which compose its nature—what make it *ex-sist* or stand out—are, on the one hand, a glob of primal matter, an indefinite raw metaphysical stuff, and, on the other, a last extra grace or act which is

Existence itself. The primal matter[32] is not only indefinite in its own being; it radiates or exudes indefiniteness, infecting with vagueness and deficiency the properties attached to it. Existence, conversely, is supposed to be a spring of perfection and definition. The brute substratum of matter and the boon and bloom of very existence are in some wise antipodal, yet are alike in being intrinsically dynamic. They are striving, efficacious, no less aquiver with *élan* and valuation than is the aristocracy of essences. Libraries of books have been written, in the Scholastic tradition and in contemporary existentialism, about the glory and horror, the surd mystery and the strange forces, of existence *per se*.

That Santayana's cautery of the theory of existence is no less neat and salutary than of essence is obscured because, while he wrote about essence with what for him was professional abstractness, his high phrases are at their most sibylline and parabolical when he celebrates existence. Existence, he says, is "the Life of Matter," a "wind," a "surfeit of being," a "rumble," "a strain and an incubus," "a forward tension," even power and love.[33] Partly these adjectives are a function of sheer prosody; partly they are to emphasize to a superficialist generation that "existence is not so jejune as an analytic positivism would make it"[34]—to be is not to be perceived; partly they are piety toward Lucretius, who apostrophized Matter as the world Mother; but for the rest they are to stress that existents are spun out in time, "intrinsically a flux or process."[35] Underneath the innocent figures he proclaims eventually an idea of existence as accurate and austere as his idea of essence.

Existence, he instructs us, is just existence. Essences are natures, but the whole point of the distinction between essence and existence is lost if any nature is assigned to existence. Matter

[32] We need not blink the favorite Scholastic idea that *having* matter is part of the *essence* of man, for example; but this makes matter a principle of essence only as, since being a particular is a universal, the particular might be assimilated to the universal. Prime matter, "signed" by spatio-temporal location, is a favorite principle of individuation, and though this does not make it *per se* a principle of existence, the individuated and the existent are among mundane beings the same.

[33] *Realms*, pp. 280, 282, 286, 517.

[34] *Realms*, p. 844.

[35] *Realms*, p. 626.

or existence[36] is the plain fact or status of occurring; and occurrence is the irreducible circumstance that essences enter into external relations. All essences eternally possess relations which are intrinsic to their being the natures they are, as four is twice two, and purple is similar to violet, irrespective of whether there exist purple things or sets of four. But they may also have relations which are not intrinsic but adventitious, like respective location in space and time—the juxtaposition of blue and white on a flag, for example, which could never have been deduced from blueness and whiteness *in abstracto*. Existence taken thus clear-headedly as pure occurrence is utterly diaphanous and indifferent; it is perfectly "sheer," as the ladies say. It leaves the existent nature absolutely and definitely what it is, neither subtracting from it, blurring and degrading it, nor adding to it anything except itself, the sheer status of existing. It is neither noble nor ignoble, neither active nor inert, neither God nor the Devil, neither glorious nor dreadful. It is not, as the existentialists say, decision, but neither is it indecision; it is not freedom and it is not fate. It neither tends nor impedes, neither loves nor empowers. It is none of these for the same reason it is neither blue nor gold, neither chocolate nor vanilla. All those properties, in so far as they *are* at all, are essences, to which existence may happen or not; they belong on the other side of the ledger.

Since existence is a simple status which an essence either has or lacks, it cannot pertain to different things in different intensities nor promote a new hierarchy of degrees of being. As what is common to all existent things, it cannot be what individuates them, but must leave that duty also to their essences.[37]

If we can assign any positive trait to existence itself, this is only the purely logical one that it is contingent. As no external relation has any ground in the essences it connects, so existence has no ground in any essence. It is, Santayana tells us, "an unintelligible emphasis," "an insane prominence," "a truly monstrous excrescence and superfluity," an "unfathomable mystery," "odious to the logician."[38] That Santayana uses thus a somewhat derog-

---

[36] Matter is the same as existence, save perhaps in the strange half-world of spirit; see *Santayana*, p. 521.

[37] So *Realms*, p. 23; but in *Santayana*, p. 524, it is place which individuates.

[38] *Scepticism*, p. 48; *Realms*, pp. 415, 845.

atory tone where the Thomist and the existentialist use an honorific one is due mostly to the temperamental fact that whereas those metaphysicians are almost piggishly avid for existence, he does not much care one way or the other; in principle he differs from them on contingency only by being consistent. As there was originally no necessity that you or I exist, there was no necessity that anything exist at all. The notion of a Necessary Being is then a chimera,[39] whether in the frank ontologism of Anselm or the covert version of Aquinas. That an essence should be or entail its existence on the finite plane of tables and trees is finite nonsense. That it should do so on the infinite plane of God is infinite nonsense.

Finally, as there was no necessity that anything exist, so too the fact that certain things do exist does not necessitate the existence of anything else. There are regularities among events, but no transcendent power in them and no flow of being from one to another.[40] Time may end today,[41] and in the meanwhile there is "essential novelty at every step."[42] We are all on our own, every act is autonomous, and "everything is what it is by its own initiative."[43] If there be a God, which Santayana thinks very unlikely, he is *primus inter pares,* an existent responsible for himself and the world only as an upholsterer is responsible for himself and his upholstery, and inferred from his work by the same sort of contingent hypothesis by which an upholsterer may be.

We have been taught to think of Santayana as at heart a Catholic—an atheist, to be sure, but a Catholic atheist rather than a Protestant atheist or a Jewish or pagan one. He called himself Catholic.[44] He found Bostonian Protestantism "unintelligible, sanctimonious and often disingenuous, . . . thoroughly alien and repulsive,"[45] while he was always scandalized by Protestant-

---

[39] *Realms,* p. 415.
[40] So *Realms,* p. 621, and *Santayana,* p. 505. Yet we remember his lyric attribution of power to existence, and in *Realms,* pp. 273, 281-282, etc., he cannot forbear to praise matter as a true principle of derivation and generation rather than merely of succession.
[41] *Realms,* p. 500.
[42] *Realms,* p. 626.
[43] *Realms,* p. 837.
[44] *Santayana,* p. 583; in *The Thought and Character of William James, loc. cit.* (p. 321); *et passim.*
[45] *William James, loc. cit.*

ism in general as of one piece with the wild Teutonic subjectivism which is "morose and barbarous at its inmost core."[46] Philosophical Catholics, however, will avoid his seductive embrace. The Catholicism he loved was a mere moral legendry, purified by the confession that it is false. He was loyal to Rome less because it was Catholic than because it was Roman, and less because it was Roman than because it was indifferent. In his theory of knowledge, he grants to private judgment more than would the most fanatical Protestant. His dual dualisms, of universals and particulars and of spirit and body, are integral to the Platonic revival which mainly marked off the modern age of Protestantism and science from Catholic Scholasticism. The ontology I have been outlining is opposed to Catholic thought in nearly every respect save that it *is* an ontology. It is opposed in its more than Platonic realism, in its rejection of prerogative and efficacious essences, of absolutely demarcated substances, and of immanent teleologies; in its denaturing of existence, in its setting substance and essence at opposite poles, in its identifying existence (which for St. Thomas was the last act of being) with matter (for St. Thomas the first potency); in its rejection of any principle of obfuscation and indeterminateness, in its doctrine that every existent is self-existent but that none exists necessarily, and in the Cartesian conception of spirit as a being at once individual and immaterial.

If it be complained that the major question is not whether Santayana's philosophy of being is Catholic, Protestant, or pagan, of the Eastern Hemisphere or of the Western, but whether it is true, I can agree, but I am less ready with an answer. Santayana himself we might expect to take exception, for he often held that the different perspectives in which men see the truth are rather more interesting than the truth itself. He comments demurely that anyhow he understands the world Sphinx better than she does herself.[47] This is too faint praise, however, and we may prefer to remember his earlier tribute to that staunch old common-

---

[46] *Little Essays*, p. 190. The immediate allusion here is to Shakespeare as exemplar of "the northern mind." But compare pp. 80-83, *Realms* p. 534, *Santayana* p. 537.

[47] *Realms*, p. xix.

place realist, Herbert Spencer, that it is after all an advantage for a philosophy to be substantially true. It is easy for us to surmise a hundred inconsistencies and excess complexities in his ontology which must be denuded of the rich cloths of his metaphor before they can be aptly criticized or corrected. True or false, however, his theory of essence and existence is a pure type which deserves to be a landmark and is likely to be his most lasting legacy. For the rest, his philosophy is "substantially true" in the modest sense appropriate to our profession, that it is not easily demonstrated to be false. This is almost the best than can be said of the best philosophies, and better than can be said of the philosophies of essence and existence which we have been pitting against him.

Pure Being

GEORGE SANTAYANA

The intuition of an infinite pregnancy in pure Being came to the Indians, as to so many mystics, because in them dialectic was not mere dialectic, but part of a spiritual discipline leading to the highest sublimations of character and experience. Naturally in that path I can follow them, if at all, *non passibus aequis:* but from my lower station I seem to see a fact to which their very holiness might easily blind them: namely, that they were not as yet the pure Being in which they aspired to lose themselves, but men of flesh and blood, rapt in austere contemplation. Pure Being to their ascetic souls was an equivalent for all the interests of life and for all its joys. Above all, it was the one haven of safety. They therefore saw in it, in spite of their logic, not what it is in itself but what it was to them. It became *all* reality in their eyes, although it excluded appearance, which is our only witness to

George Santayana, "Pure Being," *Columbia Manuscript Collection,* XIV:2.
© 1967 by Daniel Cory.

existence, and excluded flux, which is the principle of existence itself. It also became bliss, although its simplicity excluded consciousness. These contradictions are not contradictions to the spiritual man seeking liberation: he thinks of reality as the opposite of illusion, and of bliss as freedom from evil.

If pure Being were self-conscious (which is impossible logically because it is simple and ontologically because it is an essence) it would not find in itself any hint of the diversity with which it is said to be pregnant. This pregnancy is imputed where there is properly only simplicity. A human mind, familiar with diversity and change and simmering with them by virtue of its living organs, carries this pregnancy with it to the contemplation of pure Being; a sense of suspended animation suffuses the object, which in itself is clear and pellucid, like a jewel enlarged into an infinite sea; and the contemplative spirit, when it returns to verbal consciousness and tries to give an account of its experience, reports that in pure Being it saw all things contained potentially. They are all contained, not indeed potentially, but formally, in the realm of essence; but in pure Being, which is only one of these essences, nothing is contained save pure Being. That this essence is in its way supreme, that it expresses the most perfect fusion and harmony of all vital processes, without any trace of contingency or division, is very true; intensity and infinity are united in it with simplicity. Those who identify it with nothing are simply playing with words; it of course excludes all existence, and they may never have collected their thoughts enough to come face to face with this pure essence, or perhaps with any other. On the other hand those who in contemplation have reached those higher stages can speak of them only in metaphorical terms, which they wish to make as eulogistic as possible, since they have found there a miraculous freedom and rest. They are compelled to be poets, without always having the gift; and we must not blame them too much if their myths are stale and monotonous. Contemplation is not eloquence, and must be practised by each man for himself. The artist may be repelled by the saints who love the formless better than any form; the moralist may be shocked or puzzled by the infinitely greater importance which they give to the abyss of non-existence over any existence; yet artists and moralists are themselves practising the same sort of discipline in a different sphere:

they are finding principles in cases and images in things, and discovering a glory in these essences which makes the sole rightness or the sole beauty of existence.

Inevitable Contingency of All Fact

GEORGE SANTAYANA

Indetermination is usually thought of as something exceptional and marginal. Nature, we assume, is ordinarily regular; but we hope that sometimes free variations may break in, and from a moral point of view, totally change the issue. The brave lame boy may win the race, and God, for once, may be on the side of the small battalions. Yet such is the complexity of mundane events that the cynic can always suspect that some unobserved natural cause may have produced the happy result, without any miracle. There is one place, however, where the lover of metaphysical liberty may always find it, and that is at the beginning. Suppose we admit—what a romantic libertarian like Faust would hotly deny—that at the beginning was the Word, understanding some overruling principle of order and harmony. But why that Word? Why that plan for the universe, rather than some other plan? Why that choice on the Creator's part? If we say, Because that was the best plan, the question recurs: Why was that thought best? Is there no point of view, no direction of love, from which some very different plan indeed would have seemed better? And even abstracting from the radical irrationality of every radical preference, supposing this plan were somehow inherently the best, Why was the best realized? Why not something less good? Because such was the will of God; or if you prefer, Because so it happened, and such is the fact. So that contingency of existence, no matter what you may believe to exist, always remains absolute, and the uni-

George Santayana, "Inevitable Contingency of All Fact," *Columbia Manuscript Collection*, IX:13. © 1967 by Daniel Cory.

verse as a whole, having nothing before it or beside it, necessarily rejoices in the freedom of indifference, and is as it is without any cause.

This fundamental contingency of the world is multiplied and endlessly repeated as it moves through time. A timeless reality, if it could have been said to exist at all, would only have had one chance, so to speak, to declare what it was. But a world in flux has to renew its allegiance to its own character at every moment. Even if, as a matter of fact, nothing were ever added to substance or changed in natural law (as most materialists have supposed), this very constancy would be a contingent fact, which conceivably might have been otherwise: so that determinism itself, if it rules the world, rules it by chance. The necessity or inertia which compels things to go on as they have gone hitherto is but a challengeable habit; and the fatality that first adopted this constitution for the universe may have adopted it with a sly wink and for a time only, to be exchanged, after so many revolutions of the engine, for a different rhythm. Ultimate elements and ultimate laws are inevitably arbitrary. If they are given, they need not have been given, and if they are constant they need not have been constant. Nothing but routine and biological inertia makes us sure that the future can never belie the past.

Addition to Comparisons in Substance

GEORGE SANTAYANA

So much for those views of substance which, while containing some element of insight, confused physical with moral terms and are metaphysical. It remains to say a word about the theories of

George Santayana, "Addition to Comparisons in Substance," *Columbia Manuscript Collection*, IX:14:II. © 1967 by Daniel Cory.

matter which scientific philosophers have entertained. The clearest is that of atoms: and, in a methodological sense, it is safe to
say that it is the correct theory: because a flux, such as substance
certainly is in, cannot be studied or sensed (even if it can exist)
otherwise than as a redistribution of relatively constant elements
—and the atomic theory, with its prodigious recent developments
proves how accurately this hypothesis may be applied at deeper
levels. When it comes, however, to the conception of an ultimate
unit, we are afloat again: for any chosen or discovered unit may
have parts and be itself a system of elements in motion. As we
start from the outside in this investigation, we are soon confronted
with an object in which the sensible units have disappeared, and
only a certain numerical and dynamic construction remains, relative to the gross observable phenomena. Hence some thinkers, taking their science as a game of expression dealing with appearances
rather than a serious anticipation of the form of discoverable
things, and in views of substance from which substance has disappeared: and this methodological jest sometimes passes for a
proof of idealism. If the parts of houses and trees did not exist,
the houses and trees certainly would not: but if the vulgar objects
are real, anything which is truly a part of them is real in the same
sense, and matter is just as real as wood or bricks. But speculation,
for fear of the vulgar, is sometimes coy, just as to please the vulgar, it is often meretricious. Galileo and Descartes, for reasons of
prudence, proposed these principal discoveries as *jeux d'esprit;*
and so they were, in their transcendental status, as all thought
must be; but if Columbus had regarded the new world as a construction, to which a method of fictitious explanation of the geog-
raphy of Europe had led his fancy, but prophetic of nothing
substantial and on the same plane of natural reality as the coasts
and stars he had already sailed among, he would never have set
forth on his voyage of discovery, and would have missed his vocation. So those views of matter which protest that they regard it
as a methodological fiction have a certain mock modesty and visionary cowardice about them. They say: We are mere fancies
suggested by what everybody sees: and yet, in their honest intent
and often in their destiny they are prophecies of new things that
everybody might or shall see—with a microscope, or a telescope, or

with a mind made plastic by study of the known parts of nature, so as truly to imagine some of the parts unknown.

The little cubes, spheres, pyramids, and prisms of the Pythagoreans and of Democritus even when provided with hooks, were certainly very crude images of atoms: but it may be observed that these little crystals never really helped out any calculation, they were fictitious not because calculation required them, but because, when calculation did not require them, a hasty fancy supplied them, as it had supplied the gods. It is for more studious mathematicians and physicists to tell us what kind of atoms it is reasonable to believe in, or what substitute for atoms.

As matter is the substance—ex hypothesi—of what we perceive daily about us, the formidable reality that confronts us inside and around houses and trees, we know by common experience what it most concerns the philosopher to know about it—that it circulates through space, is permanent in quantity, methodical in movement, docile to well-adapted labour, and full of potentialities of life and mind. The rest will be curious and wonderful but in this short life not indispensable to the moralist.

Note on Οὐσία

GEORGE SANTAYANA

Οὐσία is traditionally rendered by "substance"—but it is rather the subject of discourse, Socrates, the horse; a logical entity with physical functions, i.e., something metaphysical. What corresponds to what I call substance is not Οὐσία, but ὑποκειμενον or ὕλη. Οὐσία is not "essence," except in the preferential and metaphysical sense which I have rejected. If spirit, or rather each individual soul, is a "substance" in Aristotle, or in the Scholastics,

George Santayana, "Note on Οὐσία," Columbia Manuscript Collection, IX:14:II. © 1967 by Daniel Cory.

it is only because, instead of fluid matter, they took a lot of ideal and merely morphological units to be the groundwork of existence.

The Order of Genesis and the Order of Discovery

GEORGE SANTAYANA

The order of discovery is normally the reverse of the order of genesis. Discovery becomes possible only when something to be discovered already exists: otherwise it would be invention. It also presupposes a creature capable of curiosity and memory, by whom the discovery may be made. This new contact can then come to enlarge the experience of that creature, and to enlighten it concerning the conditions of its existence and fortunes. Discovery renews the spirit, turning it upon facts that were previously unknown; were there no consciousness of fresh knowledge, there might be a new adjustment, but no discovery. Spirit must be engaged: and spirit is last in the order of genesis, being a spark kindled by a thousand biological tensions, the voice of a formed animal will, an act of prospect, retrospect, or self-knowledge.

First in the order of genesis comes essence since it spreads out the field of forms through which existence may travel and may pick up one form after another along its special path. Matter in this order is second and truth third; for truth is the ideally complete description of the existing world, as it is, has been, and is to be. Finally spirit with all its discoveries comes last, because the psyche—without which spirit could not arise or live—is a trope established in matter; that is to say, a truth concerning the order

George Santayana, "The Order of Genesis and the Order of Discovery," *Columbia Manuscript Collection*, XIV:2. © 1967 by Daniel Cory.

and cohesion of certain events in the flux of nature. The tropes proper to spirit—the passions expressed in morals and in literary psychology—are truths about spirit which of course presuppose its existence: but the discovery of these tropes is itself subsequent to them; so that even here, when spirit considers its own career, the relevant spiritual act, the moral sentiment or psychological insight, chronicles a prior truth, and brings into the light of consciousness an order in events which, though the events were spiritual, had hitherto uncoiled itself unnoticed in the natural world.

On the other hand, in the order of discovery what comes first is matter. Undoubtedly a pure and free spirit, could such a spirit exist, would distinguish essence at the first dawn of consciousness, and would never distinguish anything else; since any datum of intuition, overt and actually possessed, is *ipso facto* a pure essence; and the very nature and function of spirit is to distil pure essence, simple or complex, from the flux of existence. Yet in an animal life intuition is hatched in a nest of pressing occasions; intent precedes intuition; the actual sensible data, in their internal quality and intensity, are traversed by attention without being arrested or distinguished; the not-given, the eventual, absorbs the mind; all definite intuition is submerged in a fluid uneasiness or alarm about the outer world, where the instinctive action of the body, by which consciousness is governed, finds its stimulus and opportunity. Thus matter, before its aspects are clearly discerned, is vehemently posited in the beginning by every passion of the soul; and a quick and sure response to its operations dominates the spirit with a sense of urgency, of distress, or of triumph, long before it comes to any clear intuition of what all this trouble is about, or what may be the fruits of this labour. Ultimately, however, in the very act of adjusting some response more accurately to its occasion, animal attention may come to rest for a moment on the pure forms of things and on their essential relations. Then, in distinguishing what the object of intent exactly is, where it lies, how it moves, in the place of what different thing it has arisen, in what direction it has vanished, or into what different thing it has turned, truth begins to assert itself above existence, and to be as it were the sediment, or surviving reality, which existence leaves

in the mind: and perhaps at the same time the mind itself begins
to be discovered and to become self-conscious.

Naturalism and Agnosticism in Santayana

STERLING P. LAMPRECHT

Repeated readings of Santayana produce in me the mood of
exasperated delight. Perhaps this is as he would intend. Surely he
could not write with the charm of a style that almost distracts
attention from content unless he meant to delight; surely also he
can not be averse if others find in his writings some of that delight
which he obviously finds himself in his own philosophic pursuits.
Yet he is no sentimentalist and would not have any reader soothed
by his books. Has he not himself said that it is not the aim of
philosophy to feed us on sweets and lull us in errors?

The delight I feel is due chiefly to two factors. One of these is
the happy precision of phrase in which some important insight is
summed up with trenchant force. This precision is more than the
charm of style of which I just spoke: it is primarily a matter of
such complete intellectual grasp of a topic that the entire essence
of the topic, separated from accidents and irrelevancies, can be
succinctly stated. Indeed I find it hard to avoid some of Santayana's phrases in dealing, even in my own thinking, with subjects
on which his epigrammatic utterances have captured my imagination. I shall never be able to think of fanaticism except as the
blunder of a man who redoubles his efforts when he has forgotten
his aim, nor of art except as those perfected human operations in
which the purpose is conscious and the method is teachable. I find

Sterling P. Lamprecht, "Naturalism and Agnosticism in Santayana," *The
Journal of Philosophy*, 30 (1933), pp. 561-574. Reprinted by permission.

new significance for education and politics as well as morals generally through conceiving piety as the serious attachment to the sources of one's being and the steadying of life by that attachment. I do not know how much my opinions of current events may be colored by the wicked jibe that in a democracy every one does as he wishes and no one gets what he wants. In these and a host of similar felicitous phrases Santayana opens up for me lines of profitable inquiry. His sentences, more than those of any other contemporary philosophic writer, have the finished form of great art.

Then again he delights me by the richness with which he has illustrated the truth that "in the Life of Reason, if it were brought to perfection, intelligence would be at once the universal method of practice and its continual reward."[1] His writings are far more than a series of pregnant utterances on detached points of interest. He has pursued a great theme, perhaps the greatest theme of "the philosopher," through many important fields of human interest,— domestic and economic and political institutions, industrial and fine arts, religion, science, and the growth of rationality itself; he has heightened the significance of Greek philosophy by restating the life of reason in connection with various modern concerns and problems. The persistence with which he has followed his controlling theme through all these vital phases of our common human experience makes, as it seems to me, his *Life of Reason* one of the masterpieces of modern philosophy.

Yet I have ventured to say that repeated readings of Santayana produce in me the mood of *exasperated* delight. And my present purpose is not to praise Santayana, but to air the grounds of my exasperation. The more I reread the books that Santayana has written, the more perplexed I am concerning his attitude on certain fundamental issues of metaphysics. Of course he would protest that he has never been guilty of writing metaphysics at all. For he chooses to use the term "metaphysics" to mean unverified speculations about the nature of existence. I hasten to agree that in that meaning of the term, metaphysics is a spurious science and an illicit and vain performance. And I recognize further that much "metaphysics" in recent times is just such an illicit perform-

[1] *Reason in Common Sense*, p. 5.

ance and warrants that peculiar (though, I believe, unfortunate usage) of the term. But I am using the term in a different sense. I am using it in the sense in which I think it was originally used when it meant the kind of reflection which is to be found in the unnamed work of Aristotle to which the term happened to be applied. In that sense metaphysics is a body of "first principles" about existence which we find to be warranted by observation and experiment. Or, in other words, metaphysics is a systematic statement of the fundamental assumptions that lie at the base of any and all sciences about existence, provided that we have made those assumptions explicit and have tested them out by all the tests by which any principles can be tested. And when I say that I am perplexed by Santayana's attitude on certain fundamental issues of metaphysics, I mean that I am left, after repeated and careful (and I believe sympathetic) reading of his books, in a state of uncertainty as to what he really means to say. I think that on some of those issues I know the truth; I think, moreover, that the brilliant insights of Santayana are not simply consistent with, but actually depend upon, what I regard as true solutions of these metaphysical issues. In fairness I must hasten to say that at times I find in Santayana's writings a recognition, often implicit and occasionally explicit, of these very principles. But I also seem to find—and this is the cause of my exasperation—a virtual denial of these principles and a formulation of alternative principles that are incompatible with the former principles and are really false. These latter principles would often weaken or annul the force of Santayana's distinctive treatment of the life of reason and the enterprise of intelligence. Perhaps I am at fault in taking figurative language too literally or in missing some of the elusive irony of Santayana's words. But in the later writings I find a growing emphasis on what seem to me the unsound and unfortunate metaphysical assumptions; and therefore I am regretfully led to believe that the seeming equivocations of the earlier volumes are really what the language makes them seem to be. So I conclude that Santayana is not clear in his attitude to what I call metaphysics and must meet certain metaphysical issues before his philosophy is at all consistent or satisfactory in its implications. The sound metaphysical principles which he at times expresses I would call his naturalism (in the sense in which Aristotle is the great naturalist); the unsound metaphysical assumptions that creep in and grow increasingly obvious in successive books are a kind of agnosticism which, absent from Plato and Aristotle, arose in modern philosophy under Descartes' influence, controls the *Essay* of Locke, and reaches a kind of culmination in Spencer. At least I shall develop the contrast between two attitudes that Santayana seems to me at different times to assume, even though I run the risk of merely showing my own inadequate reading of his books. The question is important, whether or not I raise it in correct fashion.

In the first volume of *The Life of Reason* we find a brilliant introductory statement of what has always been the leading theme of Santayana's thought. He there gives us a discussion of what has been happily called "crises in the life of reason." Our human experience begins with a chaos of strange qualities and inexplicable sequences, and is almost overwhelmed by "the crushing irrationality of existence." Impulse and ideation are so lacking in correlation that the first is disastrously vain and the second is pathetically visionary. Then training begins under the pressure of the need of adjustment to the menacing threats that crowd upon the human animal from what lies about him; and eventually, through a discipline that is never wholly complete, there comes to be discerned an intelligible order. The pains and pleasures that follow upon thwarted and satisfied impulse compel attention to certain items of the "loose elements" of experience and transform them into "things" or "conceived realities" of relatively permanent status in the environing world. Exigencies of practice lead men to neglect "the irrelevant infinity of ideas" and hence to distinguish between the realm of nature and the sphere of the imagination. The dramatic values things have for human life require men to seek for control and thus teach them to discern causes and to discover the principles that tie together various things in an integrated nexus or cosmos. Thus the passing sensation becomes but an appearance of a reality that, as a term of discourse, is "a psychic complex of memories, associations, and expectation."[2] And the increasing integration of human life, es-

2 *Reason in Common Sense*, p. 82.

pecially as political organization gives rise to concerted and comprehensive planning, produces the idea of a unified nature, from which are banished all those "parings of experience" that do not fit into its systematic totality.

The wealth of detail with which Santayana develops this growth of reason in man's attitude towards existence need not be reviewed here. But we must take note of the metaphysical principles with which his theme is constantly accompanied. He never lapses into any of "the noble ambiguities of idealism." He never breaks with the naturalistic position according to which substance is prior to life, consciousness, and reflection. He insists that common sense is right against all subjectivism in "regarding nature as the condition of mind and not mind as the condition of nature."[3] He does not conceive substance as artificially constructed out of experience, but holds an antecedently existing substance to be the source of all the rich complexities (including the moral and spiritual facts and processes of the human world) that come to pass in the course of history. Hence something we may call "nature" is the matrix of whatever time and change bring about in the way of composite bodies and their consequent functions. Nature is "a set of conditions" for the appearance of all sorts of happening, physical, mental, good and bad. He does not first denaturize nature and then (and as a consequence) mythologize mind. He so regards nature that all distinctions pertinent to existence fall within it; and he thus avoids the two false extremes of annulling actual differences by formulating some vapid monism and hypostatizing some selected difference into a hard and fast dualism. He cuts with true wisdom under the superficialities of much current popular philosophy.

And yet I am far from satisfied with certain ways in which Santayana amplifies his conception of nature. At times he is thoroughly Aristotelian and sound. He says explicitly that "nature is the sum total of things potentially observable, some observed actually, others interpolated hypothetically."[4] He takes the development of reason to involve the progressive discovery of reality as one element in the progressive discipline of the mind. To pass

3 *Ibid.*, p. 104.
4 *Ibid.*, p. 104.

from the fleeting enjoyment of a "sensation" to the perception of a relatively permanent "thing" is to move out of subjectivity towards objectivity. Reason infers an order of nature vaster and more regular than the items of immediate experience; but it does so by taking those items as a part of the natural order to be known. But this Aristotelianism of Santayana is curiously mixed up with foreign conceptions borrowed from Cartesian traditions of modern philosophy. According to these traditions the data of experience are not aspects or phases of things in the cosmic order, but items from another order altogether. In the earlier of Santayana's writings this other order is usually conceived as a series of psychic states and in the later writings it is conceived to be the timeless realm of essence. But in both cases the immediate content of experience falls outside of the cosmic order. Thus there is "an *external* material world"[5] that is hidden from direct observation. Santayana never becomes so romantic as to suppose that mind builds the cosmos out of psychic states or essences; but he treats knowledge sometimes as a transitive process from part to part of the cosmos and sometimes as a transitive leap from realm to realm. He acknowledges the paradoxical character of the latter position when he ejaculates "Strange that the only possible object or theme of our knowledge should be something we can not know."[6]

In the former or Aristotelian position nature is the larger whole of which experience is a fragmentary and disordered part. In the latter position nature is an equivocal affair. It is not immediate experience; for that is lacking in stability, coherence, unity, and integrity. It is not the "external material world" which supports experience; for that is something we can not know. It is a "Platonic system." When we build up "such atomic and astronomical theories as science is now familiar with," we are dealing with "an abstraction."[7] Take as a sample of this equivocal position the following passage. "When you distinguish your sensations from their cause and laugh at the idealist (as this kind of sceptic is called) who says that chairs and tables exist only in your mind, you are

5 *Ibid.*, p. 87. Italics mine.
6 *Ibid.*, p. 76.
7 *Ibid.*, p. 122.

treating a figment of reason as a deeper and truer thing than the moments of life whose blind experience that reason has come to illumine."[8] Nature (for nature is the whole congeries of objects of which chairs and tables are homely instances) is here spoken of as a "figment of reason"!! And science is then an arbitrary enterprise of fabricating symbols that have pragmatic value but no ontological status. Without the dogmatic insistence upon the reality of independent substances, this second position would easily lead into such romanticisms as Santayana often deprecates in French and German thought. Even with that dogmatic insistence the position makes nature into a conventional fancy that reason accepts only because real knowledge of "external" reality is impossible.

What indeed does it mean to say that "the real sun is so far from being an original datum from which roundness is abstracted, that it is an ulterior and quite ideal construction"?[9] Does it merely mean (what is quite true) that the real sun could not be known unless intelligence worked with the fragmentary data of sense? Or does it mean (what seems also to be said) that "real" objects are built up out of those data? Is Santayana in this passage talking psychology and giving us the natural history of intelligence? or is he talking metaphysics and distinguishing the "nature" we come to know from the external realities we at the same time fail to know? The latter would appear to be his momentary intent; for in the same chapter he writes that "to discover a physical object is to pack in the same part of space, and fuse in one complex body, primary data like coloured form and tangible surface."[10] He speaks of an object's qualities as "its original and component elements": indeed he speaks of the qualities discerned in sense as "themselves the true particulars." Hence he is led to contradict his ordinary position and to speak of "the immediate flux" as the "substance" out of which we manufacture both mind and nature.[11] Even in this agnosticism about external reality Santayana remains a kind of naturalist; for he never forgets that some

8 *Ibid.,* p. 80.
9 *Ibid.,* p. 168.
10 *Ibid.,* p. 162.
11 *Ibid.,* p. 126.

"external" substance is always generating this experience of ours and giving us "raw experience" as a material from which to construct what we will. But he is not in these passages an Aristotelian naturalist; for he treats the nature we know as a human fabrication that is distinct from the nature that produces us and our deceptive fabrications.

The equivocation with which Santayana shifts from one to another of these two metaphysical points of view is not absent from any chapter of the first volume of *The Life of Reason*. Perhaps this is simply because he is here so preoccupied with the moral aspects of knowledge that he never meets squarely the question of the ontological validity of knowledge. At times he compares religious interpretations of the world (such as the Christian Epic) with scientific interpretations in one way and at other times in another. Religious interpretations he always asserts to be symbolic of the moral and esthetic rôles that things play in human life. Scientific interpretations he sometimes treats as the efforts to reach the literal truth about things, which (even where they fail of reaching that truth in any final and authoritative fashion) are yet headed in the right direction and yield a degree of assured and genuine knowledge of the cosmos. And then again he treats them as utilitarian devises of no more ontological value than the moral and esthetic pictures of religious faiths. It would be plausible to say that Santayana was caught in the meshes of his own brilliant analysis of the growth of human rationality. For in making that analysis he naturally speaks in psychological language: he talks of objects as "the cohesion in space and the recurrence in time of recognizable groups of sensations."[12] But one can not properly transfer to ontology the enlightening metaphors of psychology. One can not legitimately treat nature as constructed in the fashion by which we reach our concepts of it. But unless the nature we come with the growth of reason to understand and to know is identical with the reality that supports experience, it is only a fabrication of our own minds. And in that case reason would be no more than conventional fancy.

As we pass from *The Life of Reason* to the more recent series on *Realms of Being* the equivocations are no less frequent, but

12 *Ibid.*, pp. 82-83.

the emphasis is considerably changed. Whereas in *The Life of Reason* Aristotelian naturalism is the dominant attitude and agnosticism intrudes largely in metaphors and illustrative material, in *Realms of Being* agnosticism is boldly and explicitly proclaimed and Aristotelian naturalism appears only occasionally in what seem like lapses where Santayana has not taken pains to maintain his agnostic position. Indeed the agnosticism is set forth almost as a pose which can not be dialectically circumvented (as indeed no philosophical standpoint can be overthrown when its defenders hold consistently to the implications of their first principles). Thus the new series is more enlightening as a revelation of the implications of Santayana's own intellectual development than as a resolution of the metaphysical difficulties of the earlier work. Santayana has turned from preoccupation with moral problems to a direct interest in epistemological theory; and in so doing the non-Aristotelian elements in his thinking become more prominent. Yet even here equivocations keep emerging in the exposition of various points.

One recurrent theme of *Realms of Being* is that "nothing given exists." In other words the immediate data of experience are timeless essences rather than aspects of the enduring substances of the "external world." Yet Santayana betrays in frequent phrases that he is far from accepting the implications of this major theme. Even in assuring us that the child's sensuous experience is not the moon for which he cries, he offers as proof of his contention the child's "fixed gaze and outstretched arm" which any one of us is evidently supposed to be able to see.[13] The argument is not that a child can not directly see objects that are visible to mature eyes. For the child's "bodily attitude" not only *"identifies the object in the discourse of an observer,"* but also *"identifies the object for him, in his own subsequent discourse."*[14] The argument is that substances are not directly perceived; but the argument proceeds to appeal to substances that are directly perceived. Surely there is equivocation here. Similarly when Santayana assures us that "the only facts observable by the psychologist are physical facts,"[15] or

---

[13] *Scepticism and Animal Faith*, p. 172.
[14] *Ibid.*, pp. 173, 174. Italics in the text.
[15] *Ibid.*, p. 257.

when he finds it significant to remark that "what I tuck under my pillow at night, I find there in the morning,"[16] he is giving himself away. Such assertions are hardly compatible with the agnostic contention that "nothing given exists" and that belief in substances is due wholly to "shocks" that interrupt our intuition of timeless essences.

The fact of the matter, at least as repeated readings of Santayana's books make it appear to me, is that in turning to theories of knowledge and ontology Santayana remains essentially a moralist. He would reconcile us to accepting the universe with humility and patience and would encourage us to live bravely and spiritually. He says of himself: "I myself have no passionate attachment to existence, and value this world for the intuitions it can suggest, rather than for the wilderness of facts that compose it."[17] And as for himself, so (in spite of his geniune tolerance and appreciation of alternative ways of life) he would have it for others. It is difficult not to guess that the strange dictum that "nothing given exists" is an epistemological *tour de force* to turn our thoughts from substances that change to meanings that are eternal.

But whether such reflections are just or not, the equivocations remain. And another instance of them is to be found in his treatment of the principle that "existence is irrational." He uses this dictum at times, with entire wisdom, to warn us that existence is not usually moulded according to the heart's desire or the idealist's dream. "Existence," he says, "is accordingly not only doubtful to the sceptic, but odious to the logician."[18] We not only may, but must, doubt with empirical modesty concerning existences that lie beyond experience. And when we come through experience to know some few existences, we should not try to account for them as if there were a reason for their being at all or being in particular what they actually are. We must accept them; and only after accepting them may we make them the basis of our inferences and the test of our beliefs. Hence it is correct to say that "if there is any existence at all, presence to consciousness is

16 *Ibid.*, p. 236.
17 *Ibid.*, p. 171.
18 *Ibid.*, p. 48.

neither necessary nor sufficient to render it an existence."[19] But it does not follow that existence in some of its phases may not be directly presented at times and under certain conditions to a consciousness that may observe it. Perhaps we come here to an ultimate matter of fact that can not be argued but can only be asserted in accord with what we find experience to be. Only I find that much that is given does exist and must reject Santayana's dictum that "nothing given exists." And I make the charge that Santayana is guilty of equivocation because I detect him taking for granted at times the same Aristotelian naturalism I profess and he at other times explicitly denies. I would agree with him that "the only critical function of transcendentalism is to drive empiricism home."[20] But transcendentalism performs this function, it seems to me, by forcing us to note carefully what existences are given and what are not, rather than by enabling us to assert that nothing given exists. Indeed unless some existences were given, transcendentalism would be legitimate and inevitable; and in at least a large part of his writings, earlier and later, Santayana himself is unwilling to grant any such thing. One may well enjoy the playful mood in which in the first few chapters of *Scepticism and Animal Faith* Santayana shows how impossible it would be to refute the consistent advocate of "solipsism of the present moment";[21] but unless Santayana broke with his own agnosticism at times, he would himself be unable to know so clearly that existence is foreign to many human hopes and dreams and relentless in its inevitable course.

In some of his detached essays Santayana reveals significantly his intellectual kinship with certain historic figures. For example in his Herbert Spencer Lecture on *The Unknowable* Santayana pays generous tribute to Spencer for insisting on the reality of an external substance that is the source of life and mind. He doubts a bit whether the term "Unknowable" is a suitable word by which to designate this substance. For we know *that* it exists: we know it operates in infinite modes and produces in us the phenomena we call "appearances." Yet Spencer was, he tells us, on the right

[19] *Ibid.*, p. 45.
[20] *Ibid.*, p. 4.
[21] *Ibid.*, p. 17.

track. For he recognized that appearances are only "secondary facts and not, as is often alleged, the fundamental or only realities."[22] Appearances are, no more than the names we apply to objects, any real part of them. Substance works by "secret operation" and never reveals its inner nature. If our ideas are more than symbolical of the effects things produce in us and the expectations we may rightly entertain of their future actions on or in us, that is merely a happy chance and can hardly be distinguished as such when it may occur. Experience may explore the world adventurously and science may describe it with precision; but "after you have wandered up and down it for years, and have gathered all you could of its ways by report, this same world, because it exists substantially and is not invented, remains a foreign thing and a marvel to the spirit."[23]

Santayana ought indeed to be more generous to the memory of Herbert Spencer than most of Spencer's critics have been. For he shares with Spencer the fault that those critics have pointed out with wearisome repetition. As in Spencer, so in Santayana, the "nature" that the physical or existential sciences claim to know is not the underlying substantial world that brings all things to pass in its countless changes, nor is it the confused mass of isolated sense-data that are said to be the "raw material" for knowledge. It is neither flesh, fish, nor fowl, nor good red herring. The sciences thus are "about" nothing that is real at all except in so far as we pretend to forget that we are feigning. When we do so forget, we identify nature with the ultimate substance of the world outside experience, and our grandiloquent generalizations then gain dignity and power. Spencer chose to forget most of the time; and so his generalizations are uttered with pompous eloquence. Santayana forgets but seldom; and so his generalizations are tentative and his conclusions ironic.

The more obvious kinship of Santayana, however, is not with Spencer, but with Locke. The kinship is not a moral one. For when Locke came to realize that his theory of ideas was making it logically impossible for him to know real substances (other than the self by intuition and God by demonstration), he exhibited a genuine ontological distress; and when Santayana displays the

22 *The Unknowable,* p. 6.
23 *Ibid.,* p. 29.

agnostic implications of his theory, he indulges in a whimsical esthetic playfulness. But a kinship of metaphysical standpoints is clearly discernible. In the Herbert Spencer Lecture, Santayana is almost quoting Locke when he writes that the "intrinsic character of things," though undiscovered or inexpressible by us, would yet be disclosed at any moment "if a new observer turned up with the requisite organs, and a more sympathetic imagination."[24] Neither Locke nor Santayana pauses to explain why other sorts of organs would be more ontologically satisfactory than the ones we happen to possess. Both seem to be trying to defend the empirical appeal to sense as a corrective of the vagaries of fancy at the same time that they disparage the findings of sense for metaphysics. In any case they are akin in that they both hold to empiricism while they mutilate the sound grounds on which empiricism must rest.

Santayana's kinship with Locke has just been corroborated in his delightful tercentenary lecture on Locke and other essays that have appeared in his little book on *Some Turns of Thought in Modern Philosophy*. No animal, writes Santayana, can be "aware of what goes on beyond him, except as it affects his own life."[25] As in Locke experience was both a basis for all knowledge and a screen which cuts us off from the real world, so is it with Santayana. "Science," Santayana acknowledges, "when it is more than the gossip of adventure or of experiment, yields practical assurances couched in symbolic terms, but no ultimate insight."[26] We may even have alternative sciences of existence as of geometry; and we may choose between these alternative systems on grounds of convenience or convention. Science is "a human language" of symbolic character; and if we would deal with existence itself, we must resort to faith. Of course, Santayana continues, "the appearance of things is always, in some measure, a true index to their reality"; for it is possible for us "to discount appearance and to correct illusions," so that external fact may indeed "come within the range of consciousness, not indeed by being contained there, but by being aimed at."[27] That is, we can not know all things, but only those that concern our station; and though we

24 *Ibid.*, p. 16.
25 *Some Turns of Thought in Modern Philosophy*, p. 9.
26 *Ibid.*, p. 79.
27 *Ibid.*, p. 37.

can not plumb the depths of existence, we may know enough to live well and to save our souls. (Of course the kinship evaporates and gives place to sharp antagonism as soon as we ask Locke and Santayana what our souls are and in what our salvation consists!)

The difficulties that exasperate me appear once more in Santayana's fascinating book, *Dialogues in Limbo,* though they here have a new context and perhaps a slightly new form. Santayana proclaims himself a follower of Democritus "in respect to the substance and origin of things."[28] He had already said that "in natural philosophy I am a decided materialist—apparently the only one living";[29] and he here reveals the basis of his materialism in the atomism of Democritus. In the very spirit that gave birth to the Epicurean philosophy Santayana deals with human life as a form of madness. For life tends to be too much in a hurry with its passionate cravings to note "the distinction between things as they exist in nature, and things as they appear to opinion."[30] The being of things "is indomitable substance and motion and action, and to add thought, impalpable and ghostly, is to add madness."[31] The illusion to which life leads is not inevitably an evil: indeed it may be a great and glorious good, since it makes possible love and beauty and religion. It only becomes an evil when we take our religion for science, our art for nature, and our love as the sure and certain goal of the cosmos. Victory over the cosmos is possible even to men in their madness, provided that they know how to be mad with discipline and to laugh at their own limitations. At least this seems to me to be the central teaching of this wise and penetrating series of dialogues.

But the exasperating difficulties come to the fore as soon as I begin to analyze the notion of madness. What, I am prompted to inquire, is the antithesis to madness? Good and bad, right and wrong, beautiful and ugly, long and short,—these are obvious antitheses. The antithesis to madness is not easy to specify. Indeed I suspect that Santayana was again too preoccupied with moral problems to pose this question to himself. And as I have read the

[28] *Dialogues in Limbo,* p. 29.
[29] *Scepticism and Animal Faith,* p. vii.
[30] *Dialogues in Limbo,* p. 37.
[31] *Ibid.,* p. 41.

dialogues in repeated efforts to settle this question (which may of course only prove my own madness), I find an alternation between two incompatible answers. Sometimes the antithesis to madness is reason; sometimes it is death.

Madness gives place to reason, the dialogues seem to say, when with Democritus we learn to enjoy legitimate illusions without attributing them to the nature of things. Dionysius was really mad; for when he listened to Democritus invent a liturgy for a newly invented religion, he would at once "account it veritably an ancient mystery."[32] But Alcibiades was a convert to reason when he exclaimed: "I like a youngster who falls in love or makes verses because he can't help it"![33] To recognize the inevitable madness of living is to rise in reason above the deception, and hence to grow in character above the degradation, that make madness a tragedy. If it is natural for animals to be mad, it is the moral privilege of men to be reasonable. Reason recognizes all substance to be ultimately material and finds this substance the source of life and madness; and in the training that this rational insight produces, philosophy may escape from superstition and men may become sane.

But again, as soon as Santayana goes beyond morals to theory of knowledge and ontology, equivocation appears. It would seem that there is no cure for madness except death. "Life is at once the quintessence and the sum of madness."[34] "Images in sense," just as much as "love in youth, and religion among nations," are a form of madness;[35] and "to add thought" to the other motions of substance "is to add madness."[36] There is here no choice open to men except to indulge in some fantastic and eccentric madness and to discipline themselves in accord with "normal madness." Sense and thinking are surely the only tools whereby men can hope to surmount the conditions that make for madness; and with the condemnation of these tools, men are doomed to madness as long as they continue to live. To outgrow the petulant folly of rebellion against the inevitable limitation of human nature, to

32 *Ibid.*, p. 65.
33 *Ibid.*, p. 82.
34 *Ibid.*, p. 37.
35 *Ibid.*, p. 46.
36 *Ibid.*, p. 41.

conform with moderation to the institutions of the society to which one belongs, to take all one's opinions as subjective preferences,—to do all this may be wisdom, and to sulk irresponsibly may be folly. But it is not to escape from subjectivity to objectivity: it is not to rise above madness altogether.

Santayana seems to me to be undecided as to which of these theories of madness he would espouse as his own. He wishes to maintain his materialistic faith; he also adopts an epistemological point of view which condemns his materialistic opinions as mad along with all other and alternative opinions. Sometimes he treats illusions of sense as subject to correction by more and different sense-experiences. For example: "To the innocent eye the six stout spokes of a chariot-wheel revolving rapidly are merged and blurred in one whirling disc; but the philosopher, though no less subject than other men to this illusion, on seeing the disc will remember the spokes, and in all his fevers and griefs will be mindful of the atoms; his forced illusions will not deceive him altogether, since he knows their cause."[37] But again he generalizes more sweepingly and concludes that all our sense-experiences are as illusive as the vision of the blurred spokes; he denies the possibility of getting from the madness of sense to any foothold in existence that does not involve an inevitable subjectivity of all life. And thereby he undermines the intellectual basis of his own confidence in the being of material substance and reduces his own materialism to the same unjustifiable dogmatism as the assertions of the idealists and transcendentalists he denounces and dislikes.

In commenting some years ago on Royce, Santayana wrote (and with perfect justice): "He has not seen his way to any one of the various possibilities about the nature of things, but has remained entangled, sincerely, nobly, and pathetically, in contrary traditions stronger than himself." Something of the same criticism might well be passed on Santayana himself. He is naturalistic in his major persuasions and agnostic in his exclusion of the data of experience from a status in the real or "external" world. These two traditions he does not bring into peace with each other. Hence the constant equivocations that I have seemed to find in the pages of his books. He enjoins on us the life of reason; but he

[37] *Ibid.*, p. 46.

makes reason unable to ascertain the nature of the world in which that life must inevitably occur. He insists that matter is the matrix of life and mind; but he allows life no direct contact with matter except in the reception of various "shocks" and denies to mind the data by which to know that these "shocks" come from matter. He proclaims with firmness that mind arises within nature; but he treats mind as an ontological orphan doomed merely to intuit essences and to guess, without evidence, of existence. Of course he does not do all this constantly; for he is so realistic as often to forget his own sophisticated agnosticism and then to deal empirically with the substances that are the environment of life and the normal subject-matter of much of our human thinking. His own sanity is proof that madness is not as universal as he feigns to believe. His own philosophy reveals that much existence has come directly within the range of his experience. His proneness to irony makes me wonder how seriously he means to maintain that nothing given exists.

Maxims

GEORGE SANTAYANA

Life falls upon us and awakes us: it is an incident; and the incidents in it are more important and more beautiful than the imaginary goals which it presumably never reaches.

A goal is the terminus of some incidental movement, forming a moral trope, and positing its completion as being a good. If realised, the end becomes actually a relative good: but the desire for such a good remains incidental. If the whole world had a goal, the whole world would be a moral incident. Its morality would not save it from being "un défaut dans la pureté du non-être."

George Santayana, "Maxims," *Columbia Manuscript Collection,* IX:12. © 1967 by Daniel Cory.

The intrinsically possible is more extensive and indestructible than the potential, the potential more lasting and firmly rooted than the actual. Essence is deeper than matter, and matter deeper than the human world.

The present bloom of being is always withering and turning to ashes; but in the ashes are seeds from which being flowers again into some second summer. Yet this whole long heredity is but a wraith in the infinite, like a shooting star in the night.

When all things are possible, what wonder that some things should be actual? (This is my sole deduction of existence from essence.)

The importance and beauty of any incident lie in itself: and morally they transcend its accidental function in time and belong in the realms of truth and of value. These realms, being determinate and excluding many features that figure with equal right in the realm of essence, are contingent and, viewed from outside, unnecessary. Yet their importance and beauty, being intrinsic, are inalienable and forever actual in their own being.

The web of Nature has two strands or strata, as a tiger skin has hide and hair. The lower level is matter, the upper, thought. The hairs are held together only by the hide, yet the fur, to stroke, is smoother than the leather. So the intermittent and loose aspects of things, held together by continuous secret processes in substance, are nevertheless smooth and easy for discourse to glide among; and idealism and rhetoric love to slide over that surface, and stroke it.

There are no substantial qualities, and no adventitious qualities, in essences, because quality is essence itself. The distinction arose, among the Platonists, from the false supposition that some essences were powers. The others would then be accidental to the work or expression of those powers. But when we understand that all essence is indifferent, and the degrees of essence infinite, we see that every combination of qualities is an essence, to which all those qualities present in it are essential, the quality of the combination being the essence itself.

Agnosticism—or the theory that substance is heterogeneous from every essence discernible by the human mind—is partly wise and modest, partly absurd and superstitious. It is wise and modest in so far as it reflects the persuasion that substance has much more in it than we perceive or can imagine: it is absurd and superstitious in so far as it suggests that nothing of substance can be perceived or imagined at all. The perceived qualities of substance are some of its real qualities and every quality of it, to a fitly endowed and sensitive intellect, would be apprehensible. The essentially unpresentable is the essentially null.

The substance of our world may well be called matter because it has not merely the logical function of an unknown substance, but known qualities like distribution in space, persistence, quantity, and specific potentiality: qualities which are designated by the term material. We know, therefore, that the substance of our world is a material substance. But that is not to say that this substance has only specifically material attributes. We know that, sometimes, at least, this substance is conscious; and this not apart from its materiality, but, on the contrary, just when its material elements fall into a certain arrangement which we call a living body. And just as this extant consciousness proper to bodies would remain unknown from without if the observer had no kindred consciousness, or no body, so many other concomitant qualities of matter may remain unknown to us for want of suitable faculties in us to reproduce or to impute them.

No qualities, however, can be unknowable essentially: for every essence is knowable to an intellect properly disposed, intellect being (by definition) no less plastic than form, and as infinite as essence. But to extant *human* intellect much is unknowable, even in the matter of the human body and of the human environment.

It is characteristic of existence that it unites irrelevant essences. The compound, to be sure, has its total essence, which is one; but while the essence of an existence (a nominal essence) has elements merely *conjoined*, the elements of a pure essence or Idea are mutually *implied* (when the whole is given).

From this it follows that irrelevance among the various attributes of existence is normal and not exceptional. To exist is in itself irrelevant to essence: and, in a concretion in existence, every quality is more or less irrelevant to every other. Colour is irrelevant to weight, consciousness to extension, pain to knowledge: yet in existence these things are conjoined.

Consciousness has a describable dimension and an indescribable one: it presents some essence, and it creates some value. By existing consciousness gives psychic presence to essence; by caring, it gives importance to change. Yet the specious existence which essence thus acquires is inconsequential: it has no lien on duration or on further events. These are redetermined, at every step, by material substratum. (The power which consciousness has to lend specious existence to essences by perceiving them, is a borrowed power; what lends this power is the prior embodiment of other essences in the matter of the body.) The material situation also determines the values given.

Secondary qualities are possessed by imputation: that which imputes them, consciousness, is the tertiary quality of some living body: and this tertiary quality is defined by what it perceives. Hence (the quality perceived and those imputed being the same) consciousness and secondary qualities are the same in act; yet the quality imputed by consciousness cannot be predicated of consciousness.

It is proper to matter to be sensible, because it is proper to attention to be perceptive. To any specific organ of perception much in matter may be unknowable; but another organ of perception might know even that feature of matter.

"Sensible phenomena" is a pleonasm used to remind the reader that all phenomena, though perhaps unknowable to man, are knowable essentially and immediately.

Matter is a potentiality which is continuous (in time and space), specific, quantitative and dynamic.
"Dynamic potentiality" is a pleonasm, but the phrase may be useful in emphasizing the distinction between the potential and the intrinsically possible.
Matter is dynamic, since it alone suffices to produce changes in

itself and to produce life; the organ and the object, properly constituted, creating feeling and perception without further conditions [*sic*].

Aristotle's "matter" is not dynamic in this sense, and hardly specific.

Men give cold praise to animal excellences; but to human excellence they give the name of merit, and think it incomparable. It consists in having machinery to coordinate many half-formed and conflicting instincts. This machinery is called "reason" or "freedom"; but in truth it is an endowment like any other, only compound and in unstable equilibrium, so that the issue of it is hard to predict.

(Note on a thesis comparing Plato, Aristotle and Emerson on Friendship):

Does Emerson really seem to you to have written about friendship? I should call what was in his mind *esteem* and trust, not any experience of "living together" or of the joy of it. The Puritan or the Transcendentalist merely notes that there seem to be other godly men in the world, and considers how far their visioned presence can aid him in his self-development. He does not really love them or believe in their existence. He catches nothing from them, yields nothing of himself. He is incapable of conversation. His tenderness is the sentiment he might have towards a flower or a gnarled oak. He has no entrain, no youth, no grace, and no laughter.—As to Plato and Aristotle, the contrast is obvious: yet the agreement is profound. Take the two together and you have all Hellenism. Friendship is the flower of it—the liberated soul wholly at home in what is liberal.

A *Phaenomenon*, properly understood, is the occurrence of an essence, not the appearance of a substance.

Poetry is not to be spread on things like butter, but must shine on them like dew.

God is a name the world gives to the devil when he is victorious.

The religion of the optimists is one long lazy lie.

There are three traps that strangle philosophy: the Church, the marriage-bed, and the professor's chair. I escaped from the first in my youth; the second I never entered, and as soon as possible I got out of the third.

Rationalistic idealism is swagger; empirical idealism is impotence.

Spirit is self-discovered, it is not self-generated.

The transcendental essence of matter is to be the ground of appearance.

Animal life has an aesthetic function. It brings intuition into the world, and the value of intuition is intrinsic.

The energy of intellect is moral not physical, not dynamic but cognitive. It reveals everything and adds nothing except itself.

Language makes fools of those who profess to employ it accurately.

IV

PERCEPTION, KNOWLEDGE, AND ANIMAL FAITH

Three Proofs of Realism

GEORGE SANTAYANA

I. DEFINITION OF REALISM

Realism in regard to knowledge has various degrees. The minimum of realism is the presumption that there is such a thing as knowledge; in other words, that perception and thought refer to some object not the mere experience of perceiving and thinking. The maximum of realism would be the assurance that everything ever perceived or thought of existed apart from apprehension and exactly in the form in which it is believed to exist: in other words, that perception and conception are always direct and literal revelations, and that there is no such thing as error. If this is the range of realism, I think we may say that any reasonable theory of knowledge—any theory that does not abolish its own subject-matter—will occupy some point between these extremes, and will be more or less realistic.

The various degrees of realism, however, cannot be arranged in a single scale, for there are two distinct questions that may be answered more or less realistically: one, what measure of inde-

George Santayana, "Three Proofs of Realism," *Essays in Critical Realism* (London: Macmillan, 1920), pp. 163-184. Reprinted by permission of Macmillan & Co., Ltd.

pendence or separate existence shall be ascribed to the object? and the other, what degree of literalness and adequacy shall be claimed for knowledge? These two applications of realism by no means go hand in hand. The most decided realist in respect to the independence of objects may be a sceptic in respect to the accuracy of his ideas. He may be a believer in the unknowable, like Kant: or he may be a materialist, who thinks that most of the notions entertained by the human mind are either illusions or conventional symbols. On the other hand, the most imperturbed realist in respect to the accuracy of his ideas, who is sure that things are just what they seem, may for that very reason be tempted to drop the other strand of realism and to maintain that his experiences and their objects are identical. Then the only difference between him and an idealist will concern the genesis and duration he attributes to those neutral or epicene "facts of experience" which they both recognize: the naïve realist will deploy these objects naturalistically, in their own medium of space and continuous evolution, whereas the idealist will admit that they exist only intermittently and in single file, as perceptions in some mind.

A critic might perhaps suggest that the two strains in realism are positively contradictory, since the tendency of the one is to oppose appearance to reality and the tendency of the other is to identify them. But this happens in very different senses. In the first place appearance is perfectly real in its own way. We may leave to one side for the moment the physical realities implied in appearance: the animal that must exist for things to appear to, and the things that by their impact appear to him, attract his attention, and are the objects which appearance reports and prompts him to investigate further; for although without the animal body appearance would lose its seat and its focus, and without an external object would lose its significance, yet these physical realities are not contained in appearance taken absolutely, as we may take it when, in its presence, we inhibit as much as possible all reaction and understanding. But even the passive and immediate data of appearance, its bare signals and language when stupidly gaped at, retain their aesthetic and logical character—the primary sort of reality or being. Moreover, the fact that any such data appear or are thought of at all, however ideal and non-existent in themselves, is an historical event, with undeniable existence in the empirical sphere. It seems clear, therefore, that the special and invidious kind of reality opposed to appearance must mean an underlying reality, a *substance:* and it had better be called by that name.

In view of this complexity proper to appearance, of its own special kinds of reality, and of its various internal and external bonds with substance, the alleged contradiction between the two tendencies in realism is easily solved. For these two tendencies appear in the treatment of two different problems. One problem is whether substance and appearance are distinct in their existence and have different conditions; to which the answer of the realist tends to be that their existence is quite distinct and their conditions entirely different. The other problem touches the degree of similarity between the immediate data or symbols of sense or thought and the intrinsic qualities of the substance which is its object: and here the tendency of the realist is to reply that the similarity is great, and may even rise to identity of essence.

Now there is obviously no contradiction in maintaining both that knowledge is something added to its subject-matter, previously unknown, and at the same time that this acquired knowledge describes that subject-matter correctly. Indeed, how could there be any description, correct or incorrect, if it were not in existence something new, and in deliverance and intent something relevant? A portrait, to be a portrait, must be distinct from the sitter, and must at the same time somehow resemble or be referred to him; the question how good a portrait it is, or what are the best methods of portraiture, would not otherwise arise. So knowledge could not be knowledge at all unless it was a fresh fact, not identical in existence with its object; and it could not be true knowledge unless, in its deliverance, it specified some of the qualities or relations which really belong to that object. Even to fall into error and misconceive its object, the cognitive process must first select that object unequivocally, by designating its real locus or some true circumstance that will suffice to identify it.

The two tendencies in realism are therefore perfectly consistent, and truly complementary: the one tends to separate appearance from substance only in existence; the other tends to identify them only in essence. But neither the separation nor the identification can ever be absolute, else the theory of knowledge would prove that knowledge was impossible, and all good sense would go by the board.

If we regard things ideally and ontologically, we may say with Hume that whatever is distinguishable is separable. In this sense the events that common sense regards as inter-dependent are just as separable as those which it regards as disconnected. Every one admits that earlier things are independent of what follows upon them, since evidently annihilation or a different sequel might, for all we know, have intervened at any time without changing anything in what had occurred up to that point. But on the same principle later things are also independent of their antecedents, since they might have arisen from other causes or might have existed from all eternity, or might have been suddenly created *ex nihilo*. Yet all this is true only if we abstract from the world as it happens to be constituted, on the ground that it is contingent and irrationally complex, and might as well not have existed, or might have been wholly different from what it is. The moment we consent to admit the order of nature as actually established, all this independence of thing from thing disappears. Even earlier things cannot then be called independent of their consequences, since they are pregnant with them, and may be inferred and reconstructed by those to whom the consequences are known.

The same ambiguities infect the question of the dependence or independence of knowledge and its object. Regarded abstractly, substance is independent of appearance, since it might have existed unperceived: and appearance is also independent of substance, since it might have arisen without any occasion, as idealists believe is actually the case. But, taking the world as God has made it, neither can exist without the other. Even at the time (if there was a time) when substance moved about alone, like Adam without Eve, it was constituted and predestined for the future partnership; for its structure involved changes of structure which in due season would involve the genesis of appearance; as still happens daily when any one is born or awakes. Dialectically considered, all this involution and evolution is full of redundancy, arrest, and open alternatives; but considered naturally there is nothing paradoxical about it or not shrewdly to be foreseen by one whose acquaintance and sympathy with nature were deep enough: for the standard of naturalness is nature itself. Therefore a realist who is also a naturalist will not hesitate to admit a mutual dependence between substance and appearance, although certainly they are not the same thing nor logically inseparable; but they hang together and reflect one another like a poet and his works. Only if arrested and isolated would the material world and the bodily life of animals seem not to involve sensation and thought and not to be involved in them; but to arrest and isolate these parts of nature would be to denaturalize them.

If the independence of substance and appearance maintained by a realistic philosophy is thus deeply qualified, so is the identity postulated between them. This identity in any case touches essence only, not existence; it is not his knowledge or his mind that the naïve realist identifies with the object, but only the essence immediately intuited by him that he identifies with its *essence*. Even when he is right in this, as he is when knowledge is adequate, the act of attention is not similar to what it attends to. Knowledge has an essence of its own which it is far from reporting when it reports on any chance object. Ideal relevance consists precisely in this power to intuit an essence which we do not embody, but which may be embodied in some other suitable thing, as the essences pea-green, sphere, similarity, and duality may be naturally embodied in two peas. In any case, even when the essence intuited is identical with that embodied in the object, the intuition and the embodiment remain different in existence, origin, date, place, substance, function, and duration. An essence may appear in any number of instances without forfeiting its identity; it may now have the ideal status of an object of intuition, and again the material status of the form of a thing. It is precisely this ideality, this amphibious but incorruptible quality, that distinguishes any essence from any fact, and makes essence (as Socrates discovered) the key to the problem of knowledge.[1]

1 By "essence" I understand a universal, of any degree of complexity and definition, which may be given immediately, whether to sense or to thought. Only universals have logical or aesthetic individuality, or can be given directly, clearly, and all at once. When Aristotle said that the senses gave the particu-

Realism accordingly is the union of two instinctive assumptions, necessary to the validity of knowledge: first, that knowledge is *transitive,* so that self-existing things may become the chosen objects of a mind that identifies and indicates them; second, that knowledge is *relevant,* so that the thing indicated may have at least some of the qualities that the mind attributes to it. These two kinds of realism, though they may rise and fall reciprocally, like the pans of a balance, are like those pans necessary to each other: if either disappeared, the other would collapse. If relevance were wholly denied, it would be in vain hotly to assert the independence of the object; that independence would be undermined. An unknowable substance, even if it existed, could not be the object designated by a conception which, being by hypothesis wholly irrelevant to it, could not specify even its place, date, or relation to anything else. Similarly, if transcendence or transitiveness were wholly denied in its turn, so that the object could neither subsist when not known nor become the object of any other thought than the one which now knows it, relevance too would be eliminated; for the thought and its object would have become identical, and a thing cannot be relevant to itself. Knowledge in this case would perish by compression, by ceasing to aim at anything, as in the other case it would perish by futility, being condemned to aim always at an unattainable target. Some remnant, therefore, of each kind of realism must always persist, if knowledge is to be posited or to be actually valid at all: and the defender of realism, or of the possibility of genuine knowledge, has merely to show to what degree transcendence and relevance are achieved in particular instances. It is quite conceivable that the proportion of these two necessary ingredients should vary, as knowledge is addressed to various kinds of objects. I will attempt

---

lar, he doubtless meant by the senses the complete fighting sensibility of animals, with the reactive instinct and sagacity which posits a material object and places it in its external relations, here, now, and in such a quarter. But the senses as understood by modern idealism suggest rather a passive consciousness of some aesthetic datum, and this (which I call intuition) can never find anything but an ideal individual, which being individuated only by its intrinsic quality, not by any external or dynamic relations (since none are given), is also a universal. This object of pure sense or pure thought, with no belief superadded, an object inwardly complete and individual, but without external relations or physical status, is what I call an essence.

to show how the case stands in respect to three important spheres of knowledge: and the proof that in each our knowledge claims to be, and actually is, in some measure, both transitive and relevant, will be a triple demonstration of the truth of realism; though the exact force and scope of the demonstration will differ in each instance.

II. BIOLOGICAL PROOF

When the proverbial child cries for the moon, is the object of his desire doubtful? He points at it unmistakably; yet the psychologist (not to speak of the child himself) might have some difficulty in fixing exactly the sensations and images, the gathering demands and fumbling efforts, that traverse the child's mind while he points. Fortunately all this fluid sentience, even if it could be described, is irrelevant to the question; for *the child's sensuous experience is not his object.* If it were, he would have attained it. What his object is, his fixed gaze and outstretched arm declare unequivocally. This attitude of his body identifies his object *in itself,* in its physical and historical setting; for it shows what particular thing, in the same natural world as the child's body, was the object of this particular passion. If the object which the body is after is identified, that which the soul is after is identified too: no one, I suppose, would carry dualism so far as to assert that when the mouth waters at the sight of one particular plum, the soul may be yearning for quite another.

The same bodily attitude of the child identifies his object *for us.* In perceiving what his senses are excited by, and which way his endeavour is turned, we can see that the object of his desire is the moon, which we too are looking at. That we are looking at the same moon as he, can be proved by a little triangulation: our glances converge upon it. If the child has reached the inquisitive age and asks, "What is that?" we understand what he means by "that" and are able to reply sapiently, "That is the moon," only because our respective bodies, in one common space, are discoverably directed upon one material object, which is stimulating them simultaneously.

The attitude of the child's body also identifies the object *for him,* in his ensuing approaches or references to it. When in stretching his hand towards it he cannot touch it, he learns that this bright good is not within his grasp, and he makes a beginning in the experience of life. He also makes a beginning in science, since he now adds the absolutely true predicate "out of reach" to the rather questionable predicates "bright" and "good" (and perhaps "edible") with which his first glimpse of that object had supplied him. The active and mysterious thing, co-ordinate with himself, since it lies in the same world with his body and affects it —the thing that attracts his hand, is evidently the same thing that eludes it. His failure would have no meaning and could teach him nothing—i.e. could not correct his instinctive reactions—if the object he saw and the object he failed to reach were not identical; and certainly that object is not brightness nor goodness nor excitements in his brain or psyche, for these are not things he could ever attempt or expect to touch. His instinct to touch the moon is as primitive as his instinct to look at it; and the object of both efforts is the same, because the same external influence arouses them, and with them the very heterogeneous sensations of light and of disappointment. These various terms of sense or of discourse, by which he expresses the present agency, under whose attraction and rebuffs he is living, are merely symbols to him like words. They are miscellaneous in their intrinsic character—sights, sounds, smells, contacts, fears, provocations—and they are alternative or supplementary to one another, like words in different languages. The most diverse senses, such as smell and sight, if summoned to the same point will report upon the same object; and even when one sense bears all the news we have, its reports will change from moment to moment with the distance, variation, or suspension of the connection between the object and our bodies; and this without any necessary change in the object itself. Nay, often the very transformation of the sensation bears witness that the object is unchanged; as music and laughter, overheard as we pass a tavern, are felt and known to continue unabated, and to be no merriment of ours, just because they fade from our ears as we move away.

The object being thus identified by our bodily attitude and by its other physical relations, the aesthetic qualities we attribute to it will depend on the particular sense it happens to affect at the moment, and on the sweep and nature of the reaction which it then calls forth in us. This diversity of experience and of symbols is normal, and when it does not amount to a direct contradiction, it irritates us only if we are unreasonable and egotistical; and even the contradiction which may arise, and which truly demands a solution, resides in the implications of our terms concerning the movement and powers of the object, not in the sensuous or rhetorical texture of these terms themselves. Looking at the moon, one man may call it simply a light in the sky; another, prone to dreaming awake, may call it a virgin goddess; a more observant person, remembering that this luminary is given to waxing and waning, may call it the crescent; and a fourth, a full-fledged astronomer, may say (taking the aesthetic essence before him merely for a sign) that it is an extinct and opaque spheroidal satellite of the earth, reflecting the light of the sun from a part of its surface. But all these descriptions envisage the same object—otherwise no relevance, conflict, or progress could obtain among them. What that object is in its intrinsic and complete constitution will never be known by man: but that this object exists in a known space and time and has traceable physical relations with all other physical objects is given from the beginning: it is given in the fact that we can point to it. If it did not so exist and (as sometimes happens) we were suffering from a hallucination, in thinking we were pointing at it we should be discoverably pointing at vacancy; exploration would satisfy us of that fact, and any bystander would vouch for it. But if in pointing at it we were pointed to it, its identity would be fixed without more ado; disputes and discoveries concerning it would be pertinent and soluble, no matter what diversity there might be in the ideal essences—light, crescent, goddess, or satellite—which we used as rival descriptions of it while we pointed.

Animals, then, in pursuing, touching, or recoiling from surrounding things, evidently know them. This knowledge is transitive, since the things known exist side by side with the animal they stimulate, and prior to the reaction and perception which they occasion. This knowledge is also relevant, no matter what sensible essence may be called up by it before the mind, since such essences are the apparent qualities of the thing perceived. The senses of all animals supply them with such signs and their thoughts can often rehearse and anticipate the movement of things by reckoning it up in symbolic terms such as words. It is evident that all animals have relevant and transitive knowledge of their environment; so that realistic knowledge is but another name for vital sensibility and intelligence.

III. PSYCHOLOGICAL PROOF

Modern philosophy, without being very sceptical in spirit (it has not been disinterested enough for that) has undertaken a psychological criticism of science and common sense, calculated to show that all supposed facts are only ideas constructed by the human mind according to its own principles, and having no further existence. This criticism, since it was psychological, could not consistently go on to deny the existence of the human mind, its successive ideas, and it habits of interpretation. It could not deny, except by committing suicide, that knowledge is transitive within the psychological realm, and truly describes the march and structure of experience; it could reject the claim of knowledge to be transitive only in respect to certain physical, metaphysical, or religious objects, which the modern mind had become suspicious of, and hoped to feel freer without.

Even in regard to these traditional burdens, however, the psychological reform of human faith was somewhat ambiguous and halting. It professed to discredit the operations of the intellect, but not to suspend them. We were not asked to abolish our conception of the natural world or even, in practice, to cease to believe in it: we were to be idealists only north-north-west, or transcendentally; when the wind was southerly, we were to remain realists. The pronouncements of the practical intellect had no doubt been reversed in a higher court, but with this singular proviso, that the police and the executioner, while reverently acknowledging the authority of the higher tribunal, must unflinchingly carry out the original sentence passed by the lower.

When this sort of criticism is applied to the biological facts invoked in our first proof, it evidently will change nothing in the aspect of those facts. In the picture of the world which we shall still continue to frame, we shall see the senses of every creature reporting to him sundry objects and changes in his environment; and the cognisance he takes of these outlying matters will be, in that sphere, obviously transitive and true. Theoretically, however, our proof will be invalidated; because we shall have learned that, at bottom, no animals and no world of the sort necessarily conceived exist at all, and no realistic knowledge. If the idea we have of the world—and must continue to have—were true, then indeed the knowledge possessed by those who would live in that world would be realistic; but as this idea is only an idea, as it is objectless and (since it professes to have an object) is false, only intransitive knowledge, that is, the possession of objectless states of mind, will exist in reality.

But this consequence, accepted by the psychological critic when material objects are concerned, is not accepted by him in principle, or applied consistently. As I have already indicated, he does not regard his own theories also as objectless and false; these he thinks true realistically. There are human minds, apart from his idea of them, and they were endowed, before he or they discovered the fact, with a particular transcendental logic, which they were bound to apply to their progressive experience; there are unknown numbers of centres in which this experience is gathered in various degrees; and there are successive shocks or sensations, inexplicably distributed in a real time, to which those minds may apply their innate categories. And not only does the psychological critic assume that he possesses transitive knowledge of all these historical matters, but his criterion of criticism itself is dogmatic: for instance, he assumes that when he feels two things to be incompatible, nature cannot combine them, and that when he finds it easier, in obedience to his instinct of intellectual parsimony, to get on without some idea, God cannot have been so lavish as to create the corresponding reality. Naturally it is not on such dogmatic assumptions of its own that his criticism of knowledge is directed.

In empirical idealism criticism of knowledge is thus frankly arrested at the threshold of psychology and history; successive sensations, or selves, or phases of experience exist, and are aware of one another's existence in a realistic fashion. Even transcendental idealism in its more popular forms inherits this realistic outlook. This is especially plain when the transcendental principle is reduced to a mere teleology present in human experience, or in universal history: the distribution of facts and existences then remains the same as in empirical idealism, and the knowledge that vouches for them is just as transitive: all that is added is the belief, that, by a miracle of finality, all these facts have, from the beginning of time, expressed certain very human principles of dramatic logic and moral purpose, and that they must continue to express the same for all eternity. Similarly in the theistic interpretation of the transcendental philosophy. Here the transcendental principle becomes an eternal existence and power, over and above the detail of its manifestations in time. In this case realistic knowledge not only bridges the chasm between the various centres and episodes of finite experience, but unites them individually with God, who exists consciously and unchangeably in himself, as well as ideally or formally in our destiny.

A more resolute attempt to banish transitive knowledge is made in the pantheistic and mystical forms of transcendentalism. We then hear that the absolute spirit alone exists, and either neutralizes all the details of universal experience in the unity and simplicity of his being, or thinks them all at once and eternally. In either case time, which is the great principle of perspective and distribution in empirical idealism, is synthesized into timelessness; and the divisions and successions which made realistic knowledge possible as well as requisite are reputed to fall away. All knowledge (if it still deserves that name) will be intransitive possession by the absolute of its own nature.

This theoretical escape from realism is vitiated, however, by a radical defect. It does not represent what even its advocates habitually and honestly believe, but only what, in a warm argumentative moment, they imagine they ought to believe. Parmenides and the Indians themselves were obliged to admit laws and methods of illusion or opinion, and to offer the world a sure prescription for ultimately getting rid of itself: so that not merely as men, and by virtue of an excusable weakness, but as adepts of their moral disciplines, they remained realists. The case of our modern transcendentalists is still more desperate: for while they must deny the reality of time (they would be realists otherwise), their whole moral inspiration is notoriously bound up with the sense of time, progress, and evolution; indeed, it often issues in little else than a philosophy of change. It is certainly possible, in abstracted contemplation, to survey change without believing in it: the surveying glance in any case must span the distance it takes note of. But transcendentalism is not contemplative, it is vital; and of all vital assurances and vital necessities the most imperious is the belief in time. A living being, enduring the flux of events and living in constantly varying retrospect and expectation, especially a breathless, busy, hopeful, experimenting modern, can hardly bring himself to doubt that the very past he recalls was once present, and that the very future he expects and works for may become present in due time; but this belief is the purest and most radical instance of realism.

The critic of realism, on the contrary, must maintain that the past and the future exist only in the present idea of them, else, according to his principle, they could not now be known: in knowing them he cannot admit that we know more or less inadequately realities as self-centred and self-existent as the present thought that knows them. Hard as the doctrine is, he must bring himself to say that the past and the future are nothing but ideas in the present. Conscience, especially his own modern conscience, requires him to admit the equality of all phases of life in respect to reality and intrinsic status. Yet his whole method of philosophizing remains subjective. He cannot purge his distrust of the intellect, which makes him deny transitive knowledge, of its egotistical insolence; his romantic and rebellious impulse is to say that if he cannot contain things external to him such things cannot exist. But egotism, when practised by the present towards the past and future, loses half its evil by losing all its plausibility.

Belief in time is, I think, the deepest belief we have: it is requisite for the acceptance of the witness of memory, and for rational action and hope. It is the soul of introspective psychology. Yet there is another belief which critics of knowledge have been even

more loth to question, indefensible though it be on their principles: the belief in other men's minds. While their method ought
evidently to establish not so much solipsism as a solipsism of the
present datum, yet it never consents to doubt the whole comedy
of human intercourse, just as the most uncritical instinct and the
most fanciful history represent it to be. How can such a mass of
ill-attested and boldly realistic knowledge fail to make the critics
of realism uncomfortable in their own house? Is it because the
criticism of realism in physics, without this realism in psychology,
could never so much as begin? Or do they love to attack dogmatism so much that, if need be, they will become dogmatists in
order to do so? Or is it simply that their criticism at bottom was
a work of edification or of malice, not of philosophic sincerity,
and that they keep this particular social realism without a qualm,
because they need it to justify their moral reflections and to lend
a false air of adequacy to their egotistical method?

IV. LOGICAL PROOF

The backsliding of critics does not impair the principle of criticism: had they been more intrepid, perhaps they might have
impugned consistently the reality of time, origins, and evolution,
and escaped the realism which the assertion of such a reality
involves. This might have been done by retreating into the immediate, in order to rest in the direct and minimal datum of
consciousness. Such a disintegration of intelligence, to be instructive, ought to be radical; more radical, for instance, than that
which Hume or Fichte accomplished. What, according to them,
was the ultimate datum of experience? Hume said: some perception, as of heat, colour, or pleasure. But why, we may ask, a perception, and not merely the heat, colour, or pleasure? Simply
because criticism had not quite disintegrated convention. Hume's
expression was correct enough, but what was correct in it was
naturalistic. Everybody knows that the specific qualities of heat,
colour, and pleasure are never actualized, never intensively present, unless a perception (and a perceiving organ) exists. A living
body must focus itself, or some part of itself, on an appropriate

stimulus before heat, colour, or pleasure can be intuited. Hume knows this, however, by looking over his shoulder and remembering what sort of a world he is living in: it is not the pleasure, colour, or heat that says so.

Similarly, what Fichte divined about an absolute act of the ego positing a non-ego, and then by reflection positing itself, conceals some modest truths about nature. The actual datum has a background, and Fichte was too wise to deny it: hence this myth about the birth of knowledge out of unconscious egos, acts, and positings. It is quite true that the throb of being which we experience at any moment is not proper to the datum—a purely fantastic essence—but to ourselves; it is out of our organism or its central part, the psyche, that this datum has been bred. This living substance in us has the gift of sensibility and is reactive; and being intent, in the first instance, on pursuing or avoiding some agency in its environment, it projects whatever (in consequence of its reactions) reaches its consciousness into the locus whence it feels the stimulus to come, and thus it frames its description or knowledge of objects. In this way the ego really posits the non-ego: not absolutely, however, as Fichte imagined, nor by a gratuitous fiat, but occasionally and for the best of reasons, when the non-ego in its might shakes the ego out of its primitive somnolence.

All this, however, is ulterior natural history, which Hume and Fichte instinctively import into their criticism; it does not help them to the truly immediate datum. On the contrary, it prevents them from discerning this datum in its purity. The datum is no perception, state of mind, or bit of experience; it is not a moment of life both the existence and the character of which are obvious. A present conscious moment is so called in view of other moments and of a past and future conceived to surround it, but not given in it. Without these extraneous associations and interpretations the absolute datum would cease to seem an event, new and contrasted with what went before. As it is given, the datum lies wholly in its own category: if a sound, it is just such a sound; if a pain, just such a pain. There is no indication whatever of a thing that emits the sound, nor of a self that hears it; there is no indication of a flux of sense-data in which this sound turns up; or, if the datum is itself a change, there is no indication that this change supervenes upon something permanent or upon other changes. We have come upon a present object without roots that we can see, without conditions, seat, or environment. It is simply an essence.

The being proper to essences is not existence. When the datum is said to exist something is added to it which it does not and cannot contain—the finding of it, the assault, the strain, the emphasis, the prolongation of our life before and after it towards the not-given. These concomitant contributions of the psyche weight that datum, light it up, and make it seem at once substantial and incidental. Its imputed existence is a dignity borrowed from the momentum of the living mind, which spies out and takes alarm at that datum (or rather at the natural process that calls it forth), supposing that there is something substantial there, something dangerous that will count and work in the world. But essences (as Berkeley said of his "ideas") are inert. Even in the most excruciating pain, it is not the quality of the feeling that can injure us, but only the organic process which it betrays. For, undoubtedly, whenever an essence is given an existence is involved, or rather two: one is involved logically—the fact that this intuition is taking place; the other is involved according to the constitution of the world we live in—the organic process without which intuitions do not arise. But no existence was given to that existing intuition; and if, like that intuition, we absorb and lose ourselves in the essence given, we shall find no evidence of any existence. Events are instinctively assumed; we move through them, rehearse them mentally, and gather that they are going on; but only qualities are given absolutely.

This purely ideal character of the datum appears not only on a close scrutiny, but it turns out on reflection to be inevitable. The great characteristic of what exists is to be in flux; not only does it continually lapse and move forward, abandoning some part of its essence, but it is jostled laterally by a crowd of neighbours alien to its nature. It is a creature of circumstance, compacted and surrounded by external relations. Now a datum may have any degree of complexity, and may figure a whole universe; but no external relations can be given in it connecting it as a whole with anything foreign to it: in other words, the datum cannot appear under the form of existence, but only as a pure essence. Certainly the essence, when the fact that it was given is reflected upon, is seen to have touched existence at one point, and to have acquired this one external contingent and unstable relation—that it was given then, there, and to that person. But this circumstance was not part of its given nature. By virtue of his own existence and instability that man now saw and now ceased to see that essence. His intuition existed and lapsed like any other event, but the essence did not change its nature when he abandoned it for another, nor did it acquire existence because he thought of it.

That existence is not immediately given has not escaped the mystics. Many of them have felt that existence is an adventitious emphasis cast upon ideal objects by will, love, or sin. Relieve the pressure of these personal forces, and the illusion disappears: for in truth (so they would say), apart from our sin, love, or will, nothing exists. Even Kant, who was no extreme mystic, thought all he could think of was imaginary. Existence is imputed to data —correctly or incorrectly—by our obsession with them. And it is not they that exert this magic over us, but quite different subterranean forces at work in the world and in ourselves.

For naturalists and men of science, too, existence is something more than the logical or aesthetic quality of what is found—a quality which they often slight. To exist, for the naturalist, means to exert force, to push one's way through the world. *Die Wirklichkeit,* said Schopenhauer, *ist das Wirken.* But to operate is to be unintelligibly entangled in external relations called history, evolution, causation; and no such operation can be given in that absolute datum to which criticism must appeal in the end.

If we once see clearly that the datum is not an existing thing, nor a state of mind, but an ideal essence, a very interesting corollary comes into view. The sort of being that essences have is indefeasible: they cannot lose it or change it, as things do and must if their being is existence. Therefore intuition, or pure acquaintance with data, has an object whose whole reality is independent of such a perusal of it. This independence is not physical, because the object here is ideal, and never exists at all. But its logical or aesthetic character, which is all the reality it has, is inalienable: for that reason, perhaps, it was called by Plato τὸ ὄγτως ὄν; being which is intrinsic, essential, and contingent on nothing else, least of all, of course, on knowledge. So that when our roving thought lights up one of these intrinsic possibilities, it discovers an object ontologically far more necessary and fundamental than are physical things or pulses of feeling. It follows that acquaintance with essences or ideal terms is pre-eminently realistic knowledge. The circle of essences which human faculty can bring before us is limited, not by the absence of other possible themes, but by the bias of our endowment and the circumstances of our life. Pure intelligence within us—if we have such a thing—is by no means hostile to what, so far, has remained outside. Those yet unintuited essences can be brought into our experience, of course, only by an enlargement or shift in human nature. But human nature is elastic, and the realm of essence is infinite; and if we grew more imaginative and less egotistical we might be more ready to pour out our spirit, in sacrifice or in playfulness, on what is not relevant to our own fortunes. What we have not intuited has as much ideal reality, and for other possible souls as much possible charm, as what we call beautiful. In hugging our humanity, as we very properly do, we need not grudge a speculative respect for what remains non-human. For it surrounds us on every side, ideally as well as materially, and we know that it surrounds us.

Even the essences we take some note of have many necessary ideal relations which escape us. Logically the essence of a right-angled triangle involves the Pythagorean proposition, but psychologically we may have no occasion or no power to discover it. Nature herself, like our thought (which for the most part expresses nature), is selective in respect to essence, and reproduces only a part of that infinite labyrinth. If physical (or at least terrestrial) space had not happened to be Euclidean, Euclid certainly would never have thought out Euclidean space: yet all he says of it would have been just as intrinsic to that essence as it is now.

Even ideal contemplation, therefore, is realistic. The relevance of knowledge in this case is absolute, since our object is simply what we happen to think of. The transitiveness of knowledge is indeed wanting in one sense, since the object does not exist materially, but in another sense is complete, because this ideal object is immutable. Transitiveness in knowledge has two stages or leaps: the leap of intuition, from the state of the living organism to the consciousness of some essence; and the leap of faith and of action, from the symbol actually given in sense or in thought to some ulterior existing object. The first leap, which is primary and fundamental for knowledge, alone concerns us here. It reveals some universal term, which borrows nothing whatever from the observer except its presence to him, which is perfectly adventitious to its nature, and not indicated there. Essences, like things, become objects by accident. Consequently knowledge of essence too is transitive, terminating in an object which is self-determined in its logical sphere and essential relations, and may be revealed to many minds at different times, in various contexts, and with more or less completeness.

V. CONCLUSION

It appears from these various considerations that all reasonable human discourse makes realistic assumptions; so that these proofs, as I venture to call them, are necessarily circular: without assuming realism it would be impossible to prove realism or anything else. What I have endeavoured to show is merely that biology, psychology, and logic require and fortify this assumption, not that a person willing to dispense with biology, psychology, and logic need be a realist. You cannot prove realism to a complete sceptic or idealist; but you can show an honest man that he is not a complete sceptic or idealist, but a realist at heart. So long as he is alive his sincere philosophy must fulfil the assumptions of his life and not destroy them.

The Proofs of Realism

JOHN LACHS

It might seem difficult to imagine a more disappointing essay than Santayana's contribution to the well-known manifesto of critical realists.[1] The cursory reader is encouraged by the title to

Expanded version of John Lachs, "The Proofs of Realism," *The Monist,* 51 (1967). Reprinted by permission.

[1] George Santayana, "Three Proofs of Realism," in *Essays in Critical Realism* (London: Macmillan, 1920), pp. 163-184 [pp. 171-189, above]. "Three Proofs" hereafter.

expect rigorous proofs of realism. Yet the essay contains neither compelling logical arguments nor overwhelming empirical evidence in favor of the realist hypothesis. Much of what Santayana says is interesting, and some of it is important, but one has the feeling throughout that none of it has the least tendency to demonstrate the truth of realism. One's worst suspicions seem to be confirmed at the end of the article, where the author appears to make a mockery of his own exertions by the disarming confession that his position cannot at all be proved to sceptics or idealists. If only he had thought of this at the beginning, we may feel, he could have saved himself the effort of writing such a thin, confused essay. Incidentally, he could also have spared us the embarrassment of seeing through the threadbare thought of an allegedly great philosopher.

We may be inclined to file away some mental notes on Santayana and perhaps on critical realism, and then let the matter drop. Yet this would be a mistake. The hypothesis that Santayana set out to prove realism, but later recognized the impossibility of the task is too easy to be credible. And the view that he would allow the damning record of such a change of mind to be published is so improbable as to deserve no serious attention. The reason why the essay might seem baffling at first is simply that it presupposes too much. Because he is a systematic philosopher, each element of Santayana's thought is organically connected with every other. It should come as no surprise, therefore, that his theory of perception is largely unintelligible in abstraction from the system as a whole. Because he is exceptionally single-minded, almost every one of Santayana's essays is a portrait in cameo of his system. Since the depiction is both unannounced and in miniature, it should come as no surprise that much of what he says seems at first incoherent, and becomes clear only when the general context is supplied and the fine lines have been sketched in.

The function of this essay is to provide the context and the refinements necessary to see Santayana's critical realism as a consistent, though not fully defensible, whole. Since the appearance of Marten ten Hoor's study over forty years ago,[2] there have been

[2] Marten ten Hoor, "George Santayana's Theory of Knowledge," *The Journal of Philosophy*, 20 (1923), pp. 197-211 [pp. 220-236, below].

only scattered and minor attempts to present a critical assessment of Santayana's theory of knowledge. Even those who paid particular attention to his epistemology showed only passing interest in his theory of perception. He has received not so much as the uncertain compliment of attempted refutation; Lovejoy and Drake have long been singled out as prime targets for raids on critical realism. I hope to convince the reader that Santayana's version of the theory is well worth serious study by showing that it is a sophisticated, and in some respects persuasive, attempt to give an account of the facts of perception. I shall try to do this without concealing the difficulties of the view: only in that way will it be possible for us to understand the sort of proof Santayana proposes to give of realism, and to assess the force and adequacy of his arguments.

I

If realism, in the widest sense of the term, is the view that there is nothing whose *esse* is *percipi,* Santayana must be counted among its most determined and single-minded advocates. His realism has its historical roots in Plato and, to a lesser extent, in Aristotle; its closest contemporary analogue is the G. E. Moore of "The Refutation of Idealism," with whose analysis of consciousness into diaphanous act and non-mental object Santayana fully concurs.[3] But there are two forms of realism we must distinguish. One is a theory about universals and their relation to thought; the other is a theory about particulars and their relation to sense. The first maintains that universals are neither mental in nature, nor dependent on thought for their being or existence. The second contends that spatio-temporal particulars are non-mental, and exist independently of our perception of them. The theories are similar in making the essential realist claim that consciousness does not create its objects: they differ only in the type of consciousness, and hence the type of object, concerning which their claims are made.

[3] G. E. Moore, "The Refutation of Idealism," *Philosophical Studies* (London: Harcourt, Brace, 1922), pp. 1-30.

It is worth remarking that the two types of realism are logically independent of each other. Either one could be maintained while the other was denied, without involving us in self-contradiction. Descartes, for example, was a realist in his view of perceptual knowledge, but he maintained that universals were dependent on the mind. At least one reading of Spinoza, on the other hand, would have us see him as a realist about the universals that were the objects of his second and third kinds of knowledge, while he held that the time-bound objects of perceptual cognition were creatures of the human imagination. Santayana is explicit in subscribing to both theories of realism. On the one hand, he insists that essences or universals are independent in their logical being of the intuition that summons them to mind. He spends long chapters, on the other hand, in the attempt to show that there are enduring, substantial things whose existence is independent of, and unaffected by, our knowledge of them.[4] In this paper I shall not spend time on Santayana's Platonic realism about essences. I shall concentrate my attention on his realistic view of sense perception. To focus our inquiry, let me begin by discussing his two central, and apparently contradictory, methodological commitments.

The two methods to which I refer structure and dominate the first and the second part of *Scepticism and Animal Faith,* respectively. The first is the sceptical method of refusing to assent to any proposition whose certainty has not been demonstrated. The second is the method of accepting, after some rational reconstruction, the beliefs of sound common sense.

Sceptical doubt leads Santayana to solipsism of the present moment, in which nothing beyond the immediately given is admitted. Since the existence of a past, a future, and of outlying contemporary events is always subject to doubt, we are left with the changeless qualities and relations we intuit. They justify no inference to anything beyond themselves. If to exist is to stand in changeable, external relations,[5] the features (essences) which constitute the only possible objects of consciousness themselves

---

[4] See especially, George Santayana, *Scepticism and Animal Faith* (New York: Dover, 1955), ch. 18, 19, and 20. *SAF* hereafter.

[5] *SAF*, p. 42.

turn out not to exist. This does not mean, of course, that what is given in the specious present is *nothing,* but only that any such complex essence is simply what it is and stands, as essence or group of qualities, in no temporal or dynamic relation to anything. Essences, not being enduring objects, cannot be changed: a "changed" essence in the field of attention is one that has been exchanged, viz., one whose place has been taken by quite another.

Consciousness of the immediate objective manifold, then, yields only acquaintance with essence, not knowledge of existence. Intuition that is free of the transitive force of intent is, indeed, incorrigible; but this certainty is bought at the price of significance. In pure intuition nothing is meant and nothing is asserted: since no judgments are made, no mistakes can be committed, and all is open-eyed trance and docile enjoyment. Santayana's sceptical method thus leaves him stripped of the knowledge of change, existence, mind, and God. Even the possibility of knowledge evaporates as the world contracts to the moment's changeless essence and the silent self is swallowed in the object. Ultimate solipsism ends without an *ipse;* although as a theory scepticism ends with the singular conclusion that all theories are unjustified, as a method it is successful in reducing us to ignorant and ignominious silence.

Now the point that may be the source of great puzzlement in the reader is Santayana's repeated claim that scepticism is both irrefutable and untenable. On the face of it, this involves an outright contradiction. To say that a theory is untenable is to contend that someone is in a position to refute it, or has already done so: to say, on the other hand, that a thorough investigation has failed to reveal any compelling argument or evidence against a view is to commit ourselves to considering it eminently tenable. If Santayana is in fact guilty of such a contradiction, we have good reason to maintain that his concessions to the subjectivistic, sceptical tradition of modern philosophy are incompatible with the positive tenets of his ontology. And if this incompatibility can be substantiated, it is evident that the most distinctive element of his philosophy, the attempt to implant the private life of spirit in the rich soil of the natural world, must inevitably end on the rocks.

A close reading of Santayana should make it clear that he is careful to avoid the imputed contradiction. He holds that from the standpoint of rational argument scepticism is irrefutable. From this point of view it is not only a tenable, but the only tenable, position.[6] When he says, by contrast, that the sceptical stance is insupportable, he speaks from an entirely different frame of reference. Just as the reflective man cannot escape scepticism, the active man cannot escape belief. Suspension of belief is an impossibility for the animal engaged in action: his impending actions, his expectations, the rhythmic patterns of his life impose beliefs on him or express his tacit commitments.

The sceptical method hinges on the rationalistic criteria of knowledge. If only what is self-evidently true or demonstrably certain may be known, we shall end by knowing nothing. Although this is the note on which the first part of *Scepticism and Animal Faith* closes, it would be a mistake to construe it as a conclusion of Santayana's philosophy. It is, instead, to be read as a *reductio ad absurdum* of scepticism, and hence of the rationalistic criteria of knowledge. The fact that these criteria leave us with no knowledge and no justified belief[7] is enough to show their absurdity; it is clear that in beginning with them we have made a false start. Doubt, as the voluntary withholding of assent in the absence of ideal evidence, is an intellectual exercise which can only show that our ideal of evidence has been set too high, viz., that natural knowledge of the natural world cannot meet the demands of unbridled reason. But scepticism does not suspend life: doubt is not disbelief. Belief is the involuntary active attitude of an animal engaged in the business of life, as well as the expression of that attitude in consciousness. On its physical side, it is the psyche's attitude of expectation and her readiness to react. Mentally, it is neither a quality of ideas nor the vivacity of our conception of them,[8] but the felt presence of intent or transcendent reference, which is the counterpart in consciousness of the vectorial energies of the psyche.

6 *Ibid.,* p. 101.

7 *Ibid.,* pp. 110-111; George Santayana, "Literal and Symbolic Knowledge," *Obiter Scripta* (New York: Scribner, 1936), p. 129. "Literal" hereafter.

8 *Ibid.,* p. 18.

In sum, then, scepticism is irrefutable so long as we move in the realm of reason or discourse, but untenable if we take three-dimensional man and ubiquitous action as the starting points of our philosophy. Though reason finds all doubts legitimate, good sense and candor pronounce the sceptic dishonest. The dishonesty comes of an essential conflict in the sceptic's life: in his theory he suspends his commitments, while in practice he happily acts them out. A philosophy that will not abandon us the moment we take it out of the study must be based on the "large facts" of temporal existence, it must be free of crippling discrepancy between theory and practice, and it must include a criterion of rational belief which allows for legitimate (though not indubitable) natural knowledge.

"Animal faith" is the phrase Santayana uses to denote the commitment, the confidence in the constancy and plasticity of the environment, which is tacit in spatio-temporal action. When we act we silently assume the truth of such principles as (1) there is a world which consists of enduring things, (2) there is a future which will resemble the past, (3) the things we seek can be found, and (4) the things we see can be eaten.[9] These and other principles implicit in action are the tenets of animal faith. Their progressive unravelling, careful formulation, and organized presentation are the tasks of the second method to which I have alluded. This constructive enterprise undertakes the restoration of the views of common sense, using as its criteria the beliefs tacit in animal action. Everything Santayana says about the general features of the natural world is meant to have its justification, directly or indirectly, in the natural beliefs unavoidably implicated in action. These beliefs, in their turn, cannot be justified by evidence or argument: their validity is assumed in the acts of collecting evidence, as well as in the processes of reasoning. Although practical success often bears them out, they have the status of ultimate, inescapable commitments. They are the natural beliefs of the active man: if they are false, human action and the world of flux are radical deceptions, and we are back at a feigned scepticism.

That the two methods Santayana uses are not incompatible or contradictory should now be obvious. They are not coordinate

9 *Ibid.,* p. 180.

and rival methods at all: Santayana's positive conclusions are all reached by the method that may be alternately called the critical reconstruction of common sense or the eduction of the principles of animal faith. Scepticism is used exclusively with destructive intent: it clears the field of dogmas, establishes the impossibility of rationalism, exposes its own criteria of knowledge as irrelevant to life, and ends in a self-stultifying silence that invites neglect. Once the sceptical phase of his investigation is completed, Santayana can begin the positive enterprise of framing a natural philosophy. Scepticism has served to eliminate blind alleys, to set limits to his inquiry, and to focus his task.

II

The sceptical phase of Santayana's analysis leaves him with essence only. Since essences, the immediate objects of consciousness, are logically prior to the cognitive acts which apprehend them, Santayana is led naturally to hold the realistic position that universals are neither mental nor dependent on intuition. But essences are changeless qualities and relations, not existing material things: they cannot be the objects of natural knowledge. The existence of a world of substantial and enduring things is, accordingly, the primary assumption implicated in action. In affirming the existence and detailing the properties of such a world, Santayana pays special heed to the realistic assumptions of common sense and animal action. When the notion of substance is first introduced, it is simply that of whatever exists independently of thought, but is open to cognition.[10] It is only later that this realistic skeleton of the concept of substance is fleshed out to become that of being that has "a place, movement, origin, and destiny of its own,"[11] viz., that is, at least potentially, both agent and patient in a field of action.[12]

We thus find ourselves with the classic trichotomy of dualistic

---

[10] *Ibid.*, p. 182.

[11] *Ibid.*, p. 203.

[12] For a more complete treatment of the notions of substance, see my "Matter and Substance in the Philosophy of Santayana," *The Modern Schoolman*, 44 (1966), pp. 1-12.

realism in the theory of perception. There is a mental act (intuition) directed upon non-mental immediate objects (essences). The immediate objects serve in some way as the vehicles of perception: the ultimate object of knowledge is the independently existing physical world (substance). It is at this point that the critical realist must face his two most fundamental problems. The first is the provision of a general account of the nature of knowledge and a formulation of its criteria. The second is the explication of the relations which obtain between intuited essence and perceived substance in veridical as well as in erroneous perception. Although the two problems are intimately connected, I shall consider Santayana's answers to them singly and in succession.

Let me begin with the problem of the nature of knowledge. In light of his view of the realm of truth, it might seem rather simple to provide a Santayanan account of knowledge. Facts are existing things or events against which we may run up[13]: as such, they are objects not of intuition, but of belief. Such belief must be the outcome or expression of living in the flux. Now a proposition p which serves as the vehicle of belief about some fact a is true if and only if it consists of essences which also occur in the standard comprehensive description of a. The standard comprehensive description of a fact is the truth about it: it is a part of this truth which is or can be brought to a person's mind when he is said to know that fact. It may appear, therefore, that knowledge, for Santayana, is simply true belief founded on experience.[14]

Unfortunately, this view will not do as it stands. Knowledge, Santayana assures us, is symbolic in character. The relation of the essence intuited to the essence embodied, therefore, need not be that of identity, as the strict form of the correspondence theory of truth would demand. The two essences need have no intrinsic connection for the one to constitute knowledge of the other, and in fact they rarely do: the only thing important is for the one intuited to be taken as the symbol of the one that is actually instanced. If this view is taken as seriously as Santayana's repeated insistence on it demands,[15] the nature and limits of knowledge

13 *SAF*, p. 229.
14 *Ibid.*, p. 180.
15 *Ibid.*, pp. 176-178; "Literal," pp. 141-146.

must be sought in the rules of symbolism. But we search in vain for a clear and complete theory of symbolism in the works of Santayana. He places no limits on appropriate symbolization and presents no criteria by which the adequacy of a symbol may be determined. Instead, he shows the greatest permissiveness about what may with legitimacy be considered symbolic knowledge. Any essence intuited in the presence of an object upon which we react is an acceptable sign for it, he informs us.[16] And since any object has, "at least partially and relatively,"[17] the characters we assign to it, we are apparently free to assign any feature to anything without running the risk of being found in error.

This view raises serious problems, to which I shall come presently. For now, however, we may welcome it, for it eliminates the apparent contradiction between the symbolic nature of knowledge and the criterion which demands that knowledge, as true belief, repeat a part of the truth about some fact. The truth about a fact *a* is *a*'s standard *comprehensive* description. As such, it is infinitely extended and includes all *a*'s relations to everything existent and eternal.[18] The essences, therefore, that constitute the perspectives of any and every being on *a* are all parts of the truth about it. Now whenever some being takes a view of *a*, it intuits exactly those essences which are enshrined in the realm of truth as constituting its view of *a*, and those essences are a part of the truth about *a*. The obvious but disquieting conclusion is that in spite of all the ignorance and stupidity in the world, no one can be in error in any judgment he makes about anything.

The most remarkable feature of this view is its tendency to move away from judging the adequacy of knowledge by an ideal standard. The truth as the ideally accurate description of facts seemed, at first, to be such a standard. But the comprehensiveness of the description strips it of its value as a norm, and the condition and circumstances of the knower appear to assume supreme importance in determining the adequacy of knowledge. The excellence of a representation is thus a function of the situation which gave rise to it: to judge it good or bad apart from that con-

---

16 George Santayana, "The Unknowable," *Obiter Scripta, loc. cit.,* p. 181.
17 "Literal," p. 131.
18 *SAF,* p. 267.

text is simply meaningless. It is, accordingly, not as a matter of irony that Santayana calls a blatantly inaccurate assessment of his opinions fair and good, in view of the fact that it is a photograph "taken of my system in a bad light at a great distance."[19]

This view, held without a corrective, ends in irremediable relativism. If the circumstances and limitations of the knower are allowed to enter into our assessment of the adequacy of a piece of knowledge, cognitive achievements become incommensurable, understanding cannot be enhanced, and the collective enterprise of science is ruled impossible. To avoid such a vicious relativism, Santayana introduces two criteria in terms of which we may establish the comparative excellence of cognitions. The first is the test of action. Given two beliefs about the same configuration of circumstances, one is more adequate than the other if it traces the generative relations of the substances involved more accurately than that other. The measure of accuracy is the degree of success that may be achieved by acting upon the belief, since such success is thought to depend upon the correct estimate of the balance of ambient forces. It is this compelling structure of power that constitutes the "control by outer facts" Santayana considers essential for knowledge.[20] Since prosperous animal operation is the only possible touchstone of the relevance and appropriateness of the symbolic cognition of the dynamic, Santayana's claim that "knowledge of nature is a great allegory, of which action is the interpreter"[21] may be readily seen as a perfect *précis* of his position.

The second criterion should be prefaced by the comment that, even though he sometimes speaks of their "ultimate elements," Santayana does not distinguish between the essential and the accidental properties of existing objects. Any and every property that characterizes an existent is enshrined in the realm of truth as pertaining to it: none is more relevant to it than any of the others, save in the eyes of an observer with special interests. Every part of its standard comprehensive description is equally and irrevocably a truth about it. For this reason, it is impossible to

19 George Santayana, *The Realm of Spirit* (New York: Scribner, 1940), p. 273.
20 *SAF*, p. 180.
21 "Literal," p. 140.

characterize advance in knowledge as movement from the apprehension of peripheral properties to cognition of the object's central features. Santayana's second criterion for judging the adequacy of knowledge is designed, therefore, as an alternative to this characterization. It is simply the claim that, without there being degrees of truth, there are degrees of knowledge.[22] On this view, the adequacy of knowledge must be judged by its completeness. The completeness of a piece of knowledge, in turn, is a matter of how much of the truth about a fact it manages to include. Since the truth about any fact is infinite in extent,[23] complete knowledge must always remain an ideal limit for mortal man.[24] But the finite segments of truth we rehearse are susceptible of comparison on the simple quantitative scale of greater or lesser inclusiveness, viz., they are essences of greater or lesser complexity.

It should now be possible to formulate a relatively precise description of the nature and criterion of knowledge, as Santayana conceives them. As we have seen, we can accept the view that knowledge, for him, is true belief about facts, if we introduce the necessary qualifications and place the right interpretation on this general formula. Thus the detailed description might run as follows. A belief may be said to constitute knowledge if and only if (1) it is the projection by intent into a bounded region of existence of more or less complex intuited essences, (2) the essences thus projected are parts of the standard comprehensive description of the given region, and (3) the belief, if it were translated into behavior, would make it possible for the animal to engage in action that is both successful and relevant to the region. It is important to note that knowledge is always of some past, present or future segment of existence, that it is always mediated by projected essences, and that the segment of existence or fact that is its object is always logically prior and dynamically independent of it. Both the intuition and the projection of essences are mental acts, and the mental realm is that of free construction and discourse, for Santayana. It is for this reason that (3) is of central

[22] "Literal," p. 132.
[23] *Ibid.*
[24] George Santayana, *The Realm of Truth* (New York: Scribner, 1938), p. 79. *RT* hereafter.

importance in his account of knowledge: only through the medium of action can a conscious belief make contact with the hard facts which constitute its only check and control.

Knowledge, then, is a cooperative enterprise of body and mind: it is the "intellectual transcript" of the reaction of an organism to its environment.[25] The concept of belief itself is amphibious in the work of Santayana: sometimes it stands for a mental act, on other occasions it designates a behavioral disposition or bodily attitude. Since beliefs in the first sense are units in discourse, consistency, a requirement of organized thought, is a necessary condition of knowledge. The ultimate test of the truth of a belief in the first sense (as act of mind), however, is the successful discharge in action of the corresponding belief in the second sense (as latent tendency). The unfailing correspondence of beliefs as occurrent acts of mind and as behavioral dispositions, which is necessary to maintain this view, is a postulate of Santayana's philosophy of mind: its defense properly belongs under that head. Finally, the ideal of knowledge, as imposed by the prolixity of the realm of truth, is unattainable omniscience; but as much knowledge as is requisite for us not to be entirely in the dark about nature,[26] or to enlighten us about our natural good,[27] or to develop a useful but tenuous natural science[28] should suffice for men whose bodies were forged for action, and whose minds have been framed for contemplation and not for belief.

The most remarkable omission in Santayana's account of knowledge is the lack of reference to evidence or reasons. We would not normally be said to know *p*, unless we were able to offer some evidence for it or some good reasons for thinking it true. Now Santayana is, I am quite certain, in full agreement with this view. He fails to make much of it, however, for a simple and perfectly good reason. His view is that perceptions and beliefs, with the exception of totally deceptive ones, are the causal consequents of their intended objects. For this reason, the very occurrence of a perception or belief must be taken as prima facie evidence of the

25 "Literal," p. 115.
26 *Ibid.*, p. 134.
27 *SAF*, p. 102.
28 *Ibid.*, pp. 178-179.

existence of its objects, and hence of its own truth.[29] Given this view, it is not surprising that Santayana does not think it important to stress the evidential element in knowledge. The tenability of this view, however, turns on the fate of Santayana's beliefs about the connection of mental acts to antecedent physical processes in general, and on the case for his causal theory of perception, in particular. Since I have already considered the former issue elsewhere,[30] I now turn to the theory of perception proper.

III

At first sight, Santayana appears to be of two minds about the relation of intuited and embodied essences in perception. Since essences are repeatable universals, the way is open for the identity of the perceived features of the epistemological object with the characteristics of the surface of the independent substance. And indeed, Santayana often writes as if veridical perception consisted in just such a reduplication of essence in two distinct realms of being. At one point, he identifies the ideal of realism as the view that appearance and substance are distinct in existence but identical in essence.[31] In another place, he firmly maintains that perception, if adequate, describes the whole essence of its object: the diversity between perception and natural substance then amounts to no more than "the separable existence of each."[32]

In direct opposition to the above view, we have the Santayana who spoke of the "fantastic inadequacy of our perceptions,"[33] who wrote an entire chapter to show that nothing given exists, and who boldly affirmed that "no quality in the object is like any datum of sense."[34] For this Santayana, all knowledge is symbolic, and the most we can achieve is "appropriate description," which is "no incorporation or reproduction of the object in the mind."[35]

I attribute this apparent contradiction to Santayana's free and

---

[29] "Literal," p. 131.

[30] See my "Santayana's Philosophy of Mind," *The Monist*, 48 (1964), pp. 419-440.

[31] "Three Proofs," p. 165 [p. 173, above].

[32] "Literal," p. 114.

[33] *SAF*, p. 6.

[34] *Ibid.*, p. 84.

[35] *Ibid.*, p. 178.

evocative use of language, which verges, on occasion, on the philosophically irresponsible. I call the contradiction "apparent," because a study of our author's general intent makes it relatively easy to detect his deliberate position. If it conceived veridical perception as consisting of the reduplication of the world in sense, Santayana's theory would be subject to all the obvious and fatal objections to copy dualism. Santayana knew the force of these objections too well not to have taken them into account: his repeated insistence on the symbolic nature of cognition was in fact prompted, at least partly, by the desire to sidestep such difficulties. The claim that knowledge is symbolic,[36] the reminders that there is a great disparity between human ideas and natural things,[37] and the reason he gives for the fact that intuited essences are seldom if ever identical with the essences embodied in substance[38] are the best indications of Santayana's actual belief. If we add to this his claim that sensation works "in a conventional medium, as do literature and music," and is presided over by the Muses,[39] no reasonable doubt can remain that he repudiates the view that in veridical perception envisaged and embodied essense are identical.

Santayana's reason for thinking the qualitative identity of the data of sense with the properties of substance vastly improbable is not only the negative one of avoiding the difficulties of a Lockean view. He hints at his positive reason in several places where he speaks of the discrepancy between the scale of nature and the scale of our senses. Since he nowhere discusses the topic in detail, I am forced to fill in the missing steps in his argument. The scale of our senses is established, he maintains, by "the interaction of gross living bodies."[40] Nature, by contrast, is minute in the scale and texture of her ultimate processes. Now it is highly probable that processes whose scales differ do not embody or give rise to intuitions of the same essence. For this reason, Santayana appears to conclude, it is highly probable that human perceptions cannot capture the essences embodied in the ultimate natural units of substance.

This argument involves too many unsupported assumptions to

36 *Ibid.*, p. 103.
37 "Literal," pp. 133-134.
38 *Ibid.*, p. 133.
39 *SAF*, p. 102.
40 "Literal," p. 133.

be convincing. First of all, that the scale of the senses is established by the interaction of macro-bodies is both a vast and a dubious simplification. It is, of course, true that to the best of our knowledge there are always some medium-sized bodies involved in perception. But it is rather probable that the ultimate causes or immediate conditions of intuition are not gross objects, but submicroscopic processes, whose scale may be not very different from that of the ultimate units of substance. And, further, even if the difference in scale were granted, it remains dubious that processes of different magnitude cannot embody at least some of the same essences. Mathematical and geometrical properties are examples of essences that may be embodied on various scales, and there are many more among those most familiar in our experience.

The weakness of Santayana's argument on this point convinces me that we should leave open the possibility of the identity of intuited and embodied essence in veridical perception. However, I feel inclined to agree with Santayana that even if the identity ever obtained, it would be impossible to verify it. At any rate, he assures us, qualitative identity is not the usual relation between intuited appearance and substantial reality when perception is said to be correct in its deliverance. Their relation is that of a symbol to what it symbolizes. To say this, however, and no more, is singularly uninformative. What we need is a theory of symbolism, and although Santayana claims to have made use of Peirce's work in this field,[41] his scattered statements are not easily collated into an adequate, consistent, and defensible view.

The two greatest hindrances to understanding Santayana's theory of symbolism are its incompleteness and its verbal boggles. It is best perhaps to begin with the remark that Santayana considers the data of sense to be symptoms of changes and adjustments in the psyche.[42] In another place, he calls such intuited essences "signals to the animal of his dangers or chances"[43]; an unhappy locution, since the "signals" are sent by the psyche to the spirit which, consisting of intuitions only, has no Ego to receive, inter-

[41] In a letter quoted in Justus Buchler, "One Santayana or Two?" *The Journal of Philosophy,* 51 (1954), pp. 52-57 [p. 68, above].
[42] *SAF,* p. 64.
[43] *Ibid.,* p. 102.

pret or act on them. Then, again, essences are "messengers" or "signs" for existences of which they provide descriptions.[44] But messengers presuppose an audience and signs some interpreter: consciousness can provide neither, since it consists only of momentary acts. Once more, sense qualities, like exclamatory words, are elicited from the psyche by the pressure of external events: by another unhappy turn of phrase, Santayana calls such qualities "spontaneous symbols."[45]

Verbal and conceptual confusion seem to rise to a crescendo when Santayana introduces the notion of an index without the least explanation, and quickly proceeds to tell us that an index, when it is used, becomes a symbol.[46] If we take this in conjunction with his claim, made elsewhere, that an index used becomes a sign,[47] we must inevitably conclude that Santayana makes no distinction between symbols and signs. This conclusion is borne out by his constant and easy shift from "symbol" to "sign" throughout his "Literal and Symbolic Knowledge" and elsewhere, as well as by the frequency in his work of such phrases as "sign or symbol."

Can we disentangle any positive account of what it means for an essence to be a sign or symbol of existence, from Santayana's cryptic and perplexing suggestions? The bare outlines of such an account may be detected in his hints, I believe. His use of map-reading as the model for symbolic cognition suggests that he conceives of symbolization as a four-term relation.[48] In the case of the map, the terms are obviously the chart itself, the countryside, an interpreter, and the interpreter's conception of the relevance of the chart to the countryside. In the more general case, the essence as symbol and some substance as thing symbolized are clearly two of the terms. The other two terms, however, are not as easy to identify. The key is in Santayana's insistence that in symbolic cognition there is always some "material instrument of information."[49] The remaining terms, therefore, must be the "momentary map" drawn somewhere in the nervous system of the

44 *Ibid.,* p. 155.
45 *Ibid.,* p. 56.
46 "Literal," p. 141.
47 *SAF,* p. 87.
48 "Literal," p. 141.
49 *Ibid.,* p. 142.

organism, and the active psyche which fills the role of interpreter.

Now in reading a chart we do not assign its properties to the geographical region it represents: the features we project are ones correlated with the properties of the map and suggested by them. Similarly, the essences we read into nature in symbolic perception are not those embodied in the brain-region which probably serves as the material instrument of information, but those whose intuition that activated brain-region creates. There need be no pictorial or qualitative similarity between symbolized substance, brain-region, and intuited essence. The connection between a substance and our brain-"map" of it, and a brain-"map" and its associated intuition is a dynamic or generative one. The foundation of symbolism is thus the natural or dynamic correspondence of certain material objects with certain intuitions. Any essence may become the sign of any substance, therefore, so long as (1) the presence and activity of the substance regularly evokes (through intermediary brain-"maps") intuitions of that essence, (2) the absence or inactivity of the substance is regularly accompanied by the absence of intuitions of that essence, and (3) relevant changes in the substance regularly evoke changes in the intuition of that essence. The central role of the dynamic tie between the significate and the sign of its presence it creates, as well as the lack of resemblance between them, together exhibit this concept of symbolism as closely similar to Peirce's notion of an index.[50]

The relationship I have so far described suffices for a perception to be minimally symbolic of its object. Since it was caused by its object, the perception may be called a symptom, signal or index of what it cognizes. However, in favorable circumstances we claim to know more than the mere presence or absence of substances. Such knowledge is not based on any simple pictorial or qualitative similarity, but rather on some "methodical correspondence" between the sign and its significate.[51] What Santayana seems to have in mind is a structural correspondence: certain systems of

[50] Charles Hartshorne and Paul Weiss, eds., *Collected Papers of Charles Sanders Peirce,* Volume II (Cambridge: Harvard University Press, 1932), pp. 160-165, 170-172.

[51] "Unknowable," p. 172.

relations that obtain between symbols in perception are supposed to match, point for point, systems of relations in existing objects.[52] Such one-to-one correspondence of selected groups of relations is the basis of our closer knowledge of nature, and particularly of the dynamic interactions of substances. The fact that appearance is the child of reality guarantees the frequency of their, at least partial, correspondence: when such analogies are exploited, appearance yields representative knowledge of reality.[53]

My first objection to this theory derives from the peculiarity of introducing the material psyche as the symbol interpreter in cognition. Since the psyche is not conscious and consciousness is not a material thing, the view makes it impossible for the symbol interpreter to be in any way cognizant of the symbols it is supposed to interpret. The symbols are intuited essences: since the psyche's organic intelligence cannot detect their tenuous presence, it cannot interpret their message or use them to light up the darkness of nature.

The difficulty is clearly a result of Santayana's epiphenomenalism, but he never attempted to deal with it explicitly. A possible answer to it may run as follows. When an animal encounters another natural thing, a "map" corresponding to that thing is established in the creature's brain. But the reaction of the animal to such an external influence goes far beyond the creation of a transient brain-"map": the entire organism is vibrant with nerve and muscle movements, chemical changes, and rapid bodily adjustments. Physiological processes decode the brain-"map" and compute the location and potentials of its external cause: others use the brain's memory-stores to calculate the form and magnitude of the appropriate response. This or something like this may be a fair general description of what, on the basis of its "innate instinct" and "training and experience,"[54] the psyche does to the material instrument of information in the symbol relation. All the intelligent "symbol-interpreting" occurs at this point and on the physical level: the actual symbol, as well as its felt projection on the environment are but mental "transcripts" of the psyche's

52 "Literal," pp. 139-140.
53 *Ibid.*, p. 141.
54 *Ibid.*, p. 115.

activity. The intuited essence is the counterpart or reflection in consciousness of the brain-"map"; the intent or belief which seems to project the essence unto a region of existence is the mental, and hence only apparently active, counterpart of the psyche's attempts to decode and respond to the information carried by the brain-"map." Since consciousness reflects the activities of the psyche without re-enacting them, the symbol, as it appears to us projected unto the world, must be but an image in a pellucid medium of action in the dark: its ground is the reaction of the psyche to the outside world.

This defense of Santayana's position suffers from the vagueness of the notion that consciousness is a "reflection" or "transcript" of the psyche's movements, as well as from a surfeit of speculative physiology. Instead of pressing these points, however, I shall move on to my next objection, which raises even more serious difficulties. All the immediate objects of our experience are non-existent essences. These essences, Santayana tells us, serve as symbols of ambient substances. Yet symbolization presupposes some form of contact between symbol and thing symbolized. The simplest form of contact is the sort of juxtaposition of thing and symbol which we establish when we teach the meaning of words by ostensive definition. The contact between the two elements may, of course, be much more tenuous, but everything symbolized must be tied, directly or indirectly, to something that appears in our experience. Without some such point of contact, we end with a free-floating system of symbols, which have neither relevance nor application to existence. Now since on Santayana's view nothing given exists, there seems to be no possibility for an existing substance to enter the sphere of consciousness or of experience. The system of our perceptions forms a charmed circle: no symbol can break out of it to touch the ebbing flux, and no substance can break in without being turned, as if by magic, into the bloodless essence of itself. Even if we were inclined, therefore, to accept the testimony of animal faith and to construe the existence of an independent world as unavoidably implicated in action, we could not claim to have the least knowledge of that world. Ideas can have no relevance to substances which always elude them, and symbols have no application to what cannot be tied to some object of consciousness. If nothing given exists and if cognition is symbolic, knowledge of nature is impossible.

This objection, if it remains unanswered, is devastating for Santayana's realism. Now a first attempt to give an account of the way in which symbols link up with the reality they depict may be hinged on the distinction Santayana draws between intuition and intent. Intuition is passive consciousness: it is the contemplation or enjoyment of essences without commitment and belief. In perception, by contrast, we find that presented essences are taken as indicative of absent existing things. There the immediate objects of our consciousness are not enjoyed for their intrinsic nature: they are used in the attempt to characterize some segment of a complex and changing world. The belief element present in such perceptual (and other) judgments is what Santayana designates by the word "intent." This belief element is the detectable difference between the receptivity of intuition and the active symbolic cognition which occurs in perception. Intent seeks out and fixes in attention the region of existence we are moved to explore; by projecting intuited essences unto a dynamic field, it establishes the indispensable contact between substantial thing and its fine-spun symbol.

The analysis of judging into the element of intuition and the element of intent bears close resemblance to Descartes' view.[55] Tacit in it is a theory about the constituents of judgments. Although he never explicitly defended this theory, it seems that, for Santayana, intent identifies the subject of the judgment (some existing thing or event), and intuition provides the predicates assigned to it (intuited essences). This view is borne out by such claims as that we posit existence first, and then color it with whatever essences the mind can provide.[56] However this may be, it is clear that intent alone cannot tie symbol to substance. In focusing upon an object, intent can no more escape the charmed circle of experience than can direct intuition. Its sensible endeavor does not carry it beyond the object of experience: it falls far short of

---

[55] Compare with Descartes' account of judgment in his *Meditations on First Philosophy*. René Descartes, *Philosophical Works* (New York: Dover, 1955), Vol. I, pp. 171-179.

[56] *RT*, p. 51.

reaching independent substance. The essences it seems to project on nature are projected only on a specious backdrop of pictorial space and sentimental time: intent is impotent to further the cause of correlating sensed time and space with the space and time which characterize substance.

IV

Santayana's main attempt to link symbols to their existing objects takes the form of a theory about the role in perception of bodily attitudes.[57] He appears to realize that nothing purely mental, such as intent, can bridge the gap between intuited symbol and independent substance. It takes an amphibious being, part mental and part material, to connect a system of symbols with a system of things or events. Santayana believes that, luckily, man is just such an amphibious creature. The human mind provides the symbols of perception, the human body identifies the substance which is the cause of that perception and of which those symbols may form relevant knowledge. The object of perception lives and moves on the same plane as the body: its influence on our organs is what makes us respond by pointing at it or assuming some posture of pursuit or avoidance. This discoverable direction and attitude of the human body picks out and fixes the object of the mind's concern. Once the body's endeavor and heed are riveted on the foreign substance, intent projects alternative or complementary essences on the region of the field of action which that existent occupies. In this way, the relevance of knowledge is assured, and we can safely proceed with the task of choosing the most adequate among alternative descriptions.

I am afraid this solution simply will not do. If no existent ever enters the sphere of our consciousness, the human body cannot play the role Santayana ascribes to it. In order to play this role, the body would have to fulfill two requirements: (1) it would have to exist in a field of action continuous with external substances, and (2) it would have to be presented or presentable to the mind. But, according to Santayana himself, (1) and (2) are incompatible.

[57] "Three Proofs," pp. 169-173 [pp. 177-180, above]; *SAF*, pp. 172-179.

If nothing given exists, the body presented to consciousness is but a complex essence within our perceptual field. As such, it cannot be the body that is an existing substance in its own right within the field of action. The body whose "discoverable attitude" identifies the object of intent is, therefore, the phenomenal body: it is a unit in discourse which occupies a position in pictorial space and is devoid of dynamic properties. This body is the only one we can observe, and it is altogether unable to escape the charmed circle of our thoughts. The attitudes of this perceptual object can only be directed upon other objects in perceptual space; its motions, changes or developments all take place in sentimental time. It could be used to identify the existing substances which surround the *material* body only if we could show, on independent grounds, that there is an exact correspondence between the elements and the relations of pictorial and physical space, sentimental and physical time, and the phenomenal and the physical body. Yet, since only one of each of these three pairs of terms is a possible object of consciousness, there is no way in which such a correspondence could be established.

Santayana's attempt to tie the symbolic terms of perception to their putative objects thus fails on account of the impossibility of using the specious endeavor of a phenomenal body to fix in mind the movements of a substance. But in addition to this difficulty, Santayana's theory of perception suffers from another serious weakness. The complication to which I refer springs from his claim that any sensuous image which fills the mind when the body reacts to a substance is adequate to express that reaction and to signal the presence of an alien force.[58] But any sensation that expresses some actual relation in which an object stands to the self is said to be true of that object.[59] An immediate consequence of this view is that perceptual error is limited to total delusion. "An animal vision of the universe is . . . never false"[60]: so long as there is some object which confronts the self on the plane of action, it is impossible to attach an essence to it which will not yield a true description. A perceptual judgment can be false only

[58] "Unknowable," p. 181.
[59] *SAF*, p. 180.
[60] *RT*, p. 50.

if its constituent essences have been bred spontaneously in the psyche, viz., if their presence in intuition is not causally tied to immediately preceding motions in external substance.

Now it may well be true that the presence of material things is open to the test of action: what we can or cannot do is often adequate indication of the existence of substances in our environment. The way to find out about what appears to be water in the desert is to try to drink it, and it is reasonable to be sceptical about the existence of pink rats which cannot be touched or caught or caged till a sober morning. But this by itself is not enough to establish Santayana's position, which remains open to two serious objections. First of all, it seems wrong to insist that no perception that has an object may be in error. The truth, borne out by the common and correct distinction between error and delusion, appears to be the very opposite. Since error is failure in rendering the nature or properties of some existing thing, only perceptions which have such objects may be liable to it. Secondly, it is unfortunate to suppose that, given an external object, any essence is as good as any other to characterize it. In addition to being counter-intuitive and abolishing the well-established difference between the more and the less accurate in the realm of sense-experience, the view that all the perceptions of an object are equally veridical leads to one or another of two conclusions. The first is that physical objects possess no properties other than those attributed to them by the senses; perceptions are true of objects because they or their components constitute them. The second is that each perception is relative to the position and predicament of a percipient animal; as such, it yields knowledge only of some of the relational properties, but none of the hidden core characteristics, of its substantial object. The first conclusion tends to undercut Santayana's realism; the second moves from total perceptual relativism to scepticism about the power of the senses to give knowledge of reality. Both, therefore, are evidently incompatible with Santayana's views: they are also objectionable on independent grounds.

Santayana may try to avoid the first objection by claiming that action is a test not only of the presence, but also of the dynamic properties of perceived objects. This, however, will not work.

The dynamic properties of substance are potentialities or dispositions which, in the nature of the case, cannot be perceived. A disposition is not the sort of thing that is sensed or experienced or encountered: it is, rather, suspected or posited or inferred. We usually take the presence of a certain group of sensible qualities as evidence of the existence of a certain disposition in an object. When the evidence is adequate and the object actually has such a disposition, our inference is warranted and our belief is true. But this conviction, although based on perceptions, is not itself a perceptual belief. An invalid inference from sensible qualities to disposition does not turn the consciousness of those sensible qualities into an erroneous perception of the disposition, for the simple reason that they were not a perception of it in the first place. To perceive the dynamic properties of substance is impossible in the same way and for the same general sort of reasons as it is impossible to walk or sneeze or store a jump. Since no such perceptions can exist, it is absurd to invoke them in the attempt to expand the class of perceptions which may be erroneous.

In answer to the second objection, Santayana introduces his theory of the degrees of knowledge.[61] He appears to be of the opinion that we can avoid the view that all the perceptions evoked in the presence of a substance are equally veridical by arranging our perceptual experiences in a hierarchy of greater and lesser adequacy. There seem to be two independent measures of the adequacy of perceptions. Both of them measure the magnitude of the segment of the realm of truth reproduced in a given experience. The first concentrates on the range of truth encompassed: the wider the context of "substantive being" in which the perception places its material object, the truer the perception will be. The second gauges the articulateness of the essences intuited: the more richly developed and minutely specific the essences, the truer the perception will be. A view of Monticello from a high flying airplane may give us range without much articulateness: the house is seen in its relation to a large number of other physical objects, but most of the details of all of them are missing. A close-up picture of my right thumb, by contrast, may yield minute articulateness with not a great deal of range: the pattern of lines

61 "Unknowable," p. 181.

detected is richly elaborate, but the breadth of "substantive be-ing" encompassed is negligible. Most of what I have said so far is a development of mere hints in Santayana: how he would rate the relative weights of the two criteria, however, is an issue about which I cannot even hazard a guess. All one can say is that the measures are additive: any perception which has both range and articulateness is more adequate than a perception which has one of them only, and any perception which has one of them is more adequate than a perception which has neither.

I am afraid these criteria, no matter how far or how well they may be developed, cannot remove the grounds for my second ob-jection. It is only by a subtle, and perhaps unintentional, slip that Santayana may speak of perceptions as being more or less true.[62] On his own view truth is not a matter of degree: any judgment which repeats a part, no matter how small or large, of the stand-ard comprehensive description of a fact is true, and any judgment which contradicts a part is false.[63] For this reason, range and ar-ticulateness cannot measure how true our perceptions are, but at best how much of the truth (standard comprehensive description) about a fact they reproduce. They are thus gauges of the informa-tion content of our perceptions. But it is evident that truth and information content vary independently: the richest perceptions and the most articulate judgments may be false, while many true perceptions remain stark and unadorned. It is not open to Santa-yana, therefore, to argue that his two suggested criteria suffice to avoid the unwelcome consequences of the view that all percep-tions which have objects are equally veridical. The criteria do not measure the accuracy of perceptions: the adequacy they do meas-ure is not that of the perception to its object, but of the intuition to the total truth about the fact upon which intent directs it. And that the accuracy of a perception has no significant correlation with the amount of information it conveys should be evident to anyone who wishes to invest a few minutes of his time in reflec-tion on this topic.

There are two additional points that need to be made here. The first is that there seems to be an element of absurdity in the at-

62 *Ibid.*, pp. 181-182.
63 *SAF*, p. 267.

tempt to hinge the accuracy of sense-experience on the complexity of the essences which appear in consciousness. I am reasonably certain that whatever absurdity there may be here was unintended, and remained undetected, by Santayana. The reason for this is that his mind, moving in a characteristically intuitive and verbal medium, has probably never worked out the discursive details of his position. The combination of imaginative sweep and relative carelessness about detail is frequent, and perhaps unavoidable, in synthetic thinkers whose first goal is a vision of the world.

The second point is that as far as internal elaboration is concerned, I can see little difference between such perceptions as that of Monticello from an airplane and such as that of my right thumb from a distance of two inches. The essences intuited appear in both cases to be vastly complex: there seems, in fact, to be no ready way of determining which of the two has more components or is more articulate. Nor is it possible to decide, on the basis of the perceptions alone, which of the two encompasses a greater range of "substantive being." The difficulty which arises from this is the following. The criteria of range and articulateness are meant to be ways in which the adequacy of a perception may be measured by reference to the essences present in sense-awareness alone. However, the articulateness of the essences frequently does not reflect the complexity of the physical objects they report, and the range of substantive being encompassed cannot be known by a study of essences only. For this reason, range and articulation cannot function as epistemic measures of the adequacy of perceptions. We can use them to gauge the adequacy of a perception only if we have more information than that perception, or any group of perceptions, can provide. To know if the articulateness of our essences is relevant to judging the adequacy of sense-experience, we must know the articulations of substance. And to know the range of substantive being our essences depict, we must have independent information about the landscape of ambient substance. I need hardly remind the reader that Santayana himself maintains that neither one of these requirements can in fact be met.

This last point leads me to what I think is Santayana's only possible defense against the sort of difficulty I have been urging.

Most or all of my objections, he might argue, are subjectivist in nature: they are based on the anomalies of the private knowledge-situation. But he condemned and abandoned the attempt to do epistemology by beginning with the knower and his ideas when he condemned and abandoned systematic scepticism. His interest, Santayana might continue, was in founding his epistemology on ontology, and not vice versa: he wished to begin with a world populated by animals engaged in dodging, fighting, and eating one another. He framed all his theories, and hence also his theory of knowledge, by viewing active beings in a moving flux from the standpoint of an objective observer. How they perceive and know was sketched as if it were a story told by an omniscient third person, or a report of his findings by a biologist. Objections, Santayana might conclude, which are based on the peculiarities of the epistemic situation or on the difficulties of the egocentric predicament are, therefore, irrelevant to his account of knowledge and perception.

The final judgment of the adequacy of this defense must rest with the reader. If the reader agrees that my objections are based on peculiarities of the egocentric predicament, he must decide whether or not he thinks it possible and legitimate to found epistemology on ontology, and to treat the subject-matter of the theory of knowledge with the same objectivity with which we can treat the objects and processes of biology. Whatever the reader's convictions on this account, I cannot forego the remark that Santayana himself appears more deeply committed to a subjectivist (or at least a "privatist") emphasis than he would, at times, like to admit. He holds, after all, that intuitions, the ultimate units of cognition, are the invisible fruition of life. They cannot be observed as essences are observed, and they cannot be encountered as natural objects are encountered[64]; they are not even events after the fashion of natural events.[65] These undetectable, evanescent moments of consciousness constitute our being as minds. Privacy and total isolation are thus the burden not only of each mind, but of each separate intuition; and it is with these intui-

[64] *Ibid.*, p. 274.
[65] George Santayana, "Some Meanings of the Word 'Is'," *Obiter Scripta, loc. cit.*, p. 208.

tions and the panorama of essences open to them that our account of knowledge must begin. It seems, therefore, that Santayana is no less pledged to the "modern" subjectivism, which takes as the ultimate data for its theories whatever private consciousness reveals, than he is dedicated to the task of resuscitating the sound naturalism of the Ancients. If his philosophy fails at this point, its ill success is due to precisely this attempt, arduous but perhaps unavoidable, to marry Cartesian commitment to the inner life to Aristotelian insistence on the primacy of nature, and to see the world as an amalgam of public substances and unapproachable mind.

V

Our discussion has now come full circle, and we are in a position to answer the question with which we began. What sort of proof does Santayana propose to give of realism? It is evident that by "proof" he means the provision neither of compelling arguments nor of overwhelming empirical evidence. His view is that no arguments are so compelling as to withstand the onslaught of scepticism, and that philosophical theses cannot be confirmed by observation. What Santayana wishes to show is not that realism is absolutely or demonstrably right, but that it is among the theories animal faith reinstates after sceptical doubt has been abandoned as self-stultifying. The object, thus, is to exhibit that realism is a tenet of animal faith. The method of proof must, therefore, take the form of showing that realistic knowledge is implicated in action. And this in fact is what Santayana attempts to do in the first and most important of his three proofs of realism. This "biological" proof consists in showing that pursuit and flight, animal desire, and intelligent action all involve realistic, viz., transitive and relevant, knowledge of a moving environment.[66] The knowledge is transitive, because its objects exist independently of it in the physical flux: otherwise action on them would be impossible. The knowledge is relevant, because appearance cannot leave us entirely without a clue as to the nature of

66 "Three Proofs," p. 172 [pp. 179-180, above].

surrounding substance: otherwise successful action would be impossible. The animal engaged in the business of life naturally believes, or acts as if he believed, in the existence of a knowable external world: to show that realism is such a "natural opinion" implicated in action is all the proof an honest philosophy can or need give of it.

The second proof is a characteristically Santayanan attempt to show that critics have succeeded in the verbal denial of realism only: realistic commitments and distinctions inevitably reappear in their rival theories. The modern denial of realistic knowledge in the physical sphere, Santayana argues, was possible only on the assumption of it in the psychological realm of minds and their ideas. Even those who wish to maintain that a changeless Absolute Spirit is the only reality must make room for a world in which action and transitive knowledge are possible.[67] This proof is clearly ancillary to the first one: its function is not to show that realism is a tenet of animal faith, but to buttress the biological proof, and perhaps to secure its flanks, by the capsule demonstration that the facts of practical life and the tenets of animal faith permeate even the theories specifically designed to prove them illusory. To prove a proposition p in this context, then, is not to exhibit that the truth of p is implicated in action, but to display that if p is a corollary of action, it will be inevitably present in any theory which can lay the least claim to plausibility or adequacy. The proposition may appear in many guises: it may be denied in its usual formulations while it is affirmed in uncommon language, or it may be overtly rejected while it is covertly unwittingly embraced. But, Santayana believes, in one way or another the proposition must be present in or implied by every theory: that knowledge is transitive, for example, is a view to which each philosopher is unavoidably committed by the claim that his theories are true of a world they did not create. The latent materialism of idealists may thus be supplemented by their latent realism, and we see at once that, for Santayana, every philosophy, with the exception of total scepticism, consists of the same hard core of honest beliefs, along with varying amounts of verbiage and dross.

Santayana's third proof is an attempt to show, by a method not

[67] *Ibid.*, p. 176.

unlike phenomenological reduction, that the immediate objects of thought are universals of mind-independent status. Since the realism he wishes to prove there differs from the one which has been my topic, I shall not spend time on it now. Instead, I shall sum up by remarking that it should now be clear why Santayana ends his essay with the admission that his proofs are not compelling to sceptics or idealists.[68] Scepticism is an irrefutable position, and it is always open to the idealist to suspend the hard facts of practical life in a solvent of what Santayana preferred to call "egotistical" theories. To the "honest" man, who wishes his philosophy to accord with his daily practice, scepticism has always been a forced pose, and idealism will always remain an implausible construction. His "natural opinions" which, though logically indefensible, are "honestly expressive of action"[69] make him a realist in epistemology, as they make him a materialist in metaphysics. His "belief in nature, with a little experience and good sense to fill in the picture, is almost enough by way of belief. Nor can a man honestly believe less."[70]

It is very difficult to disagree with Santayana on this last point. To see the spectacle of nature as a play of which spirit is the gay or bemused spectator[71] is not without its attractiveness and satisfactions. To see ourselves as parts of a great flux whose ways we vaguely trace in our terms is a condition of due measure and fit modesty in a human being. To admit that the mind is a weak, fitful beam in the encircling dark is sanity itself. In its inspiration and in its outlines Santayana's view is indubitably right: it is only when we begin to work out the details of his critical realism that severe problems arise. But here Santayana may at once reply that in philosophy no less than elsewhere, we may have to be satisfied with a general picture which furthers scope in contemplation and harmony in life. And in this contention he may well be right.

68 *Ibid.*, p. 184 [p. 189, above].
69 *SAF*, p. 308.
70 *Ibid.*, p. 308.
71 *Ibid.*, p. 274.

George Santayana's Theory of Knowledge

MARTEN TEN HOOR

I. THE LEAP OF INTUITION AND THE LEAP OF FAITH

By far the most complete and important statement of Mr. Santayana's epistemological beliefs is contained in his recent essay, "Three Proofs of Realism."[1] The principal distinction made here is that which critical realists claim as their particular contribution. It might be described as an interposition of a transitive medium between the idea and its object. The three persons of this epistemological trinity, then, are the external object; the symbol of this object actually given in sense or in thought, that is, the datum; and the mental state of awareness or consciousness of this sense-datum, what might be paraphrased as the appreciation of it. It is obvious that the naïve realistic definition of knowledge as the direct intuition of the object is insufficient and quite unsuited to explain this process. In a certain sense, the ultimate conclusion is the same, namely, that external realities exist independently of thought and that such existence can be defended and satisfactorily explained; and it must also be apparent that the ultimate ground of critical realism suggests quite the same confidence in such independent existence. The difference is principally one of technique: the two views differ in their explanations of the knowledge process; critical realism, as the name implies, claims to be less intuitive and more critical in its exposition. Whereas naïve realism feels that we cross the chasm between idea and object in one leap, the critical realist has not this high acrobatic confidence and feels the need of an extra leap. "Transitiveness in knowledge," says Santa-

Marten ten Hoor, "George Santayana's Theory of Knowledge," *The Journal of Philosophy*, 20 (1923), pp. 197-211. Reprinted by permission.

[1] In *Essays in Critical Realism* [pp. 171-189, above].

yana, "has two stages or leaps: the leap of intuition, from the state of the living organism to the consciousness of some essence; and the leap of faith or action, from the symbol actually given in sense or in thought to some ulterior existing object."[2] The first problem suggested here concerns the definition of these two stages or leaps, which in turn implies a clear conception of the respective points of departure and arrival. The second question is the more fundamental one, to wit, whether the description of the knowledge process as developed by Santayana makes necessary and inevitable the assumption that external facts exist independently of experience.

Viewed from the standpoint which Santayana assumes, the transitiveness of knowledge involves both the identification and the independence of substance and appearance. They are independent only in an abstract sense; since the world is what it is, it is apparent that the genesis of appearance had to follow from the nature of substance. To express this in his own terminology, the flux of appearance, the Personal Flux, which is the flux of mind, was bound to arise in the Absolute Flux, the flux of nature. It is evident that Santayana does not mean here that the Personal Flux is a part of the Absolute Flux in an idealistic or pantheistic sense. He says clearly on page 167 of this essay that appearance arose as a result of "changes of structure," which can mean nothing else but that the flux of appearance is merely a phase of the flux of nature. Now how does this "appearance" differ from "change"? And what is the exact relation involved? "Appearance" is merely a particular form of change which we describe as "mind." Just as a mind is born in a baby, so appearance is the product of changes of structure in the world. Now it is to be noted here that already in the external world change is distinguished from structure, even as the mind is distinguished from the body. Change is ascribed to reality. In the individual mind we find merely a phase of it. Behind change in the Absolute Flux there is substance.

It follows, then, that appearance and substance can not be existentially identified, even if they "exist" in the same world. Identification is here a matter of essence, not existence. ". . . it is not his knowledge or his mind that the naïve realist identifies with

2 *Idem,* p. 183 [pp. 188-189, above].

the object, but only the essence immediately intuited by him that he identifies with its essence."[3] This can mean nothing other than that here we must distinguish two "essences," an essence intuited and an essence embodied. Santayana explains this further: "It [the essence] may now have the ideal status of an object of intuition and again the material status of the form of a thing." In a footnote he defines essence as "a universal, of any degree or complexity which may be given immediately, whether to sense or to thought."[4] The issue now becomes clear. Since knowledge is always a "salutation" and never an "embrace," the essence as intuited by thought can not be existentially identified with the object. Since an "essence can also be given immediately to sense," the same reservation must be made here. In what sense, then, can an "essence," a universal, be embodied in an object? It must be apparent that the term "embodies" can mean nothing except "ascribed to," and then it follows that our concern is with appearance and not with substance. To "ascribe to" for the critical realist can mean nothing else but that an idea is referred to a datum, and then the problem of knowledge is merely a matter of discovering the connection between "ideas" and "data," between thought and appearance rather than between appearance and substance.

But Santayana does not mean to have the transitiveness of knowledge thus limited and he meets this objection by insisting that both transcendence and relevance establish the truth of the realistic assumption. He acknowledges, however, that these are *"instinctive* assumptions necessary to the validity of knowledge."[5] Transcendence, for example, can mean nothing if the thinker can not escape from the subjective circle of his opinions. If knowledge does not refer to something outside of itself, it can be nothing but an idle dream. Nor could it be relevant. It is interesting to note here that for the moment one instance of escape from subjectivity, the distinction between idea and datum, is lost sight of. This kind of transitiveness is not sufficient, although even Santayana does

---

[3] *Idem*, p. 167 [p. 175, above].

[4] *Idem*, p. 168 [p. 175, above].

[5] *Idem*, p. 168 [p. 176, above].

not deny that all our knowledge of the sensible world is given to us in terms of "sense data."

This sudden extension of transcendence to something beyond the sense data is most clearly brought out in the distinction made by Santayana between concretions in discourse and concretions in existence. Instead of the qualities of an object being derived from an actually conceived object, the object is constructed out of concretions in discourse, that is, out of universals derived from repeated sensations. These universals are frankly recognized as ideas, for in *Reason in Science* they are referred to as "imposing upon the flux . . . what we call ideas . . . terms employed in thought and language."[6] Then "concretions in existence," which are combinations of such universals, are seen to represent external and independent existences. And on what grounds? Some answer is contained in the assertion that a "permanent sensation helps to disclose a permanent object."[7] Now, first of all, by the very definition of the flux, no sensation is permanent and certainly is never assigned permanent existence in the outside world. The confusion here results from the persistent "instinctive assumption" referred to above: the terms "datum" and "object" are identified with the persistence of a naïve realist. This same confusion of terms is implied in the statement, "Existence reveals reality when the flux discloses something permanent that dominates it."[8] Should not this be revised to read: *"Experience* reveals reality when the flux discloses something permanent which dominates it"? In short, what Santayana sets out to prove, it seems to me, is persistently assumed as already proved.

A particularly suggestive discussion of the datum, the middle term of Santayana's epistemological trinity, is contained in the aforementioned essay. The datum is here defined as purely mental: ". . . the datum lies wholly in its own category."[9] It is an object of immediate intuition "without conditions, seat, or environment."[10] Existence can not be predicated of it in the sense

6 *Reason in Science*, p. 28.
7 *Reason in Common Sense*, p. 130.
8 *Idem*, p. 130.
9 "Three Proofs of Realism," p. 179 [p. 185, above].
10 *Idem*, p. 179 [p. 186, above].

that existence is predicated of material things. Nor is it a state of mind. It is an *ideal essence*. It is this essence which is intuited and it is this intuition which makes ideal contemplation thoroughly realistic.

Now there are several interesting points to be noted here. First of all, the term "realistic" is given an unusual connotation, for no "real" reality is intuited; no object is intuited, only an ideal essence. Such a realistic conception might very well be accepted by the idealists. Secondly, just what are we to understand by this "essence" which is used synonymously with "datum"? It is ideal, therefore it is no object of experience as such, but merely an object of thought. Is it a concretion in discourse or a condition of such a concretion? It must be more than a mere sense-datum to be a concretion, for genetically, a concretion is something having ideal permanence, evolved from the flux of appearance, that is, from a series of sensations; and an essence is defined as being a universal. Is there then a fourth term, the sense-datum which is referred to an "essence" before it is intuited, that is, given dignity as a valid bit of knowledge? This is unlikely in view of the assertion that we are concerned here merely with "the leap of intuition, from the state of a living organism to the consciousness of some essence."

The term "state of a living organism" can not very well be interpreted genetically and psychologically as referring to an organic disturbance which somehow ends in the first stage of knowledge, namely, the consciousness of some essence, in accordance with the accepted psychological explanation that the process goes from sensation to perception. I take this to mean that ideas or essences are generated automatically in the flux of the mind, that is, that they are products of organic processes and only in the second instance become objects of thought. Santayana's deep-rooted objection to interactionism and his frankly avowed epiphenomenalism would seem to forbid any compromise at this point. Although knowledge is presently to be applicable piecemeal in a world of independent objects, its origin is not to be found there except in a very vague sense, namely, that it is a phase of the flux. As a process it belongs there, but its materials are self-generated. For Santayana, to account for knowledge existentially in terms of its working materials would mean to hypostatize them, that is, to ascribe vulgar existence to what is only ideal.

Now up to this point it must be evident that Santayana is a frank subjectivist. Genetically, ideas come from within. Yet they have mental momentum and because of this, which Santayana names "intent," the ideas escape from these apparent limitations and become ideally relevant in a world of external things, that is, of actual material existences. They do not leave the mind and take up residence there; they merely apply there. In short, their function is still ideal; they are true to their nativity. This leap is "the leap of faith and of action, from the symbol actually given in sense or in thought to some ulterior existing object."[11] "Self-existing things may become the chosen objects of a mind that identifies and indicates them."[12] Now it is to be remembered that this is no intra-mental relation between a particular appearance and a universal; here the reference is to an actual material existence. The arguments to be offered here may be summarized in the form of a question: How does mere mental reference of ideas to things establish the external existence of things? The answer is that existence is not established, but implied. To this we may offer the objection: What proof is there to offer in support of an assertion that an idea of which I am aware refers to an object, the notion of the existence of which is nothing more than an awareness of the same kind, a concretion in existence, a mental product of the psychic flux? Since essences developed independently of existences, why are existences implied in them? In short, the genetic independence of ideas and essences from external existences would seem to have established their self-sufficiency once for all. Had external objects been the cause of the genesis of essences, the latter might properly be referred back to their causes. This the critical realist of the type of Santayana can not allow because such an admission would vitiate the value and import of his epiphenomenalism. Thought must at all costs be saved from mechanism and materialism.

Santayana himself is fully aware of the fact that the real issue becomes clear at this point, even though he asserts that the first

11 *Idem*, p. 183 [pp. 188-189, above].
12 *Idem*, p. 168 [p. 176, above].

step discussed above is "primary and fundamental for knowledge."[13] He agrees in the concluding sentences of the essay that the reality of an external world, independent of experience, is in the first place an assumption, and that all proofs of realism have value only in so far as they "require and fortify" this assumption. For example: the meaning of biology disappears if we deny that organic sensations point to external things. Why isn't the child satisfied with his "sensations" of the moon if there is no real moon, he asks. First of all, this is dodging the issue. The point is not what the moon really is, but what for the child constitutes the existence of the moon. Does the child know the moon at all except in terms of his own experience of it, in terms of his own knowledge of it? Does he ever get beyond his data? Are not his organic sensations data? His experience is realistic, as Santayana himself agrees, in so far as he intuits his data, but in what other sense can it be realistic?

The logical proof advanced in this essay establishes nothing more than this intuitional character or quality of knowledge. "Events are instinctively assumed . . . but only qualities are given absolutely." Then comes the real proof. Since existence can not be ascribed to essences, it follows that "the sort of being which essences have is indefeasible: they can not lose it or change it, as things do and must if their being is existence, . . . therefore, intuition, or pure acquaintance with data, has an object whose whole reality is independent of such a perusal of it."[14] The essences, too, therefore, are independent of their being intuited. We have, then, this interesting situation. Essences are intuited, but they have independent "ideal" existence. They exist in an independent logical sphere. They become objects of intuition by accident, "consequently, knowledge of essence is transitive."[15] Now no idealist would especially quarrel with the antecedent of this statement, but the acceptance of the consequent would certainly hinge on further proof. If the second leap of intuition is from this ideal realm to the physical world, how is it accomplished? Some transformation certainly must be involved. What Santayana has

[13] *Idem,* p. 183 [p. 189, above].
[14] *Idem,* p. 181 [p. 187, above].
[15] *Idem,* p. 183 [p. 189, above].

in mind here is suggested by his description of the second leap: ". . . the leap of faith and of action from the symbol actually given in sense or in thought to some ulterior existing object."[16] Here then the leap is not ideal. It is not from a "state" to a "consciousness of some essence," but a leap from a "symbol" to an "object." Here the leap becomes truly realistic. This leap could be realistic even if there were no real external bodies, for, says Santayana, an image would have real existence if there were no external bodies, for then *it* would be the object. Now what is the situation? If symbols were "real" there would be nothing to leap to mechanistically, and if symbols are not "real" there would be nothing to leap from, mechanistically. Since Santayana himself denies thought a mechanistic character, this leap must be ideal and then it certainly could not actually reach an object. The relation would always be saltatory, as the pragmatists say.

The conclusion is evident. The assumption of the external world is gratuitous and the real end of the knowledge process is the datum which has purely ideal existence. To insist that thought would be pointless, and would devour itself, is not apropos, for Santayana himself carefully distinguishes the act of awareness from the data or essence.

The "psychological proof" acknowledges the intuitional character of the first leap and only *assumes* the existence of bodies, but does not prove their existence or establish the necessity of the assumption. Why the idealist must give up his sense of time because he refuses to accept external existence, as Santayana argues in this essay, has point only if a purely ideal appreciation of time is denied. Yet this is already implied in Santayana's conception of the flux of appearance.

Before leaving this phase of the discussion it may be interesting to examine Santayana's description of the acrobatics of thought from a more literal point of view. He himself finds in realism the freshness and sanity of scholastic common-sense. To ask whether his own logic reveals this is therefore quite apropos. His summary of his theory of knowledge in the essay referred to above is as follows: "Transitiveness in knowledge has two stages or leaps: the leap of intuition, from the state of the living organism to the

16 *Idem* [pp. 188-189, above].

consciousness of some essence; and the leap of faith and of action, from the symbol actually given in sense or in thought to some ulterior object."[17] It has already been pointed out above that there is no evident connection between these two leaps. It will suffice here to call particular attention to the terms of these two propositions.

The leap from "a state of the living organism to the consciousness of some essence" may be considered a leap from one "state" to another. Although to call this a leap is somewhat of a rhetorical exaggeration—for what happens here is merely a change of one state of the organism into another, that is, a continuous process—the sudden transition in terms to a "symbol" from which the leap is made to an object must appear rather unexpected. There is no better illustration to be found in Santayana's writings of the logical breach between these two steps in the knowledge process. Certainly, the last named can not in any such way be logically connected with the first. The failure to explain satisfactorily the knowledge process by means of a succession of leaps, over or through a transitive medium, would seem to suggest that critical realism is not yet "critical" enough.

II. RELEVANCE AND TRUTH

The first part of this paper attempted to examine critically the mechanics of the knowledge process as outlined and defended by Santayana. At this point we are naturally led to a more careful examination of Santayana's conception of relevance and truth. It must be remembered that for Santayana "consciousness is an attitude which the body assumes and which supervenes upon the body's elements and can not be contained within them."[18] The basis of mind "lies in the body's interest rather than in its atoms." The metaphysical implications of these assertions will not be discussed here. What concerns us here is how thought comes to apply, how it becomes relevant, and in what its validity consists.

According to Santayana, it is "intent" which gives meaning to

17 *Idem*, p. 183 [pp. 188-189, above].
18 *Reason in Science*, p. 148.

thought, it is "intent" which makes thought cognitive and practical. Now intent can not be finally explained and must be accepted as a mystery in the same sense that we must accept the flow of water and the gravitation of bodies. It is not a mechanical force, but an ideal pointing. By virtue of language, which is "an overflow of the physical basis of thought," thought becomes a power in the very world from which it drew its being, and the cry of reason to be reunited with the world is answered. An examination of intent reveals essences to us, what *is* rather than what happens. Since thought is ideally relevant only, it can not be practical in a mechanistic way.

It will be seen from the above brief paraphrase of Santayana's conception of intent that intent bridges the chasm between symbol and object, between datum and external thing, for by virtue of it thought becomes cognitive and practical. Intent is the stick by means of which the critical realist makes his second leap. Suffice it to say here that since this has already been denominated a leap of faith, no such rationalistic assistance is necessary. The insistence upon the epiphenomenalistic conception drives thought out of the very world from which it is derived, and intent is a confession of that. In this doctrine of intent, which is meaningless if taken realistically as Santayana would have us do, intent can have no meaning outside of the ideal realm of essences, in which case it is truly not practical in a mechanistic sense. But when it is embodied in language and thus made an agent in the physical world, its purely ideal character is denied and it becomes vulgarly mechanistic. To object that thought "supervenes" and that "language is merely an overflow of the physical basis of thought" does not destroy the power of ideas expressed in words. This doctrine is very evidently a compromise. Intent rescues the ideal character of thought; language saves its practical potency in the world. Intent bridges the chasm between datum and object, but only at the cost of the ideality of thought and the "saltatory" relation. Thought no longer "points," but it strikes out and by impact makes the wheels go 'round.

With this conflict clearly in evidence, let us examine what Santayana understands by truth and by the validity of thought. His final definition of the function of thought is very significant because it points much more clearly than does his epistemological doctrine to the general point of view which he represents. This is summarized in the assertion, "Thought organizes itself, not the world." The mind, then, has its own life, independent of external realities. This seems to fit well with the converse of this statement —that external realities have their own life independent of mind. But there are far more general assumptions contained in the first than in the second. The *Life of Reason* is a "biography of human reason," not of human life.

A preliminary question which might well be asked here is this: What is the exact relation between this activity of thought, which is refinement of the Immediate Flux, and the Absolute Flux, the great mechanistic "parade of earth and sky"? What part does the Life of Reason play in the greater life of the universe? Santayana's general contention is that thought supervenes on bodily processes, and that in it ideal form is given to the chaotic flux: moments are fixed, essences are developed, purposes are discerned. There is here a definite ideal or psychic realm, which has its own movement, its own purposes, its own directions. The analysis of this life and the discovery of its direction is the business of dialectic.

Now this explanation is complete in itself and could not be well attacked were it not for the fact that Santayana also recognizes a realm of physics next to the realm of discourse, and this realm of physics reveals an empirical validity in thought in addition to the logical validity which holds good in the realm of discourse. Science may be said to be accurate if it correctly reports the direction of the flux in nature. "Its validity is of the same order as that of ordinary perception, memory, and understanding. Its test is found, like theirs, in ordinary intuition."[19] But "science follows the movement of its subject matter . . . ; . . . it verifies and solves inference by reaching the fact inferred."[20] Now it has been pointed out above that this term, "intuition," can correctly describe only the transition from a state of mind to an act of consciousness, to an awareness of an essence; that is, it reports only the act of the mind in appropriating the contents of the Immediate Flux. As such, validity can mean nothing more than "ideal

[19] *Idem*, p. 37.
[20] *Idem*, p. 15.

relevance," the agreement, not of thought with reality in the realistic sense, but of certain refinements of thought with' the flux of raw materials. Santayana himself well expresses this: "Reason must be practical, that is, it must fit experience. . . . Speculative reason, if it is not practical, is not reason at all."[21] The distinction implied, then, is between two phases of the psychic flux, not between a phase of the flux of mind, and a phase of the supposedly external and independent flux of nature. The confidence—one might almost say, naïveté—with which Santayana accepts the realistic hypothesis and thus thinks to save the "empirical validity" of thought is clearly brought out in statements such as these: "Logical methods of comprehension must prove themselves fitted to the natural order and affinity of facts. This natural order and affinity is something imputed to the ultimate object of thought—the reality—by the last act of judgment assuming its own truth."[22] It is quite apropos to raise the question here: By what is this "last act of judgment" guided in this assumption? How does it come to accept certain constructs of the reason as true and others as purely speculative? In other words, does this ultimate reality play any part here except that of an innocent victim of hypostasis?

If it has been demonstrated that there is here no such thing as empirical validity if validity is to be taken in a realistic and representative sense, there remains nothing but logical validity. This kind of validity, then, is just as applicable to ideals as to facts in Santayana's system, and rightly so. That these two kinds of validity are but varieties of simple intuition is proved by this quotation: "Its [science's] test is found, like theirs, [i.e., perception, memory, and understanding] in *actual intuition*, which sometimes consists in perception and sometimes in intent."[23] Ideals are true when they correctly present the native direction of mind, that is, when they truly express intent; as such, "the Life of Reason gives preference a direction."[24] But this direction is purely "ideal; . . . only by virtue of a false perspective do ideas seem to govern action." The mind seeks not to control life but to "perfect its own

21 *Reason in Common Sense*, p. 176.
22 *Idem*, pp. 180-181.
23 *Reason in Science*, p. 37.
24 *Reason in Society*, p. 151.

existence." In the ideal realm, then, as in the realm of physics, thought reports the flux and as such contributes its bit to the establishment of the end of human life, equilibrium.

The insistence upon this ideality of the reason and upon its mechanical or practical inefficacy is so frequently affirmed that occasional suggestions of a more pragmatic conception are somewhat a surprise. "Science gives the mind dominion over matter by discovering its form."[25] This might be interpreted as connoting ideal dominance, were it not for the fact that industrial art is defined as giving a "more propitious form to matter." Since the flux of nature was elsewhere defined as being a succession of forms, how can art of this kind which alters nature be said to be practically or mechanically ineffective? The objection is cleverly met in an article entitled, "The Efficacy of Thought."[26] Here Santayana's peculiar conception is thus formulated: "Thought might still be called efficacious in the only sense, not magical, in which its efficacy would be at all congruous with its intent, namely through the natural efficacy of the creature whose life it expressed."[27] That is to say, thought is efficacious only if it correctly reports efficacious action. Only the cerebral processes, however, are mechanically efficacious.

The first thing to be noted here is that Santayana himself hesitates to take the second leap discussed above, which would have to be a magical one in a truly mechanistic universe unless thought actually touched reality. Thought is merely the froth and foam on the surface of the flux. Although a part of nature, it is itself mechanically helpless. Secondly, it might be objected that Santayana fails to note that certain facts, true enough about thought in its genesis, are not true about thought in its maturity. Although action is purely instinctive in its first stages, a consciousness of its purpose makes it a power where it was a force. Ideas, in a certain sense, become directive in a mechanistic universe when they are conscious.

That Santayana himself accepts this view in his practical philosophy will be suggested by a consideration of his theory of art.

25 *Reason in Science*, p. 29.
26 *The Journal of Philosophy*, Vol. III, p. 410 [pp. 246-250, below].
27 *Idem*, p. 411 [p. 248, below].

An emphatic statement is the following: "Art is that element of the Life of Reason which consists in modifying its environment, the better to attain its end."[28] This is, of course, no contradiction of the thesis ascribed to Santayana if ideas are understood as having no influence in cerebral processes.

The strongest evidence of the naïveté of Santayana in the matter of his own views concerning the practical efficacy of the reason is the volume *Egotism in German Philosophy*. The central thesis of this work is that the transcendentalist vagaries and "visionary insolence" of German Idealism are to be held responsible for the war. The somewhat unusual course of reasoning followed in this volume is summarized in this statement: "Theories in their own ethical essence can have no influence on events. But the men who conceive and adopt a theory form, in doing so, certain habits of discrimination and of reaction to things. . . . The explicit theory, however, is a symbol and omen of their practical attitude."[29] Now what is meant here by reaction but practical activity following as a result of, and even controlled by, ideas?

If it is objected that "cerebral processes" were responsible and that ideas are merely the reports of these processes, why then blame German Idealism? If the cause was lack of organization of thought, that is, of the development of speculative ideals, then *they*, not cerebral processes, were responsible, and the Germans should be blamed for not developing better directive ideals. If not, they can be blamed for nothing more serious than their unwillingness to accept, let us say, critical realism.

In explanation of such instances of stupidity and obstinacy as this one asserted of the Germans, and of others of the same kind, Santayana suggests that the Reason, in the case of such apostasy, is lacking in docility: it is egotistical and therefore unreasonable. Since the reason is denied an active part in practical life and ascribed an "histrionic rôle" in its own sphere, its principal business is to discover and follow its cues. Only then can it hope to attain its part in the organic equilibrium.

But in what sense of the term must the reason be docile, and to what superior directing force? The most logical answer seems to

28 *Reason in Art*, pp. 16-17.
29 *Egotism in German Philosophy*, p. 162.

be contained in these words: "Theory must revert to the Immediate Flux for its sanction, whereas dialectic is a centrifugal emanation from existence and never returns to its point of origin."[30] It is clear, then, that the reason must be docile in two ways: First, in science or physics it must fit the facts as they appear in the flux. This is paraphrased by Santayana in an interestingly realistic way a few pages later: ". . . sense ought to correspond in articulation with the object to be represented."[31] The only meaning this can possibly have, however, follows from the interpretation of his epistemological position as outlined above, namely, that thought must be docile to the materials given it in the Immediate Flux rather than to the objects in the external world.

But the second kind of docility is not so clearly explained. In dialectic it is the "ideal" value of the ideas that counts, and it is the purpose of science in these fields to discover "how things hang together perspicuously and how the later phases of any process fill out—as in good music—the tendency and promise of what went before."[32] Here, then, ideas must be docile to "intent," intent being here interpreted as the ideal direction which thought has, this direction being embodied in the speculations of the mind which disclose and elucidate values. This can not be checked up scientifically with such a definitely revealed process of the flux as mechanism, that is, in terms of fact, since our working materials here are meanings—purposes and values rather than essences—but it must be judged from the standpoint of the equilibrium of the mind. The "practical reason" then is docile in so far as it is guided by the ideal of the mind, harmony. In refusing to recognize this docility of thought, and in substituting for it egotistical phantasies, transcendentalism and its irrational offspring fail to live the "Life of Reason." Thought becomes even more irrational when it leaps beyond itself and hypostatizes these values. Thought in the realm of values becomes most truly docile when it is most frankly sophisticated.

It must be apparent from the above discussion that truth can not involve a transitive relation which shall extend beyond the

---

30 *Reason in Science*, p. 78.
31 *Idem*, p. 80.
32 *Idem*, p. 171.

datum, for both essences and purposes are intra-experientially derived and can be said to refer to external existences only by a leap of faith. Santayana implies this when he says: "For truth at the level at which it arises means not sensible fact but valid ideation, verified hypothesis, and inevitable stable inference."[33] Since the mind's interest is to perfect its own existence, its favorite themes are not the body's relations to nature, but its own notions; it prefers to be occupied with its own problems of synthesis. Synthesis, says Santayana, is the real problem, for "the thoughts of men are incredibly evanescent, merely the foam of their labouring natures."[34] We have here a definition of truth which at first glance seems definitely pragmatic: Where essences are concerned, ideation is valid if it fits the flux of perceptual experiences; where purposes are concerned, it is valid if it promotes the ultimate synthesis of meanings and values. Truth is truth if it fits the Immediate Flux and if it correctly reports the soul's constitution. It is pragmatically definable if we rule out interactionism and limit our pragmatic sanctions to purely ideal sanctions.

In this connection, note a definition of truth given in *Reason in Science*: "The hypostatized total of rational and just discourse is the truth. Its ideal consistency and permanence serve to make it a standard and background for fleeting assertion. Like the physical world, the truth is external and in the main potential. . . . What exists of truth in direct experience at any moment is infinitesimal, as what exists in nature is, but all that either contains might be represented in experience at one time or another."[35] What is here implied seems to be a thoroughly idealistic conception of truth, something which Santayana himself describes as having a "static ideal constitution." Such a constitution would include both "literal" truth, that is, ideally representative essences, and "symbolic" truth, ideally representative values, but in neither case could there or would there be any escape from the intramental, that is, from ideal existence. Here as everywhere in Santayana's writings, external existences are gratuitous.

In conclusion, it seems just to summarize the definition and

[33] *Reason in Common Sense,* p. 201.

[34] *Reason in Science,* p. 127.

[35] *Idem,* p. 182.

criticism of Santayana's epistemological position in these statements. Thought is the progressive differentiation and organization of mental contents according to laws in the mind itself and
controlled by a vital directive force called intent, aiming at an
ultimate synthesis and equilibrium, which is the mind's contribution to the grand equilibrium of the organism. This is a long and
tedious process which might be summarized by the term "idealistic empiricism" as opposed to "idealistic absolutism." Although
there is change in the universe, this change in experience is frac-
tional, and behind and over all is truth, having a "static ideal
constitution," which can not be contained *in toto* in any one experience, but which is contained potentially in experience as a
whole. The realistic assumption of external realities must be
judged wholly gratuitous and this aspect of his thought denominated an epistemological affectation, for if we do not do so,
thought can be considered nothing but a well-intentioned but
helpless being imprisoned in a beautiful garden, whose only interest in life is to watch the course of the "real" world outside,
through the bars of its prison—a pathetic, pale, emaciated, and
bloodless ghost. Why the realist should be concerned about this
pathetic figure at all, since real life goes on so jollily and pleasantly outside, is a mystery. And, on the other hand, why this
pathetic figure should be so concerned about this gratuitous world
out there, a world of imagined and hypostatized reality, a figment
of an active brain, instead of being happy in this entrancing and
stimulating garden of thought, is quite as much a mystery. That
some kind of choice must be made is clear: either thought must
be released and allowed to rejoin the "real" world, or this world
must be shown to be an imaginative fiction and the heated fancy
freed from occupation and concern with it. That Santayana himself makes a very real choice, a choice which involves a virtual
confession of this epistemological affectation and a recantation
of faith, must, I think, be clear to any one who, during the reading of the brilliant volumes of *The Life of Reason,* has observed
the poet gradually turn his back upon the mechanistic and realistic universe—constructed with so much creaking of dialectical machinery—and finally take refuge in the platonic realms of "Ideal
Society."

Animal Faith: Practical and Visionary

GEORGE SANTAYANA

Serious ambiguities were introduced by psychologism and idealism into the language of modern philosophy, ambiguities for which social reformers like Marx are not responsible. What, for instance, is "materialism"? Does it mean the belief that things are just as they look, and that there is nothing invisible? Or does it mean, on the contrary, that things are temporary formations in an automatic flow of matter, and that our senses and our intellectual powers, themselves incidental to such formations give us relative and partial views of that cosmic process? It is this second assumption that is involved in action, in the arts, and in natural science. The impact or the attraction of matter from without provokes this assumption in all animals; and every success in science, art, or action confirms it. Matter, for such animal faith, is the dynamic element in things which renders them persistent, mutually influential, and inwardly fertile. Sceptical analysis may indeed reject the word "dynamic" and the word "things," as lending a false substantiality to the observability and order of phenomena. But the naturalist preserves the primal assumptions implied in being alive, such as that perception may be indicative, and action may be efficacious. He trusts that tolerably reliable world of which his body is an evident part and, for him, a constant but movable centre. His mind travels with his body, when he is awake: but when he dreams or is lost in thought, he seems to travel, carrying the sense of his body with him, into unrecoverable regions; and even in his waking hours it may be habitual with him not only to

George Santayana, "Animal Faith: Practical and Visionary," *Columbia Manuscript Collection*, XIV:3. © 1967 by Daniel Cory.

imagine many wonders he has never seen, but to conceive other worlds, above or below, before or after, the one in which he ordinarily moves. His animal faith may then become speculative, poetical, or religious; and nothing in his worldly experience can absolutely exclude the possible truth of those other visions, which he will then call revelations. But no sane spiritual life that he may develop can ever rescind that animal faith with which he first questioned and explored the world. Did he rescind this animal faith, and attribute all his discoveries to the groundless fertility of his absolute spirit, he would thereby condemn all his metaphysical beliefs also as spurious; and his whole existence would evaporate into the ignominious passions of a dream.

Substance Not Composed of "Data of Sense"

GEORGE SANTAYANA

That substance has an ultimate texture other than the data of animal sense appears in this: that these data are, even when reduced to *minima sensibilia,* products of organs and stimuli of a very complex structure: the elements of these cannot be those which, when in elaborate organic movement, they place before consciousness. The essence of a *minimum sensibile* might be identical with that of a material atom; but it is infinitely improbable that it should be so, save in the abstract characteristic of being an ultimate ingredient in something else.

George Santayana, "Substance Not Composed of 'Data of Sense'," *Columbia Manuscript Collection,* IX:14:II. © 1967 by Daniel Cory.

V

THE IMPOTENT MIND

Review of *The Life of Reason*

A. W. MOORE

In the addresses delivered last year at the many memorial celebrations of the late Herbert Spencer's life and work, there was one
very common theme: it was the anachronism of such an encyclo-
pedic program as Spencer attempted—an anachronism which even
the Hegelians of Spencer's day discovered in the similar ambition
of their master, and one, it was said, which Spencer would have
avoided had he possessed a larger historical knowledge and appreciation. And it was freely predicted that Spencer's attempt would
be the last of the kind to be seen for many generations.

In the face of the extended currency of such comment among
philosophers, to say nothing of the cynical attitude of scientists, it
must be as significant as it is interesting that one who can not be
suspected of any lack of large historical orientation—one, indeed, whose method is historical—deliberately, 'with malice afore-
thought,' sends through the press within a year a volume of what
may be called first principles, a philosophy of society, a philosophy
of religion, a philosophy of art and a philosophy of science.

A. W. Moore, "Review of *The Life of Reason*," *The Journal of Philosophy*,
3 (1906), pp. 211-214. Reprinted by permission.

To be sure, we are in the midst of a great revival of metaphysical interest. But the products of this revival thus far, as presented in the works of Mr. Bradley, Professor Royce, Professor Fullerton and Professor Taylor, have been in the main of the systematic formal type inevitable in abstract metaphysics. Professor Santayana's work, however, is of a different character. He is interested in tracing the effect of the method upon the content. He is concerned in showing the connection between the general conceptions of reality, truth and goodness and their conditions and effects in society, religion, art and science. In his own sentences, "The problem is to unite a trustworthy conception of the conditions under which man lives with an adequate conception of his interest"; again, "Starting with the immediate flux in which all objects and impulses are given, to describe the life of reason; that is, to note what facts and purposes seem to be primary, to show how the conception of nature and life gathers around them, and to point to the ideals of thought and action which are approached by the gradual mastering of experience by reason" (I., p. 32).

And Professor Santayana is fully aware of the proportions of his task. He hastens to nip in the bud any suspicion of quixotism by saying that such a program "would be beyond the powers of a writer in this age, either to execute or conceive, had not the Greeks drawn for us the outlines of an ideal culture at a time when life was simpler than at present and individual intelligence more resolute and free."

In general, of course, Professor Santayana's courageous attempt, as all others, must be justified by its fruits. But I can imagine it quite possible for him to say that such an attempt is not only justified but necessitated in advance by his very conception of the place of reason in experience. An inkling of this appears in the subtitle itself, the whole caption being "The Life of Reason, or the Phases of Human Progress." The implication is that the character and function of thought is to be discovered not by isolating it and attempting an analysis of it as 'pure' reason, but by observing reason at work in the world, catching it in the act, taking it in its context in the whole concrete stream of experience. The attempt to discover the nature of reason apart from its products leads to a monstrous misconception of it and the proposal to substitute this changeling for normal reason, for reason as it is in operation, is called "visionary insolence." "Retrospective self-consciousness is dearly bought if it inhibits the intellect and embarrasses the inferences which in its spontaneous operation it has known perfectly how to make" (I., p. 29). If, then, the nature of reason is to be discovered only by observing it at work in science, in religion, in art and in social organization, is it, after all, presumptuous to propose to describe the processes, the phenomena and the results in which the nature of reason, even for one proposing to give the most abstract account of it, must be revealed?

What, then, is the life of reason, or, conversely, what is the rôle of reason in life? The reviewer has to confess that in the end the answer does not appear so univocal as the introduction promises. The problem centers in the relation of reflection to impulse. In other words, in the sort of 'efficacy' ideals have. In the introduction ideals, ends, constructed in reflection, are apparently regarded as actually organizing the material of habit and instinct. Here reason is defined as 'efficacious reflection.' And the 'efficacy' here consists not merely in an 'added content' which it brings, but in the added *function* of control. Hence we read, "To the ideal function of envisaging the absent, memory and reflection will add . . . the practical function of modifying the future. Vital impulse, however, when it is *modified by* reflection and *veers* in sympathy with judgments pronounced on the past, is properly called reason" (I., p. 2). "The life of reason will, then, be a name for that part of experience which perceives and pursues ideals, all conduct *so controlled,* and all sense so interpreted as to perfect natural happiness" (p. 3). Again, "In the life of reason, as it were brought to perfection, intelligence would be the universal *method of practise* and its continual reward. All reflection would then be *applicable in action* and all actions fruitful in happiness" (p. 5, italics mine). Here we are very properly warned that this controlling, instrumental character of thought does not make it a mere means. It does not prevent its having an immediate value of its own. But though reason may in this sense be 'its own excuse for being,' yet in order to *be,* it must *do;* and its 'doing' is just the work of converting isolated impulses and instincts into a mutually stimulating and checking, i.e., controlled, system.

But when we reach the chapter on "How Thought is Practical," one is puzzled to find thought losing this character of control and becoming a mere 'expression,' 'effect,' 'register,' 'celebration' of 'mechanical,' 'material' activity, into which now all dynamic efficacy is transferred. We now read, "Thought is nature's concomitant expression or entelechy, never one of her instruments" (I., p. 223). "Consciousness itself is not dynamic. . . . It is merely an abstract name for the actuality of its random objects. All force, implication or direction inhere in the constitution of specific objects" (I., p. 220). "Preferences are in themselves, if the dynamic order alone be considered, works of supererogation, expressing force but not producing it, like a statue of Hercules" (p. 221). Yet near the close of this puzzling chapter we read that the function of thought is "to lend utility to its causes" (p. 233), which here are material. "It is potential energy *producing* life and becoming an actual appearance." Again, in Chapter XI, on "Conditions of the Ideal," "Reason and the ideal are not active forces, nor embodiment of passion at all" (p. 265). Yet on the same page, "This suggested peace (for the conflict of impulses) . . . is the ideal which *borrows its practical force* from the irrational impulses which it embodies" (italics mine).

It may be said that the mere appearance of a 'sense of value' in a process 'bestows utility,' simply by giving the process a limit, a *terminus ad quem*. But even so this involves some sort of reaction of this 'sense of value' upon the mechanism, otherwise why should the process not simply go on grinding out 'senses of value,' without using them as limits? It is Aristotle's problem of the unmoved mover.

This discrepancy, as it appears to the reviewer, can be charged to an oversight of the distinction between consciousness in general and reflective, cognitive consciousness. 'Consciousness,' 'thought,' 'mind,' 'reason,' are freely interchanged throughout the chapter. Recognizing that the 'sense of value' belongs to consciousness-mind, it is apparently inferred that this is *all* that belongs to it and that all dynamic efficacy must therefore be referred to material nature, of which thought is the mere 'symbol,' and which even "can hardly lie in the same plane of reality with the thought to which it appears" (p. 219). Value is obviously a category of conscious activity, and as immediate 'content' is perhaps not dynamic. But is it not just the business of reflection to convert this 'sense of value' into an ideal, an end? And as an ideal it surely must be regarded as dynamic in the sense of being an essential factor in a system conceived as 'dynamic.'

In its more general form this question which divides the first and the last four chapters of Volume I is, How can the ideal be both an 'expression' and a reconstruction of instinct and habit? How can it arise out of and yet be the standard for impulse? In logic it would be the old problem of universals. Now one of Professor Santayana's theses,—indeed, one might say, the fundamental one,—is that the ideal, whether in government, religion, ethics or art, must grow out of, must be an 'expression' of, impulse. The clearness and force of his exposition of the vanity of an absolute ideal given to the impulses from without could not be surpassed. "Demands could not be misdirected, goods could not be false, if the standard by which they are to be corrected were not constructed out of them" (p. 258). Again, "Whence fetch this seminal force and creative ideal? It must evidently lie already in the matter it is to organize. Otherwise it would have no affinity to that matter, no power over it, and no ideality or value in respect to the existences whose standard and goal it is to be" (III, p. 83). The ideal, then, must be an expression of the matter, in order that it may have enough 'affinity' with it to organize it; this despite what is said above about thought not lying in the same plane with its material.

Corresponding to these two conceptions of the ideal, the one as an 'expression,' the other as control, there are two conceptions of the 'matter' to be organized. Where the controlling, organizing character of the ideal is emphasized, as in the introduction and in Volume III, impulse, instinct, immediate flux, etc., constitute the 'matter.' But where the ideal is expounded as an 'expression' of impulse, the matter appears as 'physical,' as 'body,' in opposition to consciousness and as the latter's 'cause,'—and this, too, apparently in quite an ontological Cartesian sense. Indeed, the whole treatment of the distinction of mind and body is to the reviewer as equivocal as that of reflection. Sometimes the distinction appears to be a rational construction within a process of experience which can not be described as either or merely both (e. g., I, pp. 39, 234). But again, and perhaps oftener, 'matter' appears as an existential *prius,* as "the antecedent of human life" (II, p. 200) to which somehow "mind accrues."

The present writer is well aware of the enormous capacity of reviewers' quotations for misrepresentation. He is also aware that there are many passages which could be cited to show that what has been described as different and discrepant conceptions of reason and its place in experience, are simply two supplementary phases of one conception, namely, that reason is *both* an 'expression' and a control, and must be the one in order to be the other. However, the reviewer can only record his impression of ambiguity in the account as it stands . . .

The Efficacy of Thought

GEORGE SANTAYANA

Professor A. W. Moore, in his courteous review of my book on *The Life of Reason,*[1] has pointed out what he feels to be a discrepancy in my language, and perhaps a difficulty in the subject-matter itself, touching a point of very great importance. This point is the sense in which mental facts may be called influential, may have a function or power.

There are many possible readings of this problem, some of which may be distinguished as follows:

1. It is a function of thought to give an intrinsic value to the moment in which it occurs. Thought has an esthetic or ecstatic quality. This function, inefficacious as it is, would suffice to make thought the most important thing in the world.

George Santayana, "The Efficacy of Thought," *The Journal of Philosophy,* 3 (1906), pp. 410-412. Reprinted by permission.

[1] *The Journal of Philosophy,* Vol. III, No. 8 [pp. 241-246, above].

2. Thought has the power of asserting ideal verities; it has a contemplative and dialectical function. An ephemeral seraph, alone in the universe, might recite the multiplication table and die. His thought would have possessed two ideal functions, one beatifying, the other self-explicative or discursive.

3. Thought may have a transitive but merely cognitive function; it may represent, and mean to represent, some independent fact, as when I say to myself that Caesar died on the Ides of March. The eventual test of this truth, its consistency with other judgments, its prevalence, its destiny, or its being a thought that would subsist permanently in an organism usefully adapted to a special environment—all this does not enter into the cognitive pretensions of the thought. These are ideal; but as the truth of the thought hangs on the existence of the external fact to which it refers, its truth remains always an assumption from its own point of vantage; though a third person might perhaps have further means of deciding for himself whether that thought had been true or false.

4. Thought may have prophetic scope: it may foretell what is about to take place. This harmony, purely speculative in itself, would, if at all frequent, very much increase the inner wealth and dignity of thought mentioned in 1 and 3.

5. Mingled with prophecy may be desire; and if to confident prophecy and eager desire an eventual verification accrues, the result is a sense of power. Thought is then supposed to have brought about its own realization, and to be responsible for it. This felt efficacy is always moral, or rather magical. It is a power attributed to thought, in its ideal capacity and by virtue of its intent, to bring about what it calls for, as an incantation or an exorcism might do, through empty reaches of time and space.

6. Thought, taken as a psychological existence, might have a causal influence on a succeeding state of mind, quite apart from the ideal burden of either. Thus, a dialectical argument might bring on a headache or (if mental association were directly efficacious) hearing others speak with a certain accent might cause me to hear myself later speaking with the same, no physical links intervening.

7. Thought might be carried on for a while by dialectical pro-

gression, the meaning constituting an evolutionary 'force.' The thought might then be transformed into another irrelevant state of mind, as in 6; but a moment later this state of mind might become a cerebral process, which, in turn, might be propagated for a while mechanically, but might finally evaporate out of the physical world altogether, the 'force' of it going to constitute a fresh mental event, either irrelevant or, by preestablished harmony, cognitive of the physical fact that caused it; and so on as before.

8. Thought might be without efficacy, either in its moral or in its existential capacity; yet the bodily function, the instinct or habit, which it accompanied, might involve the maintenance of that thought, or its dialectical development in time. In this case the thought would be so grounded as to vouch for its occasional reappearance, whenever the juncture reoccurred at which it was evoked originally. Thus books, customs and works of art insure the perpetuity of spiritual experience as, in a larger sense, do the unchanged face of nature and the hereditary structure of animals. Thought might still be called efficacious in the only sense, not magical, in which its efficacy would be at all congruous with its intent; namely, through the natural efficacy of the creature whose life it expressed.

As to my personal opinion in this matter, which I am sorry to see Professor Moore finds ambiguously expounded in my book, it is probably plain enough from the above statement of the various possibilities. 1, 2, 3 and 4 describe purely ideal functions of thought, all of which it undoubtedly reaches at certain moments. 5, on the contrary, describes a superstition; yet it is this superstition, clung to by the unreconciled childishness of man, that alone induces anybody to defend the extravagances and confusions of 6 and 7. People wish thought to be mechanically efficacious because they think it would be a *better guide* than the cerebral process which underlies it; yet why a better guide, unless it operated miraculously, by its intent, and not by virtue of some irrelevant evolution of its substance? 8, accordingly, represents the conclusion to which I arrive; and it explains certain phrases which I have not studied to avoid, thinking that their metaphorical character would be obvious to the reader. We all speak of Malthus's ideas 'governing' the movement of population, yet hardly expect to be accused of maintaining that poor Malthus's hard thinking caused Israel's fecundity or the congestion in our large cities. A thought is said to govern those portions of existence the movement of which it serves to predict or to describe. One may well say that 'reason is vital impulse modified by reflection.' It is certain that when a man 'reflects' his action changes in consequence, just as he turns aside when he 'sees' an obstacle in front of him; but as his seeing was an impression on his organs, without which his fancy would have pictured nothing, and as his turning was an instinct or habit of his organism, without which the image would have signified no danger; so the pause in reflection was a physical event, accompanied by an oscillation of projects in the mind (for reflection can not decide when reflection shall arise, nor how long it shall last, nor what course it shall take). The consequences of reflection are due to its causes, to the competitive impulses in the body, not to the wistful lucubration itself; for this is mere poetry. People's thoughts are most inadequate and choked just when their action is most rapid and urgent. That consciousness is a lyric cry, even in the midst of business, is something which must be felt, perhaps, to be understood; and they that have feeling, let them feel it.

I may add that the ambiguity which others as well as Professor Moore find in my book seems to come, at least in part, from their generously attributing to it loftier pretensions than it ever puts forth. They begin by reading into my words two doctrines which perhaps they think highly of, namely, that the genesis of knowledge is the genesis of things, and that truth is useful illusion; but they soon find that my expressions contradict these doctrines, which I not only never entertained, but can not even conceive. For in assigning any origin to nature we assume another nature operating behind, while it is hard to see how one illusion could be more useful than another in a vacuum; yet if a determinate environment existed, the true idea of it would be determined by what that environment was, not by the uses which the idea of it might have. What I can readily conceive, however, is how puzzled and disappointed a reader must be who begins by taking for a complete cosmogony what is merely a biography of human reason, and how miserably this whole drama of thought must seem to him to end, if it ends in discovering what has always been true.

Purposes and Results

GEORGE SANTAYANA

Human actions often have some purpose, and they always have some result; but the purpose is one thing and the result is another. Even when there seems to be a perfect correspondence between them, they are separate facts having different conditions, because the purpose is bred in a psyche by the private forces operating there whilst the result is produced in the open world, at a later time, under the cross-influences of many an alien circumstance. Actions animated by the most precise purposes are immediately compounded, in their effects, with these alien forces, and in the hurly-burly of events they issue in some new posture of affairs to which they are no longer relevant, and in which they are lost without recognition.

Rhetorical sciences, such as history, philosophy, and even natural history, are not able to trace the true complex and miscellaneous web of events, but are compelled to attribute them impressionistically to some purpose, as if purposes could directly and miraculously compel events to realize them. This way of conceiving things is superstitious resting on ignorance of the true derivation of events and on casual rhymes struck in the fancy: yet it is rendered almost inevitable by two circumstances: one, that events often do correspond to actual purposes within a narrow field, and that field the most familiar to moralists; the other, that the moralist in surveying any important event, synthesised it in conception by the unifying force of his own passions; he sees it fulfilling or

George Santayana, "Purposes and Results," from the *Manuscript Collection of the Clifton Waller Barrett Library of the University of Virginia Library.* © 1967 by Daniel Cory.

thwarting some purpose of his own, actual or possible; and he instinctively reads into it a corresponding purpose, human or divine, which in fact has never existed.

There might be some justification for this practice, as for any
reasoning by analogy, if the familiar instances of fulfilled purposes
had been rightly understood: but this is seldom the case; for even
here purposes never produce events, but only prefigure them. The
purpose itself arises by virtue of the ripening of certain actions, or
impulses in the organism; these impulses, before the sort of action
in question has been often performed or observed, come clothed
only in vague feelings of uneasiness or impatience: but when the
appropriate action is well-known, they come clothed in images
picturing that action by anticipation: and the purpose in that
case can prefigure graphically its probable or normal fulfilment.
The issue is not called forth or shaped by that image in the mind:
but the first images accompanying the purpose may be very like
the images which perception of the result will arouse in the end:
and this natural congruity in two pictures will be transformed
by superstitious haste into the power of the first image—whose
causes are ignored—to produce the material event which the second image reports to the same minds. A man's ability to say what
he thinks or to do what he likes is itself dependent on the normal
continuity of his bodily life. Interrupt this continuity, by a blow
or by simply whistling, and the most impetuous eloquence will
stop short, and the mightiest purpose will have no sequel at all.

The Realm of Spirit

GEORGE SANTAYANA

That spirit is no primary substance or force, but is generated in
living bodies and follows their fortunes, appears clearly in certain
lights, by both external and internal evidence. Yet the special

George Santayana, "The Realm of Spirit," *Columbia Manuscript Collection,*
XIV:3. © 1967 by Daniel Cory.

nature of spirit, as a moving centre of survey and an inner light that makes light visible, renders that evidence easy to elude, or may even seem to nullify it by a contrary and more immediate assurance. This is not really the case: even from the inside, spirit bears continual witness to its created and dependent condition: and the very privilege of knowledge, by which spirit may threaten to absorb and incorporate the universe, would cease to be a privilege and become an insane obsession, if there were no universe to know. It is not in this radical transcendental form that the independence of spirit seems plausible to the natural man, but incidentally and partially. From the outside, spirit is invisible: we cannot observe it actually kindled in an organism, like a fire in the chimney, nor being secreted like bile in the liver. Since it belongs essentially to another realm of being, we imagine it perhaps as pre-existing there, and merely descending and interweaving itself for a while with the motions of the body, sorrow heaving the breast, and the breast oppressing the spirit, and finally expelling it, or freeing it, like a bird from its broken cage. In all these ancient images we assimilate spirit too much to matter, while meaning to distinguish it and make it a separate force. We almost *see* the dove issuing from the dying man's mouth; we actually *watch* our own will and resolution struggling with temptation, like a man trying to lift a weight almost too great for his strength. The fact of effort is a physical fact: in attaching it to spirit, we are thinking of a sort of release of potential energy, and thereby turning spirit unwittingly into potentiality, that is, into the very essence of matter. Thus the realm of spirit would become in our hands a tenuous extension of the material world, a realm of astral bodies, ethereal currents, and magnetic influences working from a distance all sorts of material changes. The spiritual side of will is not effort but prophecy, desire, consent, command, and proud self-assertion. Spirit says the word: and then—if God also is willing —the body and the whole obsequious world perform the intended action.

Santayana's Philosophy of Mind

JOHN LACHS

The history of philosophy resembles a convention of deaf-mutes. Each participant attempts to communicate the secrets of his private imagination through a swirl of silent gestures. Intent on disclosing his own insight, each is confined in his own world: he has no ear for the language of others and often little knowledge of how to make them understand his. The carnival of controversy which ensues is grotesque in the eyes of the outsider but tragic for the thoughtful participant. For in the history of philosophy many more messages are sent than are received, and the ones that are received come to us mutilated, infected by our own perspective and interests. In our own way each of us distorts or discards the central judgments of almost everyone else. The dead sign-language of the printed word is inadequate to span a century. Philosophers signal like wild semaphores that lost their common code.

If the philosopher who attempts precision and rigor is often misunderstood, the fate of the thinker who writes as though he were a poet is still worse. A picturesque style rich in metaphor invites misapprehension not only of its content and detail but also of the author's general intention. The result of such misunderstanding and of the frustration attendant upon the attempt to explicate poetry in prose is disdain and eventually the total neglect of the thinker's work. The supposition is soon advanced that the author did not mean to write serious, systematic philosophy or, at least, that his thought is not a significant aspect of his work. In precisely this fashion, George Santayana has long been celebrated as a consummate stylist, a poet, and a literary psychologist,

John Lachs, "Santayana's Philosophy of Mind." Reprinted from *The Monist*, Vol. 48, No. 3 (1964), LaSalle, Illinois, pp. 419-440.

while the view that his philosophy does not warrant serious study
has been gaining ever wider acceptance.

It has become fashionable to pay cursory homage to Santayana's
'courageous naturalism' and, at most, to follow this by the expression of regret about the vague and almost mystical things he
said about the realm of spirit. But, the official view runs, such
mysticism, incoherence, and ambiguity should not surprise us for
Santayana was, after all, a poet, and it would be rash to look to
him for philosophical enlightenment or to judge him by the rigorous standards of rationality. I contend that this 'official' view of
Santayana's philosophical achievement is radically mistaken. If
my purpose were to present a general refutation of it, I would
begin by arguing that style and content cannot be dissociated,
and that Santayana's picturesque mode of expression is not an
accidental feature of his work. In his view neither literary psychology nor philosophy is a source of clear and adequate knowledge, and it would be vain pedantry to affect precision of language
where such is inappropriate. An imaginative style which evokes in
us the intuition of particularly rich and comprehensive essences is
singularly appropriate for Santayana who believes that existence
is ultimately unintelligible, knowledge is always symbolic, and
one of the tasks of philosophy is to articulate 'the large facts.'

I will, however, not take this occasion to present a general
rebuttal of this most influential of the current appraisals of Santayana. Instead, I hope that the destructive task of showing the inadequacy of this appraisal will be accomplished in the course of
the constructive enterprise of developing a central segment of Santayana's philosophical thought. The segment of his system which
I wish to explore is what may be called 'the philosophy of mind,'
viz., his views on such subjects as the nature of mental acts, the
nature of the immediate objects of consciousness, and in this
paper especially, the relationship of mental acts to the animal
organism. In essence I propose to do three things. First of all, I
propose to point out some of the fundamental concepts of Santayana's philosophy of mind, along with the technical terms which
fix these concepts in the public language. Secondly, I intend to
exhibit the structure of Santayana's thought, the strong skeleton
of a system which may be discerned once the bedizenments of

style, all embellishment and vagary are cut away. This will be the major task of my paper. In order to accomplish it I will attempt to clarify his language, systematize his statements, and throw some light on his scattered arguments. Whenever necessary, I will introduce distinctions or make explicit the ones Santayana drew. In some discussions I will be reduced to conjecturing what he would or might say: in all such cases I will try to stay within the largely unstated intent of his thought. Finally, by a critical examination of some of its concepts and theories I hope to demonstrate that Santayana's philosophy of mind has a unity of purpose and structure which is a considerable source of strength. Even though I will not hesitate to level serious criticisms against it, I hope to show that the easy dismissal of this aspect of Santayana's mature thought is as unjustifiable as it may be injurious to future progress in the philosophy of mind.

I

By careful and elaborate ontological analysis Santayana distinguishes four 'realms' or irreducibly different kinds of being. First in the order of being there are an infinite number of essences: this infinity of the forms of definiteness Santayana calls 'the realm of essence.' Essences are universals and as such they do not exist. By existence Santayana means location in a space-time network with the consequent possibility of causal action. Essences do not exist because neither spatial nor temporal properties may be predicated of them. They are timelessly and hence changelessly self-identical forms of every degree of determination. Such timeless, changeless universals, Santayana maintains, are necessary conditions of the possibility of time and change and action, and therefore of the world as it exists.

In the order of generation matter has primacy, even though its operation presupposes the availability of a plenum of essences. Matter is the principle by virtue of which essences are instantiated: it is the incalculable force that confers existence on the forms. In a fundamental sense matter has no characteristics or nature. As the principle of selective instantiation it is merely the undifferentiated and inarticulate other of essence. No essence can yield an adequate description of its inner dynamism, and it does not derive its inexhaustible creative power from participation in some form. Matter is a primordial existential flux; it is an indescribable and unintelligible surd.

The world of substance, of physical objects acting and reacting in space, can be analyzed into the two components of matter and essence. The blind thrust of matter embodies, 'existentializes' set after set of essence. And we must be careful not to put narrow limits on the conception of essence: Santayana claims that even events have essences. The essence or form of an event as distinct from its occurrence he calls a 'trope.' Substance may, then, be described as a set of instantiated tropes or, in plainer language, a large number of physical events. The realm of truth is the total inventory of essences instantiated by matter. It consists of the possibly infinite set of universals which have been, are being, and will be exemplified in the history of the world. In Santayana's view, then, truth is fully objective: it does not presuppose the existence of a knowing subject or mind. On the contrary, truth as an objective standard is a necessary condition of the possibility of true opinions. Judgments are true if and only if they faithfully reproduce a portion of the descriptive properties of the world-process.

The fourth irreducibly different realm of being Santayana distinguishes is that of spirit. By 'spirit' he means nothing more mysterious than consciousness. However, the notion of consciousness, I am afraid, is mysterious enough for some philosophers. For this reason, I will presuppose in my discussion as little as I can, perhaps no more than their and my human experience. Human experience consists of a series of conscious acts, and consciousness is the total inner difference between being asleep and awake.[1] This difference itself is never the sole object of consciousness, but in retrospect it can be discerned with sufficient clarity. In conscious events we must draw a distinction between the objects of consciousness and our consciousness of these objects. The consciousness or consciousing of the object is a pure act of apprehen-

[1] George Santayana, *The Realm of Spirit* (New York: Charles Scribner's Sons, 1940), p. 18. Hereafter referred to as RS.

sion. As such it exists only in being enacted, and can never be its own object or the object of another conscious act. It is because the act of consciousness is never, and can never be, among the objects of our experience that so many philosophers tend to deny its existence. But its presence, though not all of its properties, is undeniable even on a Humian theory of mind: it is a necessary condition of experience and the correlate of every object of awareness.

Spirit in a man, then, consists of a series of conscious acts, each with its own manifold of objects. Santayana calls these conscious acts 'intuitions.' The objects of consciousness are always changeless and impotent essences. Since no conscious act can exist without some objects, and since any essence implicates through the internal relation of difference an infinity of other essences, the entire realm of essence is a necessary condition of the possibility of intuition and hence of spirit. In another and even more fundamental way, intuitions presuppose the existence of both matter and essence. Although consciousness is first in the order of knowledge, it is a late arrival in the causal order of nature. Its emergence presupposes the instantiation by matter of a set of enormously complex essences. This system of tropes, the hereditary movements and physical organization of an animal, Santayana calls 'the psyche.' The psyche is the mythological unity of the sum total of significant tropes embodied in the life history of an animal. Since it is wound up to aim at self-development and self-maintenance, the psyche has diverse groups of functions which conjointly define its nature. Being present in the seed, its first function is embryological and vegetative. Biologically, it is a self-regulating and self-repairing mechanism. In the search for food and shelter it is the source of locomotion. Surrounding itself with a web of organs, its psychological function is to grow perceptive and intelligent in its responses. Socially, it is the agent in all interaction and the cause of all behavior. Morally, it underlies all choice, impulse, and interest, and is the natural ground of the distinction between good and evil. Its physiological and endocrinological function is to maintain the internal health and equilibrium of the organism. Finally, one of its neurological functions is to give rise to consciousness.

Spirit is thus totally dependent for its existence on the system of embodied tropes that constitutes the psyche. "Spirit, or the intuitions in which it is realized . . . [requires] the existence of nature to create it,"[2] Santayana says. And again, "The life of the psyche, which rises to . . . intuition, determines all the characters of the essence evoked. . . ."[3] In the light of this generatively secondary or derived character of intuitions, it is important to remark that even though spirit is causally reducible to the psyche and exerts no causal influence over anything, it nonetheless constitutes an ontologically irreducible and ultimate mode of being. At a later stage I will discuss Santayana's reasons for maintaining the irreducibility of consciousness to neurological process, of spirit to psyche. At this point, however, I must content myself with an unembellished statement of what Santayana holds.

II

The significance of Santayana's distinction between psyche and spirit is best brought out by directing attention of the properties and functions of each. The psyche as a set of embodied tropes is a relatively stable vortex in the universal flux. Each psyche is a system of vital events: each system of this sort is a material organism. To say that something is material is to assert at least that it is publicly observable, that it is in a field of action continuous with the human body, and that under favorable conditions its behavior may be predicted and even controlled. To say that something is in a field of action is to say at least that it has a specific locus in physical space and a specific locus in physical time, that the behavior of its spatio-temporal neighbors may bring about changes in it, and that its changes may modify the behavior of its neighbors. A psyche, then, is an observable, spatio-temporally located system of operations which stands in close and constant interaction with its environment. No psyche is a substance: only the physical universe as a whole is a substance in the sense of being an enduring and independent existent. Psyches are modes of

[2] George Santayana, *Scepticism and Animal Faith* (New York: Charles Scribner's Sons, 1923, reprinted 1955), p. 274. Hereafter referred to as SAF.
[3] SAF, p. 130.

substance, limited centers of dynamic equilibrium which the flux of existence temporarily sustains.[4]

By contrast with its material organ, spirit is immaterial and imperceptible. It is "the actual light of consciousness,"[5] "the light of discrimination,"[6] or "intelligence in act."[7] The essence of spirit or mind is cognitive awareness. Let me warn at once against two possible misunderstandings. First of all, by 'spirit' Santayana does not mean a single individual being or some cosmic Consciousness. Instead, he uses the word to refer to a category or type of being, the class of occurrences of which every particular thought, feeling, and sensation is a member. Secondly, the fact that he speaks of 'minds' should not mislead us into supposing that he thinks of minds as substantial, independently existing things. Nothing could be farther from Santayana's intention than to admit the existence of enduring mind-substances or mental continuants. Consciousness exists only in the individual acts Santayana calls 'intuitions.' A mind, therefore, is simply a set of intimately connected intuitions. The intimate connection between the intuitions that constitute a single mind is at least of two sorts. Firstly, all of them share the same psyche as their source of origin. Secondly, the essence disclosed in any intuition of the set is qualitatively similar to, or in some sense continuous with, the objects of intuitions which precede and succeed it. Since both the occurrence of intuitions and their specific objects are dependent on the psyche, it is clear that the continuity of our experience is due to the continuity through change of the animal organism, and the unity and identity of the mind is but a reflection of the unity and identity of the psyche.

Intuitions are intentional acts directed upon objects. The objects of intuitions are non-existent essences of varying complexity. At this point a problem arises. If all intuition is of essence but knowledge is always of some state or process of substance, how is knowledge possible? If nothing that is presented to the mind exists, how can we discern the phases of existence? If the immedi-

4 George Santayana, *The Realm of Matter* (New York: Charles Scribner's Sons, 1930), p. 140. Hereafter referred to as RM.

5 RM, p. 139.

6 SAF, p. 273.

7 *Ibid.*, p. 274.

ate is, without exception, a changeless and eternally self-identical universal, how can we perceive the growth and the corruption which gnaw at the heart of each particular? Let me begin an answer to this problem by expanding the act-object terminology which has been adequate for our purposes until now.

Santayana needs a threefold distinction here. He cannot be satisfied with distinguishing the act of consciousness from its immediate object. He must also draw a sharp line of separation between this immediate or 'immanent' object of consciousness and its transcendent object in the knowledge-situation. The framework of distinctions Santayana has in mind parallels rather closely Meinong's act-content-object scheme. Intuition is the act of consciousing, changeless essences constitute its content or immanent object, and the enduring substance of the physical universe functions as its most frequent, though by no means only, transcendent object. It is important to insist that by speaking of intuited essences as the 'content' of experience I do not mean to imply that for Santayana experiences form total and inseparable wholes of which such essences are parts or in which they are in some way contained. On the contrary, Santayana is a realist in the extreme sense of maintaining that both the immediate and the mediate objects of consciousness, both essence and substance, are logically as well as causally independent of mental acts.

Under what conditions will an intuited essence constitute knowledge of material substance? Intensely aware of the overwhelming difficulties of any copy-dualism, Santayana claims that knowledge presupposes neither the qualitative identity nor even the resemblance of what is "in the mind," and what physically exists. There are no reasons to suppose and there are excellent reasons to doubt that the simple, dramatic pictures of the eye trace faithfully the movements of the flux. If the animal organs and occasions of knowledge are taken into account, the probability of such a reproduction of the world in sense is at once seen to be infinitesimal. Literal possession of the object or of a replica of the object, however, is not a necessary condition of knowledge. The relation between the immanent and the transcendent object of consciousness is symbolic: the data of sense function as symbols of the presence and processes of physical objects. Santayana has never made a sustained attempt to explain the nature of symbols or to formulate the rules of symbolism. I suspect that in the claim that essences appearing in intuition are symbols of the modifications of matter, the word 'symbol' is used in a quite non-technical sense. It is used primarily to call attention to (a) the fact that the intuited essence and the properties of the encountered physical object are not numerically identical, and (b) the fact that the animal whose psyche gives rise to a series of conscious acts does not accept the essences intuited at face value, but habitually deputizes them to stand for and report the movement of ambient forces. As a test of the adequacy of such symbolism we do not need to compare the given with what is physically real and hence irrevocably beyond the reach of mind. The ultimate criterion of successful symbolization is appropriate action.

Knowledge, then, is always symbolic in character. Intuited essences serve as the vehicles of symbolism: the movements of substance, the phases of the world-process, are symbolized. I will not concern myself with special problems that arise in this connection, but I cannot avoid dealing with at least one issue of general significance. Intuition in its pure form is enjoyment of self-identical essence. How is it possible for an essence, intuited in its meaningless aesthetic immediacy, to acquire meaning and become a symbol of something other than itself? What is the factor or force that transforms the contemplation of essence into knowledge of substance?

In its current form the question is misleading. It can readily be interpreted as implying that there is some mysterious psychic force which harnesses, at a certain point in our development, innocent intuition to the practical life. This interpretation of Santayana's point is incorrect for two reasons. First of all, common human experience does not consist of a string of pure intuitions. Probably even the earliest conscious experiences of the child are symbol-cognitive: for the adult, at any rate, the uncommitted contemplation of essence is an infrequent and difficult achievement. Secondly, since most of our experiences are substance-directed and hence involve symbolic cognition of facts or things beyond the experience, it would be clearly inappropriate to speak of the intuition of essences and of the factor which makes it possible for the essences to function as symbols as if they were in some sense separable. The factor which is present in all experiences that are symbol-cognitive and in no experiences that are not, Santayana calls 'intent.' Now even though intuition can exist independently of intent, as it does in moments of aesthetic enjoyment, on occasions of symbolic cognition the two exist inextricably interwoven. When our consciousness is symbolic, intent and intuition are at best distinguishable elements in the experience: it would, however, be a mistake to speculate about the way in which intent transforms essences into symbols. Strictly speaking, such a transformation does not occur. A pure intuition exists while it lasts: it can never be transformed into an act of knowledge. Similarly, moments of symbolic cognition cannot be stripped of their referential element and transformed into pure essence-directed acts. Like Athena out of Zeus' head, each moment of consciousness springs into existence full-grown out of the psyche's substance.

What then, it might be asked, is the nature of intent? It is the expression on a mental plane of the outdirected concerns of the psyche. Intent is the counterpart in consciousness of animal fear and the psyche's natural urge to live. The hidden agencies of the environment must be feared and fought: animal life is eternal preparation for the impending blow. This preoccupation of the psyche with the distant, the absent, and the latent is reflected in the mind in our tendency to take the qualities of the given as revelatory of what is not presented. Intent thus is an agent of animal faith: it is external reference, unthinking belief in the not-given. Such tacit reference to what is not presented or what is yet to come is an essential condition of all perception, memory, and science. In the case of perception intent takes the form, first of all, of the supposition that the essence presented stands for a physical object, and secondly of the belief that this object far outstrips in complexity the essence that is its symbol. In the former instance intent deputizes an essence to stand for an existent, in the latter case one or a small group of properties is taken as the symbol of a larger set. In general, intent is the animal urge to use what is present and presented for the representation of the absent: by its means essence may become the symbol of existence, and the changeless may be made to yield knowledge of change.

In view of the central significance of the concept of intent in his account of the conscious life, one could reasonably expect Santayana to be detailed and specific in his explication of it. Unfortunately, however, such expectations are disappointed. Santayana leaves the matter on a level of high generality with almost all the technical details missing. Here Santayana might argue that since the major task of philosophy is the evocation of particularly comprehensive essences, once such an essence has been elicited little more can or should be done. This argument sounds hollow, and I suspect it had little to do with Santayana's scanty attention to the theory of intent and symbolism. A far more obvious explanation is at hand. Santayana was simply not interested in issues relating to the nature of intent. Even though he showed intense interest in certain special fields of symbolic activity such as religion and art, he had never managed to develop any great concern with the general problem of how symbolic cognition is possible.

The reason why Santayana has so little to say about intent is that its study does not further his central interests in the nature of spirit and of the spiritual life. The study of intent gives practically no direct insight into the nature of spirit. Even though intent can only exist in conscious experiences, it is not for that reason indigenous to consciousness. Spirit in its purest form is pure intuition. Pure intuition is free of all symbolic reference and all belief in the absent. Intuition with intent is a form of spirit, but it is not spiritual. Intent strips intuition of its spirituality by subjecting it to the principle of practical interest, the prejudices of its psyche, the grotesque limitations of a single perspective. If a mind could ever be fully spiritual, it would have no special interests, no predilections, and no preferences. If a life of detached contemplation could ever be sustained, it would consist of the impartial readiness to conceive without the urge to posit or possess. "All essences are grist for the mill of intuition": spirit, as the principle of universal sympathy, would never be motivated on its own account to go beyond what is immediately presented.

As spirit is purified it approaches the ideal of what it would be if it were left alone: pure contemplation of essence or *Wesenschau*. In a strict sense, of course, if spirit were left alone it would not even exist. The psyche, after all, is the sole and adequate source of consciousness, and it is this humble origin of spirit in the heat of organic adjustments that makes prolonged spiritual living an unattainable ideal. If it were free of external influence, intuition would be fully and solely essence-directed. Intent represents alien interests, the interests of the struggling body, in the realm of mind. It diverts the attention of spirit from essence to substance, and impels it to follow the fortunes of its organ. Santayana's interest in intent is slight because it is only the study of intent-free intuition that yields an insight into the nature of spirit. Once the nature of spirit is clearly conceived, the ideal of the spiritual life becomes inescapable. The central concern of Santayana's philosophy is with life, not theory, and specifically with the uniquely human, or divine, life of disinterested aesthetic enjoyment. In this subordination of theory to practice, Santayana is in the best tradition of the Ancients. As a consequence, the standard by which his work is to be judged cannot be the single one of theoretical adequacy. Like any philosophy that has at its heart a conception of the good life, it has to be judged at least partly by the satisfactoriness of the life it advocates.

III

Santayana uses a general argument to show that mind and matter, knowledge and object known cannot be identical. The physical world is a spatio-temporal process. Change, coming into being and passing away, pervades the innermost recesses of every material thing. Change is substitution of event for event and quality for quality in relatively permanent surroundings. In the material world this substitution is total in the sense that the termini of change cannot coexist: whenever there is a change from any state S_1 to another state S_2, there is a time at which S_1 is actual and S_2 is not yet, and a later time at which S_2 is actual but S_1 exists no longer.

If the mind mirrored this total physical substitution of state for state, knowledge of change would not be possible. Change can only be known by "arresting" its temporal passage. Since it is a relation, it cannot be conceived unless its terms, separate and successive in physical time, can coexist in the conscious mind. The state that is no longer must be remembered, and the state that is not yet must be anticipated: only by such time-spanning, synthetizing actions of the mind is knowledge of temporal process made possible. Change and knowledge of change differ, then, in a fundamental way. Apprehension of the changing is synthetic and hence exempt from alteration and passage; change, on the other hand, involves successive substitution which is possible only in physical time. But the temporal and the non-temporal cannot belong to the same ontological realm, Santayana maintains. The act of intuition is not an event located in physical time, nor do the essences intuited in any way undergo substitutive passage. Each act of consciousness occupies what Santayana calls "the transcendental position appropriate to viewing";[8] each is "withdrawn from the sphere of the categories which it employs."[9]

This argument appears to me to be an exceptionally strong one. It is a reason sufficient by itself to justify the initial distinction between mental act and physical event, quite irrespective of what our ultimate theory of the mind-body relation will be. Santayana contends that no theory of the relation of consciousness to the physical world can disregard the difference between the temporality of change and the time-spanning vision or time-independence of the cognitive act. The pair of concepts that seems most succinctly to express Santayana's view of the contrasting nature of physical existence and mind is that of agent and spectator. Agency in a space-time field is the very essence of substance, and spirit consists of nothing but cognitive acts. Since all causation and generation belong in the sphere of action, it is here that we must look for the origin of consciousness. Since all cognition belongs in the realm of spirit, it is to spirit that we must look to discover the organ of consciousness and the laws or circumstances of its emergence.

No reasonable philosophy can ignore the fact that cognitive awareness arises on the occasions of physical existence. Santayana

8 George Santayana, *The Realm of Essence* (New York: Charles Scribner's Sons, 1927), p. 128.
9 RS, p. 46.

contends that consciousness emerges as a by-product of the activities of the psyche. This appears to be a difficult view to uphold. What specific sense can be attached to the claim that the spirit depends for its existence on the psyche? Since all generation is material, the psyche-dependence of spirit must be total: each moment of consciousness must be individually produced by some process in the physical organism, and no cognitive act can sustain itself in existence, change anything, or beget its own successor. The correlation of neural events with conscious acts, no matter how complete, would never suffice to establish such generative dependence. By the claim that *a* generates *b* we mean more than that *a*'s and *b*'s are highly correlated, although it is by no means clear what more. In any case, it is evident that if by causation Santayana meant nothing more than constant conjunction or regular sequence, he could not consistently maintain that all generation is physical. Consciousness precedes physical changes no less regularly than psychic process ushers in mental acts.

It is clear, then, that no science, not even the ideally complete unified science of physical nature whose possibility Santayana foresaw, can adequately support a theory of the unilateral generative dependence of consciousness on the material organism. There appear to be at least two reasons why Santayana's epiphenomenalism is not a scientific hypothesis. The first is that in speaking of the generation of spirit by psyche Santayana means to convey more than that there is a functional relation between the two: he wishes to maintain that in addition to the discoverable correlation between mental acts and physical events there is also an imperceptible though real derivation of the former from the latter. All such generation occurs 'in the dark' of the realm of matter. As such, generative process is, in principle, unthinkable. Since only forms or essences may be intuited and they are the termini of change, the actual process of alteration, the process that renders essences existent, the process of the embodiment of forms is closed to inspection by the mind. Such generative process permeates the psyche and surrounds it. The body encounters it at every turn even though the mind finds its existence conjectural and can at best adumbrate it by the use of symbols. Generation is matter itself, and matter is the unintelligible other of essence. The unintelligible cannot be an object of scientific inquiry.

The second reason why epiphenomenalism is not a scientific hypothesis is that it is a theory about the relationship of two types of occurrences only one of which falls properly within the field of scientific investigation. Conscious acts are private in a way no physical object or particle is: their imperceptibility is not on a logical par with the imperceptibility of electrons. There is something logically odd even about the correlations between physical events and mental acts, for a direct correlation can only be established in the single case of the investigator's own experiences. For the rest, we must be satisfied with the indirect and tenuous method of attempting to correlate physical events with experiences through the verbal, introspective reports of others. Santayana's theory of the mind-body relation, then, cannot look to science for confirmation because one of the terms of the relation cannot be investigated by the scientific method, while the relation itself cannot be understood by the mind.

I will not hold it against Santayana's mind-body theory that it is not a scientific hypothesis: no mind-body theory is. However, I do wish to call attention to the difficulty Santayana has to face in his attempt to give an account of the relationship of consciousness to the physical organism. What appears to be needed first and foremost is a theory of causation. Santayana rejects the entailment view,[10] and his epiphenomenalism makes it impossible for him to hold either the activity theory or the regular sequence view.[11] He is left with the conviction that constant conjunctions are signs of causal connections, but that the generative act itself is beyond the pale of mind. When late in life he noted the fact that on the issue of the emergence of consciousness he has "not seen much new light,"[12] he should have felt no surprise or regret. There is nothing new to be discovered here for the simple reason

10 RM, p. 111.
11 On this issue see my "Epiphenomenalism and the Notion of Cause," *Journal of Philosophy*, 60 (1963), 141-146.
12 George Santayana, "A General Confession," in *The Philosophy of George Santayana,* "The Library of Living Philosophers" (La Salle, Ill.: Open Court Publishing Co., 1940), p. 17.

that there is nothing to be known about the causal process that gives rise to intuitions. The most we can hope for is a more adequate knowledge of the physical occasions and the physiological antecedents of the emergence of consciousness. But no matter how much we may eventually learn about the psychic tropes that are the necessary and sufficient conditions of consciousness, we will never be able to understand the dark process by which something new, a mental act, is brought into the world.

It is tempting to terminate Santayana's credit at this point and file for theoretical bankruptcy. There is good reason to be dissatisfied with Santayana if this is all he has to offer. I tend to think he is quite correct in his contention that reality outstrips the human mind or that existence is a surd. But this single contention does not constitute a philosophy. In fact, if it is not to be construed as an outright denial of the possibility of philosophy, all avenues of rational inquiry must be explored until exhausted. If the principle of the ultimate unintelligibility of existence is not to beget wild mockery of reason, we must avoid seeking its protection at every turn.

I now wish to argue that Santayana in fact does not have direct and immediate resort to the unintelligibility of generation in his attempt to explain the relation of spirit to psyche. He conceives the mind-body relation in terms of concepts which, while they are inadequate to render a complete account of the generation of consciousness, at least confer upon it a degree of intelligibility by connecting it to the coherent system of concepts and theories which constitutes his ontology. The key to my argument is Santayana's distinction between what belongs in the realm of spirit and what is properly spiritual. Every type of consciousness belongs in the realm of spirit, but only intuition free of intent or animal faith is truly spiritual. Feeling, belief, and memory are forms of consciousness, but they do not possess the spirituality of pure intuition. Unbiased and uncommitted contemplation, aesthetic enjoyment of the immediate reveals most clearly the inner, spiritual nature of spirit. Spirituality is freedom from the concerns of animal life, release from the anxious selectivity of the psyche, liberation from the practical intelligence which is incessantly at work adapting means to ends. It is precisely this temporal separation of means and ends that is the most pervasive feature of the physical world. By contrast, for spirit in its purity each mental act is its own end: each is whole and complete in itself and a means to nothing beyond itself.

The difference between the physical and the mental is best expressed in terms of the contrast between the Aristotelian concepts of process and activity. A process (*kinesis*) is an event or series of events with internal reference to time. By this I mean that each process is temporally diversified: each consists of heterogeneous segments or parts, and cannot be considered complete until its last part has occurred or its end product has been brought into existence. No part of a process can meaningfully stand alone, for a process is only complete when completed, it is 'whole' only in the whole time required for its occurrence. But since processes are changes or motions, there is an important sense in which they are never whole at all. For although they are 'whole' in the whole stretch of time necessary for their existence, that stretch of time never exists as a whole. Being temporally variegated, processes are condemned to move from birth to death, from beginning to end, essentially incomplete.

An activity (*energeia*), by contrast, is a being or occurrence with no essential or internal temporal reference. Activities contain no heterogeneous or separable parts. They are complete and self-contained at each moment of their occurrence: their actualization is not accomplished piecemeal and by parts. Although an activity may be said to last a shorter or longer period of time, such time is not an intrinsic measure of it: the profound irrelevance of time to act is clear if we recall that activity is whole not only in the whole stretch of duration through which it exists but whole also in every measurable part of that duration. Activity, in brief, is act without motion (*energeia akinesias*), or an occurrence that is not a change.

The relation of spirit to the world of nature generally is that of activity to process. Borrowing further from Aristotle, Santayana describes the system of operations that is the psyche as the first actuality of a natural body possessing the power to live.[13] Consciousness, accordingly, is the second entelechy of the living body,

13 SAF, p. 217.

or the psyche in act.[14] The relation of a particular spirit to its organ, then, is that of the second entelechy to the first or, in what is perhaps a less precise but more direct way of putting the matter, that of the actual to the potential. The ideal of spirit is pure actuality: Santayana models the spiritual life on the divinely active but unproductive existence of Aristotle's Prime Mover. Such divine perfection will, of course, be powerless in the sense of being unable to create change. Impotence is the price of perfection. For if existence is the movement from potentiality to act,[15] pure actuality once reached cannot give rise to any more existence. When the laborious process of physical life is transmuted into synthetic vision, existence achieves its aim and apex in actuality. In actuality motion ceases and existence comes to rest. The actual light of consciousness is a terminus of life: beyond this act of final consummation existence has nowhere to go.

IV

In the last few pages I have presented what I take to be Santayana's constructive account of the mind-body relation. On the whole, I have refrained from raising objections: I have reserved until now the task of critical assessment. The first difficulty that appears to be involved in Santayana's view is that the Aristotelian concepts he adopts have acquired their distinctive significance in a framework of teleological explanation. Concepts cannot readily be torn from the context that is their natural habitat. Aristotle is very plain in stating that potentiality exists for the sake of the actual and that the soul is the formal and final cause of the body. But Santayana, as an epiphenomenalist, cannot and does not leave room for formal or final causes, even though he wishes to retain the notion of the mind as the form or actuality of the body. Now what explanatory force do the concepts of potentiality and actuality possess if they are divested of all connotations of purposiveness and hence of value? Is purposiveness not tacitly assumed even in Santayana's own attempt to account for the impotence of mind by

14 RS, p. 94.
15 RM, p. 93.

the claim that once existence achieves the actuality that is consciousness, it has nowhere to go, or that the end of a causal chain can only be something that is an end-in-itself (note the ambiguity of 'end')?

This objection is readily answered by recalling Santayana's distinction between scientific and literary psychology. The science of the psyche consists of the description and explanation of the behavior of animals. Psychology can only be scientific if it aspires to be a part of biology: its aim is a system of theories that would be ideally adequate to explain the vital operations of animals in space. Since consciousness does not consist of publicly observable events in space and time, it cannot be an object of scientific inquiry. In clear contrast, then, to the behavioristic or physiological science of the psyche, the art of literary psychology is the imaginative exploration of the feelings and intentions of other minds. The literary psychologist divines the existence of thoughts and purposes in nature: the hallmark of his art is that it yields a reading of the flux of nature in terms appropriate only to spirit. The result of literary psychology is myth.

Now myth, properly understood, is adequate to convey a moral about regions of fact which are opaque to the intellect. It is, in reality, the only means at the disposal of the mind for gaining knowledge of what is recondite. If it is taken literally, however, it presents a grotesque and untenable view of the world. Teleology is a myth of the literary psychologist: it is the interpretation of nature in spiritual terms, the projection of desires and aspirations into the flux. Reading the fortuitous concourse of events from its own perspective, spirit might easily see a moral direction to history and believe that its own existence has from the first been the goal of evolutionary change. Such myths should be taken seriously but not literally. They should be made to yield whatever insight they can, but we ought to be wary of accepting them as accurate descriptions of reality.

Santayana's defense on this point consists, then, of the claim that the relation of consciousness to the body belongs in the sphere of literary psychology. Here the mystery of the generation of spirit by matter is transformed into the myth of the attraction of matter for the ideal and its potentiality to make it actual. It must be remembered that this is no more than a myth, and therefore less than knowledge, and even this myth has to be discounted and stripped of its teleology to bring it to fighting weight. But, it may now be objected, does the claim that psyche and spirit are related as first and second entelechy, or as the potential is related to the actual, in any way help us attach clear meaning to the 'generation' of intuitions or specificity to the psyche-dependence of spirit? Is the concept of potentiality of any theoretical significance, or is it merely the ponderous expression of our conviction that things manage to bring into existence what we think they do?

This objection is well founded. A statement *ex post facto* that X had in itself the power to generate Y is not an explanation of the occurrence of Y. The claim that consciousness is the operation of a psychic power conveys no information about methods of action or modes of generation. But what kind of information are we looking for? What sort of 'explanation' of the generative process would satisfy us? Santayana urges, rightly I think, that there are no ultimate explanations,[16] and that sooner or later we must face the facts and make our peace with the insane and inexplicable emphasis that arbitrarily raises some possible states of affairs to the status of existence. It is certainly true that we can only think of generation as "a transformation of one thing into another, involving two natural moments, and leaving the bond between them obscure."[17] If this is the best the human mind can do, it would be thoroughly unreasonable to ask for more. I, for one, do not find it difficult to conceive that the human mind may identify the unintelligible without understanding it, and that it lives by framing spontaneous myths to assimilate each recalcitrant fact into its structure.

Santayana's positive contribution to a better understanding of the mind-body problem was his recognition that epiphenomenalism is incompatible with any of the significant views of causation. While he was by no means the first philosopher to abandon the category of causation in the attempt to explicate the precise connection between consciousness and the animal organism, his introduction of the potentiality-actuality framework in its place was both adroit and auspicious. Not only was his epiphenomenalism made self-

16 SAF, p. 208.
17 RM, p. 90.

consistent in this way; the concepts of process and activity made it possible for his view of the mind-body relation to be incorporated in a coherent and comprehensive system of theories which derives its strength from, among others, a cogent ontology and a persuasive view of the nature of the good life.

The strength of epiphenomenalism is that it preserves the experienced duality of consciousness and physical fact, while it leaves the material world exempt from interference by non-physical agencies and therefore open to total scientific scrutiny. The epiphenomenalist takes full account of the obvious facts of the physical dependence of consciousness, as well as the no less obvious fact that consciousness as we know it is a product of evolutionary, biological advance. There is no theoretical reason why any physical action or change could not be explained in terms of previous physical actions and changes, or why science could not develop a system of concepts and theories ideally adequate to account for the behavior and distribution of all physical things. Santayana's philosophy of mind has the advantage of allowing for this autonomy of science in the physical realm, while it retains as categoreally different the private and intentional mind. I also consider it a strength of Santayana's position that it avoids the pitfalls of the view, now in vogue, that phenomenalistic language and physicalistic language differ only in connotation but agree in referent, and that introspection and the observation of brains are but two ways of examining the same thing. Epiphenomenalism has its difficulties, and it will certainly not appear plausible to the man who has not seen himself forced out of other, initially more promising positions by overpowering objections, but these difficulties are relatively slight when compared with the problems of the monistic identity view.

The weakness of Santayana's philosophy of mind is the weakness of any system. No system is an open-ended set of theories that leaves room for investigation or research. There is nothing tentative about a system: it is not a dynamic tool or stimulus to inquiry, for it is nothing if it does not claim to give a full and authoritative account of all the facts. A system is a clear and total crystal; it may be beautiful but it is dead. Since it has to account for everything, it tends to establish an orthodoxy or a status quo and become a harassment to much-needed research. To bring but one example, Santayana's concept of intuition cuts across the distinction between thought and sensation. The system tends to sanctify the concept, and the significant differences between sensing and thinking are suppressed. The result is that the little known and rather complex similarities and divergences of sense and thought are no longer deemed worthy of serious investigation. The issue is considered as resolved once and for all. The instances could be multiplied, even though in such systematic dogmatism Santayana is by no means the worst offender.

I will not use his dogmatism, clearly an unavoidable attendant of every philosophical system, as a general argument against Santayana's philosophy of mind. For the weakness of systems is at once also their strength: like castles and manor houses they are recognizable landmarks for the mind. A hundred or five hundred years after the architect has died, we may still study the structure of the walls and spend an evening in his living castle. What is of import is not that we divine with accuracy the builder's every thought. His work belongs to the public treasury of mankind, to be used by each as his wits will allow. In this way, history sometimes converts the voiceless monuments into starting-points for another age. New thinkers will begin where Santayana left off. They will transcend or reject him; they may distort his thought or not even know that they are in his debt. All of this, I am certain, matters not the least: all of them will have profited from Santayana's work, and it is such facts that justify the man, not our eulogies.

Philosophy, like the human mind itself, lives only in being continually refashioned and recreated. The question of ultimate historical accuracy is irrelevant to the progress of philosophical thought. What matters is the continued integrity of the inquiring mind. What matters is that we should use the past the way we use food, for the sustenance of life. If in the last analysis our intuition will disclose essences which differ from those that constitute his philosophy, Santayana would have no regret. Man is not a disembodied searcher after truth: each must mirror the world in his own way. Every man must seek to make his thought the adequate expression of his personality: this is the sum and substance of philosophy. In this enterprise of self-fulfilment Santayana would be the first to wish us luck.

Living Without Thinking

GEORGE SANTAYANA

A learned man is apt to overestimate the scope and importance of the subject in which he happens to be versed, but Professor Watson in his "Psychology from the Standpoint of a Behaviorist"* rises entirely above this prejudice. In fact, he runs to the opposite extreme and seems to reduce his subject to a modest minimum. Thinking, according to him, is simply "subvocal" speech, feeling is visceral effervescence, character is bodily habit, nothing goes on in any man not essentially observable by others, and psychology gathers only statistical laws of behavior, because there is nothing else in human life to discover.

Does Professor Watson, then, deny the existence of the human mind? It would seem so, if we take him at his word; yet, I hesitate to attribute that opinion to him and this for two reasons. One reason is verbal. He does not deny the existence of mind in his own sense of the word "mind," but only in the sense which everyone else gives to it. This is an old trick of reformers who are more conservative in their vocabulary than in their ideas. When they are on the point of discarding something that has a familiar or a hallowed name, they hasten to transfer that name (lest it should be missed in their works) to some other object in which they still believe. In this way, the words God, freedom and immortality may come to mean almost anything in the mouth of a philosopher. In the mouth of Spinoza for instance, (one of the greatest and most honest of them) we may almost say that immortality meant mor-

George Santayana, "Living Without Thinking," *The Forum*, 68 (1922), pp. 731-735.

* "Psychology from the Standpoint of a Behaviorist," by John B. Watson, Professor of Psychology, The Johns Hopkins University; Philadelphia and London, J. B. Lippincott Company, 1919.

tality, freedom meant necessity, and God meant matter. This sort of equivocation is a consequence of the fact that modern philosophy is theology attenuated rather than science filled out. Of late years, the Pragmatists, instead of announcing boldly that there is no such thing as truth (which is what their doctrine amounts to) have maintained that truth is verification; and the New Realists, whose system excludes the existence of consciousness, have preferred to say that consciousness is that portion of the material world on which some animal is reacting. In strict logic, nothing can be anything else; but we all commonly say that a table *is* wood, or that sound *is* vibrations, meaning that such is the substance or the origin of these objects. Such slippery use of language is inevitable and involuntary but it becomes confusing when we try to reflect or venture to dogmatize.

If Professor Watson, without transferring the name of thought or of feeling to anything else, should be satisfied with asserting that their entire basis is found in bodily habit and that only this bodily habit can be perceived externally or can be caught in the net of science, I for one should heartily agree with him. Perhaps this is really all he claims; for he assumes that if mechanisms enough could be discovered running on while we think, his case would be proved. I believe that such sufficient mechanisms exist, and that they do all the work and even do the thinking, although they are not the thought. The larynx does the talking, the ear and brain receive the consequent vibrations; but I mean and hear what I am saying and therefore I am a mind as well as a body.

In the effort to remember or express my thoughts, or to imagine those of other people, I am consequently driven to indulge in quite another sort of psychology, very far from scientific. A picture of human experience rises before me (called up and carried no doubt by my verbal habits) a sort of autobiography of man or universal historical novel, composed and recomposed continually. It starts with scraps of reminiscence in which conversation abounds; it goes on to find dramatic expressions for what various persons have felt, might feel or ought to feel; and it ends in formal history, theology, poetry, and fiction. Such literary psychology, in a warm sympathetic mind, may become very exact and very plausible; but there can never be any evidence that it literally reproduces anything that has ever existed before. The interèst of it does not lie in its fidelity to actual facts, but in its inward humor and vitality. Who cares whether Cleopatra in Shakespeare utters the actual sentiments which that mummified queen of Egypt may have uttered when alive? The truth of literary psychology is graphic truth, like that of William James's descriptions of experience, or of Bergson's appeal to our fundamental sense of merely existing and lasting, in the midst of infinite vibrations and a universal flux. We applaud such expressions of experience when we feel that they hit off just what we might imagine ourselves feeling under the pictured circumstances. Of course, there is nothing scientific or final about them, and the next literary psychologist will naturally express things differently, though perhaps no less truly. Eloquence, reflection, pleasant conversation, and witty fiction can refine sentiment and fancy in all of us, as the fine arts can refine the senses. They kindle in us those high lights of thought which alone are communicable or worth communicating. Literary psychology, though not a science in method, constitutes our knowledge of the human mind and of the moral world. I should accordingly learn, if I could, my scientific psychology in Professor Watson's school, and accept the limits which he sets to it; but for my insight into what goes on in people's mind I should turn to my private experience, to the novelists, to the poets, and to the ladies.

The other reason why I should hesitate to affirm that Professor Watson denies the existence of the human mind goes much deeper and involves the whole confused heritage of modern philosophy. Although he disparages philosophizing and disregards the problems involved in his own doctrines, I am convinced that he could never have reached these doctrines nor accepted them, if he had not tacitly assumed a general philosophy and one which, in my opinion, is false. This philosophy is that species of idealism or empiricism which teaches that experience is identical with its objects. Professor Watson is very wide awake and he makes no bones of assuming that the rest of us also see, hear, and feel as he does; otherwise he could not appeal to us to accept the evidence of scientific psychology proving that all we know of ourselves is the way we behave. We do, then, observe ourselves and others behaving; and this antecedent wakefulness or lucidity on our part, which surveys all things so grandly, is presupposed throughout. We must be minds, if we can come to the conclusion that we are only habits in matter.

Professor Watson, I should say, is implicitly an idealist; he fuses the light of thought and the actuality of experience with all the objects which he mentions and which he only *seems* to regard as existing materially. He does not need the human mind in his world because his world is already in the human mind: as at the theatre we need not be addressed by the actors or be admitted on the stage in order to know what is going on, because the whole play is addressed to us from the beginning, and is only a play. If it were real life, this clairvoyance on our part would be impossible: we should not dominate the scene, but should see it, at best, as the characters themselves might, each with his perspective and limitations. And then it would be indispensable that the actors should not be puppets but should have minds of their own: an invisible item which, so long as we were spectators on the other side of the footlights, did not concern us, and might be nonexistent.

Apart from these technical questions I find Professor Watson's book impressive and almost ominous. In its style, illustrations, humor, and outlook it has a very strong American flavor. We catch glimpses of a breezy, active, healthy, sensible society. Everyone works, everyone helps, everyone typewrites. Indeed, the chief test of proficiency, and of behaviorist psychology, seems to be how many words an hour, for how many hours, a person can typewrite without error. It is evident that what recommends this science especially is the use in organizing work and in getting as much work as possible out of everybody. A wonderful future seems to open before us, in which everybody will be wound up to do a great number of things, always the right things, all of them perfectly, and all of them on time. We can almost see Congress hypnotized by the "laryngeal activity" of some professor of behavior, and decreeing how many human animals shall be bred to cotton-picking habits, how many shall be turned out as living gramophones (popularly called singers) how many as sub-vocal talkers (popularly called thinkers), and when each shall be set to fall in love, and when to run down smoothly and die. For we learn that if only the right situation is arranged, such habits as may be wanted can be established at will; and there is no such thing as fatigue, only efficiency temporarily reduced, and easily restored after short intervals of organized rest.

I foresee a behaviorist millennium; countless millions of walking automatons, each armed with his radio, will cross and recross a universal telephone exchange, all jabbering as they have been trained to jabber, never interfering with one another, always smiling, with their glands all functioning perfectly (which *is* happiness) and all living to a sunny old age, when instead of vocal behavior before one another, or sub-vocal arithmetic at a desk, they will separately indulge in pedal behavior before a pianola, or will typewrite, at the vertiginous rate of life-long experts, pages and pages of short lines (which *are* poetry). Truly a wonderful exhibition, which for all I know might last forever. But alas! I was never brought up to behave, and when I *think* of that exhibition, my ill-regulated language-habit leads me sub-vocally to add these two syllables: what for?

Comparison with Other Views of Spirit

GEORGE SANTAYANA

The words entelechy and act or actuality, which I have used often to designate consciousness are borrowed from Aristotle; and indeed I think no other philosopher has conceived the relation of the body to the mind that animates it so fairly and squarely. He saw that spirit was something spiritual, an expression and not a substance: and as a part of that view he saw that spirit was al-

George Santayana, "Comparison with Other Views of Spirit," *Columbia Manuscript Collection*, IX:14:II. © 1967 by Daniel Cory.

together inseparable from body, and relative to the vital functions which it was to express. But two chief obstacles existed in his philosophy to the pure and consistent development of this doctrine. One was the Socratic enthusiasm for final causes; the other the popular habit of confusing the status of spirit with that of its deliverance or object. The first prejudice led Aristotle to suppose that a non-psychological sort of mind, a soul, the type or norm of what the living being should be, preceded the body and magically presided over its formation: this doctrine being perhaps confused also with the merely verbal (but correct) point, that it is the interior form and function of an animal that determined its name or species, and in that sense *makes it* the animal which it is. The second prejudice led Aristotle to say that a part of the mind (the intelligence that enables it to think things as they are), comes to the mind from without, and is divine and immortal. Consciousness, in its deliverance, is not attached to the body, or to an individual or temporal or human field: the whole realm of essence, and *a fortiori,* the form of all nature, is open to its possible intuition and interest; so that it can look at things from the point of view of eternity, it can play the god, affect to nod, and learn to rule the spheres, and the more it does so the more it deserves the name of mind or spirit. But this emancipation of consciousness, as Spinoza afterwards admirably explained, regards the objects of contemplation and interest only, not the seat or basis of that activity. Spirit does not come from without into the house, but from within looks outward, forgetting itself: it does not outlast the body, but while radiating from the body may disregard it, and its own duration. If these matters were amended in Aristotle, in conformity with Spinozistic doctrine, the immaterial expressive cognitive nature of spirit would appear in all its purity, while its material seat, organs and other conditions would be frankly confessed, without subterfuge or forced exceptions.

This is not to say that the artifices of Spinoza, to keep body and mind parallel, are to be substituted for the humanistic fallacies of Aristotle, which superposed them awry and made them separable. Mind (at least what I am calling so) is no impartial accompaniment of matter, whether in motion or at rest, dead or living; it is a rare, local, and fragile expression of animal life. It is very far from representing, on another plane and point for point, all the determinations of material being. If it is parallel to anything that thing is not matter or space, but morphological units or biological processes. When these are suspended, spirit ceases to inhabit nature, or to accompany motion. This is said not merely because spirit is not then discoverable, a mere negative presumption, but because the internal nature of spirit is expressive of dramatic, animal vicissitudes in such a manner as to render it absurd to suppose spirit existing when nothing dramatic is brewing in nature. The tremendously complex and tense machinery of perception, reproduction, hunting and war are what give consciousness a station sufficiently equipped for thinking and something to think about: an atom crossing another atom cannot salute it: it has nothing to covet or to fear from that encounter and no hat to doff.

The parallelists, to be sure, in order to avoid this absurdity, tell us that there are perceptions which are not apperceptions, or forms of consciousnesss which are sub-conscious: there are kinds of white, in a word, which are black. The essence intuited may indeed have, in relation to the type or ideals of other intuitions, any degree of tenuity, vagueness, or dullness: but it must be a perfectly luminous and standard essence in itself. The relative clearness of intuition is like the relative clearness of sounds: in view of a given expectation, or a given type of sound, a different one may be called confused and inchoate; as the sounds of each language seem inarticulate and unseizable to an ear accustomed to a different articulation. Every language is the standard of clearness and purity to itself. Every intuition that really exists reveals a self-sufficient essence: and only in the eyes of foreign prejudice or convention can it be called sub-conscious or incomplete.

The counterfeit notion of unconscious consciousness was coined to disguise the bankruptcy of idealism. It is obvious to any honest survey that life, even in its most rational business, is not carried on through conscious machinery. To a few pious immediatists, like Berkeley and Malebranche, this suspension of our conscious existence over an abyss of nothingness was a welcome stimulus to religious faith and a sense of perpetual dependence on Providence: since consciousness was so frail and scattering, and nature (being unconscious) could not exist, it was admirably evident that the Spirit of God was our only sustainer and companion. Such intrepid piety, however, is rare among men, and hard even for the mystic to stick to: but the subjectivist dogma that nothing but consciousness can exist had become almost axiomatic in the herd of philosophers: and hence the expedient of saying that much consciousness existed of which at the same time we were unconscious.

Nature may be as thick set with intuition as she will, and any one of these may not be reflected upon by any other of them, being lost for historical purposes; or (which is the commoner form of retentiveness) parts of what they perceived need not remain parts of subsequent objects; but intuition, a moment of consciousness, must perceive some essence or other, and cannot be unconscious of that essence however little later experience may repeat or recall it. Furthermore, if this had meant that of much actual feeling or ideation there was no subsequent review or appropriation, the contradiction would be only verbal: but, there were motives at work driving the psychologist to find a *substance* for human experience; he gradually dropped the mental qualities out of mind, and substituted material qualities until, in the motion of mind-stuff, he crossed the chasm and began to speak again of matter under a bashful psychological name. Real confusion remained, however, in this view: for instead of looking for the matter of consciousness in the organs and the circumstances of animal life, they looked for it in qualities abstracted out of sensible essences, lending them prolonged existence when they were no longer intuited: so that the mental image—a spiritual unit—was treated as a tapestry of half-hidden threads all of which, when out of consciousness, might nevertheless retain their existence and colour.

But this pre-natal or posthumous being of sensible qualities is either the being of their essences—which is nothing temporal or existent, much less substantial—or the occurrence of fresh intuitions, having these sensible essences for their object. To suppose a great wealth of such ambient intuitions is not only gratuitous, doing violence to the significance of consciousness, but it is useless for natural philosophy: because however continual and similar those intuitions might be, they would not supply the required canvas on which to paint experience: no multiplication of auditors at the concert of sense would help us to discover what makes the music. The fullness of experience comes at each moment afresh out of the pulses of the body; only in matter is movement consecutive or cumulative; in the spirit there is simply the instantaneous, the actual, the synthetic, perhaps the supreme. But the psychic stuff of the panpsychists was avowedly not spirit, so that besides having introduced a sort of substance which was undiscoverable and equivocal, they had still to explain like any materialist, the emergence of spirit out of that mass.

The English psychological philosophers had naturally little to say about spirit, except that it was "nothing but" something else. What may seem strange is that the German idealists who pronounced the word *Geist* so often and with such unction, should also have hardly discerned it. *Geist,* to them, was a certain divine afflatus or destiny swelling the universe, and precipitating the various forms of religion, art, and polity: and *Bewusstsein* was the seat of this process, or rather of the apprehension of it—for the two things were systematically confused in their philosophy, the soul of which was that experience created its object: what existed was a universal consciousness imagining a world, with its parts imagining parts of the same. But here the loose hold which these enthusiasts had on themselves, a certain solemn charlatanry which pervades them, began to appear. A consciousness has no parts: and if God imagines the world, and we imagine parts of it, that is only a world in fancy: the real world, which neither God's imagination nor ours creates, would be the collection of our experiences and of his; the mutual relations of the two, both in existence and in deliverance, would have to be studied by literary psychology, in a sort of historical romance or natural history of experience. This romance some of these philosophers actually tried to formulate; but the result was rather an excerpt from political history, limited to those parts which could be made to fall within an ideal scheme of moral development. The actual destinies of spirit—its flickering, passionate, incoherent career in innumerable distinct persons —was hereby lost, or deposed to the rank of subjective illusion, only significant where these persons illustrated the stages of the

divine destiny previously conceived: so that the end was a monstrous idolatry, in which all actual moments of happiness and
insight were subordinated morally to an imaginative principle of
evolution. And this disregard of actual spirit was not accidental;
it could never have been built into such grotesque systems of "all
possible experience," if its authors had not been unchastened at
heart—at once force-worshippers, dreamers, fanatics, and pedants.
This barbarism in their blood was easily wedded with their hereditary religion—a Christianity reduced to Hebraism. Religion is
not always a form of spirituality and as there is a practical religion
of thrift, so there can be a speculative religion of world-worship
and world-service.

Where we find Spirit fully expressed is in Indian and Platonic
philosophy; and perhaps we should add, in the quick intuitions of
many an artist and poet, who has not given it philosophic expression. Greek poets, Homer first of all, are full of spiritual feeling;
because the ultimate beauty and preciousness of life are there proclaimed without being denaturalized, inflated, or uprooted from
their conditions. But it would require an interpretation, perhaps
too intentional, to detach that element from all the others that
naturally jostle it in a popular mind, as the mind of a poet must
always be. The Indians, on the other hand, erect the Spirit into so
absolute a judge of things, that while magnificently expressing its
ideal demands, and enforcing them heroically, they run the risk
of undermining its natural foundations. The spirit has no principle or pregnancy in it by which to select or produce its objects: it
is ready like rain to fall on everything that happens to be spread
out beneath it; and the taint by the subjective medium which all
material apprehension suffers from is due to the organ, to the
senses and passions of the animal, not to the spirit itself. Therefore where the object is an essence and not an existence, no subjectivity and no error can intervene; for though consciousness still
has an organ, it then has no natural object and the bias of the
organ does the whole work *ab initio*. It freely selects and therefore
cannot vitiate the object to be intuited.

If now we supposed an intelligence so angelic that it was not
compelled to care for any body, or to study material things, nor
to view them from a particular angle, nor to care for what is going

on in any crazy world: still that intelligence, if it considered anything at all, would be considering objects arbitrary, imposed, and
alien: it would have just as much reason as an avowedly animal
intelligence for kicking against the pricks, and saying it was a
winged bird shut up in a cage of circumstance: and if it cared for
any of its chance visions, it would have the same reason as it has
in animals for feeling itself sinful, and wondering what attached
it so irrationally to things with no claim to be called precious.
The only recourse of spirit, if it is too proud to be the voice of
matter, is not to exist. It will not do to suggest that the whole
realm of essence would be a proper object for free consciousness
to contemplate: first, because the contemplation of all essence,
without movement or emphasis, would not be contemplation, but
the realm of essence itself, and second, because to contemplate all
essence is itself a particular fate, excluding all others, possibly
more congenial; and Spirit is not in itself more akin to all essence
than to such particular essences, for instance, as unity, goodness,
or change. In truth, actual spirit is far more akin to these latter
essences than to all essence; not because all essence might not be
spiritually apprehended, but because actual spirit, being the expression of animal life, hovers most joyously over those things
which animal life happens to be enhanced and sustained by:
whereas the contemplation of all essence is radically impossible
to any animal, and would excruciate him. To rebel against the
animal, warm, and humane pre-occupations of the spirit is to
rebel against the only possible exercise of it; and therefore, the
choice lies between animal consciousness and unconsciousness.
To choose unconsciousness, like ordinary suicide, is a revulsion
against particular circumstances, not a condemnation of all possible life. The mystic should not say, therefore, do not have delusions, but do not have the *wrong* delusion; do not have delusions
that spoil one another: for by delusion he means, I suppose, any
object of experience that does not in itself imply the existence or
value which we find in it, but is a contingent and groundless fact.

The desire for salvation, for insight, or for immortality is no
desire especially native to spirit, nor indicative (as the fable has
it) of its celestial origin. It is a desire borrowed, like all others,
from the impulses of animal life. This is notably the case with the

wish for immortality. Spirit is *in actu* instantaneous and *in potentia* eternal: spectator alike of change and of duration, it can undergo neither of them. It will arise and vanish with equal celerity as occasion may command, and always with the same readiness to survey ingenuously whatever may be offered next. So we see it born afresh every morning in every new creature; absolutely innocent and fearless, inexhaustible and uncontaminated by the thousand ruins it has looked upon. But the life of each animal, its labouring soul or psyche, is quite a different affair. This the measure of a waxing or waning organisation, the seat of passions, the confederate or slave of a thousand external contingencies and unstable natural supports: and it involves, or rather it is, a continual positing of the will, a perpetual claim to exist, and to attract things into its vortex. This is often called the effort after self-preservation; but the "self" to be "preserved" is always changing, and is an ideal not ordinarily determinable at all: now this eventual object and now that is envisaged with craving or horror, and by a series of skirmishes, the psyche, while it is growing, manages to swell its resources, and extend its field of influence; and then in illness, old-age, or defeat, it suffers retrenchment, disperses and dies. But the momentum of the psyche, while she lives, remains prospective: she posits a future, and in planning what shall happen at least virtually plans to be. There is therefore a sort of assumption of immortality, not in the remote future, but continually at each step. The spirit has the same merely cognitive relation to these movements of passion or hope, as it has to any other object; it undergoes them by watching them; it raises them to actuality, without determining their character or duration. All is determined by the animal psyche breeding experience; for consciousness is no substance, no concrete particular force, but only a new status and intensity of being which certain terms of animal life assume on occasion.

Spirit, then, cannot be disembodied: if it does not express the dynamic object which arouses it, it expresses the spontaneous life of some slumbering organ. Nevertheless, there is a difference between more or less spiritual forms of experience: there is a realm of Spirit in which are many mansions, and perhaps a standard of subordination among them. Knowledge or love, for instance, might each be thought of as possibly such a principle; and after choosing between them we might have to choose in each between purity and scope. Ascetics have always conceived progress in spirituality to be connected with mortification of the flesh, or escape from the body. This escape being impossible, we may ask ourselves what sort of liberation of the spirit from nature and the individual might constitute a true ascesis.

Consciousness seems to be aroused either by external stimulation, or by internal remodelling—as in dreams or in those developing passions which people ordinarily call their thoughts. Now if consciousness comes and goes with instant action, merely catching a glimpse of things in transit, as action presents them, consciousness has added nothing, achieved nothing of its own: it has merely taken note of a mechanical process that might have gone on just as well unnoticed, or even better: for the ground of the alert attention is some uneasiness, some strain in the machinery. Now the indignity of this servile attention does not lie in the fact that the things perceived are material, or transitory, or practical. In material things we might see beauty, into movement we might read grace, music and destiny, from practical affairs we might learn art and understanding. These would be spiritual fruits of contact with things material; and the cause of missing them, if we do, does not lie in the externality of the things, but in their ill-adjustment to one's organs. A stimulus is brutal only when it provokes consciousness to no purpose—is a consciousness of no value in itself: for consciousness is never of value in expediting the flux of matter —if such acceleration of matter were to have any value. Let the stimulus, coming from the same quarter, enhance the life of the organ: then consciousness will dominate and survey the object, not merely feel its passage or weight. The object, though existent, will have delivered up its essence, and become an object of speculation, a passive form. Hunger will have become taste, lust will have become love, and life will have passed into knowledge. The existent world may fill the imagination quite as worthily as any ideal thing, provided it is the imagination that it fills, and not merely the nerves that it agitates, occasioning a vain and hounded consciousness in that perturbed automaton, the worldling. Spirituality is not separation from the life of man, but requires detachment from it. A free spirit may study, like a curious painter, every sordid detail of the world; but it is lost if it becomes passive, dragged about by this or that, and not contemplative. The spirit of practical men is passive, and that of contemplative men active: for the activity proper to spirit does not consist in an alleged magic influence on the motions of matter but in the spontaneity of that organic life which consciousness expresses; a life which (either by virtue of a happy constitution in the animal or of civilisation having humanised the influences under which it operates) receives only such and all such stimulations as its native fertility requires to expand under: and so is at once free and clear. Its commerce with things is entertaining to it, and its conception of them true, as far as it goes (which is far enough): but it is not *pressed* to know them, either in their ulterior extent or in their absolute quality: its view remains human and poetical. *Pressure* in investigation is unspiritual, and bread-winning or fame-winning rather than philosophy; and so is the craving to be converted, and supplied with all truth all at once; this craving is an incident to spiritual fatigue and the last form of that life-long pressure, that tiresome flurry to know of the would-be convert, for fear of missing some rare bargain, either in this world or in the next.

VI

THE SPIRITUAL LIFE

Why Does Spirit Aim at Its Own Purity?

GEORGE SANTAYANA

Because life aims at its own equilibrium or entelechy.

Spiritual confusion and ruin of which the world is full are accordingly not evil to the spirit but to the flesh: for to the spirit nothing is either good or evil—an animal distinction altogether. The spirit does not therefore *condemn* moral bias, any more than it imposes it; for to condemn morality is to have it. It merely *feels the glow* of the moral passions, as of the others, and among them of the moral passion for purity of will and vision—for sanctity.

It is a mistake to suppose that Spirit has any interests whatever —even in its own existence. But if some animal cares for Spirit, and makes the realization of Spirit his goal, then this attainment becomes one of the aims of Spirit, and may, by an excusable ellipsis, be called its interest in itself.

How then shall we express this spiritual aim of human beings, to realize Spirit? And what would such a realization be?

1. Greek spirituality, or suspense and measure. Because to yield

George Santayana, "Why Does Spirit Aim at its Own Purity?" *Columbia Manuscript Collection,* IX:14:II. © 1967 by Daniel Cory.

to each impulse without reserve makes a sort of conflict in the
total soul, like that produced by simultaneous conflicts in the
body, before reason has made the succession simultaneous. It is
this emergence of equilibrium that is health and resource. The
mind expresses it by sweet reasonableness and philosophic *ethos*.
It does not quit nor electrify common life, but merely moderates
or melodises it.

II. This smug rationality (cf. Aristotle's ethics) is possible to
a prosperous middle class, in a civilised state. There are *higher
tensions* latent in human nature, and each, taken as a standard,
regards the others as mean. So military, adventurous, or religious
passion. Is it a gain in spirituality? Probably it is, at certain
points; but in respect to the form of the whole and in principle it
is a retrogression. After all, the things life seeks, in becoming
spirit, are intensity, clearness and security. The effort to perceive,
the effort to possess, in body or soul, ends and justifies itself in
adequate intuition: and when we enlarge the scale, and take the
circumstances of life for the thing looked to, we end, if at all, in
the same adequacy: which the Greek synthesis in suppression
realised—for by synthesis it retained the various *motifs* of life,
and by suppression it kept them all in the potential phase, and at
a distance, and in a form fit for contemplation. By heightening
any element, and straining to make it supreme at the expense of
the others, we are either providing a new balance (if we succeed
in establishing the spiritual aristocracy we aim at) or we are falling into spiritual *vice;* that is, for the sake of a special sort of
spiritual achievement, ruining natural life, and so undermining
that very achievement itself. Predatory habits exist in the jungle
of Spirit: fixed aspirations and fanaticisms that prey on the un-
wary multitude of little goods that common life might be filled
with but for that fierce visitation, and that if finally devoured
would bring about starvation for the tyrant spirit itself. To exist,
therefore, such a predatory ideal must be double and inconsistent:
it must say; let there be no other will to stay me; but yet, let
there be other wills to keep me strong. So despotism, and idleness.
The *beau geste* of each of these self-assertions is delightful: they
give colour to the comedy of ethics, and supply genuine ideals to
the imagination, without which—see Protestantism—it would be

stiff and empty, and the slave of external things. But they seldom have the courage of their full convictions; they do not say either: Let me be so, and perish: nor: Let it be so for me, while you, pleasing yourself thereby, follow a different maxim, to enable me to follow mine. You work and serve and beget children, that I may be indolent, and rich, and free from sorrows and bonds. This is the way we all treat the inanimate, and even the brute creation: with a little courage we might treat the bulk of mankind in the same way. But the question would ensue: which had the better part, and in whom [was] spirit . . . more notably realised? The lilies of the field might be the more gloriously arrayed and some enslaved Epictetus might be the better philosopher. And this not in their judgment, or in that of some third party, but in that of the enthusiast himself, who might not be altogether comfortable in his ticklish supremacy.

The more satisfactory way of breaking through the classical ideal is to re-establish it with heightened elements. The shrill extravagances of the zealots must be disregarded, as the Greek moralists did not disregard the inspiration of oracles and poets and the dark irrationalities of ancestral cults and mythologies: but these stray notes must be fused, subordinated, and tamed into orthodoxy. A richer system of suspended impulses and divine messages reverently listened to but not rashly obeyed, must supervene on these insurrections of sectaries: in other words, the actual must not be ignored, it must be understood: because the essence of spirit being understanding, it has not reached its goal so long as, to understand more readily, it brushes aside, as not existent or horrible, half of what exist to be understood.

I have been called many names—pragmatist, poet, intellectualist, dualist, mystic, epiphenomenalist, phenomenalist, brutish materialist, atheist, papist, amateur—but no one, I believe, has yet called me an optimist. Nevertheless, I will say this: that if everything could be understood, it would form a harmony. Not a harmony, to be sure, for those who suffer and go down, i.e., for the old Adam in all of us, but a harmony for the Spirit that understands. Not merely that it would be intelligible—which is a truism, since intelligence is sympathy with the facts, whatever they may be, and contains, in its date and axioms, contingency and surds enough for any world. Besides finding the world in this empirical sense intelligible, and of a describable nature, the spirit would find both the efforts and the checks of life acceptable: the impulses positing goods and beauties, the checks, in forbidding this realisation, publishing their unimportance. Nothing is important, except to itself. Spirit is impartial here, feeling both the manifold wills that weight everything with values, and the omnipresent indifference, that turns those values to nought. There is peace beyond these wars; not only the cold peace of death, but the warm and living peace of understanding. It was Justice, said Heraclitus, that imposed change, because what exists, being irrational or unstable, merited to perish: that is, while with one voice it asserts an ideal of special fulfilments which would be beautiful, but which are impossible, with another voice it asserts an ideal of order which to realise is inevitable, and which in its way is beautiful too. Thus all efforts and sorrows in being intelligently shared are shared poetically only, at a distance, by a spirit that has regained its inviolate purity: and if the reader thinks this is a heartless and immoral doctrine, let him remember the received opinion that God is all-knowing, happy, and unmoved. Of course, I do not suggest that either God or man can have this purely spiritual life after or apart from natural existence: what I mean is that natural existence has for its inherent entelechy just this emancipation and impartiality of the spirit. It can be reached only in moments of perfect equilibration and internal harmonious movement: and on the ways in which this may be approached or almost touched, I will yet say a few words.

Equilibrium through abstention (memory, elegiac feeling, old age, etc.)

Equilibrium through contemplation in the *act* of material occupations and party warfare, through an intention or dedication to what undoes them. (The sacrifice of Abraham.)

The two *not alternatives*. Abstention requisite beyond a certain point. Action requisite within a certain field.

There are two chief methods by which salvation or perfection or happiness may be pursued: that of the ascetics: retrenchment, with a contemplative life, and that of the Stoics: endurance with action in the world. But there is no opposition between them, if we have really entered the field of spiritual life, which would not be the case either if we renounced everything, or if we accepted everything. Renunciation is fundamental, since harmony must have some principle of synthesis and demarcation; however numerous and varied the orchestra, the difference must subsist between it and pandemonium. In the same way, however, renunciation cannot be absolute. We renounce to achieve, and a treasure to be saved subsists however much we disencumber ourselves of earthly baggage. This apart from the material necessity (which spiritual men might well not perceive) of a brain in tolerable health and vigour and a society not too pervasively savage, if spiritual life is to dawn at all. On the other hand, endurance and action would be mere brutishness if contemplation did not accompany and consecrate them. The question is simply what kind of action, and how much of it, yields the most satisfying consciousness. And by satisfying is to be understood self-sufficient, adequate to its own ideal and at peace with its conceived destiny: not at all, adequate to its ground or its environment, in any descriptive sense. Health involves far more consciousness than consciousness of the body: spirituality indeed implies utter unconsciousness in this respect; because consciousness of the body, except as a fact among other facts, is an *obsession* incompatible with serenity and unselfishness: it implies cravings, vanities, fears, disappointments, animosities. These things all are unavoidable, however, so long as the body is diseased and persecuted and not sufficiently provided for: so that the spiritual rule of life, in regard to hygiene, should be to reduce material economy to a mechanism that will insure support without requiring attention. Begging is an attempt to do this; but not successful; because begging, and even praying for daily bread (when not otherwise assured) is an agitating business, and fertile in little sordid hatreds and envies. But life in a community is a great help: because the ordinary brother is provided for and kept in shape, while the officers are concerned with impersonal provision for the community in which (especially if rival communities were not in view) little passion need be involved: and business, when carried on disinterestedly, is as good an object of attention as any other science or art. Anxiety is the primal curse of consciousness. The tormenting both in knowledge and in ignorance

lies in the anxiety they bring. To remove anxiety is a prerequisite
to spirituality: but it cannot be removed, and secure spirituality
[*sic*], by a total denial of the will; for then animal existence and
consciousness have vanished together. The only other way, apparently, is to secure all possible supports in nature, and to renounce all impossible wishes. Should philosophy meditate on life
or on death? Surely on life: but only after, by long meditating on
death, life has been purged of all that causes anxiety, and the
sting of death taken away by limiting the will to live to living as
is possible: not on the circumstances of life—again a preoccupation of those anxious about the means of living: but on the issues,
rewards, and beauties which life can have and create.

Out of anxiety comes rebellion.

Elements of the Realm of Spirit

GEORGE SANTAYANA

1. Intuition.

2. All things lighted up by intuition.

(*a*) The sensuous quality of these things (even if not found in
the external objects) is no obstacle to perfect spirituality in the
vision of them: neither the subjectivity nor the warmth and immediacy of the apparition is anything against it. In fact, these are
rather the *typical* objects of spirit—essences not things, and values
not uses.

(*b*) The fugitive quality of things is also not calculated to defeat
the spirit. The spirit is not addressed to existence, and therefore
not to duration of existence. The instinct to hoard or accummulate
is an animal impulse run wild, and defeating its own uses. This is

George Santayana, "Elements of the Realm of Spirit," *Columbia Manuscript Collection*, IX:14:II. © 1967 by Daniel Cory.

as true of hoarding knowledge as money: and it is true of hoarding experience also, of wishing to taste, and know, and store up
everything in one's own person *ad infinitum*. Things are not
more fugitive than breaths: and the spirit is a thing of breath.
If at each moment it finds the beautiful and good—that is enough.

(c) Nevertheless, the life of the senses and the mutability of
things are thorns in the spirit's side: why? Because the senses are
ordinarily not fields of intuition so much as paths of allurement:
and the fugitive character of things confuses the impression of
them as they flow, and *cheats* the affection they may have begun
to inspire. Now to be lured, confused, and cheated are woeful
trials to the spirit. Hence that religious dread of the senses, and
those lamentations about change.

(d) But how can the spirit have woes? Consciousness can actualise pain, as it can actualise anything; but is not the ground or
reason why one thing hurts and another pleases: this ground lies
in the contractions and instincts of the body. If then we say the
spirit suffers from the deceits of the flesh, we must look for the
rebellion against such deceits in the body itself, which requires
a certain steadiness if it is to feed the spirit. The woes of the spirit
are then not its own, but those of the natural life it illuminates,
and whose colour (being colourless) it is said to take. If the bodily
life were not impeded by cheats, confusions and lures, these would
cease to obscure the spirit: for in each it would find a separate
and appropriate object. It is not a sign of brutishness (as bad
critics suppose) but on the contrary of diffused spirituality, to
find delight and sufficiency in sights, sounds, fancies, and incidental loves. That a creature should be able to pass without distress or remorse from moment to moment of pure sentiment and
vision, among simple pleasures and clear passions, is not a sign of
dissolution but of a plastic and tender organisation; a childlike
method pursued with a man-like courage and zest—a sort of
Epicurean or Saracenic chivalry. When the brain is more synthetic, and the mind wiser, spirituality remains of the same sort,
only more widely based. Every dashing adventurer has something
of this desultory wholeness of soul; in blackguards it is mixed
tions and debts unpaid to the world, while only in artists or

with shreds of ugly and clouding preoccupations—impure ambi-
poets or a certain sort of saint does it appear birdlike and pure—
a sort of angelic freedom from care, a genial unconcern, united
with a high intensity of insight and enjoyment. The defeat of this
kind of spiritual naturalism comes from the *insecurity* of human
health and fortune. This is not a philosophy to live by long in this
treacherous world: we need much heavier armour, a much larger
capital, on which to draw even a pittance securely. We cannot
live on the fruits of the hour; the birds and the lilies of the field
would not, if they had any more far-reaching apprehension. This
greater scope is in the first instance, like the complexities of modern society, a defeat of spirituality; but it makes room for a
spirituality with a greater sweep—when poetic sentiment of the
Oriental sort has yielded to philosophy or to sanctity. It is then
that the fugitive comes to seem vain, and the sensuous delusive
and sinful. It has become an obstacle to a certain discipline, now
recognised as necessary, to certain sacrifices found to be requisite
for establishing purity and simplicity on a higher plane. *'Entbehren sollst du, sollst entbehren,'* then becomes *'der ewige Gesang.'*
What might have been a perfect life in isolation may, unpruned,
be a disturbing element in the life which has absorbed it. This is
the Fall from Eden: or the laborious and confused beginning of
human salvation.

The moral confusion and obliquity of man are physical mal-
adjustments: the spirit is neither responsible for them nor tarnished by them in its own person: but when there is this disorder
beneath, spirit can be realised only imperfectly and with difficulty.
As old age and death dry up the spirit, so business and passion
stifle it. But let these new activities once attain balance, let the
business and the passion be clarified and thoroughly understood,
and they have become new materials and objects for spiritual
consideration: they are more life to save. For it is folly to suppose
that without business of some sort there could be any attention,
or without passion any devotion. Spirit (extraneous as it may
seem to animal life) is really the fulfilment of it; animal life is not
motion; it is a focussing of motions into sparks of light, a con-
spiracy of instincts that meet in an ideal. Consciousness is spiritual

from the beginning; it does not arise until there is something in life capable of expression and it is a form afresh with wider and wider fields of vision as more and more articulation is introduced into the machinery of life, until it becomes the hypostatic expression of the whole process, when this has been integrated enough to be expressed in a large imagination and a wise rule of life.

It may well be said that on this theory health, youth, and vigour would be spiritual, whereas the mortified life of the saints would be misguided. And so I maintain that it would be, if the penance, and asceticism were the end; but in the true saints they are not. There is an issue out of them which is seraphic. In savage asceticism, violence is done to the body, by bleeding its tormenting passions into repose, or venting some overpowering frenzy: and this method is doubly blind, because it does not extinguish lawlessness in the members, but merely cows them for a moment: while it does not advance towards a reasonable life, in yielding to new sorts of hideous impulse. Disciplined asceticism often retains vestiges of these errors, and good rule on the contrary retains *sympathy* with the passions it suppresses, so that it remains sweet *and* intelligent: its severities are not casual or cruel, but rather exercises in detachment and self-contempt, together with the practice of a simplicity which is really a deliverance from a thousand troubles. Suffering—because suffering is the birth out of nature into spirit—and joy, because the spirit is born [*sic*]. The most spiritual of saints or poets will use images drawn from nature and from passion. What else should he clothe his thoughts with? Surely those would not be more spiritual if nakedly logical or mathematical. So in the world, in the very midst of orgies and battles, a pure spirit, a Socrates or a Hamlet, turns everything into images, into the pageant of a strange, lovely, and poisoned world. That is, such a mind sees essences and examples where fleshly men see things and opportunities. He can renounce the existence of what exists even before the existing thing has renounced it (which is soon enough). He distils existence while still in white heat, into infinitely variegated light of ideas. It is not necessary—even if it were possible—to abolish the senses or passions or fashions of our poor humanity, in order to live in the spirit. It suffices to accept them for what they are, and not for what they promise to the unteachable animal in us: to disdain the material and temporal substance and the selfish illusion beneath them, and to gather from them their flower or essence—i.e., their truth.

Note on Morality versus Spirit

GEORGE SANTAYANA

What is called morality is an expression of reason, like science and art: in fact it is a province of politics, which is a province of art. Men have a destiny which they know in the gross long before they have an ideal of life; for we all repeat that men are mortal, but only two or three great philosophers have attempted to conceive what a mortal life is or might be. Now this ideal, when it becomes articulate, even when it seems merely personal dream, is the expression, more or less comprehensive, of human impulses which are those of a particular gregarious animal. First, it demands courage and a certain warmth of nature—it expresses self-defense and the will to live. Secondly, it demands helpfulness and fidelity, that is, it expresses the need of cooperation to carry on a prosperous society. All this is indifferent to the spirit. There is nothing unspiritual in self-defense, or inquisitiveness, or sexual propagation, or politics, or commerce, or sport: as there is nothing unspiritual in coral formations. In a sense, all this and the prudent ordering of it called morality, is food for the spirit; if there were no coral reefs, or other natural and social bodies, there would be no soil for it to spring from and nothing for spirit to consider, since the realm of essence is not open to inspection save through the realm of existence, which brings some samples of essence, as it were, to our notice, though not always those that exist

George Santayana, "Note on Morality versus Spirit," *Columbia Manuscript Collection,* IX:14:II. © 1967 by Daniel Cory.

[i.e., what is noticed may not exist, but then something else (say, the brain) must exist to stimulate that illusion]. On the other hand, the most perfect morality may be a perfect spiritual death: for it may veil and passionately deny the fact that it is utterly indifferent in itself whether there are coral reefs or not, or whether men, or sexual embrace, or civil laws exist or do not exist. What is important is that if by any of these instruments the light of spirit is kindled at all, it shall not by that very act be tarnished, or be brought forth flickering, agonised and impure. In other words, the spirit being perfectly contemplative, should seem so: as it can do nothing, it should not writhe to do anything; as it can see all things, that it should contract itself passionately to see only some particular thing. Spirit is vision; unspirituality is attachment.

Spirit in Indian Philosophy

GEORGE SANTAYANA

To India, rather than to Europe, we should turn for understanding of spirit; yet the several doctrines that we actually find there, notable for maturity and elevation, are developed under the influence of fanciful metaphysics, and carried out into a wealth of detail that is purely inventive. It is therefore hard but necessary to distinguish two parts of the Indian philosophies of Spirit; one of unmatched authority, on account of the spiritual integrity, unworldliness, imaginative courage, and prolonged intense meditation which it enshrines; the other part negligible in view of its childishness and insanity.

Indian metaphysics is not the abuse, like ours, of grammar and psychology, but rather of the moral imagination. Of nature those spiritual philosophers took a disinterested, poetic, attentive sur-

George Santayana, "Spirit in Indian Philosophy," *Columbia Manuscript Collection*, IX:14:II. Title supplied by editor. © 1967 by Daniel Cory.

vey; they watched it loom, labour, and vanish before them; they divined in sensation the play of vast numbers and minute subdivisions; but they did not rise from their meditation to follow up and study this structure, as the objects, when handled, anatomised and experimented upon might reveal it. What the pageant did not offer on its surface, they were content to ignore, or filled it up with stupendous dreams which they deputed to be miraculous perceptions, vouched for by an intuition which could dispense with ordinary organs. Hence it was easy for them to admit that nature might be composed of substances corresponding to our moral states (such as exaltation, struggles, empathy), or might be unsubstantial altogether; they also imagined that experience was governed by a magic principle of retribution and that the world was evoked (at least for our perception) by the power of ancient acts, inevitably fertile in sorrow, or in that other kind of pain which men call pleasure. Life was a continual expiation of continual follies, till wisdom called a halt.

We can see, in the very wantonness of these physical dogmas, how well the nature of the spirit was understood—especially [by] the Sankhya philosophy, which admitted the reality of the material world, [and] posited spirit over against it with admirable boldness. To be sure, it posited spirits as substances; but this error too was a sort of homage to the mind, since its alleged substantiality was far from degrading it into a physical force or confusing it with the psyche. The psyche (buddhi, ahamkãra, manas, or antahkarana) was material; but each spirit (atman) was an eternal impossible self-subsisting light, or potentiality of consciousness, needing to shine on nothing; and the great sorrow was that the nearness of some portions of matter caused the latter to be lighted up, [and] a reflection of this illumination stained the soul, or seemed to stain it, so that the illusion arose that it was proper to the soul to follow with anxiety the fortunes of that illuminated portion of matter. Here we have several obscure or absurd notions: the *nearness* of a soul to matter of any kind; the *illumination* of this portion; a change in the matter only, thus kindled to consciousness, passing rather an act of the soul, which yet remains unchanged [sic].

It would have been better to say that actual consciousness is only the incandescence spontaneous to the body—the entelechy of its life; and the separate soul, as the Buddhists soon taught, is non-existent. That Nirvana, however, or absorption in Brahma, is the alternative to slavery to the flesh, is a piece of mysticism, grounded (so that nothing definite could seem good) partly on a dreamful illiberal nurture and partly on ignorance of the expressive nature of spirit, which has bodily life for its ground. Absorption in Brahma, we are told, leaves joy standing, and even Nirvana is not quite annihilation: but we may suspect that this *mere* joy, or *mere* salvation, are felt to be positive goods because that from which they are an escape is felt to be so immense an evil, and that they, in their very negativity, seem the more real and true, because the phantasmagoria of earthly life is so acutely felt to be a delusion. After this mockery and distraction, the alternative, however blank in itself, becomes joyful and deeply real. It is a refuge and a sanctuary in the profound immovable truth.

Excellent too is the insight that the aim of spirit is not to know, say, the truth, but to be or live after its own nature, whatever that may be. The knowledge of truth is the aim of spirit only by accident, in so far as this knowledge is a sign of prosperity and safety in the destinies of spirit; for a mind full of errors indicates a body full of maladaptations. But if once the body is well adapted, and by its heart and habits ensures a prosperous life to the mind, the *truth* of intuition becomes indifferent; for all intuitions are true to themselves, and reveal their chosen essences, and it profits the happy mind nothing to possess reports of the machinery by which it is supported in being. Nevertheless, the notion that the proper being or life of the soul is to withdraw from all contact with the body, and employ itself in thinking about nothing, is doubly chimerical; first because such withdrawal is impossible, and would abolish the soul in its ground: and then because a spirit without thoughts is a false abstraction and spiritual freedom consists in thinking about the congenial and beautiful, not in not thinking at all. The congenial or the beautiful, however, is not (as an idolatrous religion has taught us in the West) what happens to exist; the essence of God, of the

world, or of destiny, these matters of fact are at best shabby
fatalities, full of sadness, absurdity, and wrong: consider, for instance, the Creator and his creation as religions conceive them,
with their restless plottings, tinkerings, pedagogical habits, moral
obsessions, hatreds, redemptions, conversions, and hells. If that
were the real world, it would be a blessing to forget it. The actual
underpinning of the spirit is not so positively mean and odious:
it is an ethereal flux, swift, complex, and infinite; but even this,
with the moral incidents which grow out of it, is for the most part
uninteresting and better unknown. So that the withdrawal of the
spirit within itself is really, as the Sankhya teaches, the salvation
to be hoped for; only this spiritual emancipation must be based
on the health of the body (since spirit cannot be severed from it
materially), and must terminate in the free life of art and imagination (since the spirit could not be if it thought about nothing).

Apropros of Aristotle

GEORGE SANTAYANA

His moral doctrine is right in substance but somehow wrong
in accent; there is something tiring and priggish about his outlook. He is thinking too much of the choice of an occupation and
too little of the nature of life: his contemplative activity is almost
synonymous with talkative leisure and the progression of science;
as if a wanderer, a singer, a saint, or a child could not be as contemplative as a philosopher. The contemplative force of spirit
does not lie in not acting but in living when you act.

George Santayana, "Apropos of Aristotle," *Columbia Manuscript Collection,*
IX:14:II. © 1967 by Daniel Cory.

Santayana, Then and Now

STERLING P. LAMPRECHT

Recent works from the pen of Santayana have made clear a distinction which compels a revision of the estimate usually put upon his philosophy by American critics. This distinction is expressed by the two contrasted ideas of *the life of reason* and *the spiritual life*. Traces of the contrast can be seen in the earliest books of Santayana, but the traces are both few and faint. *The spiritual life* is not a development of a theme familiar from pages of former writings; it is comparatively a new theme, a theme so contrasted with *the life of reason* that we may wonder at times whether it can be incorporated into the same symphonic whole. For some reason, or because of some accident, Santayana devoted himself to an exposition of the life of reason many years before he turned to elucidate his present conception of the spiritual life. Perhaps this fact is due to some prompting of his personal taste; for Santayana is a mixture of artist and moralist, and it is the life of reason which is the *locus* of all esthetic and ethical achievements, while the spiritual life, as he now defines it, has no concern with values at all. In any case, and no matter what may explain the temporal priority of the five-volumed *Life of Reason,* his critics, even his "friendly critics," have too often supposed that his philosophy was exhausted in the explanation and development of that conception. This is now clearly seen to be not the case,[1] whether happily or unhappily. The world of essence, Santayana tells us, contains infinite richness; and so his philosophy, we dis-

Sterling P. Lamprecht, "Santayana, Then and Now," *The Journal of Philosophy,* 25 (1928), pp. 533-550. Reprinted by permission.

[1] The theme of *the spiritual life* is developed particularly in the last two books which Santayana has published: *Platonism and the Spiritual Life* (New York, Charles Scribner's Sons, 1927), and *The Realm of Essence* (New York, Charles Scribner's Sons, 1927).

cover, contains at least an unsuspected variety of themes. The
great series of *The Life of Reason* carried through one conception with masterly skill. The new series of *Realms of Being,* along
with the reply which in *Platonism and the Spiritual Life* he
makes to Dean Inge, is striking out in a new direction. For any
just appraisal of Santayana's thought, we must try to make clear
the distinction between the fundamental ideas of these two series
of books.

The life of reason is "a name for that part of experience which
perceives and pursues ideals—all conduct so controlled and all
sense so interpreted as to perfect natural happiness."[2] It is a temporal career which men may at times come to live on earth. When
imagination is guided by the needs of animal life, and impulse is
disciplined by the foresight of ideal possibilities, then the life of
reason comes to pass. It is the intelligent utilization of raw materials for the manufacture of a finished product which will more
efficiently serve the interests of man. It is the loving reshaping of
natural objects (in clay and stone, in sound and color) into forms
which will delight the soul. It requires for its achievement both
industrial and fine arts; it involves a high degree of competence
in techniques of handling the means to human welfare, and it issues in increased sensitivity to, and in heightened appreciation of,
the ends at which men aim. Also it is the transformation of human
as well as of inanimate nature, the building up from crude impulse and wild imagination of an ordered and harmonious life. It
is concerned with politics, with war, with family life, with friend-
ships, with all human institutions. It leads men beyond the "natural society" into which they are born, until they win a status in
that "free society" in which their relationships with their fellows
are reconstructed in accord with the ideal, are beautified and enriched, and become a source of enduring joy. Religions have
aimed to complete the life of reason by reshaping man's fear of
the unknown into citizenship in the Kingdom of God, even if
their proneness for superstitious form has invariably thwarted
their realization of this aim. Thus the whole history of human
culture is a record of man's stumbling progress towards and tragic
blindness to the ever-present possibilities of the life of reason. The

[2] *Reason and Common Sense,* p. 3.

life of reason has no final goal in the sense of a culminating moment for the sake of which all else occurs; it is a process of constant moral gain, in which each measure of success but opens the way to further efforts for still loftier ambitions. Yet it has many final goals, in the sense of moments of intrinsic value and self-justifying worth; for life does bring to men bits of genuine glory, moments of sheer happiness in the exercise of power nobly directed to noble ends.

The spiritual life, as outlined in Santayana's last two books, is quite another affair. It is not a matter of effort, of enterprise, of the control of nature; it is rather a matter of escape from the mundane realm. Though it can occur only at moments in the career of rational animals, it is yet not directed to temporal achievements in the refashioning of the course of events. "Spiritual life is not a worship of 'values,' whether found in things or hypostatized into supernatural powers. It is the exact opposite; it is *disintoxication* from their influence."[3] It is based on "the gleam of intuition."[4] It is concerned, not with existence and time, but with essence and eternity. It is contemplation of essence, contemplation so detached from worldly affairs, from moral promptings, from consciousness of change in the realm of matter, that it is utterly unaware of its existential basis and its temporal relations; for since, as Aristotle says, the soul is everything it knows, the man who lives the spiritual life tends to become, like the essences he contemplates, a disembodied and eternal form. Though it is true that "wherever spirit exists, it exists at some particular place and time, by the operation of its natural organs," yet it is also true that "wherever it thinks, it regards only some essence, eternal and non-existent, a more or less ample manifestation of pure Being."[5] Spirit then means loss of even self-consciousness; and this loss is, not metaphorical, but actual,—for spirit "cannot attain that ecstacy without dropping all connection with its body—that is, without dying."[6] To those who do not cultivate the spiritual life, it will always seem that "the end of the spiritual life is an

3 *Platonism and the Spiritual Life*, p. 30.
4 *Ibid.*, p. 49.
5 *The Realm of Essence*, p. 63.
6 *Ibid.*, p. 61.

end indeed: it is annihilation."[7] But to those who seek the spiritual life, its end is a liberation from existence which is scorned and a passing into that eternity which seems to offer abiding peace.

Thus the life of reason and the spiritual life are different in nature. As one is a temporal career towards ideal goods, the other is withdrawal from time and indifference to goods as much as to evils, indifference to all existence of whatever moral quality. Santayana does not seek to lead people to live the spiritual life: he is seeking for understanding rather than carrying on propaganda. "In the spiritual life there is nothing obligatory."[8] It is the good life for those whose temper leads them to seek it; but so are several other forms of life. And Santayana concludes his most persuasive chapter in *The Realm of Essence* with the confession that he himself prefers the life of reason to the spiritual life. "Much as I may admire and in a measure emulate spiritual minds, I am aware of following them *non passibus aequis;* and I think their ambition, though in some sense the most sublime open to man, is a very special one, beyond the powers and contrary to the virtues possible to most men. As for me, I frankly cleave to the Greeks and not to the Indians and I aspire to be a rational animal rather than a pure spirit."[9] Now the cynic may smile that so sympathetic an expositor of the spiritual life should thus pronounce. But the critic must not be cynical. A writer may minutely describe the way of life of some Tibetan monks or ancient anchorites without aspiring to fashion his own life on the model of his subject. And furthermore Santayana has already shown himself a zealous spokesman for the life of reason and can not therefore be a practitioner of a life so radically different. None the less, the critic, however he may eschew cynicism and seek just appraisal, will be forced, I believe, to consider Santayana's reluctance to become "pure spirit" a significant confession. Perhaps it will be found that Santayana has not drawn the outlines of the spiritual life in a way thoroughly true to the intent of his own thought. Of course if he or any one else wishes to define the term in a certain way, such is his right: definition is arbitrary. And some men have

[7] *Ibid.,* p. 61.
[8] *Ibid.,* p. 65.
[9] *Ibid.,* p. 65.

lived such a life as Santayana calls the spiritual life. Yet Santayana may perhaps have overstated his case. In preëmpting the term "spiritual life" for a life he can not himself choose to live, he is perhaps exaggerating an idea which in another form would present a more alluring prospect.

But before we discuss the spiritual life further, we must turn to an analysis of the realm of essence with which in the spiritual life Santayana tells us we are wholly concerned. Essences can hardly be defined; but they can be designated by discourse about them, especially through careful assertions as to what they are *not*. They are not metaphysical powers behind the world of appearances, nor magnetic forces which draw men and things upwards in aspiration. They are not properly to be called the natures of things; for many essences may never have been manifested in any existence, and those which are so manifested are indifferent to such a casual and adventitious accident. They are not concepts or mental events, though some of them at times happen to be envisaged in the "gleam of intuition." They are not immortal as the gods are alleged by their worshipers to be, though they are eternal in their timeless being. They are not intrinsically noble and do not deserve to be regarded as superior to existence, though some of them may serve as symbols of the values we human beings pursue and many are indeed logically prior to the situations by which they happen to be brought before our attention. They are the objects of that final form of mystic contemplation, when the existence of even God becomes too trivial to absorb the continued devotion of the emancipated soul. They remain unchanged while we shift our gaze unwittingly from one to another and say we have "changed our minds;" and they do not cease to be when all else perishes in the unceasing cycle of birth and death. They are identical and individual, universal and non-existent; they are not imaginary, nor abstract, nor, except by chance, the terms of discourse. They alone are luminous in a world where the texture of events is confused and puzzling; but they are not therefore friendly to man, but only innocent of all regard for mortals. They are not themselves truths, since truth involves predication about some reality; but whenever we try to speak the truth in science or human affairs, we must resort to essences as the only means of significant utterance. And all our scientific theories, all our bodies of knowledge, all our assertions about the world and our business in the world,—all our speech, in brief, is but an inroad into the realm of essence whereby we hope that some light from "the gleam of intuition" may fall across the dark and abysmal course of nature.

Such is the chief thesis of *The Realm of Essence*. The delightful pages in which Santayana carries the reader through his exposition of the thesis are so intriguing in their literary charm that they tend to silence dissent. Indeed the book is one of the most effective which has come from his pen. The critic might almost venture the opinion that no such exquisite philosophical literature had ever before been composed; and he could not be refuted unless some interruption reminded him that there are other volumes written by Santayana and there are the dialogues of Plato. But admiration is not the only form of criticism. And on certain points the truth of Santayana's presentation of the nature of essence may perhaps be challenged. I say *perhaps*. For one can hardly be sure that objections to Santayana's statements are fair: a style which uses so many graceful literary figures is sometimes difficult to interpret with accurate literalness. Yet even at the risk of captious criticism, two points seem to me to call for adverse comment. And if the points are not well taken, the later volumes of the series on *Realms of Being* will perhaps give the needed correction.

The first point on which I would make adverse criticism is in connection with a doctrine set forth in *Scepticism and Animal Faith* and repeated in *The Realm of Essence*. In the former book Santayana employed the phrase that *nothing given exists*.[10] In the latter book he uses no such extreme statement of the point, and I am left somewhat doubtful to what extent he still intends to maintain the point unchanged. Yet often Santayana seems to say that the whole content of experience is a series of essences and that nothing else is ever immediately present in experience. The point is not that only an essense can be intuited; for intuition is a term which Santayana chooses to preëmpt for the way in which

[10] Cf. the title of chapter VII, and *passim* in the entire book.

essences are present to the mind. The point is rather (if this interpretation is correct) that intuition is the only activity which clearly occurs in experience. And then one would be driven to assert that all the particular colors and sounds, all the immediate "impressions" of the various senses, all the so-called data of experience are essences. Possibly this is what Santayana means in speaking of "sensible essences,"[11] or in saying that "all the qualities of sensation,"[12] "the sweetness I may taste,"[13] or "the colour of the sky"[14] are essences. Surely, since essences do not exist, it would follow by rigid logic that, if only essences are given in experience, nothing given exists. Few would challenge the premise that essences do not exist. But many would challenge the premise that only essences are given in experience. Experience seems to many of us to give immediately certain existential facts. "A particular sort of colour, say Cambridge blue" is what Whitehead calls a "sense-object" and Santayana calls an essence. But Whitehead goes on to point out that this *sort* of color is an entirely different thing from "a particular patch of blue as seen during a particular second of time at a definite date."[15] And the particular patch of blue is, so it seems at least to me, as immediately present in experience as the *sort* of blue, the essence of blue. Whitehead calls the way in which the particular patch of blue is present "presentational immediacy."[16] And experience does seem directly and indubitably to give us abundant data through presentational immediacy. Much that is given would then exist. And if we need inference, cautiously checked and controlled, if we also need postulates which can perhaps never be thoroughly demonstrated, in order to go on from the given data to the supposition of an order of nature which, if it exists at all, surely lies largely beyond direct experience and concerning which we can never hope to pronounce with the certainty with which we can pronounce concerning the essences we intuit, even then we do not have the problem on our hands of jumping from essences in-

11 *The Realm of Essence*, p. 48.
12 *Ibid.*, p. 30.
13 *Ibid.*, p. 40.
14 *Ibid.*, p. 115.
15 *The Concept of Nature*, p. 149.
16 *Symbolism, its Meaning and Effect*, p. 17.

tuited to existences wholly hidden from view, but rather we have
the problem on our hands, theoretically and practically, of concluding from the existential data of presentational immediacy and
the essences thereby suggested what further existences are continuous with the existences already given. Now there may be
involved in this process of exploring the realm of nature an activity which might go under the name of "animal faith." For action
is prior to reflection, impulse to intuition. Animal life is occurring already when first some essence becomes "luminous" and
intelligence effects an awkward control over further acts. And
there are phases of this animal life which may at any minute
become data of presentational immediacy, and which may thus
disclose partially the existential complex of events within which
action is occurring and must continue to occur. But "animal
faith" is not, when thus viewed, what Santayana means by the
term: at least it does not involve any leap in the dark from one
realm of being to another realm of being. It is rather a matter of
the extension of belief from the existentially given animal actions
in the existentially given situation to the more inclusive events,
existing but not given, within which we live and move and have
our being. This extension of belief may be based on prejudice,
passion, vain desire, or sheer guessing, and will then doubtless
issue in mythologies, horrible or entrancing. But it may be guided
by tentative hypotheses and corrected by further evidence given
in further cases of presentational immediacy, and will then be
called "scientific" and be more likely to be true.

Now all this criticism may be an irrelevant protest against a
position which Santayana would not assume. He may have intended only to assert two things about experience which I for one
would not in the least wish to challenge. On the one hand he
may have meant to point out that along with what is given in
presentational immediacy is a large element of interpretation,
that perception is saturated for us adult human beings with
meanings which may or may not be valid, and that immediate
experience, until vigorously scrutinized, and perhaps not even
then in some cases, is not a trustworthy witness of the course of
events in nature around us. On the other hand he may have
meant to recognize that mystics will be mystics, that many a man

can so withdraw attention from the data on presentational immediacy as to become entirely unconscious of them, while he voyages serenely in the realm of the eternal and the "luminous." In so far as Santayana means that all we seem to have in experience is not existentially given or that all which is existentially given may at times be successfully ignored, he is on solid ground. But he seems to mean more, and to that more I must dissent. "Essences," he writes, "are the only objects of indubitable and immediate experience."[17] And thereby he not only asserts that we intuit essences, but also denies that we have presentational immediacy of some natural and existing events. I am as sure that some few of the flux of events about me are immediately given in my experience as that some few of the unchanging essences are given.[18] I believe that my fellow men have kindred experiences; and if any of them assure me they have not, I am unable to believe they are correctly reporting the facts. And so I have difficulty in convincing myself that Santayana really means what he none the less seems clearly to say on this point.

The other point on which I would dissent from Santayana's contentions is as to the basis of dialectic. According to Santayana no essence has any implications. Each essence is "all surface without substance": it is wholly and entirely revealed in any intuition in which it is revealed at all. What we falsely take to be implications of an essence are associations which lead us mortals to pass in routine fashion from one essence to another. Thus implications are "imposed on essences by human discourse,"[19] and arise from chance correlations in the realm of existence. Logis then "is a kind of rhetoric," which "marshals intuitions in ways which are irrelevant to them."[20] And the alleged force of logic is only a bias ingrained in human nature,—a bias which is largely due to congenital predeterminations and is reinforced and "rendered precise

[17] *The Realm of Essence*, p. 165.

[18] Santayana gives some dialectical reasons for his position, especially in *Scepticism and Animal Faith*. Into these I shall not go here. I must point out, however, what indeed is an *ad hominem* argument only, namely, that if dialectic (as is discussed in the next paragraph) is only the pressure of circumstances something of those circumstances must be given in experience. In other words, Santayana seems to be defending two inconsistent positions.

[19] *The Realm of Essence*, p. 81.

[20] *Ibid.*, p. 90.

and irrevocable by habits formed under the pressure of circumstances."[21] The *a priori* is what an individual finds ineradicable in himself; but it has its origins in the history of the race and was generated in the individual's ancestors by some peculiar exigency of the natural flux.[22] The urgency of dialectic is then moral,—we are trying in dialectic to be loyal to the fundamental tendencies of our own natures. "The controlling force in reasoning is not reason, but instinct and circumstance, opening up some path for the mind, and pledging it to some limited issue."[23]

This is irrationalism raising its head in an unexpected quarter. It is too easy a way of disposing of a difficult philosophical problem. The relationships between essence and existence can not be disposed of in so cavalier a fashion. Men find sometimes that the essences set forth in the postulates of their thinking lead far away from the expected outcome, and discover that they are driven by the inevitable bearing of these essences on each other to conclusions which neither congenital predeterminations nor empirical contacts with existence could account for. It is true that consistency in developing postulates is unable to lead us to a determination of the truth of our dialectical systems as applied to the course of nature. Santayana is on sound ground in emphasizing the inability of dialectic to settle matters of fact. But there is a great gap between this position and the denial of all implications between essences, and adherence to the former does not involve assent to the latter.

Santayana once took a different position himself, a position which seems more defensible. In his essay on *Three Proofs of Realism* he wrote: "Even the essences we take some note of have many necessary ideal relations which escape us. Logically the essence of a right-angled triangle involves the Pythagorean proposition, but psychologically we may have no occasion or no power to discover it. Nature herself, like our thought (which for the most part expresses nature), is selective in respect to essence, and reproduces only a part of that infinite labyrinth. If physical (or

---

[21] *Ibid.*, p. 99.

[22] Santayana seems here to be repeating Herbert Spencer's theory of the *a priori*. Cf. Spencer's *Principles of Psychology*, section 208.

[23] *The Realm of Essence*, p. 104.

at least terrestrial) space had not happened to be Euclidean, Euclid certainly would never have thought out Euclidean space: yet all he says of it would have been just as intrinsic to that essence as it is now."[24] Essences are here recognized as having implications ("ideal relations") which may not at first be apparent ("which escape us"); and indeed an excellent illustration of the relation of essence and existence is given. The Euclidean system was a development (as presented in its finished form at least) of certain essences defined in the initial postulates. The occasion for noting this geometrical system may have been, as Santayana suggests, its seeming congruity with the space which characterizes the natural events about us. Dialectically it is no more adequate than the Riemannian or Lobachevskian or some further geometry yet to be discovered. And whether it is to be preferred on empirical grounds is a question the philosopher must leave to the experimental scientist. Be the truth of these various geometries as applied to the real world what it may, at least there is an internal logic in Euclidean and other geometries which is not borrowed from observation of the "brute" course of events. And Santayana will probably not insist that the alternative dialectical systems are all alike derived from congenital predeterminations of the discoverers of these systems. As he himself so beautifully expressed the point a few years ago: "Only when dialectic passes its own frontiers and, fortified by a passport countersigned by experience, enters the realm of brute fact, has dialectic itself any claim to truth or any relevance to the facts."[25] But when it passes its own frontiers and seeks a passport, it finds all existences conforming to its wishes as no tourist can expect from the governments of the countries into which he enters. It may, of course, seek to intrude where experience refuses a *visa;* and then when detected, it will receive the deportation it deserves (as Euclidean geometry, according to rumors set afoot by some physicists, will soon be de-

24 *Essays in Critical Realism,* pp. 182-183 [p. 188, above]. There are many other places in Santayana's writings where he takes implications as following from the *intrinsic* nature of an essence, as indeed must be assumed wherever there is rational discourse. Cf., for example, the statement that there were in Herbert Spencer's doctrine of the unknowable implications which he never suspected, in Santayana's Herbert Spencer Lecture, *The Unknowable,* p. 7.

25 *Scepticism and Animal Faith,* p. 28.

ported after lingering a trifle longer on the Ellis Island of the realm of nature). But when passport and *visa* are duly countersigned, dialectic, without indeed exercising the slightest pressure, has its wishes fulfilled in every jot and tittle, and, without issuing a single order, finds its will more adequately carried out than ever any earthly tyrant. In literal phrase, the essences, though not to be taken as forces or powers in either the efficient or final sense, often stand in relations of implication to one another; and when they are embodied in the realm of nature, particular existences exhibit the connections required by the relationships among the essences. As Santayana put it in the passage quoted at the beginning of this paragraph, one essence may *involve* another, apart from any question of psychological associations.

Whether Santayana would try to reconcile his present position with his past utterance, and if so how, or whether he has deliberately departed from or "outgrown" his former opinion about dialectic, we can not say. There are such difficulties in the problem of the bearing of dialectic requirements upon natural events—and of course the preceding paragraph of criticism of Santayana did not refute him so much as dogmatically assert an opposed point of view—that a man is entitled to try out several positions in turn and experiment with them in his thinking. If Santayana has consciously changed his views on the basis of dialectic, his reasons do not seem conclusive. And the change is towards a less defensible position.

But we may return to a consideration of Santayana's present interpretation of *the spiritual life.* Though essences must be sharply distinguished from existences, and even if also they were wholly relationless or without implication for each other, it would not follow that a life devoted to contemplation of them need be wholly foreign to the ambitions of the rational animal. And indeed Santayana formerly defined the spiritual life in a quite different way. This earlier definition of the spiritual life is in interesting contrast with the conception given in *Platonism and the Spiritual Life* and in *The Realm of Essence.* Let us consider this contrast.

Throughout *The Life of Reason,* and especially in the chapter on "Spirituality and its Corruptions" in *Reason in Religion,* Santayana spoke of the spiritual life as the crown and fulfilment of the life of reason. "A man is spiritual," he there tells us, "when he lives in the presence of the ideal, and whether he eat or drink does so for the sake of a true and ultimate good. He is spiritual when he envisages his goal so frankly that his whole material life becomes a transparent and transitive vehicle, an instrument which scarcely arrests attention, but allows the spirit to use it economically and with perfect detachment and freedom."[26] According to this view, the vision of essence is regulative of human actions in the world of moral affairs. It does not involve blindness to existence and time, nor is its perfection found in ecstatic numbness to the pursuits of the rational animal. When successive crises in the life of reason have witnessed the appearance of useful and fine arts, the rise and development of political forms, the discipline of impulse by foresight, the integration of human activities in a rich and happy harmony, then there still remains an adventure of spiritual import. This adventure is the imaginative exploration of the realm of essence, in order therein to find the meaning and standard by which to appraise and justify the achievement of one's life. Or if perchance, as more often happens, the struggle towards moral reconstruction of the raw materials of physical and human nature fails and is brought to an untimely halt by the recalcitrance of those materials, still the adventurous grasp of the essential nature of the unachieved goal is an enterprise which may yet transform bare failure into sublime tragedy. Without "the gleam of intuition" such spirituality is impossible; for standards and meanings are not some existences among others, existences which we may touch or see with bodily organs. Spirituality is not here regarded as exhausted in "the gleam of intuition"; it involves comparison of the nature intuited with the character of the existential situation and appreciation of the sorry inadequacy of the latter and the radiant glory of the former.

When in *The Life of Reason* Santayana expounded this earlier conception of the spiritual life, he was following in the footsteps of Plato. Plato is always leading us towards a grasp of the ideal which enables us to appraise our acts, our institutions,

26 *Reason in Religion,* pp. 193-194.

ourselves. In the *Republic,* for example, he gains for himself and for us a vision of the perfect city which does not exist on earth, but is emblazoned upon the sky. And he does not lose himself in uninterrupted contemplation of the perfect city, nor would he have achieved spirituality in that way (in Santayana's earlier sense for the term). Rather he was spiritual precisely because he viewed his beloved but miserable Athens from the battlements of the perfect city, pronouncing authoritative judgment upon the existing city in the light of his vision of the city in the sky.

Plato is not a perfect parallel to Santayana at this point. For Plato, though he never allowed his reforming passion to pervert his vision of the "ideas," was yet passionate in his desire to effect reform. And Santayana has shown no such desire. Perhaps a better parallel to Santayana is Spinoza. Near the beginning of the *Political Treatise* Spinoza said: "I have laboured carefully, not to mock, lament, or execrate, but to understand human actions; and to this end I have looked upon passions, such as love, hatred, anger, envy, ambition, pity, and the other perturbations of the mind, not in the light of vices of human nature, but as properties, just as pertinent to it, as are heat, cold, storm, thunder, and the like to the nature of the atmosphere, which phenomena, though inconvenient, are yet necessary, and have fixed causes, by means of which we endeavor to understand their nature, and the mind has just as much pleasure in viewing them aright, as in knowing such things as flatter the senses."[27] Just this attitude, detached from all reforming zeal, yet intellectually concerned to know the nature of existence, is what Santayana expressed as making possible "ideal society."[28] Ideal society, as readers of *The Life of Reason* will recall, is not utopia: it is fellowship with ideal being, i.e., with essences. When the life of reason is sufficiently advanced, the human mind turns to a realm, beyond its physical and social environment, and seeks a "disintoxicated" and just view of the ideas and ideals, the sentiments and beliefs, the hopes and ambitions which have absorbed other men during the history of culture. It does so, not to escape the world any more than to reform the world, but to understand the world. And understand-

[27] Bohn edition of Spinoza, Vol. I, pp. 288-289.
[28] *Reason in Society,* Chapter VIII.

ing involves the intuition of essence, the choice, out of the vast labyrinth of essence, of just those essences which enable us to define the present nature of things and to discern the ideal goal of things. The vision of essence does not, in Santayana's earlier conception of the spiritual life, end in itself; rather it aims at interpretation of the values which men may properly cherish in the realm of human affairs.

Santayana's present conception of the spiritual life is quite another matter, as the outline above makes evident. It involves complete indifference to and total forgetfulness of the realm of existence: it scorns even the most just appraisal of the possibilities of existence. It craves unconsciousness as it loses itself in the eternal being it contemplates. It "regards *only* some essence,"[29] and does not employ the essence to illumine problems of existence.

The unsatisfactory character of Santayana's present view of the spiritual life may become more clear if we pause to examine a certain phrase he uses. He tells us that "contemplation of pure Being is the last phase of spiritual progress."[30] The term "pure Being" is used by Santayana without any equivocation; but it is rich in associations from the history of mysticism; and almost inevitably carries connotations for the reader which go far beyond Santayana's express doctrine. My criticism involves the point that without these further unintended associations Santayana's thesis about the spiritual life would be, if not ridiculous, at least utterly unconvincing.

Santayana's statement that contemplation of pure Being is the last phase of spiritual progress means just this. We become spiritual if we pay exclusive attention to "the positive intrinsic nature"[31] of an essence without further considering its relations to possible existence. We become spiritual, that is, if we enjoy the essences for their own sake, and resist the natural urge to make the leap of animal faith by building up on some essence a belief about the natural world. Thus the less interested we are in truth about existence, the more chance we have of being spiritual. Pure Being is, when thus used, a name for the kind of reality which any

29 *The Realm of Essence*, p. 63, italics mine.
30 *Ibid.*, p. 60.
31 *Ibid.*, p. 56.

and every essence possesses in its own right. Santayana maintains that, once we have grasped any essence in its own positive intrinsic nature, we will be led on surely to a vision of the whole infinite realm of essence. Santayana has no moral preference for any one essence over others, in his treatment of the spiritual life. To rest in unalloyed intuition of any essence whatever is to tend towards spirituality.

But though such is Santayana's position, his language is loose. Though at times *pure Being* means for him the kind of being which every essence possesses, at other times it stands for a special essence apart from the rest. In an earlier writing he said: "Pure Being is itself a particular essence, the simplest of all, clearly distinguishable, both in definition and in experience, from every other essence."[32] And in many passages in *The Realm of Essence* he continues to use the term in this sense. "Pure Being is different from all other essences."[33] Pure Being is "of all essences the most lauded and the most despised, the most intently studied in some quarters and the most misunderstood in others."[34] And while "pure Being is no purer than any other essence," it is "related to other essences very much as any essence is related to its existing manifestations."[35] In such passages pure Being is the supreme essence at the head of a hierarchy of lesser essences. And while the two meanings of "pure Being" have a legitimate bearing on each other, this second usage of the term is likely to mislead Santayana's readers.

Any student of mysticism can understand the appeal which contemplation of pure Being as a supreme essence makes to many minds. Its logical priority gives it, illicitly perhaps, but none the less forcefully, a moral urgency and religious attraction. It is The One, The Absolute, The Ultimate. But pure Being, as the kind of reality which any and every essence possesses, is hard to consider with the same affectionate and awe-struck fervor. The contemplation of the pure being of mud, and hydrogen peroxide, and mahogany, and dandruff does not really seem very noble an

[32] *The Unknowable,* p. 9.
[33] *The Realm of Essence,* p. 46.
[34] *Ibid.,* p. 45.
[35] *Ibid.,* p. 49.

occupation. And even if one then goes on to contemplate the pure being of the perfect circle and eternal justice and sheer beauty, the glory of the realm of essence is not very bright. Deprived of reference to existence, as scientific description or as moral appraisal, the essences are as democratic as Santayana rightly asserts; and the essence of beauty is no more lovely than the essence of dandruff, since their being is equally pure. The success of Santayana's doctrine that contemplation of pure Being is the last phase of spiritual progress would seem to be dependent on this point, namely, that the reader should be guilty of the equivocation in reading Santayana's language against which he successfully guards for himself. The critic can not then help but wonder whether the dual usage of the term "pure Being," though stylistically adroit, is not also a bit unfortunate.

Not only is the earlier of Santayana's two conceptions of the spiritual life a more significant moral adventure, but it is, I believe, more in line with the real intent of his philosophic point of view. Of course, the term "spiritual life" may legitimately be redefined in a dozen ways by different authors or by the same author in different connections. And it is true enough that men have at times lived the spiritual life in each sense in which Santayana defines the term. But none the less Santayana seems in his last two books to be engaged in a kind of *tour de force,* a philosophical trick more amusing than profound. Engaged in writing a volume on essence, he has been driven to press his theme with rigor and to show the extreme to which contemplation of essence may go. But his confession that he does not wish himself to live a spiritual life in his new sense of the term stands forth like an acknowledgment that when he has played his philosophic game he will return to more fruitful and profitable inquiry.

Santayana developed his present conception of *the spiritual life,* not simply as a by-product of his discussion of the realm of essence, but in connection with his reply to the neo-Platonic position of Dean Inge. And therein we perhaps discover the basic motivation of his present position. Throughout his many books over many years Santayana has always shown a strong animus against what he regards, and rightly, as a misuse of essence. Neo-Platonism he has treated as a perverted Platonism. The Platonic "ideas" or universals or essences may properly be used to define the values of natural existence and to guide the life of reason; but they are not to be hypostatised and treated as the generating forces behind the course of natural events. We should not take our vision of ideal ends as a discovery of efficient causes. Theologians have only too often been guilty of just this blunder; and their excessive enthusiasm for the ideal has thus issued in superstition. Similarly, whereas "idealism in the proper sense of the word" would be "nothing but a visionary intuition of values," most historic idealisms have usually become "a supernumerary second physics, a world to which an existence was attributed which could be hardly conceived and was certainly supported by no evidence, while that significance which it really possessed in reference to natural processes was ignored or even denied."[36] Against these mythologies and pseudo-idealisms Santayana has persistently maintained that the "moral effects" of natural events must not be confused with "their dramatic antecedents."[37] Or, in other words, "the ideal to which all forces should minister is itself no force or factor in its own realization."[38] But Santayana's earlier conception of the spiritual life is at least as effective a reply to the neo-Platonism of Dean Inge as his present conception. Indeed it seems to me altogether more effective; for it is in harmony with the life of reason and need not be repudiated by advocates of the life of reason. It would seem that, in the eloquence with which Santayana opposes Dean Inge, he has overreached the mark. He meant to insist on the reality of essence apart from the realm of existence, and he has ended in making the life in which essence is intuited unconcerned with the existential course of human affairs. Even granting the arbitrary character of all definition, Santayana's present choice of the meaning to be attached to the phrase "the spiritual life" is unfortunate.

The last few paragraphs have been concerned with possible motivations of the recent course of Santayana's thought. It must be recognized that whoever enters upon a discussion of motives behind any philosophical opinion or system is on dangerous ground.

---

[36] *Reason in Religion*, p. 134.
[37] *Ibid.*, p. 141.
[38] *Reason in Society*, p. 190.

If the critic of Santayana thinks he can detect motives, he may be but giving expression to his own prejudices; he must surely realize that he is guided by a general impression which contains elements of subjectivity rather than by clear evidence. Yet the attempt to trace motivations is an enticing venture; and the outcome, whatever it is, may in a sense be said to have a measure of validity. For even if the motive inferred as an element in the formation of Santayana's present view of the spiritual life never operated *existentially,* it is *essentially* one that some Santayana-like person might have entertained in a world more or less like our own. Thereby the critic is merely turning Santayana into an essence; or, more exactly, he is turning from the Santayana whose books he has been reading to the essence which that existing Santayana brings before his mind in "the gleam of intuition." This essential Santayana can not but interest his discoverer, and will inevitably become the theme of discourse. Even the existing Santayana can not protest too vehemently. No man is a much better judge of his own motivations than the sympathetic observer, and no man can claim infallibility in correcting his friendly critics.

However just our discussion of motives may be, at least there is no doubt that Santayana's recent works require a modification of the opinion in which he is usually held in America. The new series of books on *Realms of Being* will correct the estimate of the man which was made on the basis of the earlier series of *The Life of Reason.* Santayana is not by temperament a lover of the realm of matter. His professed materialism[39] is not an index of his personal taste. His naturalism is due to honest and reasoned argument: it is not the prejudiced expression of a love of nature. Many of his American admirers have taken him to be more of a naturalist than by intent he aims to be; and they have used his books as partisan literature in support of their more militant and aggressive naturalism, thus obscuring the other strains besides naturalism which run through his pages. His naturalism is akin to that which he attributes to Democritus: "His delight in a mechanism that can fall into so many marvellous and beautiful shapes, and can generate so many exciting passions, should be of the same intellectual quality as that which the visitor feels in a mu-

[39] *Scepticism and Animal Faith,* p. vii.

seum of natural history, where he views the myriad butterflies in their cases, the flamingoes and shellfish, the mammoths and gorillas."[40] Or as he expresses the matter in personal confession: "I myself have no passionate attachment to existence, and value this world for the intuitions it can suggest, rather than for the wilderness of facts that compose it."[41] Santayana's naturalism is only an episode, so to speak, in his Platonic enjoyment of eternal being. Nature does not tempt him to join actively in the struggle for existence, to direct the course of its shifting flux of events, to become a reformer in control of natural processes. Rather it leads him to stand aside and use events as occasions for the contemplation of certain essences which he might otherwise never intuit. While the essences are infinitely more numerous than those which find some embodiment in nature, at least nature is what directs our attention to many essences in which we can find delight. Nature is for Santayana an introduction to ideas, a prelude to intuition.

In brief, Santayana's naturalism, if that term be applied to him at all, is anything but a summons to delve into matter and to take part in active affairs. It is the recognition of hard facts from a mind unyielding in its integrity and unwilling to delude itself. But having acknowledged the existence of nature as Margaret Fuller accepted the universe, Santayana turns to things which delight him more. Even his acceptance of nature is a bit malicious: it is based on an indifference such as he tells us the essences exhibit to their chance embodiments at casual moments in the flux of events. A thoroughgoing naturalist who then proceeds to scorn nature is a much more emancipated mind than an idealist who tries vainly to read his purposes and prejudices into the cosmic processes.

Indeed Santayana is more "Platonic," in one sense of that term, than Plato ever was. Behind Plato's search for essences, as of justice or holiness, there lies a moral preference for those essences which serve to express human ideals; and there is evident in the dialogues a constant longing to enter, as the normal Greek naturally would enter, into the direction of affairs in the city he loved.

40 *Reason in Science*, p. 90.
41 *Scepticism and Animal Faith*, p. 171.

When Socrates in the early dawn saw Hippocrates blush, Plato is poignantly revealing his own soul; for Socrates had made Hippocrates seem to say that he preferred to be a talker about government rather than an active governor. But if Santayana had written the *Protagoras*, no youth would have blushed at such an offense, or rather there would have been no offense committed. Santayana is as aloof from politics as from inanimate nature. He immensely enjoys the prospects he obtains in watching the course of party warfare, intrigue, triumph, and failure; he finds pleasure in passing competent judgment upon the character of different political ambitions, programs, and performances. But these affairs are instances to him of ideas, begetters of intellectual insight into certain eternal essences. As most people who to-day read Dante regard each particular sinner in Hell, not as the real person he was in the political life of Dante's own day, but as a recurrent and oft-encountered type of human character, so Santayana takes even his contemporaries and ours, even us ourselves who are his admirers and critics, as but occasions on which his vision turns to appreciation of perennial forms. He looks through us and beyond; he sees *what* we are as well as *that* we are, and he pays no more attention to the fact *that* we are than courtesy demands. He sees *what* we are, and he smiles; and in the contemplation of our essence, he has caught up all that is of worth in us for him.

VII

REASON, MORALITY, AND
THE GOOD LIFE

Santayana's Moral Philosophy

JOHN LACHS

I

What G. E. Moore called the "naturalistic fallacy" consists in a confusion of the 'is' of predication with the 'is' of identity. The statement "pleasure is good," for example, should be taken as asserting not that pleasure = good or that 'good' means 'pleasant,' but rather that pleasure is a member of the class of good things or that whatever is pleasant is also good. Good is an indefinable and unanalyzable quality, attaching to things, events, and courses of action independently of our cognition or volition. If two men disagree about the goodness or badness of things, events, courses of action, or persons, at most one of them can be right; if they contradict each other, one of them must be right—though it is difficult to know which one.

Santayana wrote an article entitled "Hypostatic Ethics"[1] in

John Lachs, "Santayana's Moral Philosophy," *The Journal of Philosophy*, 61 (1964), pp. 44-61; reprinted by permission. An earlier version of this paper appeared, translated into Spanish, in *Convivium* (Barcelona, Spain).

[1] Section IV of "The Philosophy of Mr. Bertrand Russell," in *Winds of Doctrine* (New York: Harper Torchbooks, 1957), pp. 138-154.

which he criticized this view severely. It is indeed true that good is good and not another thing, just as yellow is yellow and as such indefinable. But from the fact that a thing is indefinable we cannot conclude that it is unconditioned. The quality good attaches to things not arbitrarily and for no reason, but only under certain specifiable conditions. The prime condition is that someone take a positive interest in or a pro-attitude toward the object. Thus things we consider good are good not absolutely and in themselves, but only relative to us. Value in all cases presupposes an act of valuing: an evaluator subject as well as a treasured object. This point seems to be valid, and it is a little surprising that it has not gained universal acceptance among moral philosophers. "One man's food is another's poison" the proverb has it; what is good for one man may conceivably be, and often is, bad for another. Shall we then conclude that one of them must be wrong: that an object that is bad for a man isn't *really* bad for him? Shall we say that the object *in itself* is good, and it is only perversion of nature or error in cognition on his part if he fails to see its goodness?

The case is analogous to that of sense perception. To say that objects are good or bad independent of our cognition of them is the equivalent, in morals, of naive realism. If we decree that some object is green regardless of circumstances, we are faced with the prospect of having to call the color-blind depraved, the physicist mistaken, and types of lighting other than the customary 'unnatural.' It is evident that we are setting up a norm: we shall call green that which, to the majority of men with sound vision, under standard conditions, looks green. Similarly, we call good that concerning the positive value of which normal men under ordinary circumstances agree. This standard is fairly compelling so long as the belief in a single, fixed human nature is retained. It may be held that the normal man under ordinary circumstances— the 'man of practical wisdom' or 'the good man'—knows the value of the object truly. Moreover, it may be considered obligatory to become as much like this standard of what a man should be as one's nature will permit. But as soon as we recognize that there is no such constant and universal human nature, it becomes evident that the ideal of one man or of one age can have no authority over another man or another age. Different natures make for

different ideals; it would be just as ridiculous to expect an oyster
to obey the fifth commandment as it would be impertinent for
me to demand of shoemakers that they become heroes, saints, or
composers of inspirational music. There is no reason to believe
that the normal man's color judgment or his value judgment is
more apt to be true to the object than anyone else's. The statements "object S under circumstances T looks green to a," and
"action X under circumstances Y seems good to b" say nothing
whatever about the object or the action as they are in themselves.
Value, like color, is a relational predicate: to say that X is good
is an elliptical way of saying that X is good for somebody b.

Santayana distinguishes four realms or kinds of being: essence,
matter, spirit, and truth. An ontological 'realm' should not be
confused with a cosmological region: the latter is a part of the
natural world, as the heaven and hell of Catholic mythology
would be if there actually were such places; the former is the result of a reflective analysis of experience. A cosmological region
is one that may someday appear in our telescopes or in our mi-
croscopes, or one that astounded travelers to other worlds may
find.

The four realms of being must evidently be present in every
facet of our experience, and I will now go on to elucidate how. In
doing this I wish to remark that Santayana has never developed a
systematic and comprehensive view of ethics, nor has he made the
attempt to relate his scattered statements about the nature of
morality to his ontology as a whole. For this reason, a good deal
of what I will say cannot be supported by reference to explicit
passages in Santayana's works. The aim of this paper is not to
present a summary of Santayana's views on ethics but to develop
and enlarge upon the ethical position that is the natural comple-
ment of his ontology.

We have already noted that Santayana agrees with Moore that
good is a non-natural quality which is both indefinable and unanalyzable. As such, good is an essence. The realm of essence is
the ultimate answer to reductionism of any type: to say that a
thing is not what it is, that it is "nothing but" something else, is
manifestly absurd. Good is good, and this is all there is to be said
about *what* good is. It is a different question to determine under

what conditions anything will be, or will be judged to be, good.

"By [morality] I mean the principle of all choices in taste, faith and allegiance," Santayana says,[2] and the principle of choice has its basis in matter. The animal organism with needs and drives of its own and a nature that is not infinitely plastic does not welcome all things, all events, all states of affairs equally. Selectivity is of the very essence of the animal: the psyche, which is a mythological entity invented to symbolize the subtle material organization of the body, endeavors to secure and maintain optimum conditions for expressing and discharging all that is latent in it.

The fact that certain things are preferable relative to the nature of the individual psyche is the basis of morality. If all things were equally valuable for me, nothing would be valuable—desire, will, and aspiration would pass out with a cozy sigh; life would cease. This is indeed, as we shall see, virtually the case in the spiritual life; but the spiritual life, Santayana believes, is supramoral. In general terms, the non-natural quality good will attach to an object if a psyche takes a positive interest in that object.

We should immediately warn against two possible misunderstandings of this view. First of all, the interest taken in the object does not have to be occurrent; it may be dispositional. This means that the object does not cease to be good for the subject as soon as it is not directly attended to. The value relation is based on a disposition of the psyche to aim at the object in question and a disposition of the object to satisfy the psyche's impulse directed toward it. Secondly, the interest does not have to be conscious. I may or may not realize that an object is good for me: the object may be 'good' (in the sense of being impulse-appeasing) without my realizing it, or alternatively it may be bad or indifferent despite the fact that I believe it is good. In general, interest is organic in nature and as such subconscious, preconscious, or unconscious. Morality originates in and is primarily relevant to the field of action; the fact that interest, the organic equivalent of value, is conferred on the object unconsciously in the darkness of the realm of matter explains why we naturally think that goodness and badness inhere in things objectively and that we *discover* them in the object instead of projecting them there. This

2 *The Genteel Tradition at Bay* (New York: Scribner, 1931), p. 54.

view is indeed correct so far as it goes, but it does not go far enough. It stops on the level of consciousness without venturing below, to consider the conditions of consciousness which, Santayana maintains, are material.

One important upshot of the above discussion is that good and bad are not subjective in the obvious sense of being relative to knowledge or opinion. The realm of truth is the indelible witness that an object with some nature X will not satisfy a psyche with the incompatible nature Y, no matter how much that psyche desires or how hard it pursues the object. Although by virtue of the interest a high value will accrue to the object, the fact that the psyche's true good lies elsewhere will not be changed. The adoption of the view that possible perfection is determined by nature, well known from Aristotle, thus enables Santayana to distinguish between 'apparent' and 'real' goods. Of course, no good is good merely "apparently"—that which is good is good. Santayana realizes this, which makes the issue more complicated but its resolution more satisfactory. I will discuss that matter under the heading of the role of the realm of truth in moral experience.

Sketching the function of the psyche in moral life and thus staying within the realm of matter, I have been occasionally forced to use moral terms such as 'good,' 'bad,' 'value,' 'perfection,' 'satisfaction.' Strictly speaking, this is unjustified and should now be corrected. Moral terms do not apply to matter in motion as considered apart from a conscious*ing* mind. The river does not denounce the dam blocking its course as inherently evil. Stones fall, walls shatter without complaint; for Nature flowering gardens are no better than a scorched siliceous desert. If the psyche did not give rise to the spirit, moral feelings and a language of morals would be impossible. Only "moral action" would persist, but it would not be considered moral—it would be blind behavior. 'Good' and 'evil,' 'right' and 'wrong' are spiritual terms: they are essences which the conscious mind apprehends but matter cannot embody. To prefer X to Y, to select, pursue, and possibly attain an object is a matter of the interplay of substances describable in purely behavioral terms. To think of X as *better* than Y, in addition to having selected it in preference to Y, brings into play a radically new and irreducibly different mode

of being. Conscious acts and their contents are transcripts of physical changes, Santayana maintains[3] in accordance with his epiphenomenalistic theory of mind. This raises a question which is perhaps the outstanding difficulty of his ethics. If moral terms, i.e.,
certain types of essences, are expressive of the state of the psyche,
there should be some discoverable transformation law governing
the change of specific kinds of physical state into corresponding
kinds of conscious state. However, such a mentalizing transformation rule or set of rules is nowhere provided by Santayana, nor
is it at all easy to see how it could be provided.

In metaphysics the problem is that of how a brain event or a
brain process can give rise to a mental act. In ethics the issue is
that of how *ought* can be derived from *is*. "The life of the psyche,
which rises to . . . intuition, determines all the characters of the
essence evoked, and among them its moral quality," Santayana
states,[4] but fails to expatiate on the nature of this determination.
Why should a budding material tendency in its organ appear to
the mind as an obligation or an imperative instead of as a rival
inclination? More generally, how can the natural give rise to the
ideal? The problem is a standard difficulty of naturalism and
Santayana has but one answer to it: "Ab esse ad posse valet
illatio."[5] If we make existence the test of possibility, the generation of the ideal from the natural will seem no great mystery.
Now I will readily grant that actuality is a reasonable test of
potentiality, but this to my mind does not in the least facilitate
the elimination of the mystery. The question we are asking is not
whether that which *is* the case may not after all be impossible,
for that is a silly question: we are rather inquiring as to what is
the case. No matter how convinced we are that the ideal has a
natural ground, if a plausible account of the interrelation of the
two cannot be produced, the position will have to be abandoned.
Thus Santayana's answer is not an argument: it is a statement of
his conviction that the ideal must have a natural ground. This
conclusion is in harmony with his general position: he never

[3] *Realms of Being* (New York: Scribner, 1942), p. x; *Scepticism and Animal
Faith* (New York: Dover, 1955), p. 277.

[4] *Scepticism*, p. 130.

[5] *Reason in Common Sense,* vol. I of *The Life of Reason* (New York:
Scribner, 1905), p. 282.

claims more than that he is a *dogmatic* naturalist.[6] However, when confronted with the task of pulling an *ought* out of a hatful of *is*'s, there is some doubt about the inherent preferability of dogmatic naturalism to some equally dogmatic version of psychologism.

I will not press the point, although it is an important and interesting one. We cannot turn to science for an answer to the question of the transformation laws that connect the physical with the psychical and the natural with the ideal, for science is concerned only with one term of the relation, viz., the regularities of the physical world. One would suspect that the answer, if there is one, would have to come from the side of philosophy. It is unfortunate that Santayana neither provided an answer nor acknowledged the insolubility of the problem.

II

Santayana agrees with the emotivists that moral terms have no descriptive significance.[7] Moral 'judgments' are hybrids containing truths about matters of fact, together with the expression of a preferential attitude. The clue to the distinction between expressive and descriptive statements in Santayana is, I think, to be found in his "causal" theory of perception. Santayana is a critical realist. The sense datum (immanent object) and the surface of what C. D. Broad calls the "ontological object" are not for him numerically identical. The content of a perceptual act is one essence or a set of essences; the objects of perception are material substances. All knowing is in terms of the symbolic language of fancy, of essences appearing in intuition. The symbols have no intrinsic reference to what they are made to stand for: it is only intent, the compelling force of animal faith and urgency that converts an essence into description of a substance. In themselves all essences intuited are equally expressions of states of the psyche. Those which can be legitimately used as descriptive differ

6 "Dewey's Naturalistic Metaphysics," in P. A. Schilpp, ed., *The Philosophy of John Dewey* (Evanston and Chicago: Northwestern Univ. Press, 1951), p. 260.
7 *Dialogues in Limbo* (New York: Scribner, 1925), p. 39.

from all others in this crucial respect: they stand in causal connection with substantial objects external to the psyche and repeat some part of the standard comprehensive description of some fact about that object. But moral essences repeat no part of the standard comprehensive description of any fact; they cannot be instantiated by matter. Moral qualities or their equivalents in the psyche are not members of any direct causal chain linking the animal with its environment. They are spontaneous (though not uncaused) attitudes or the results of such attitudes on the part of the psyche. Whereas intuition of essences correctly used as descriptive of the ambient world is the last event in a series beginning with certain material changes in some external object, the intuition of moral essences is the last event in a series beginning with certain self-originated changes in the psyche, and is thus expressive of states of the psyche due (at least in part) to ingrained dispositions of the animal. There are difficulties here which a detailed discussion could eliminate. For our present purpose, however, it is sufficient if we have a general understanding of what I take to be Santayana's point. Santayana himself is not at all explicit on the issue; so most of what I have said regarding the nature of the distinction between "descriptive" and "expressive" essences is conjectural and tentative.

If moral essences are thus expressive, it would seem that they can be neither true nor false of the world and that the realm of truth has no function in moral experience. "An ultimate good is chosen, found, or aimed at; it is not opined" (*Winds of Doctrine*, 144): opinions we hazard may be true or false; preferences we feel can be neither. However, there are various ways in which moral 'judgments' may, nevertheless, be true or false, and it will be of importance to list these in order to clarify the difference between Santayana's position and that of the emotivists.[8]

1. 'Moral' judgments that concern means and not ends may certainly be true or false. Such judgments are not moral in the strict sense of the word at all; the proposition "X is good as a means" tells us nothing about the more properly ethical question

[8] See chapter entitled "Moral Truth" in *The Realm of Truth*, vol. III of *Realms of Being* (New York: Scribner, 1942), pp. 473-484.

"What is good in itself?" or "What ought to exist?" If I say that something X will bring about a desired result Y, I may certainly be mistaken. The mistake, however, will not be a moral one; it will be a mistake about matters of fact.

2. We may say that a moral judgment is 'true,' meaning that it is true that it was made. "Jim a contemptible liar?" we may ask with incredulity. "That's right. That's what he said." Here "that's right" simply means 'correct' or 'true,' but true once again not morally but factually.

3. A moral judgment may be said to be 'true' if it is made *bona fide* and 'false' if it is uttered with intent to deceive. I may, for instance, claim that the ultimate good of man is forgetfulness and the only acceptable means to this end is the liberal consumption of opium. Now if I only *say* this without meaning it, the moral judgment will be 'false,' for then no interest exists on my part by virtue of which value would accrue either to forgetfulness as an end or to opium as a means. Similarly, the judgment will be 'true' if I am honest and mean what I say.

4. The moral judgment "X is good" may be true in the sense that for the person the non-natural, relational quality good really attaches to the object X. But on reflection this is seen to be a not very significant form of moral truth, for unless a judgment is 'false' in the previous sense of being wilfully deceptive, it cannot fail to be true in the current sense. If you honestly say that X is good (for you), you cannot possibly be wrong, just as if you honestly say you see red, you cannot fail to be right. This does not, of course, mean that X is good in itself or at all times or for everyone or even for you in the long run; it just means that X now seems good to you, which is a fact no later experience can annul, nor the shrillest chorus of dissenters affect. Thus if you say "X is good," the correct answer is "If you say so. . . ."

5. Finally, a moral judgment may be 'true' in the sense that it expresses the central and long-range interests of a man. This raises the issue of the distinction between real and apparent goods, which I shall now proceed to discuss. As I have previously remarked, on a primary level every good is a good. If to love my neighbor is a good, and so is, by hypothesis, to tell an occasional lie, the question of which, if any, of these is a 'real' good and

which, if any, is an 'apparent' good cannot even arise. A good can be an 'apparent' good only relative to other, more pervasive or more compelling, goods. Thus, to tell a lie is an apparent or short-range or lesser good, because it interferes with the acquisition or achievement of other goods more comprehensive or more satisfying. Generally, it may be laid down that the 'true' value of an object for a subject is a function of the comprehensiveness (*Winds of Doctrine,* 146), permanence, and biological utility[9] of the interest of the subject in the object.

If the most general question of ethics is "What ought to exist for its own sake?" Santayana's answer is simply "Nothing." In themselves, or ontologically, essences have neither right nor claim to existence, and there is no *reason* (though there is a *cause*) why certain selected sets of essences are actualized instead of other sets or all sets or no sets at all. From the human point of view, however, groups of essences acquire selective emphasis, and it may legitimately be said that for human beings or human beings of a certain type, these essences ought to exist. Whatever would satisfy the animating or overriding impulses of a psyche ought to exist for that psyche. The standard of what would truly satisfy a given impulse is, since it is based on definite potentialities in matter, enshrined in the realm of truth. Thus the good of a man, viz., that which would satisfy his impulses, though relative to his nature, is, nevertheless, absolute and objective in at least three senses (*Platonism,* 232). It is absolute in the sense that it is not relative to opinion but is predetermined by the fatal material constitution of the animal. Secondly, it is absolute in the sense that it is fixed and varies only concomitantly with changes in the nature of the organism or the structure of the environment. Finally, it is absolute in the sense that it is all-sufficient and total; it encompasses everything that is of the least value to that man.

The good in this sense is evidently a standard, an ideal which can never be fully realized. What can be realized is a harmony of our most persistent interests. Of course, such harmony itself is of value only if it is the object of an interest. The interest in

[9] *Platonism and the Spiritual Life* (New York: Harper Torchbooks, 1957), p. 248.

harmony is what Santayana calls "reason" (*Common Sense*, 267).
Thus reason is not a slave of the passions; it is one of the passions.
Being an impulse for order, it works to harmonize, to rationalize,
and to humanize all other impulses. A conflict of interests is made
possible in men with a passion for harmony by the fact that fancy
often suggests momentary and incompatible goods. In general, a
'moral' judgment will be false if it places the satisfaction of an
impulse that is less comprehensive, permanent, or advantageous
before that of an impulse that is more comprehensive, more
permanent, or more advantageous. Thus the problem of 'real'
and 'apparent' good is solved by being reduced to a question of
better and worse, of comparative value. The standard objection
against interest theories of value is also answered in this way. The
interest theory maintains that an object o is good (bad) if and
only if a subject s stands in a relation R to o so that sRo is the
unit of value. Now it is generally supposed that, by pointing to
the fact that the relation of interest connecting the subject with
the object may itself be good or bad, the position has been refuted. To be able to say that the positive interest taken in an object is itself good, we would have to posit a second interest having
that first interest as its object. If pushed, it appears that we could
be forced into the situation of having either to deny the commonly accepted view that desires, too, can be good or bad, or to
admit that an infinite regress of interests is necessary in order to
avoid the awkward situation in which desire for a good object
will be neither good nor bad.

The difficulty falls into two parts. First we must consider how
an interest by virtue of which the non-natural quality good attaches to an object may itself be good. Next we must consider
how an interest underlying the inherence of the non-natural quality good in an object may itself be bad. The former difficulty is
eliminated by looking upon the long-range, comprehensive interests of a man as systematically ordered and harmonized by reason. Impulses that promote or at least fit in with this harmony of
goals are welcomed, and positive value is conferred on them;
others are rejected as undesirable. The general impulse for harmony is, thus, an impulse for everything that serves to further
that harmony. But it may now be asked whether this impulse *it-*

self is good or bad. Santayana's answer is, as I have already noted above, that it is good only if desired. The admission seems to give the case away, but in fact does not. It points to two essential features of Santayana's theory of morals. The first is that ultimately the good rests on arbitrary preference, ethics on animal nature. The distinction between a humanistic ethics and the ontological consideration of morals is one of point of view adopted. What from the perspective of the former is both valuable and necessary appears from the latter's perspective arbitrary and dispensable. More specifically, when the desirability of the ultimate principle of a rational human ethics is brought into question, we have left the sphere of ethics altogether and adopted the point of view of the universe. Unless the pre-existence of at least one contingent preference is allowed, human morality will be altogether impossible.

III

This leads to a second important feature of Santayana's view. If ethical principles, though necessary in order that there be a moral life, are only contingent from the point of view of the universe, they will have no authority over anyone not professing them. If I do not desire the oyster's life of safe private pleasure or the ant's life of service to the community, their goods will have no compulsion over me. If I do not desire to live the life of a martyr, it is in vain to insist that I *ought to* live that life. Obligation, Santayana insists, must be internal and vital. It is based on self-knowledge, on the recognition of one's good as distinct from, and equally legitimate with, the goods of others. Santayana's imperative is identical with that of the Stoics. It is: "Act in accordance with nature," where by "nature" is meant the nature of the agent. Hence the first and ultimate commandment of morality becomes the Socratic dictum: "Know thyself."

This view with a single stroke eliminates moral fanaticism. Recognition that the different goods of others have as much—or as little—right to existence as our own is the first step in the direction of tolerance based on understanding, and of moral sanity.

But it may be objected that such an ethics, being both relativistic and naturalistic, leads on the one hand to moral anarchy and on the other to an acknowledgment of the incommensurability of values.

The first objection can at once be seen to be unfounded. Santayana does not believe in a single fixed and immutable human nature (*Common Sense*, 289), but, despite all individual variety, human beings have enough interests in common, a sufficient constitutional similarity, to avoid the danger of moral anarchy. Though human nature varies indefinitely, human morality is the inevitable hygienic bias of a race of animals (*Platonism*, 274). As a contingent matter of natural history and a necessary condition of classification, there is a measure of overlap of the significant characteristics of various individuals of a species; this is indeed why we classify them as members of the same species. But as nature determines perfection and the psyche selects her individual good, the core of these various goods will coincide sufficiently to make social organization possible and to provide the basis for a workaday morality.

It still remains to deal with the second objection, namely that on this view values are incommensurable. Santayana here adopts the only position open to him—which seems also a sensible one— maintaining that different types of good are indeed *essentially* incommensurable (*Winds of Doctrine*, 148, 150). How are we to judge whether it is better to be Socrates than a village idiot? To say that it would be better for an oyster to be a philosopher than a mere dull mollusc is not only silly; it is probably incoherent as well. Uniform standards of excellence for species of animals are unlikely though not impossible, but it is totally without plausibility to claim a universal standard of excellence for all things. Nonetheless, this brave stand on the incommensurability of values will not go all the way. We find that comparisons of value are made every day; no honest philosophy can ignore this. Santayana tackles the problem in two places (*Winds of Doctrine*, 149; *Common Sense*, 240-243) and suggests the following solution. Values can be compared only in the private imagination. The good of another is apprehended by imitative sympathy, or 'empathy,' as it is sometimes called. It is brought before the mind in the form of an ideal representation: a representation which may or may not be accurate but which is essentially imaginative. Comparison is then effected, and, in people who are receptive, whose imagination is vivid and whose sympathies are generous, the represented alien good may not unlikely be deemed superior.

The question of appreciating the incompatible good of another raises the problem of egoism. "Egoism is not [a] thin and refutable thing" (*Winds of Doctrine*, 150), he claims. Self-centeredness, uncompromising pursuit of a selected set of private objectives is of the very essence of the psyche. The egoist holds that he himself—and, in general, any man like himself—is qualitatively superior to any other. Thus all intolerant men are egoists, as are moralists subscribing to absolute codes of value. Santayana himself is, in this sense, certainly not an egoist. The question, however, is not a simple one and involves an explanation of how the psyche, automatic self-seeking machine that it is, can act disinterestedly. To be 'disinterested' means to be interested in the goods of others, and eventually in all possible goods. Generosity is one of our primitive passions;[10] genuine altruism and a sense of justice are impulses as real, though sometimes perhaps not so powerful, as any others.[11] The growth of sympathy is parallel to the development of spirit, and reaches cosmic proportions as spirit is gradually emancipated and approaches the ideal of a spiritual life. While spirit is substance-directed, its ultimate good is sympathy; through tears and the intensity of feeling it is champion of every cause. Sympathy, purged of its element of feeling and become tolerance and quiet understanding, is retained even in the mind's essence-directed stage, which is the spiritual life. Thus the development from egoism to a partial altruism coincides to an extent with the progression from the moral to the spiritual life. I will not now discuss the distinction between the two types of life and the problem of the *summum bonum* attendant upon it. This will be my last topic in this paper. Suffice it to say that the problem of how the psyche can act in a disinterested

[10] *Some Turns of Thought in Modern Philosophy* (New York: Scribner, 1933), p. 96.
[11] *Reason in Science*, vol. V of *The Life of Reason*, p. 246.

way is in the closest possible connection with the problem of how it can give rise to spirit.

Santayana's treatment of this problem is brief.[12] It is by exploring the possibilities of organization, by the spontaneous involution of matter that the psyche acquires a capacity for sympathy. The material sensitivity to events far off leads to an eventual sensitivity to possibilities that are not possibilities *for me here,* but represent the autonomous though genuinely different goods of others. Sympathy is, of course, limited by the fact that we can represent *sub specie boni* and assimilate only that which we find intelligible and congruous with our mind. Nevertheless, even after this reservation has been made, sympathy still remains either a wholehearted sharing of the interests of others, as is the case in some communities and, I venture to hope, in most families, or at least an appreciation of the legitimacy and inward right of the objectives of other men, even of our enemies, as occasionally manifested in chivalry in war. Such an enterprise, on the part of the psyche, of increasing the appreciation of alien harmonies, this "interest in things not edible," may well prove fatal. There is nothing strange or surprising about this: no experiment of matter is everlasting, and the experiment of the psyche—making, among other things, a high degree of social organization possible—is not lacking in momentary successes. It was neither a mistake nor a good for the psyche to have generated the spirit and acquired a capacity for sympathy. Moral terms do not apply in the realm of matter, where, in the flux, what comes to be will soon pass away and where things in their inevitable movement have not the mind to call each other vile.

IV

It will be in order here to remark briefly on Santayana's relation to hedonism. First of all, being an epiphenomenalist, he cannot be a psychological hedonist. Psychological hedonism is the doctrine that pleasure alone can be the final and the efficient

[12] *The Realm of Spirit,* vol. IV of *Realms of Being,* p. 614.

cause of action. Now final-cause terminology in the sphere of matter, which is co-extensive with the field of action, is purely mythological. Once again, I must refrain from a discussion of Santayana's views on the problem of mechanism versus teleology. It will be sufficient to note that he is essentially a mechanist. To postulate purposes and intentions guiding nature is the spirit's way of rendering intelligible the spectacle of the blind motion of matter. Thus the final cause of action is always whatever we happen to conceive the objective of the action to be. On this basis it is simply not the case that the final cause of actions is without exception pleasure; we often think we do things to gain ends other than mere agreeable feeling. The hedonist's counter-argument that such ends are the final causes of actions "only apparently" is without avail.

The case is even clearer with the claim that only pleasure can be the efficient cause of action. The epiphenomenalist is committed to the proposition that no conscious event is causally efficacious. Pleasure thus becomes a concomitant of action, but under no circumstances a cause of it. It is, of course, true that the physiological counterpart of pleasure may well be a cause of action; but the state of the psyche which *corresponds to* the consciousness of pleasure and which is probably a material equilibrium and harmony is not *identical with* that consciousness. The denial of causal efficacy and thus of biological utility to pain, however, yields an argument against epiphenomenalism, the psychological hedonist will here protest. This is certainly correct, but the argument from pain is easily met. I can see no way in which it could be proved or even made probable that the biological utility of pain—its functioning as a deterrent to actions of certain types, for example—is due to the conscious state of *feeling* pain rather than the corresponding physiological state.

Not only is Santayana no psychological hedonist; he is not an ethical hedonist either. By subscribing to the view that good is an indefinable essence, he avoids ethical hedonism with a single stroke. Generally speaking, his position with regard to pleasure[13] is Aristotelian. Pleasure is certainly a good, but it is not the highest good. Agreeable feeling is a concomitant, at best a component,

13 See *Science,* p. 269, and elsewhere.

of the good life, never the whole of it. Nothing is good unless it involves, directly or indirectly, the life of the feelings—thus in the long run the morally good life is also a pleasant life. Moreover, although happiness is pleasant, it is not for that reason identical with pleasure, nor is it valued only for the pleasure it yields. Goods are numerous, individual, and irreducible.

It is unfortunate that Santayana says almost nothing about the rightness and wrongness of actions or about the relation of the right to the good. From his general approach it seems evident that he has very little in common with the deontologists. A discussion of their work, however, would have been very helpful, both from the point of view of making explicit his objections to their view and as throwing additional light on some difficulties of his own position. Without trying to arrive at a complete and precise formulation, we could say that a right action is, for Santayana, without exception one which is in accordance with nature. In a sense, of course, we cannot fail to act in accordance with our nature, and thus the formulation should be modified to read as follows. From a set of alternatives, the right action will be that one which under the circumstances best accords with the most pervasive and permanent interests of the self. As we have seen before, this does not entail egoism. It is unfortunate that altruistic action is sometimes said to be disinterested. The interest in another's good is no less an interest of the self than is the interest in one's own good. Santayana would, of course, have to acknowledge a distinction between the objectively and the subjectively right action. One of the aims of the morally good man is to make the latter approximate as closely as possible the former. The two crucial conditions for success in this are the knowledge of Nature and the knowledge of human nature.

V

This concludes my discussion of points connected with the first part of the problem raised on page 339 above, namely with the question of how interest in a good can itself be good. With this general background we are now in a position to present a brief

solution to the second part of the problem, which is: "How can
desire for a good itself be bad?" The first point to note is that no
desire can of itself be either good or bad. It is only with reference
to other desires that a desire can be pronounced bad, or sometimes misleadingly, a desire for what is bad. No impulse has an
object that is bad *from the point of view of that impulse*, though
it may well be denounced as morally despicable from the point
of view of another, rival interest. Thus any object of any striving
will have an inalienable interest attached to it; though the comparative value of one may be less than that of another, both will,
nevertheless, be genuinely valuable.

Thus once again we see that the question of how desire for a
good can itself be a bad desire reduces to the problem of how we
can make judgments of comparative value. Comparative value
judgments are based on conflicts of interests and presuppose ultimate adherence to one group of interests in preference to all
others. From the perspective of any one impulse all conflicting
impulses are categorically pronounced evil. But in the nature of
the case one of the strongest impulses of a well-knit, healthy man
is the impulse for a rational harmony of impulses. Long-range
interests, desires that are life-enhancing and comprehensive, compatible and biologically sane, are combined in a system with the
formal impulse for harmony supervening. It is by reference to this
humanized and harmonized mass of interests that we judge of the
goodness or badness of individual desires. A desire will be good if
it is compatible with, or conducive to, the enhancement of this
core of dispositional interests; and evil if it conflicts with it. Santayana's distinction between happiness and pleasure will serve to
illustrate the point (*Science*, 251 f.). Pleasure is the result of satisfied instinct, happiness of satisfied reason. The satisfaction of any
stray impulse is accompanied by pleasure. To a bored, lonely
sailor the consumption of methyl alcohol may be an immediate
good and decidedly pleasurable. This fact is in no way changed
by the additional fact that the sailor will go blind in two weeks.
But because methyl alcohol causes blindness, the value of satisfying the impulse to drink it is small when set side by side with the
disvalue it creates by impeding the satisfaction of more permanent
and more comprehensive impulses. In contrast with pleasure,

which attaches to the satisfaction of desires generally, happiness is the fruit of a sane, rational life. It is essentially a satisfaction of long-range impulses; it is serene rather than ecstatic; disciplined, not unrestrained; lasting, not momentary. Happiness involves pleasure, but not a surrender to pleasures. The happy man has achieved a rational integration of objectives, an ideal harmonious with his nature.

There is, of course, nothing compulsory in reason. Moral objectives are optional and acquire value only when preferred. We cannot forbid anyone to be mindless. Some people do not wish to be rational, and so long as we do not get in each other's way it would be silly to insist that they ought to adopt our good. The situation is more difficult when physical contact sharpens the conflict of interests into a clash in the sphere of action. The question then arises whether we have to be fatalists and accept whatever happens with resignation, as absolutely inevitable. Can we not iron out our differences by rational means, and is there no hope for reforming the unprincipled? Santayana's answer would seem to be that there is a way of doing this: not by absolute moral legislation but by setting a good example. The first imperative of morality is to know oneself. Not even this is an unconditional rule, however, and thus it is not prescriptive for anyone who does not wish to acknowledge its authority. To the renegade we can only point out that, insofar as our natures and our needs as human beings are similar, he is not choosing the better part. If an Aristippus still persists in his preference for the immediate pleasure, or some more steadfast Raskolnikov contemplates decades of exquisite crime, profitable argument will have come to an end.

VI

The question "What ought I to do?" is thus answered "Thou shalt know thyself and act accordingly." Self-knowledge is only partially a matter of physical (or social) science. It also includes an introspective self-examination which, for Santayana, is a part of the *art* of literary psychology and not of the *science* of Nature. Socratic and Freudian (*Genteel Tradition,* 57) types of soul-searching are further ways in which self-knowledge may be increased. The *summum bonum,* the highest good, is "to have expressed and discharged all that was latent in us" (*Some Turns,* 100). The task is always definite, and it is imposed on us by nature. What Santayana conceives this definite task, the nature of the good life, to be is of the greatest interest. The characteristic perfection of human life is not moral. It is spiritual. This conclusion has its logical basis partly in Santayana's conception of human nature as dual, as involving both psyche and spirit, and partly in his epiphenomenalism. Its closest affinity is with Aristotle's distinction between moral and intellectual virtue and his emphasis on the contemplative life as the good of man.

The moral life is concerned with action, and the sphere of action is the uneven flux of the realm of matter. No enduring satisfaction is possible here. Nor is the spirit satisfied with the pathetic partiality of the psyche, with its savage loyalty to a few selected objectives. The spirit sympathizes with all goods everywhere, repudiates the violent perspective forced upon it by the natural necessity of having to view all things from a particular, limited standpoint. If preference is a necessary and indispensable condition of value, universal sympathy eradicates the distinction between good and evil—it altogether removes the ground of value judgments. It consists in the intuition of essences for their own sake; it is what may be called "the essence-directed stage" of spirit. This intuition, free of distraction and of the compulsive animal faith that hypostatizes its object, is somewhat like Spinoza's third kind of knowledge, cleared of its mystical and intellectualistic overtones. It is immediate possession of the ultimate—but this ultimate is a self-identical essence or set of essences, without meaning, efficacy, or contagious emotive significance. Though a form of contemplation, it is very like aesthetic enjoyment. To live the spiritual life is to lose all fear, haste, insecurity, but also all compulsive and demanding love. It is to lose one's self in the object and to gain not Pure Being in its infinity, but at least finite being in its purity. To live a spiritual life is to live in the eternal and to see all things under the form of eternity.

The fact that for Santayana consciousness has no place in the direction of action, viz., his epiphenomenalism, is the logical groundwork of his theory of the spiritual life. Since the mind fails to find its satisfaction in the world of nature—in experience, moral action, social living, or even natural knowledge, it must look beyond, or rather in front of (essence is the luminous foreground, the immediate object of consciousness), matter and attain its perfection in the uncommitted contemplation of the play of essences. Perhaps if Santayana had had a different view of mind, if consciousness had been given a role to play in nature instead of being relegated to the position of an impotent bystander, his doctrine of the *summum bonum* would also have been different. As it is, the spiritual life is essentially one of resignation. To the spirit no essence is preferable to any other, and ultimately the intuition of essences is not preferable to the dumb oblivion of death. "We talk of 'life' as if it were unquestionably something precious," Santayana says, and continues, "perhaps a part of the vocation of the spirit may be to overcome this prejudice" (*Realms of Being*, 615). The end of life is death, and to live spiritually is to have no painful and no binding attachments, to be always ready to die.

It is not clear whether Sanayana considered the spiritual life *livable*. It must be livable, to some extent at any rate, if it is not to be a wholly delusive ideal. But it seems paradoxical in the extreme that the good *life* should be that in which one feels that one might as well be dead. And even if this uncanny indifference to death be acceptable, the spiritual life, desiccated angelic existence that it is, seems utterly remote from and unattractive to human nature as we generally know it. The pose of the sage reflecting on the tribulations of life from a distance is not without its seductive charm, but somehow I cannot help suspecting that it is never more than a pose. No one would care to, and for that matter no one could, live spiritually for forty or fifty years of one's adult life. Thus Santayana's point may be that perfection, like husbandry, is seasonal: spring is spent in sowing, the summer in cultivating the fields, and moral action brings spiritual fruit only in the fall when the harvest is gathered and the soul prepares for the long winter journey. The spiritual life may be the perfection of old age, and old age may well be the consummation of a full life. But it is never the whole of it.

The Projection of Values

GEORGE SANTAYANA

In primitive or poetic thought it is natural that moral essences should be treated as if they had a personal unity and material subsistence (things incompatible at bottom, but loosely projected together into the same object, as into a man); so that, for instance, health might be deemed the cause of agility, or beauty a constituent of the rose or even of the oval. Such moral essences are doubly secondary: not only are they mere appearances, like all essences given in intuition, but they are appearances supported by a mass of facts with none of which they have any affinity of essence. What they express is something new: a moral truth involved in the dynamic relations between the substances at work beneath; health being a harmony in the spontaneous rhythms of an animal life and beauty a perfection in some object attuned to those rhythms and stimulating them through perception.

Such harmonies, supporting moral essences, are so far from being units in nature, or special miraculous forces, that they sprawl over various realms of being. Their basis is in the realm of matter, since they are evidently relative to the interests and instincts of animals already existing. Remove these animals from the material world, and evidently nothing in the material world can any longer respond to their passions and capacities, and by so responding deserve the name of a good. Even to imagination—if we imagine imagination surviving the body—an absent good could be such only in virtue of some preference for it over its opposite: and in the end no preference could be justified or conceived except as a blind impulse: an impulse which being blind would not know its own cause, but would have it in the habits of matter.

These habits, such as life itself, and the harmony or discord which reigns between them and their environment are formal

George Santayana, "The Projection of Values," *Columbia Manuscript Collection*, XIV:4. © 1967 by Daniel Cory.

facts spread over indefinite portions of time and space; their proper being, as units, is in the realm of truth. That arsenic is a poison or bread the staff of life is a truth of physics: it could not be a truth if bread, arsenic, and life did not exist: yet those existences render the truth true in its own sphere, which is immaterial. The further truth that bread is a good and arsenic an evil is a truth of morals: the recognition of it may be, at certain junctures, of the greatest moment to the spirit; yet what truth or importance could it have, if not backed by those blind mechanical processes that make nutrition necessary to life and death hateful to spirit?

Yet here moral essences pass over into the realm of spirit; they become objects of intuition. For intuition a good is simply and intrinsically good, and evil an evil; and he who has no intuition of these indefinable essences, in their immediate idiosyncrasy and force, will never know what the words mean. In essence they are irrelevant to their basis in nature, and for contemplation do not suggest it: which is the reason why primitive and poetic fancy hypostatises them into existences on their own account, and why superstition trembles before them as before material forces. As colours, though visible only to creatures with a certain structure of the eye, contain intrinsically no reference to eyeballs or retina, so goods and evils, though created by instincts and interests ingrained in animals, are absolute qualities to intuition; and there they will eventually colour, with their ineffable light and shade, the picture of the strange world which produced them.

Two Rational Moralists

GEORGE SANTAYANA

Two American scholars, from two different points of view, have lately revived the old doctrine that virtue is knowledge. What a change of tone from the pragmatism and instinct-worship

George Santayana, "Two Rational Moralists," *The Journal of Philosophy*, 13 (1916), pp. 290-296. Reprinted by permission.

of these recent years! It would be interesting if the present war should mark the end of that romantic infatuation which for a century has been glorifying will, work, struggle, contradiction, and instability, without any idea or hope of an ultimate good. At a moment when the dreadful corollaries of this heathenism have turned the earth more than ever into a hell, it would be some compensation to recover the true though unrealizable ideals of the race, and again to believe in harmony, in intelligence, in perfection, and perhaps even in heaven.

Professor John Erskine has collected four addresses under the title, "The Moral Obligation to be Intelligent."[1] In them he represents intelligence as both the means and the end of true progress. Affection, he says in effect, is partiality, it is a sort of animal loyalty, while intelligence is the same as universal sympathy. It unites men separated by material interests and passions; it is the one stimulus to justice. It is also the ultimate good to which our nature is addressed. We hear a great deal of the duty of service, but service should not consist in degrading the lives of the best men by subordinating them to the aims of vulgar natures. Rather, by force of example and contagion, the best men should raise the others as far as possible to an intellectual life. "True service," Mr. Erskine writes (p. 68), "lessens nothing. Not that the teacher should waste himself in the enterprises of boyhood, but that even boys should fall in love with the enterprise of truth; not that the scientist should become a commodity-monger, but that all men should enjoy the high commodity of the scientific spirit; not that the priest should be secularized, but that by a race-wide consecration man should become a nation of priests—this is the end of true service."

Even in literature, where his studies lie, Mr. Erskine judges rationalistically, with a view to what is humanly and spiritually best. Inspiration in the poet is a spontaneous gift not to be secured by any effort of art or reason, but art and reason are the surer possession, and they alone can serve to distinguish good inspiration from bad,—for vain or absurd inspiration is commoner than that inspiration which is a short cut to essential truth, a miraculous synthesis or symbol of the rational. Here we see an-

[1] New York. Duffield & Co. 1915.

other error of the recent past corrected—the notion that the esthetic realm is absolute and sacrosanct and that there a man must reduce himself to an abstract sensorium, without intellect, conscience, or a right to be deafened, bored, or disgusted. A work that is merely esthetic is indeed esthetic, but that grammatical assignation of it to its class is no title of honor. The esthetic may not be worth looking at, and the man who in certain instances thinks it worth looking at may not deserve to be alive.

That virtue is knowledge is also the conclusion arrived at by Professor E. B. Holt in his book on "The Freudian Wish";[2] but here, of course, the apparatus of the argument is far more elaborate. I will, however, pass over all those parts of this most interesting book which do not bear directly on the Socratic maxim in question. Incidentally Mr. Holt corroborates what we have just heard from Mr. Erskine. "We hear everywhere," he says (p. 149), "of bringing this and that good thing down to the unfortunate and the debased, and then of *'adapting'* it to the taste and comprehension of these same unfortunate and debased. . . . It seems to me a palpable fact that every form of philanthropy and 'social service' to-day is more or less infected with this fallacy. The idea is everywhere to bring the good *down* in the false hope that it will somehow lift the masses up. But why shall anything strive upwards, when all that is high is bidden to descend? And why is it not a striking and ominous fact that to-day the word 'aspire' is never heard?"

The unit in the psychology of Freud is the "wish," the exact definition of which is "a *course of action* which some mechanism of the body is *set* to carry out, whether it actually does so or does not" (pp. 3-4). It is evident that this is not properly a "wish"; it is rather an impulse, a disposition, a propensity, or what before the days of psychology everybody with perfect propriety called a passion of the soul—one of those passions which were the elements of life. In these impulses we have the stuff of morals. Every one of them, as Aristotle says at the beginning of his "Ethics," has an end and this end (which may be itself an activity) is a good. If these seething enterprises were either isolated or harmonious, moral life would be plain sailing; we should have nothing to do

2 New York. Henry Holt & Co. 1915.

but to follow our impulses and enjoy the goods that our nature, which they constitute, is capable of enjoying. But unfortunately they conflict, both within each animal and between one animal and another. When conflicting impulses are at work in the same body they give rise to the problems of personal morality, and to those painful and disastrous suppressions of impulse which Freud has studied.

These suppressions, as distinguished from a rational discipline that should make for harmony, are the work of chance, of a bad education, or of moral taboos. Nevertheless, suppression in some form is inevitable—*entbehren sollst du, sollst entbehren*—since it is physically impossible to actualize all these warm potentialities at once, and it is fatal to actualize them alternately, because when indulged they leave behind deepening and incompatible habits which tear the personality and the conscience to pieces. There is indeed a successive maturation in some of these impulses which allows a man who has himself well in hand, and can slough off incidental habits, to give free play to each passion in its season. This is something which supermen like Alcibiades, Cæsar Borgia, and Goethe have perhaps managed better than the conventionally virtuous; but it is a delicate business. Mr. Holt, who in this book proves himself a stern and redoubtable moralist, naturally looks for some stricter solution and finds it in *discrimination*. You should carry out all your natural impulses, but discriminating in each what is capable of cooperating with the others from what is irreconcilable with them. They should all live in one another's light, so that their too free operation, or a forced suppression of the minority, may not destroy personal integrity.

It is this light, it is complete knowledge, that alone can save the situation. If a man knows himself he can not go wrong morally, for his impulses (taboos being discarded) are all equally innocent and legitimate; but they are differently wise in view of the soul or society of impulses they are born in. Give the man pause, enlighten him concerning his entire self, and his impulses will be automatically checked and marshaled in the one possible harmony. The only difference in virtue is a difference in wisdom. In this wisdom the conscience is evidently embodied, for the conscience is either one of the impulses harmonized, or a group of them, or the very tendency to synthesis which triumphs in wisdom. Morality in the narrower and personal sense is therefore well accounted for by this theory. A man who was wise after this fashion could find nothing to condemn in himself: the economy of his soul would be perfect.

It was perhaps for this reason that Socrates and Plato embraced this doctrine. They were political philosophers by tradition, being Greeks, but private moralists by vocation, and it is only to private morality that their system really applies. In the "Republic" the problem is how to save the soul, and the political discussion is introduced only as a great parable, because the public in those pre-Christian days had a keener sense for political than for spiritual perfection. What enabled Socrates and Plato to apply their personal morality in the gross, and to imagine that they had a political system as well as a spiritual one, was a triple oversight on their part. In the first place they thought that scientific knowledge of nature was impossible, or at least irrelevant to the government of life and to the right choice of ideals. In the next place, unlike the Indians, they overlooked the whole non-human creation. Finally they assumed that human nature was single, definite, and invariable. If appearance, tradition, and religious faith enlightened us sufficiently about the universe, if no beings counted except the human, and all human beings were essentially identical with ourselves, then, indeed, the morality of the single soul would cover all public morality: all men, to be good, would need to follow the same precepts, and if all men were good, society would be perfect.

Most of us now see quite clearly how far this is from being the case. The living world is fluid and contradictory, and to assume the uniformity of human nature and the adequacy of private virtue to secure public good opens the door wide to tyranny and to political apathy. The orthodox then profess to know man better *a priori* than he knows himself by experience; everything that departs from their conventions is set down for a disease, a sin, or a contradiction; and this innate obliquity in man their zeal must hasten to extirpate. No attempt to do justice to life or society is possible on such a basis.

Mr. Holt instinctively avoids these Socratic prejudices: that is the advantage of being modern and scientific, not too humanistic and not too theological. But I am not sure how in their absence he is to meet the difficulty of integrating those potential courses of action which are not seated in any single animal body. Who is to discriminate among them? By what standard is the relative force and value of each to be measured? If this difficulty can be easily overlooked, it is only because in ordinary cases we assume a tacit governing impulse, with reference to which the others are pruned. Mr. Holt gives this elementary instance: a person impelled to eat mushrooms, but not knowing whether those before him are edible or poisonous, hesitates and fumbles, misses a good chance or runs a foolish risk, all for not knowing the exact marks of the poisonous variety. Give him this botanical knowledge and his course is clear and free, no temptation to taste the bad sort, no qualms in enjoying the good. But this solution is possible only because that person is decisively and superabundantly impelled to live. On this massive root the knowledge is grafted which helps him to accept or reject easily his minor desires. Enlarge the mushroom into a kingdom, a great reputation, a religion, or a lady-love, and the proof that it is poisonous decides nothing. The impulse to live has now a dangerous rival, and the man may say: Better this sweet poison and death, than life without this sweetness. Can knowledge of itself harmonize *ultimate* impulses? Can it pronounce on the relative importance of different souls?

Let us suppose that in conformity with Mr. Holt's theory knowledge is merely a physical response, and further that it could be possible for some one creature to know and respond to the impulses of all others; this response and therefore this knowledge would evidently be a process in that particular creature. The response would seldom resemble and never coincide with its object; it would always remain a dog's response or a man's response, and the response of this particular man or dog at this particular moment. The alien impulses responded to would not be synthesized, but only the responses they provoked in one special creature under special circumstances. What would govern "discrimination" would be the vital equilibrium and total movement of this dog or man, not any comparable absolute weight of the alien impulses as they exist outside. Mr. Holt wishes to abolish subjectivity in psychology, the subjectivity of ideas, but he seems to be all the more plainly committed to a physiological subjectivity in morals. Knowledge and virtue, which are the bodily response itself, need not be sympathetic; to understand need not be to forgive; on the contrary, it may be to hate more impetuously, whole-heartedly, and deliberately than ever. The only principle of social morality, on this theory, would seem to be a savagely systematic egotism.

I do not say this as condemning Mr. Holt's theory; at bottom I think every animal must be egotistical, in the sense that it must determine organically the limits and intensity of its sympathies. If we go so far as to maintain that only sympathy or good-will is a moral motive, that contention simply proves that the sympathetic impulse in us, at least ideally, has overwhelmed the no less virtuous impulse to call some preferences vile and wicked. Knowledge, however, which is not the substance of the human soul, but a sort of celestial guest that may visit it, knowledge is really sympathetic, even when the ultimate response of the soul to the thing known is hostile; because, as I venture to think, it is not our ultimate or total response that is the ground of knowledge; the ground or organ of knowledge is a preliminary or included or residual movement, as of a fly-wheel, wherein our system reproduces, as well as it can, the movement of the object; and this imitative reaction is at once enlightening and sympathetic. But its function in our total animal life is merely to be a signal or, if we turn contemplative, to be a by-path and a sanctuary of peace. Our total response is animal, practical, egotistical, and in it our sympathy and knowledge are submerged. Macbeth feels for a moment how peacefully Duncan is sleeping, but his total egotistical response soon drowns that feeling, and he murders him.

Accordingly the knowledge requisite for "discrimination" is only one half of what is usually called virtue—hence the paradoxical character of the assertion that virtue is knowledge. The other half is a relative goodness, dependent on the degree of cooperation proper to various souls. The first part of virtue is integrity and this second part is beneficence. Beneficence is not knowledge;

it must issue from a preestablished harmony; no amount of knowledge and Platonic sympathy, integrated in the soul of the cobra or the mosquito, could render them beneficent to man. And man in his turn, with increased knowledge, will only go more systematically to work to exterminate *them*. His intelligence, or their inability to express their principles in words, may prevent him from calling them wicked; his total impulse must always call them odious. Both parties, in their mutual malevolence, will be pursuing an ultimate harmony, but harmony may be established in many ways. You may make a desert and call it peace, or give everybody half a loaf and call it justice. It will always be only such justice and such harmony as your own integrated impulses demand. Your virtue will be beneficent only in so far as your nature is "good," that is, fundamentally harmonious with such other natures as it affects. Thus we see that the essence of political virtue is not knowledge, but humanity. Beneficence is not obtainable by rational discrimination among the impulses of each soul; it presupposes a natural cooperation among all the souls concerned. This harmony must preexist; for nothing would be more malevolent than the attempt to establish it artificially. That attempt is war.

When a rational morality finds itself face to face with this great field of irrepressible conflicts, in which it is impotent, it has generally taken refuge in retrenchment. Among the ancients knowledge came to be prized for a new reason: not that it integrated natural life, but that it offered an escape from the vexation and maleficence inseparable from natural life. If we regard our animal career and the integration of its impulses as a vain and bitter good, which will never liberate us from egotism and from an almost universal cruelty, then we may see in our incidental capacity to know and to love the strait and narrow path of salvation. We shall not save our whole soul, but we may decamp, as it were, from the infected parts of it into that corner where goodness and understanding can really live. I need hardly say that this is not the spirit of Mr. Holt's ethics; but I do not think he has altogether appreciated the difficulty of transferring his principle of "discrimination" from an organic body into the world at large.

A Note on Moralities in the Philosophy of Santayana

LOUIS HARAP

The notion of morality in the writings of Santayana has passed through an interesting dialectical development. Between the time of the composition of *The Life of Reason* and the *Realms of Being* it is evident that a change has taken place. One can only conjecture as to the cause of this change; whether it can be ascribed to the dialectic of Santayana's own mind or whether it was wrought by the war. "This war will kill the belief in progress,"[1] he wrote while it was still going on; and, prophetic as this may have proved to be, it may also have been a reflection of the effect of the war on himself. For he had turned from *The Phases of Human Progress* (the sub-title of *The Life of Reason*) to the detachments of *The Realms of Being*. The tendency is entirely in the direction of transcending the urgent care for human affairs. Santayana is of course himself fully aware of this alteration, and acknowledged it in the preface to the new edition of *The Life of Reason* (1922). Contrasting his earlier and later views, he wrote, "I now dwell by preference on other perspectives [than those of *The Life of Reason*], in which the same objects appear with their relative bulks reversed, and inversely hiding one another; what lay before in the background—nature—has come forward, and the life of reason, which then held the centre of the stage, has receded."

The preoccupation with human affairs in the earlier work was so predominant that its effect was to render the realism of this

Louis Harap, "A Note on Moralities in the Philosophy of Santayana," *The Philosophical Review*, 44 (1935), pp. 577-581. Reprinted by permission.

[1] *Soliloquies in England and other Soliloquies*, p. 207.

period hesitating and indeterminate, a tendency which later gave way to the unequivocal affirmation of the independence of matter. *Reason in Common Sense* gives a genetic interpretation of knowledge such that Santayana sometimes appears to hold the view that objects of perception are ideal objects generated by the mind, instead of the later critical realistic view that perception gives the signs of material existences. This inconclusiveness in the conception of the object pervades the crucial chapter on "The Discovery of Natural Objects." "Natural objects" are not there shown definitely to be material and diverse from essence. "A reality," he says, "is a *term of discourse* based on a psychic complex of memories, associations, and expectations, but *constituted in its ideal independence by the assertive energy of thought.*"[2] A natural object is also referred to as "an ideal term" and as an "ideal representative" of a group of sensational appearances.[3] The discussion seems to indicate that the natural world is a structure raised by induction from repeated perceptual and mental experiences. But in the later writing this preoccupation with the genesis of knowledge has disappeared, with the result that there is no indecisiveness as to the status of the natural world. Santayana had finally achieved that detachment which makes realism palatable, and he no longer found it necessary to interpret the world in terms of human effort. The shift in his epistemological position is thus correlative with the development of his ethical views, and indeed the two are mutually influential in their determination. In the beginning it was the life of reason which claimed the devotion of Santayana, while latterly his detached, "post-rational" outlook has closed in upon an ambivalent faith in a stoical ideal and in an unattainable "spiritual life" as the resource for human beings all sorrow-laden and cosmically disillusioned.

In the dialectic of ethical philosophy the life of reason is not the moment of ethical youth nor of old age, but of ethical maturity. At the one extreme is the primitive, savage code of brutality and magic, while at the other is the asceticism of advanced

2 *Reason in Common Sense,* p. 82. Italics mine.
3 *Ibid.*

religions or the rejection of pleasure in ethical decadence. The life of reason stands between these two with its acceptance and enjoyment of nature and its determination to modify that nature in the interests of man. The life of reason is the vigorous re-formation of nature by sophisticated men relatively free both from the resort to magic prompted by a youthful faith in easy solutions made possible by an unsuspecting ignorance of nature, and from the resignation of a decadent people which has tried everything and found the outcome to be satiety or frustration or disillusionment. During the maturity of ethical development the energies are still exuberant and the prospect of joy in variegated forms is capable of arousing whole-hearted interest and effort. The life of reason is eminently hopeful: it is the melioration of nature by agencies originating in that very nature toward the realization of a more ideal conformation of objects and events than is found in nature in its natural state. Essentially the life of reason is epitomized by the principle of the technological machine: one part of nature is exerted upon another part in order to reduce to a minimum the inclemencies and tediums of nature, in order to ease the physical life of man and to fill the life of the mind with engrossing occupation.

Santayana's life of reason is in many ways the modern expression of Aristotle's good life through studious observance of the mean course between the too-muchness of lack and excess. This way of life can be likened to the circle in which the center—the natural man with his equipment and capacities—generates radials —the many and varied interests which are the expression of this complete nature—which terminate on the circumference—the realization of the ideals springing from these interests. This circle symbolizes the harmonious fulfilment of man. On the social side the life of reason issues in the state, in the economic structure, in friendship; on the intellectual side in science and philosophy; on the side of cosmic awareness in religion; and on the side of the immediate, but sophisticated, life of the senses in art. The Aristotelianism of his view is implicit throughout and only occasionally rises to the surface as when he says, "In the history of Jewish and Christian ethics the pendulum has swung between irrational extremes, without ever stopping at that point of equilibrium at which alone rest is possible."[4] And as the form of the life of reason as the articulation of nature in man made consonant is represented by the circle, so the irrational life in its magical and brutalized forms is symbolized by the eccentric, inasmuch as relations among the interests of man are mutually distorted. In the ethical maturity of the individual or of the race the life of reason predominates and flexibility of interest and achievement in all directions is the condition for happiness.

But happiness is after all relative to the state of consciousness, just as a probability-judgment is dependent upon the evidence for that judgment. As the mind grows older and the passions colder through satiety or disappointment there is a change in moral demands and in the conditions for happiness. Instead of seeking after positive goods of the body and mind, the man who has reached the ethical old age wishes to be let alone and to sever the dependence of his hedonic condition upon the attainment of the objects of his desires. In Santayana's later writings this ground-tone of stoicism sounds throughout like a drone bass. As he has himself written, "nature has come forward, and the life of reason . . . has receded" in importance. The resultant stoicism is not as explicit as the ancient variety, or even as in Spinoza, that philosopher so much admired by Santayana. For better or for worse it must be owned that Santayana is rarely explicit in the full, analytic sense. He is too deeply and inexorably subtle, and is too inclusive in his observations to bring them all within coherent, sharply defined conceptual limits. Thus we can say at best that Santayana is stoical *in spirit,* and has passed beyond the doctrine of the mean, the fundamental principle of the life of reason, when he says, "Religion of the sober, practical sort, Roman piety, is emphatically reverence for the nature of things, for the ways of substance. Piety is on the side of belief in substance: the existence of substance is the basis of piety."[5] The end of the moral life is to make oneself over in nature's image, to act under the reign of substance unhampered by the hedonic scruples of consciousness. The ideal existence of the stoic can in a sense be

4 *Reason in Religion,* p. 80.
5 *The Unknowable,* pp. 20, 21.

said to be that of inanimate nature. Inanimate beings are perfectly subservient to nature, untroubled by fear or desire, and they are a nature personified without the psychological interferences that impede the fulfilment of nature in its animate personifications. The closest approximation by human beings to a perfect oneness with nature is to act as though unconscious while yet retaining consciousness. The stoic ideal is a passivity transcending the intense activity requisite for the attainment of this passive attitude towards the sequences of an unconscious nature. One may get the feeling of what it is to be one with nature in the stoical fashion if one imagines how it feels to surrender one's body to the impetus of a high wind. It is to be carried along by nature, not psychologically and impulsively, which is at the opposite extreme from stoicism, but by nature in its inanimate aspect. "In confessing that I have merely touched the hem of nature's garment," writes Santayana, "I feel that virtue from her has passed into me, and made me whole."[6] What he is now interested in is no longer the perfection of man in society, but the *imitatio naturae* on the part of the individual.

Side by side with stoicism Santayana has put forward a second "post-rational" ethic in his ideal of "the spiritual life." In his most recent essay he has identified the supreme object of human loyalty as the "Omnificent," the all-doer which is the source of all cosmic activity, "by my definition the doer of everything that is done."[7] Life is an education in the ways of omnificence. The devotion to omnificence is, however, no longer so discriminating as the stoic consecration to nature. The light of the mind is to play upon no essence with especial intensity because the objects of desire have no eminence of preferability over the objects of any other psychological process. There must not be that special effort to bring one's own nature in perfect accord with the regularities of a mother nature without deflection by impulse which is the goal of the stoic discipline. Gone, too, are the preferences implicit in the life of reason. The highest expression of man is the spiritual life which transcends both, for its first law is to enjoy the manifestations of substance as spectacle, be the attendant circum-

[6] *Realm of Essence,* p. xix.
[7] "Ultimate Religion," in *Septimana Spinozana* (1933), p. 108.

stances whatever they may. Above my lintel shall I write: "Free contemplation no matter what." Neither those essences which are favored by a stolid nature nor those elevated by the moral traditions of mankind are to be preferred. The life of the spirit is sheer unconditional contemplation of essence, "the self-annihilating contemplation of all Being," self-annihilating because all preferences relating to the self, even those conducive to preservation, are absolutely set aside and enjoyment of essences is uniformly attended to.

But the spiritual life does not actually supplant the rational and stoical ideals in the later philosophy of Santayana. On occasion he falls into the idiom of the life of reason, and more often the drone bass of stoicism is heard. But it is the spiritual life that Santayana would have us live by, so far as it is possible to man. The perfectly free spirit can never be realized by man because conservation of the body requires partiality for those essences which appear in the preservation of life. The promptings of pain and the demands of the nutritive soul must be heeded. Beyond these exigencies, however, it may be possible to approximate to the spiritual life. The ideals of the life of reason lose their force as ideals and instead are contemplated as items in the spectacle of civilization no more or less interesting or enjoyable regardless of their importance in the human scheme. The keynote of the spiritual life is "disintoxication" from all human values. Stoicism is as far from the spiritual life as Santayana has shown Platonism to be, for the stoic has not surrendered all preference. Natural activity free from impulse and its consequences in pleasure and pain is the aim of the Wise Man. Thus the stoic is not disintoxicated from love of a life affectively neutral, the life from which fear and desire and pain are absent.

If we should judge from the following statement in *The Realm of Essence,* Santayana would seem finally to adopt neither stoicism nor the spiritual life. It is not for him "to go into the wilderness and contemplate pure Being. . . . As for me, I frankly cleave to the Greeks and not to the Indians, and I aspire to be a rational animal rather than a pure spirit" (65). And yet we may wonder whether he has not left the life of reason behind, giving his last allegiance to a stoicism verging upon the spiritual life. We may ask whether his development as a moralist has not run its full course, beginning with a rounded hedonism in the life of reason and coming to rest in the detached old age of morality in a stoical devotion to the unpsychological ways of nature.

Is Immortality Desirable?

GEORGE SANTAYANA

Although the body of this address is devoted to the question stated in the title, the beginning and the end consider instead whether immortality is possible or probable. The variation in subject is not unimportant; for Mr. Dickinson, being preoccupied with the poor sorts of immortality which are empirically plausible, or for which some evidence might be procurable, has not given free rein to his fancy in depicting that sort of immortality which would be desirable. Such an ideal picture, however, if not meant to deceive, would be apt to instruct. It might prove helpful in the solution of the other question, as to the truth of immortality, for it might dissuade us from twisting reality to suit our rash fancies, seeing how far reality actually responded to our rational ideals. As it is, among the most persuasive passages in this discourse are those which disparage immortality of various undesirable or dubious kinds, such as arrested youth, endless old age, perpetual recurrence of an imperfect life, or heaven on condition that others should be enduring hell. There is, however, a profound will or implicit ideal in us which earthly life can hardly satisfy; and what would render immortality desirable would be the possibility of attaining this ideal in some later life. To this end, Mr. Dickinson continues, it would be perhaps

George Santayana, "Is Immortality Desirable?" *The Journal of Philosophy*, 6 (1909), pp. 411-415; reprinted by permission. A review of G. Lowes Dickinson, *Is Immortality Desirable?*

enough that an unconscious moral mechanism should secure an appropriate sequel to all actions, a sort of Karma that should explain our fortunes in the world and preserve our acquisitions. But it would be decidedly better if a conscious, even if partial, memory connected these successive existences, as it does the episodes of our existence here. To deny this, Mr. Dickinson tells us, "does not empty life of all its worth, but it destroys, in my judgment, its most precious element, that which transfigures all the rest; it obliterates the gleam on the snow, the planet in the east; it shuts off the great adventure, the adventure beyond death" (p. 33). Such an immortality being highly desirable, it is very important to know whether it exists or not; and we may hope to discover that it actually does exist, if we encourage and follow earnestly the investigations of the Society for Psychical Research.

This conclusion, after Mr. Dickinson's restrained and exquisite presentation of the other points, will cast a chill upon the reader, as it visibly did upon the audience to which this lecture was originally addressed. The author, with Mr. Schiller, admits sadly that people are not interested in psychical research, nor in the immortality it hopes to discover; and he seems to attribute this general indifference to spiritual sloth, prejudice, and lack of imagination. It may be worth while for me, speaking entirely for myself, to point out some other things that contribute to that feeling.

In the first place, I am not sure that the adepts of psychical research are conspicuous for that "scientific method and critical faculty" which Mr. Dickinson, without a smile, attributes to them. I make no pretensions to be scientific myself; yet I think I see the difference between science and mythology. There are doubtless currents in nature to which supersensitive persons respond; to study them might throw unexpected light on the relation of mind and body, on memory, on intercommunication, and even perhaps, on the nature of time. Yet wireless telegraphy seems to promise more in these directions than psychical research. As the latter is now pursued, it seems to be less interested in bridging phenomena with other phenomena than in attributing them all to a mythical cause. Would it be a proof of scientific method and critical faculty if some one tried to find free-will in the brain, or Apollo in the responses at Delphi? A "spirit" or "person," such as is alleged to send messages from the other world, is a concretion in discourse, a moral or rhetorical entity, a term that may be conveniently used to cover a certain cycle of phenomena, but which, taken in itself, is a word only, and a mere label for our ignorance. A "mind," in another world as in this, is undiscoverable save through its manifestations. Science consists in recording these, and tracing their empirical connections; it would stop, in the case of free-will, at some material break in causality; in the case of Apollo, at the sun or the priestess or some impressionable ether vibrating between them; and in the case of messages from the dead, at some "astral body" flitting about materially. Mr. Dickinson (p. 53) accuses Professor Münsterberg of being dogmatic and unscientific when he asserts that there can be no sensation in the mind when the body does not operate. The assertion is no doubt dogmatic in form and not qualified by the proviso, which I suppose is understood, that we are speaking of sensations that may be inferred systematically and known from without to exist, and not of such as might exist for themselves in isolation, without a discoverable basis or occasion in nature. The conditions of human knowledge have no authority to limit the possibilities of being; but science can not discover anything which, by definition, is undiscoverable. This insight may be expressed dogmatically, yet it is the essence of a "critical" philosophy. Science can only collect the phenomena upon which imagination, if it likes, may build a mythology.

In the next place, the actual communications of mediums, if we choose to interpret them mythically, suggest an immortality which is distinctly undesirable. It is that same ghostly, dismal, and helpless sort of survival which primitive men have always believed in. It is not so much another life, as a prolonged death-rattle and delirium. It makes us shudder "lest death should be," as Shelley says, "like life and fear, a dark reality." A legitimate inference, however, from this shadowy character of the supposed spirits is that they are really echoes only, not existences collateral with that of living men.

Even supposing, however, that further investigation should

make it appear that this survival is genuine and sometimes happy, it by no means follows, as Mr. Dickinson seems to assume, that it is important for us now to ruminate over that future existence, or even to know that it awaits us. A future may be as important as you choose taken in itself, and when it arrives; but foreknowledge of it is important only when useful in modelling that future or in heightening, by anticipation, the value of the present. Such foreknowledge as theosophical prophets have reached, or are likely to reach, does not fulfil these conditions. The question whether one is to marry, and whether that marriage is to be happy, is not unimportant for the individual, and is a matter far more open to calculation and prearrangement than is life in another world; yet what could be more idle, or more illiberal, than to spend one's boyhood pining for wedded bliss and consulting fortune-tellers, on the ground that, unless that happy future were foreknown and secure, football and friendship would lose their "most precious element"? As Mr. Dickinson prefers poetry to reasoning on this subject (and I agree with him), I will quote a few lines from Goethe, who believed himself too good for extinction and thought the spirit might pass through death into a fresh and adventurous existence, like a seed that sleeps through the winter. Yet he says ("Faust," Part II, Act V, Scene 4):

> Nach drüben ist die Aussicht uns verrannt;
> Tor, wer dorthin die Augen blinzelud richtet,
> Sich über Wolken seinesgleichen dichtet!
> Er stehe fest und sehe hier sich um:
> Dem Tüchtigen ist diese Welt nicht stumm.
> Was braucht er in die Ewigkeit zu schweifen?
> Was er erkennt lässt sich ergreifen.
> Er wandle so den Erdentag entlang;
> Wenn Geister spuken, geh' er seinen Gang.

Furthermore, if retribution is unjust, as the author admits, how can justice be furthered by a man's perpetually inheriting the influence of his past acts and habits? What conduces to justice, I should think, is that, wherever action is likely to have important consequences for others, that fact should be regarded in action; not at all that, some good or evil state being given, it should have had kindred causes, or should have had kindred effects. The bonds of such moral fatality, which seem to Mr. Dickinson essential to the preciousness of life, seem to me incompatible with the freedom and intrinsic joy of it. I can not see how the whole of an infinite life should be valuable when every part of it is blighted and oppressed by infinite forgotten guilt and an infinite incalculable responsibility. It is only by ignoring their immortality that those who believe in it are able to live.

On the other hand (and this is my last observation), the ideal I find implied in our instincts, preferences, and hopes is a natural, earthly, and distinctly human ideal. If it seems otherwise sometimes, that is only because it has been crushed by misfortune, in the absence of articulate art, into something utterly vague and wistful. Specify your aspirations, begin to enact them, and you will perceive that they are human and that their fulfilment can come only on earth. At the same time you will perceive that they are not selfish. The precious being which you crave to preserve is essentially an ideal, not expressible save in a flux of existences. Therefore sleep and oblivescence need not destroy it. It dwells in consecutiveness of purpose, unanimity of thought, kinship in happiness; it desires to triumph over death only as memory, heredity, and culture triumph over that mutability which, in material life, is absolutely pervasive and irrevocable. There is no ideal self so private as not to be made up of these public elements. The chimera of a soul which is neither the life of the body, nor a rational object, and yet is both at once, is one of the metaphysical hybrids generated by giving a physical status to a moral entity. Such confusions are prevalent enough and traditional; yet they hardly avail to mislead instinct; and this is the fundamental reason, I imagine, why a mythical immortality, even when believed in, leaves mankind in such invincible apathy. They know it is not what their hearts aspire to; it is not really their good, much less a condition for the excellence of the universe. They are not conceited enough to believe that no one can take their place upon the world's stage to the common advantage. If I were the playwright, I confess I should hope soon to find or produce a better set of characters than any that have yet appeared. Not a single man or woman has ever existed whom I should wish to engage to play forever, rather than fill my theater from age to age with fresh faces, and new accents of nature. Continual perfection would be my ideal, not individual perpetuity; for such perpetuity, as an ideal, would imply either that perfection was unattainable or that the possible forms of it were exhausted. To the sorts of immortality, accordingly, which on closer inspection disenchant us and prove to be undesirable, I should add the finding of my own person again beyond the grave, together with the persons of all my earthly acquaintance, a prospect which leaves me cold or, rather, freezes me to the marrow. To read in such a sense the ideal of human nature, which after all *is* directed upon the ideal, seems to me far from penetrating and far from sublime.

Santayana and Humanism

GEORGE W. HOWGATE

I

Not always has Mr. Santayana been so far from humanism as he seems today. A competent observer at the turn of the century with enough of the prophet in him to foresee the new humanist movement might even have visioned at its head George Santayana, then a young poet and teacher of philosophy at Harvard, whose *Interpretations of Poetry and Religion* (1900) had just proclaimed critical canons in which there was more than a suggestion of our present humanism. In fact, Professor Norman Foerster, looking backward in order to compile a bibliography of recent humanistic literature for his symposium, *Humanism*

George W. Howgate, "Santayana and Humanism," *The Sewanee Review,* 43 (1935), pp. 49-57. Reprinted by permission.

and America (1930), lists as his first item Santayana's *Interpretations of Poetry and Religion.*

In this volume Santayana attempted to place poetry and religion on a strictly human basis as the two finest fruits of man's imagination. "Poetry," he said, "is arrested in its development if it remains an unmeaning play of fancy without relevance to the ideals of life . . . Its deepest beauty comes from its response to the ultimate demands of the soul." The poetry of barbarism, i.e., of Whitman and Browning, he roundly belabored as a "rebellion against discipline, in the abandonment of the ideals of classic and Christian tradition." Shakespeare was gently rebuked for his lack of religion, and for his lack of an all-inclusive view of life. Such pronouncements might be found in any recent humanist volume. Paul Elmer More, coming champion of humanism, writing in the *Harvard Graduates' Magazine,* September, 1900, accorded the book unstinted praise as the "wisest and most fascinating work in constructive criticism that has appeared in English for several years." He found the judgment "discriminating and profound," particularly the estimate of Browning, which he called "keen and consummately wise."

No further work of Santayana's is included in Professor Foerster's bibliography. By 1910 the praise of the humanists is more reserved and a feeling of distrust has crept in. *The Nation,* under the editorship of Paul Elmer More, finds in reviewing Santayana's *Three Philosophical Poets* (1910) that in spite of brilliant critical passages the book is marred by "a lack of central veracity in the critic's own philosophy," "a disquieting touch of make believe." A taint of aestheticism latent in *Interpretations of Poetry and Religion* is fully developed here. To the reviewer there is something naïve in the notion of the "perfect poet of the 'new religion' and the 'new art' who shall take his dreams very seriously, yet know there is nothing obligatory about them." Moreover, in the appreciation of Lucretius, humanist nostrils catch more than a faint whiff of atheistic materialism. By 1913 the same *Nation,* reviewing *Winds of Doctrine,* feels free to brand Santayana as a "materialistic naturalist," and to regret that a man of his parts sees fit to "burrow downward toward the primitive." The humanists will have nothing further to do with him.

Aestheticism and materialism, taken separately, offend them more than a little; a philosophy which combines both is simply not to be tolerated.

Santayana himself is quite aware of the effect of his philosophy upon his "friendly critics." In *Soliloquies in England* (1923) he says, "Those whose religion is of the anxious and intolerant sort . . . think my morality very loose . . . I am a pagan and a moral sceptic in my naturalism; on the other hand (and this seems a contradiction to them) my moral philosophy looks strangely negative and narrow; a philosophy of abstention and distaste for life. What a horrible combination, they say to themselves, of moral license with moral poverty."

Humanism in turn is just as distasteful to Santayana. He identifies it with the "genteel tradition," which, instead of "dying gracefully or melting into the active mind of the country," as seemed the case twenty years ago, has now become heroic in its death agonies. As early as 1911 Santayana used the phrase "the genteel tradition" as the title of a lecture delivered before the Philosophical Union in California, a lecture dealing with New England philosophy and culture at various periods of American history. The essence of the genteel tradition Santayana believes to be the Calvinism of the New England Puritans. This in turn has been softened by transcendentalism and centuries of New England culture into a tradition humane, urbane, mildly dogmatic and intensely conservative. Naturally the "genteel tradition" is essentially foreign to the instinctive, work-a-day American spirit, in the words of Santayana, the "feminine gush" and "masculine go."

It seems to me, however, that this "genteel tradition" is a synthesis too easily achieved. Any statement which can include in one breath Jonathan Edwards, Emerson, and Irving Babbitt, is somewhat diaphanous. Moreover, there is not enough distinction between academic philosophy, always derivative in American thought, and its practical applications. These applications were not metaphysical at all, but religious, literary, and even sociological. To say that New England Puritanism was merely Calvinism, that transcendentalism was merely German Idealism, explains neither the religion as opposed to the theology of Edwards

nor the literary philosophy as opposed to the metaphysics of
Emerson—nor Brook Farm, for that matter.

In spite of this objection, Santayana's comments on the new
humanism are in many instances illuminating. He shows that the
Renaissance humanism was underneath a "many sided insurrection of the unregenerate natural man, with all his physical powers and affinities, against the regimen of Christendom." Indeed
the old humanism had in it the seeds of both the unselective ex-
pansiveness of modern romanticism and the narrow specialization
of modern science. The new humanism to Santayana seems more
the descendant of medieval scholasticism than of Renaissance
humanism, even a fragment of the urn of Christianity shattered
by the three R's: Renaissance, Reformation, Revolution, the
roots of the modern world. He really defines for humanism its
pedigree more accurately than some humanists have done. With
such a pedigree humanism should openly acknowledge supernatural sanctions; in fact such a procedure would more clearly
define its relation to religion. In certain respects the humanists
have tacitly made this acknowledgment. Although they avoid the
notion of divinity, their "ethical imagination" is certainly above
natural explanation or natural control. And for the authority of
the church they substitute the authority of tradition crystallized
in the finest minds of civilization, thereby securing a universal
moral criterion, which is the aim of all religion.

Santayana meanwhile has been gradually drifting away from
universal moral criteria. In *The Life of Reason* (1905), he measured humanity for the first and last time by an arbitrary ethical
standard. Age and the war shattered his faith in any panacea for
mankind in the abstract, but his rambles about the English countryside bred in him more of a sympathy with the flesh and blood
man, a growing tolerance of the irrational instincts and longings
which are, as he says, the "atmosphere of the inner man," "the
weather in his soul."

I cannot conceive of his agreeing with Paul Elmer More that
"Happiness is the feeling that accompanies the governing of our
impulses by the inner check." That would seem to him a
strangely negative sort of morality. To Santayana morality consists in understanding the physical nature, in harmonizing its dis-

cords perhaps, but mostly in rising above it entirely. Since the spirit is free in that sense,—to impose upon all men an ideal pattern of life, however hallowed by tradition and antiquity, is nothing short of an impertinence. He says, in *Soliloquies in England* (1923), "I wish individuals and races and nations to be themselves, and to multiply the forms of perfection and happiness as nature prompts them. The good, as I conceive it, is happiness, happiness for each man after his own heart, and for each hour according to its inspiration."

The danger inherent in this point of view is that in the interests of broad sympathy and tolerance some moral strength of fibre, some critical selectivity, will be lost. Everything tends to blur in a soft twilight, wherein all cats look gray. I am reminded of a delightful fantasy of Mr. E. M. Forster, "The Point of It." Sir Michael lived a blameless life, mild, sympathetic, warmed by the love of humanity; middle age softened him into respectable mediocrity, a purveyor of lukewarm aphorisms pleasantly couched for an appreciative public. His wife, on the contrary, was a zealot for truth; age hardened her, embittered her, dried up her human sympathies. After death they found themselves in separate heavens, one for the soft, one for the hard; and Forster's comment is significant: "The years are bound either to liquefy a man or to stiffen him, and Love and Truth, who seem to contend for our souls like angels, hold each the seeds of our decay." There is a lesson here for both Santayana and the humanists.

The question has as much pertinence for the historian and critic of literature as for the moralist. The whole matter of absolute standards is bound up with the choice of the "hard" or the "soft" point of view. Santayana debated this question as early as 1890 in an article written for the *Harvard Monthly* and entitled "Walt Whitman: a Dialogue." McStout champions the "hard" cause; Van Tender, the "soft." Van Tender pleads for freshness and originality in poetry, and maintains that all themes and subjects are suitable for treatment in verse. McScout replies by upholding universal standards of what is and what is not suitable, argues for the normal as against the eccentric, for restraint as against license. To his mind the creative impulse is constantly straining at its tether, constantly alert for new pastures; it is prolific and diffuse and needs the check of the critical impulse to keep it sane and wholesome and relevant to human interests. Santayana, then under the sway of the Catholic and Platonic traditions, speaks more sincerely and vigorously through McStout than Van Tender; and it must be admitted he has always been more of a dogmatist in literary matters than in ethical.

There is still in Santayana a good deal of what Dickinson Miller aptly called "the adamant underneath." The following note I received from Santayana not long ago will show exactly where he stands today in regard to the McStout–Van Tender antinomy: "The antinomy MacStout–Van Tender has always had a clear solution—a Spinozistic solution—in my own mind. All my oscillations are within legitimate bounds. For the solution is this: Moral bias is necessary to life: but no particular form of life is necessary to the universe (or even to the human intellect, except the form of intellect itself). All contrary moralities are therefore equally acceptable *prima facie:* but the one organic to any particular species, or nation, or religion, or man must be maintained *there* unflinchingly, without compromise or heresy." In this statement there is an effort to reconcile the hard and soft points of view, to admit absolute standards on general principle but to restrict narrowly their field of application.

II

It is to be hoped that something beneficial may come from this conflict of the "soft" Santayana and the "hard" humanists, for both stand for some of the most constructive thinking of our day. I can but suggest here a few of the problems to be faced. In the first place, the conflict over first principles must be resolved. It must be remembered that Santayana, no less than the humanists, has devoted his life to the determination of the characteristically human. The difficulty is that, being human, everyone differs as to what is human. To Santayana the highest manifestation of human nature is what he calls the "spirit," to the humanists it is the "higher will" or the "ethical imagination." This is not merely a difference in nomenclature. The "ethical imagination" is one side of man's dual nature; opposed to it are his natural instincts and impulses. These are the higher and lower planes of his being, his kinship with the animal and his adumbration of the divine. This ethical imagination, deeper than reason, more stable than emotion, is his human prerogative; the remainder goes over into the category of the natural; it is nature working through man. Santayana is likewise a dualist, but his microcosm is differently halved. On the one hand is the "psyche," the "specific form of physical life, present and potential, asserting itself in any plant or animal"; on the other is the spirit, in his words, "the actual light of consciousness falling upon anything, the ultimate invisible emotional fruition of life in feeling and thought." The most important point of disagreement between Santayana's philosophy and humanism goes back to the old controversy between free-will and determinism. Whereas the "ethical imagination" is free to impose its will upon natural impulses, the "spirit" is materially bound to its roots in the "psyche" and has no causative power whatsoever. It has, moreover, no relation to any worldsoul or oversoul and is in no sense divine. In the play of consciousness it is less an actor than a spectator, or at least its rôle is completely determined for it by the individual's physical constitution, the "psyche." In its passive way, however, the "spirit" gives meaning to everything upon which it alights, transposing "essences into appearances and things into objects of belief" and giving them a "moral actuality which in their logical being or their material flux they had never aspired to have."

The difference between the humanists' point of view and Santayana's is as important for literary criticism as it is for ethics. Both the humanists and Santayana have been instrumental in taking a considerable portion of the wind from the sails of the romantic movement. Their respective attacks, however, have been based on different principles and have emphasized entirely different aspects of the movement. On what is to both the lowest level of romanticism they have united in condemning Walt Whitman, and for what seem to be the same reasons. There is, however, if one looks closer, a marked difference in their objections to Whitman. Santayana looks down upon Whitman because he is so absorbed by the pageant of existence that he forgets to see rising above the flux those ideal peaks of aspiration and contemplation which constitute the spiritual life. The humanists dislike Whitman because he reduces humanity to the level of natural impulse, the animal state from which man has gradually ascended. In either judgment Whitman has obliterated the dualistic distinction so dear to the heart of each critic; he has failed to mark off on the one hand the ideal from the material, and on the other the human from the natural. These two dualisms are not quite identical. The natural *per se* wears no garment of evil in Santayana's eyes as it does in the eyes of the humanists; in fact, Whitman's strength is, to Santayana, the very real tribute he pays the natural springs of conduct. He errs in being blind to a fourth spiritual dimension; he has no vision of a "realm of essence." At a higher level of romanticism it is easier to see the divergence of the two points of attack. Among the great romanticists the archfiend is to Santayana, Browning; to the humanists, Shelley. Browning, Santayana believes, is almost as submerged as is Whitman by the flood of transient experience; he has his finger on the quick pulse of immediacy, he feels the vibration of life as it is being lived, but he has no repose, no perspective, no sense of ideal values. The humanists, being less philosophical, are appeased by the surface Christian orthodoxy in Browning and gratified by his energetic optimism. They see in Shelley, however, a vagrant individualism, a defiance of tradition, a shallow Rousseau-like humanitarianism, and an utter indifference to discipline. Discipline, in the sense of a discipline of the human will, is of course rank Puritanism to Santayana; nature is a sufficient taskmaster; it is the human being's privilege to escape from the thralldom of matter; the spiritual life is all liberty rather than restraint or control. Thus he sides with Shelley, who, contrary to Matthew Arnold's famous opinion, has all human aspiration for the subject matter of his poems. He describes the realm of the ideal as perhaps no other poet has done; he is only naïve in expecting the realization of his ideals in a material world.

III

To return to modern America, Santayana's portrait of the American is more flattering than is the humanists'. "When the senses are sharp, as they are in the American," he says, "they are already half liberated, already a joy in themselves; and when the heart is warm, like his, and eager to be just, its ideal destiny can hardly be doubtful. It will not be always merely pumping and working; time and its own impulses will lend it wings." The humanists are unwilling to wait for "time and its own pulses," and they are right, I believe. Although they must understand the American heart better than they do at present, it will be their task to lead the American nearer to things of the center, to develop in him a greater power of selection, a stronger self-criticism and self-discipline.

But I believe the humanistic program is inadequate beyond this point. In practice its emphasis tends to be negative; its temper, coercive. Just here may a philosophy such as Santayana's, through its despised materialism and aestheticism, supplement the work of the humanists. The American, having been disciplined, can well afford to acquire more repose, more tolerance, more grace. Santayana's point of view may lead him to recognize pure beauty, pure spirit, and cultivate a steady sense of what is ideally best. The three possible attitudes toward life consonant with truth and beauty Santayana sums up in a brilliant epigram in *Soliloquies in England:* "Everything in nature is lyrical in its ideal essence, tragic in its fate, and comic in its existence." These three stops on the organ of life will give beauty and richness to every note of the human scale. The tragedy of life is never absent to him who sees it through the long vista of the flux of existence, and no one can see it steadily and see it whole without detecting the tragic cast. "The foot of the cross—I dare not say the cross itself—is a good station from which to survey existence. In the greatest griefs there is a tragic calm; the fury of the will is exhausted, and our thoughts rise to another level. . . . The dark background which death supplies brings out the tender colors of life in all their purity . . . to live in the shadow of death and of the cross is to spread a large nimbus of peace around our littleness." If, on the other hand, we do not take the long view of existence but enjoy it as it passes, life becomes a carnival of comic masks. Viewed in that light, "existence is nothing tragic or sad, but rather something joyful, hearty, and merry. . . . Existence involves changes and happenings and is comic inherently, like a pun that begins with one meaning and ends with another. The mishaps, the expedients, the merry solutions of comedy, in which everybody acknowledges himself beaten and deceived, yet is the happier for the unexpected posture of affairs, belong to the very texture of temporal being." Most lovely, however, is nature when viewed in its lyrical essence. Then can the truly contemplative mind in the song of the skylark, in the hand-clasp of a friend, in the postulates of a theorem, in the eucharist of the church lose itself, surmount its basis in nature and enjoy the free play which is the divine prerogative of spirit.

The ecstatic love of pure beauty, the calm acceptance of man's natural state, the genuine comic spirit, in the Meredithian sense, these three attitudes of a well-rounded humanity are perhaps Santayana's most substantial legacy to America.

The Psyche as Social Determinant

JOHN W. YOLTON

Early in the unfolding of the general theme of *Dominations and Powers* we find Santayana invoking his doctrine of the psyche as individual and social determinant. Calling attention to the fact that social revolutions occur in and by the effort of human beings, he asserts that each individual inherits a specific and well-formed psyche from his parents.

This new personal psyche determines all a man's powers and passions, and his taste or capacity for this or that form of association. Circumstances will encourage, re-shape, or suppress these propensities; but without the richly charged individual soul, or the souls of a thousand kindred individuals vibrating in unison, circumstances would continue to compose an empty stage, and a landscape without figures. They be-

John W. Yolton, "The Psyche as Social Determinant," *The Journal of Philosophy,* 49 (1952), pp. 232-239. Reprinted by permission.

come political circumstances when human ambition begins to move amongst them, and to enlist them in its service. Society will then become whatever the psychic disposition of its members may tend to make of it. [P. 5.]

The doctrine of the psyche has formed part of Santayana's general philosophy throughout his many books, but it receives in this latest expression of his thought new and interesting applications. The doctrine constitutes one of the fundamental axioms or presuppositions of Santayana's social and political philosophy, and as such contains the key for a full and accurate appreciation of his system. It supplies an important premise for many unpleasant conclusions of his philosophy. Hence, if we wish to criticize his social and political philosophy, it is in part to this fundamental doctrine that we must look.

In *The Realm of Spirit,* the psyche is defined as the tendency of living organisms to maintain or restore their form, a hidden power in matter which carries the potentialities of life in its various stages (pp. 15, 16). In *The Realm of Matter* it is defined as a trope of matter, an unconscious movement towards goals and objectives (p. 116). Under introspection, the psyche becomes the soul, while the self or person is the psyche in its social attachments. *Scepticism and Animal Faith* posits the psyche as a product of animal faith necessitated by experiences of external events and as a means of unifying experience around a focal center (pp. 146-147). Santayana admits that the psyche is "a most obscure subterraneous object," but believes that the hypothesis is required to explain experience. Substantializing the self thus hypothesized, he makes it to be a "nature that accepts or rejects events, a nature having a movement of its own, far deeper, more continuous and more biassed than a discoursing mind" (*ibid.*). Two approaches are distinguished for studying this postulated psyche: an external, behavioristic and an internal, introspective analysis. The latter is the more difficult and dangerous approach (*ibid.*, p. 148). He even approximates to a Rylistic concept of the self in *The Realm of Matter* where he emphasizes that the psyche is a natural phenomenon, a part of matter, insisting that the question of its locus in matter is not merely a question of the use of words: it is *a deliberate refusal to admit the possibility of any mental machinery.* The machinery of growth, instinct, and action, like the machinery of speech, is all physical: but this sort of physical operation is called psychical, because it falls within the trope of a life, and belongs to the self-defence and self-expression of a living organism. [Pp. 139-140.]

Yet he denies that the self can be just its overt behavior or just a collection of ideas, as Hume suggested.

I, if I exist, am not an idea, nor am I the fact that several ideas may exist, one of which remembers the other. If I exist, I am a living creature to whom ideas are incidents, like aeroplanes in the sky; they pass over, more or less followed by the eye, more or less listened to, recognised, or remembered; but the self slumbers and breathes below, a mysterious natural organism, full of dark yet definite potentialities. [P. 149.]

The same mysteriousness and hidden nature of the psyche is stressed in *Soliloquies in England* (no. 49, p. 220). In its relation with spirit, the psyche is that which roots spirit in physical matter (*Soliloquies*, p. 219; *Matter*, p. 139). In many contexts Santayana speaks of the psyche as a predetermining force of life (*Soliloquies*, pp. 219, 221-222; *Matter*, p. 144), although in *The Realm of Matter* he indicates that it has a certain amount of pliability: "it will bend to circumstances, but if bent too much it will suddenly snap" (p. 139). Even though he admits that the psyche can be both selfish and devoted (*Matter*, p. 144), one of the more important characteristics of this physical drive of the individual is its concern for the self in which it is housed. It becomes a kind of guardian spirit, protecting and prodding the self to make moves in certain directions for its good and to avoid evil. "In hunger and the chase, in wounds and constraint, an animal gradually learns to distinguish such objects and actions as are good, in that they further the discharge of his innate powers, from such as thwart this discharge and are evil" (*Matter*, p. 116). Similarly in *Soliloquies* he writes: "This predetermined specific direction of animal life is the key to everything moral; without it no external circumstances could be favourable or unfavourable to us; and spirit within us would have no reason to welcome, to deplore, or to notice anything" (p. 219). The psyche is "perpetually distinguishing in action, if not in words—between good and bad, right and wrong" (p. 222).

The biological or physical basis of action does not, in Santayana's naturalism, preclude a many-sided proliferation and sublimation, for the overt activity of the psyche takes place on three different levels: the generative, the practical, and the spiritual (*Matter*, p. 162). This three-leveled activity corresponds roughly with the three-fold division of *Dominations and Powers*, the generative, the militant, and the rational orders of society. The functioning of the psyche on the rational level is of most interest to us for the purposes of elucidating the role of the psyche in social determination, since it is on this level that the psyche functions not only in social formation but in the conceptualization of *ideal* social organizations. In the socio-political predecessor to *Dominations and Powers, Reason in Society,* Santayana had stated one of the basic convictions of his philosophy: "every man's ideal lies within the potentialities of his nature, for only by expressing his nature can ideals possess authority or attraction over him. Heaven accordingly has really many mansions, each truly heavenly to him who would inhabit it" (p. 97). The problem of the rational order of society is how to combine in one harmonious whole these many ideal mansions. The solution offered in *Dominations and Powers* is one which any liberal of the western world would be glad to accept, with certain reservations, for in the third part of this work it results in the ideal of an international society in which no single group subjugates the values and traditions of any other, an ideal organization in which intellectual pursuits are just as much represented as the physical activities of man, a union of diverse traditions under a harmonious central government. Conflicts of ideology are avoided by the respect which is engendered by each group's mores and ideals. The authority of such a rational government

would be autocratic but not totalitarian; for it would speak for the material conditions imposed by nature on the realisation of any ideal without dictating to any person or society what its ideal should be. Its own aim would be only to prevent conflicting desires from becoming material conflicts, fatal to both sides; while by being temporarily content with what could be obtained peaceably, nothing alien would have to be hated and crushed, but order could be preserved, and a quiet hibernation secured for the seed of every native aspiration. This is the discipline that reason, when alive enough, imposes on the individual psyche that breeds it, and might eventually impose on the world, if the world could develop a political organ of reason, an enlightened and disinterested government. [*Dominations,* p. 435.]

But the difficulty lies in the self-centeredness of the differently structured psyches composing the various groups to be united under the head of the rational international community, a characteristic which makes for militancy among its members. The militant psyche is the greatest of all evils for Santayana: it marks the egoist who demands that the whole world accept his values and his ideals. From one point of view, the greater part of *Dominations and Powers* is directed against militancy, a sin which Santayana credits most of the world with committing. Presumably, we can not, with philosophical justification, even become militant about the rational order, for all reforms must proceed naturally out of the needs and desires of the people, which means from the drives and demands of the psyches composing the groups to be reformed (*Dominations,* pp. 315-316). Santayana is not, of course, much concerned with the ways of implementing the rational order, for he believes the philosopher's task to consist in description and not in the practical application of the rational order. The ideal in this case is inevitably and admittedly tinged with Santayana's own ideals generated by his psychic structure, but the ideal follows naturally once we have defined values in terms of individual psyches. The aim of the psyche or self being to preserve its own ideals and values from absorption by and dissolution from surrounding forces, the logical goal becomes a harmony with one's environment so that these values of the self may be pursued without attack. The transference of the ideal rational life from the individual to the social level is made entire so that the social ideal becomes a simple harmony of the parts with the whole environment. Values are not created in and by social interchange. There are no social values as such, but only individual values demanding certain concessions to society or a certain organization of society to permit the individual values to be satisfied. Santayana does allow a good deal of plasticity to the psyche in this latest work (cf. pp. 43, 60, 62, 404, 414). The pre-determined, innate potentialities of the psyche stressed in earlier works are now replaced by a clear recognition that "the ultimate needs of a soul are not fully determined by its inherited disposition" (*Dominations*, p. 43), that "the great world conditions psychic life; and the psychic life so conditioned conditions the spirit" (*ibid.*, p. 60). But the conditioning which takes place does not lead the individual psyche from concentration upon self to consideration of others. If circumstances happened to produce a society in which all the members had more or less the same psyche construction and hence the same value objectives, we would have a unified and harmonious group, but the harmony would in this case arise only because a happy accident had brought similarly constructed individuals together. The doctrine of the psyche leads, in other words, into a Hobbesian conception of man.

But in human nature generous impulses are occasional and reversible; they are absent in childhood, in dreams, in extremities; they are often weak or soured in old age. They form amiable interludes like tearful sentiments in a ruffian; or they are pleasant self-deceptive hypocrisies, acted out, like civility to strangers, because such is in society the path of least resistance. Strain the situation, however, dig a little beneath the surface, and you will find a ferocious, persistent, profound selfishness. [*Dominations*, p. 71. Cf. pp. 93, 156.]

There underlies much of this analysis of the ideal rational government in *Dominations and Powers* a kind of unwritten and implicit social contract, conceived after the image of the *Leviathan*, except of course force is absolutely ruled out as a justifiable maintaining medium. A rational order of the sort portrayed here would apparently come about naturally only by the various psyches or groups of psyches perceiving that it was to their best interests so to coalesce into a common organization, and thus to achieve their ultimate objective of pursuing their own individual values and ideals, to return to the realm of spirit and essence as these are defined for each individual and for each group, and to leave aside the various burdensome cares of the political world as it is characterized today. To take any other tack is simply to court the dangers which befell Oliver Alden when he worked from the assumption that he must try to make the world better, to do good and to be militant in his goodness. If reforms can be lasting only when they arise naturally, if values are defined only in terms of the desires and needs of psyches, if to presume to prescribe for another psyche the goods and evils of its existence is to run the risk of becoming dogmatically and egoistically militant, and if, finally, all the moral and political conflicts in the world result from conflicting movements within the various psyches taking part in these disputes, Santayana's ideal of a rational government follows without labor. But the doctrine is Janus-headed. From one side, it proclaims truistic generalities which threaten to drain all significance from the doctrine. Who can doubt that each individual is driven forward in action by latent desires and objectives formed in terms of goals congenial to the self? The same propulsion operative on the individual level functions also on the social level, when man conducts his affairs among his fellow men. The doctrine of the psyche can even adjust to the tempting criticism that it fails to recognize the role of society in the formation of the values of individuals, since it can claim that whatever values the individual accepts on the level of society must be values which stand in harmonious relation with the psyche, or else they would be rejected or accepted only temporarily. How else, indeed, can we analyze society except in terms of the individuals composing and forming that society? Santayana's formulation of the doctrine in his earlier works may have stressed the role of heredity at the expense of environment in the formation of values and objectives, but it easily adjusts to both factors, as *Dominations and Powers* makes clear. These conclusions offer no challenging doctrines.

But from the reverse side, the doctrine of the psyche supports conclusions which the majority of us wish to challenge and to refute. It lends credence to Santayana's oft-expressed attitude of acceptance of matter for the sake of spirit, and the general indifference towards society which this additional doctrine entails. It also supports his preference for a ruling élite, since the ideal government is defined as the development and liberation of the "true" nature of man, a nature housed in the internal psyche.

Only specialized psychologists and anthropologists can uncover this nature, sift out the "true" from the "false" desires, although *Dominations and Powers* gives no hint as to how we are to determine when this sifting has been properly performed. When opponents insist that modern society demands a social conscience to direct the energies of individuals towards the social inequalities and injustices of the contemporary world, Santayana is able to reply, in terms of the doctrine of the psyche, that all values are individual in origin and must, to remain valid and fruitful, remain within the orbit of the individual. Even in his latest work he does not make at all clear just where moral militancy begins and moral conflicts end. We do not know just what kind of social oppression he credits to militancy and which to the clash of value systems and psyche fulfillment. He almost seems to fear more the vocal condemnation by moralists of those forms of society which have recently committed "sins against humanity" than he does the havoc wrought by those societies. It is quite easy to see and agree with his condemnation of the attempts on the part of the two major powers of the world today to force lesser nations to accept and imitate their forms of government. The western democracies have been no less militant in their proselytizing than have the Stalinist men of power. But are we to condemn the recent attempts to draw up a code of human rights, including the outlawing of genocide, as a bold act of militancy? Are we to stand aside with philosophic lassitude when we see the capitalistic system making economic slaves of vast layers of our American population, when we see that same system resorting to political witch-hunts against all liberal non-conformists, when we see slavery and oppression running rampant in the eastern areas of the world? Armed with his doctrine of the psyche, Santayana is forced to say that values or objectives are bad only when they seek to dominate the values and objectives of others. But how are dominations to be put down and what justification is there for putting them down? These are questions not clearly answered in *Dominations and Powers*. He criticizes reformers for lapsing into their own preferences, seeking to replace one social order by another patterned after their own image, instead of seeking to "improve the existing order, or bring it to its natural perfection" (p. 316), but we are nowhere told how we are to know what the natural perfection of a given group of people is. How do we determine the natural values of individuals and groups? The doctrine of the psyche does not offer answers to these questions, but the impression survives the reading of *Dominations and Powers* that Santayana is not really interested in these practical questions of his own system, that his interests lie with the condemnation but not replacement by constructive, concrete policies, of those militant moralists both east and west who constantly keep the world in turmoil by raising questions of power and morality, that, finally, he has not shaken off his moral scepticism towards the world, his belief that no lasting moral improvements can be wrought in the world. "Yet in time all ideals like all costumes become archaic and all languages die; so that it is wiser to transfer at once one's treasure to the realm of spirit, where if they were glorious once they are glorious for ever" (p. 364). It may be that the only legitimate answer to Santayana's position is to claim a radical split in our value presuppositions, to maintain that we begin our analysis from the assumption that no value can be tolerated which destroys the realization of other values except those which specifically deny the right to live to brutal fascisms and militant tyrannies. We assume as a value being militant about such things as toleration and the rights of man, even though we run the risk of subduing some natural growth with valid rights of its own. The construction of the rights of man within America and of the rights of humanity within the United Nations have been attempts to prescribe the bounds within which alone those natural perfections which Santayana cherishes can survive. These attempts have at least the merit of being more socially minded than Santayana's self-centered analysis of the psyche as social determinant allows. To understand the conflicts which do exist between the ideal of the western democracies, stated in terms of the conception of rights of man, and Santayana's social and political structure, we need to be supplied with much more detail than he has given us to date. The analysis of the fundamental drive of life in terms of the psyche contains many fine insights and provides a theoretical structure which satisfies many areas of human experience. But is

it a descriptive analysis of the various levels of society and a suggestion of the ideal of societies as we know them or does it represent the value orientation of Santayana's own psyche? That a
description can not completely escape expressing the preferences
of the author, he fully recognizes. But until we can uncover the
precise degree of subjectivity in his social and political philosophy, we are in no position to acquiesce in his charge that in
painting another ideal we have succumbed to moral militancy.
The psyche as Santayana conceives it may itself contain a bias
acquired by one grown wise but cynical about the ability of man
to govern himself or to escape the bonds of selfish drives.

VIII

ART AND BEAUTY

The Photograph and the Mental Image

GEORGE SANTAYANA

Members of the Harvard Camera Club, Ladies and Gentlemen:

I hardly know if I have done right in coming to address you here, where in my ignorance of photography I ought rather to be a listener: yet however little one may know of photography, no one can now-a-days be ignorant of photographs. They fill our rooms, shops and journals; they even take the place of actors upon the stage, and repeat for us with the movement of life whatever interesting scenes are being enacted in any part of the world. And people in their travels now carry a double sensorium about with them, and a double memory, one in their heads and another in a little black box slung over the shoulder. It is of this increase in human faculty, and of the way in which this artificial eye and memory fill out our natural experience, that I wish to speak to you this evening: and it seems to me a subject not without importance. Accordingly, I trust you will pardon a philoso-

George Santayana, "The Photograph and the Mental Image," *Columbia Manuscript Collection*, XIV:5:a. © 1967 by Daniel Cory.

pher for taking a running start and going back in this discussion to fundamentals; for I intend to be more thorough than even those pedants of Göttingen of whom Heine somewhere speaks, who, in composing a treatise on the size of ladies' feet in that town, began with a chapter on feet in general, followed by one on feet in particular, and a third on feet among the ancient Egyptians. Science has made progress since Heine's day, and we cannot be satisfied with tracing photography back to the ancient Egyptians: with your permission I will go somewhat farther back and begin with protoplasm.

The life of man, like that of other animals, is primarily an internal process: I mean, that the fundamental function of the organism is its own continuance and reproduction, or at most its development in some direction determined by its own structure and inner tendencies. Thus the vague potential life that lay dormant in Nature has differentiated itself into all sorts of curious beings, flowers and sponges and polyps and microbes of every description; and we may reasonably assume that to all these variations in form and habit corresponds an inner diversity of sentiment, a differentiation of the original infinite possibilties of feeling into particular kinds of conscious life. Some thin and diffused glimmer of sensibility, some predisposition to consciousness, would seem to hover over every organic form; although, of course, where the analogy to our own organs and functions is remote, it is impossible for our imagination to reproduce that alien experience with any fidelity, or with any assurance of truth: and when we are wholly at a loss to conceive the character of a thing we cannot have much interest in asserting its existence.

That inward core of universal life—the core of our own life as well as of that of every other creature—remains therefore vague and problematical. However impetuous and facile may be the flight of our thought among the stars, and however much at home we may feel on the surface of things, fundamentals always remain obscure, and we may know everything about ourselves and our world except what it really is and what we really are. Our simple friends the microbes and the sponges are probably in a different case; if they are aware of anything at all, they are probably aware of themselves and of themselves only. The fundamental processes of nutrition and growth could alone be represented in their sensibility; for, not having any weapons of defence nor any means of flight in the presence of danger, they float in Nature protected against destruction only by their prodigious fecundity and against fear by their perfect ignorance. When the fatal shock comes, when some unknown external force strikes and crushes them, we may imagine that they awake for an instant from their vegetative lethargy and recognise the existence of something not themselves. But that illumination comes too late and their first moment of vision is the moment of death.

There are not wanting other animals, however, for whom a shock strong enough to be felt is not necessarily strong enough to be fatal; the shock can then serve to call forth during life that prophetic power of intelligence which, as we fancied, might be aroused even in the dullest animals by the conflict with death. A shock may impress without quite destroying, and the accompanying sense of something external may endure for a while and furnish a wholly new element to the contents of the mind.

This new element is perception—the consciousness of objects among which we move and on which we react with various degrees of pleasure and profit. Perception gives the mind the picture of a world, at the same time that it denotes an adjustment of the body to its real environment. The mental image is at once the sign of a practical adaptation to things and the spiritual reward of that adaptation. Our ideas are symbols of a more far-reaching sensitiveness in our organism—of its better protection against surprise and death—and they have a value also on their own account, because they are an interesting and not insignificant development of consciousness, which by them comes to build up a world of discourse and to escape ideally (by interest in the forms it evokes) from brutish absorption in nutritive and individual processes. For the form of an idea can appear in one mind after another and is essentially eternal, just as the matter of bodies passes from one body to another and survives them all.

The mental image already carries us, therefore, from the animal to the spiritual sphere—to the sphere of practical wisdom and free speculation. But perception, however useful and enlightening for the moment, would not do us much service if it could not be revived upon occasion, just as an animal's victory over a given enemy would not do much for his safety, if that enemy could not be recognised and headed off upon a second approach. The organism must not only react upon objects, it must react upon them regularly. Reflex action must settle down into instinct. So too the mental image becomes important chiefly by becoming permanent. To acquire conscious experience we must be able to retain past images and compare them with their successors, just as to attain practical skill we must keep open those cerebral paths which were cut and cleared by our first training.

Now it happens that the body's memory is better than the mind's. The paths between act and act, the paths of habit and reflex action are better preserved than the paths between idea and idea; or rather, the connections between associated excitements are easier to revive than are the complete excitements themselves. So when we are trying to recall a forgotten name; the relation is living in the brain, the wire has electricity in it, but the ideational process is smothered and the bell will not ring. We can accordingly act in virtue of much experience which we have forgotten, and the fruits of learning are not so ephemeral as learning itself. The upper strata of the brain, on which our thoughts and images are grafted, would seem to be of an inconceivably subtle texture, and the thousand vibrations that constantly sweep through that gossamer web, tear and tangle the threads into a mesh, from which it is hard to pull out anything whole. Nothing can be repeated with exactness in the fancy, nothing accepted with literalness, nothing retained without accretion. The new is coloured by the old, the old overlaid and distorted by the new. And, what is worse, the greater part of the experiences which fill a life are lost irretrievably—although their lesson and influence may remain—because the brain, in spite of its prodigious complexity, has no room for so many impressions, has not signals and wires and energy enough for so many successive messages, for so many exact revivals of experience, as a perfect memory would require. Therefore, although everything in the physical world seems to us at times to change quickly enough, everything physical is stable in comparison with the absolute instability of images in the mind. They cannot be retained unchanged for an instant, nor recalled unchanged at any subsequent time.

This absolute flux of mental images is annoying in life and melancholy in reflection. To be sure, those images do not make up the best part of the mind nor the kernel of our individuality: if they did, we should not be able to lament their flight, which we should ourselves accompany. There is something comparatively permanent in us that takes note of mutation and is the standard of its celerity. There are instincts and ideals and intelligible truths which make a background for that flux of sensibility, as the moon and stars make a background for the drifting clouds. The moon and stars move also, but not so quickly, nor at the rate we may attribute to them by an optical illusion, when we but half see them behind those moving veils. But just because we and our interests endure, we lament the lapse of those vivid perceptions which have been the filling of our lives, the material, as it were, of our being. We survive them with a certain sense of emptiness and futility, as if we were surviving ourselves. For the very reason that the higher functions of the human mind have some kinship with the eternal [and the abstract super-structure of thought and expression can endure], we are disconcerted to find that the rest is gone. Hence we are glad when some chance encounter rekindles old memories, and makes Richard himself again. We are grateful to any art which restores that sensuous filling of experience, which was its most lively and substantial part in passing, but which now is so hopelessly past.

And this—for I come at last to our main subject—precisely this is the function of photography. The eye has only one retina, the brain a limited capacity for storage; but the camera can receive any number of plates, and the new need never blur nor crowd out the old. Here is a new and accurate visual memory, a perfect record of what the brain must necessarily forget or confuse. Here is an art that truly imitates the given nature, in the proper meaning of this much-abused phrase,—an art that carries on in the spirit of nature, but with another organ, functions which the given nature imperfectly performs. Photography imitates memory, so that its product, the photograph, carries out the function imperfectly fulfilled by the mental image. The virtue of photography is to preserve the visible semblance of interesting things so that the memory of them may be fixed or accurately restored.

Once before in the history of mankind, or rather at a time before the history we know began to gather, there was a mechanical discovery which served a similar purpose,—I mean when an artificial memory for words, and through words for events and ideas, was invented in writing. Writing was of course a more momentous discovery than photography. The farther down we pass in the history of inventions the more rapid and numerous they are, since they suggest and prepare one another: yet the farther back we go in time the more important the inventions become and the more rare. Writing preceded printing, and was more important than printing: and the invention of speech was older than that of writing and far more important; for the first steps of progress have to make that human nature which the later steps merely subserve and develop. Yet those ancient and magnificent inventions of speech and writing helped human memory to retain only those things which the understanding had already worked over: they recorded and transmitted the intelligible, the describable, what had passed through the processes of abstraction and verbal expression: our humbler art of photography has come to help us in the weakest part of our endowment, to rescue from oblivion the most fleeting portion of our experience—the momentary vision, the irrevocable mental image.

That this is the function of photography is made clear by the use to which it was first put. Photography was first employed in portraiture; that is, it was employed to preserve those mental images which we most dislike to lose, the images of familiar faces. Photography at first was asked to do nothing but to embalm our best smiles for the benefit of our friends and our best clothes for the amusement of posterity. Neither thing lasts, and photography came as a welcome salve to keep those precious, if slightly ridiculous, things a little longer in the world. It consoled both our sorrows and our vanity, and we collected photographs like little relics and mementoes of the surfaces of our past life. For many years photography had merely this sentimental function; but sentiment is akin to humour, and now for one photograph that is made to be enshrined a hundred are made to be smiled at.

Portraits are no longer the only product of photography. The technique of the art has of late so much improved that it can be turned to many other uses. It now renders for us not only monuments and works of other arts, but every aspect of life in its instantaneous truth; and as a means of enjoying travel by the fireside and a gallery of old masterpieces at home, it has wholly outstripped prints and poetry and verbal descriptions of every kind. I do not know how you may feel, but I confess that in cutting the pages of a magazine—and I never cut them unless they are illustrated—it is only the photographs that really interest me: the drawings are seldom the work of a hand that, in Michael Angelo's phrase, obeys an intellect; they are usually feeble and sketchy representatives of the fact and still more feeble representatives of the ideal. The photographs, on the other hand, are truly graphic; there is the unalloyed fact; there is what you would go to see if you had wings and an infinite circle of acquaintance; there is the proof that all they tell us about China or South Africa is no myth, but that men on two legs walk about there, looking quite recognisably human, caught in the act and gesture of life, in spite of their strange surroundings and peculiar gear. With such objects before me, I open my eyes. I look with the same inevitable interest as if the whole procession of life were passing under my windows. The sophisticated concern about art sinks before the spontaneous love of reality, and I thank the photograph for being so transparent a vehicle for things and sparing me, in my acquaintance with remote fact, the [untrustworthy and] impertinent medium of a reporting mind.

Henceforth history need not be a prosy tome in fine print without illustrations: posterity will know of us not merely what we did and thought, but how we looked and what we saw. The reportable outline of events will be filled in with the material of sense, faithfully preserved and easily communicable. Even as it is, the remnants of graphic arts of antiquity give us the most vivid notion we can have of those times; yet those works betray rather than depict the age that produced them, for they were

meant for objects of worship or were at any rate largely predetermined by traditional mannerisms, by symbolic conventions,
and by the love of absolute beauty. If such ideal works, surviving
by accident and in small numbers, yet vivify for us the records
of past time, how much more illuminating will be those innumerable reproductions of everything that surrounds and interests
us, direct reproductions uninfluenced by any human bias other
than that shown in the selection of their subjects! As students of
zoology put on their slides infinitely fine and numerous sections
of the specimens they study, so the photographer can furnish for
the instruction of posterity infinitely fine and numerous cross-
sections of the present world of men.

But perhaps I am not saying what you expected to hear; and it
may seem that in my praises of photography I miss the main
point, and say nothing about its latest successes and its highest
ambitions. Cannot photographs be beautiful? Is not photography
a branch of fine art? Cannot the impression of a sunset, snapped
at the right moment on the right day and printed on the right
paper with reagents of the right variety, have all the sweep and
subtlety of a Turner? Cannot a model's head be so posed and
lighted that the result will wonderfully resemble a Rembrandt
or a Holbein? Yes, and there is no limit that I know of to the
progress which photography may make in these directions. I have
a great faith in natural science, for being very ignorant in that
field I find it more favourable to the exercise of faith in buried
treasures, than other fields where I have rummaged more. Natural science may find in the processes of photography applications
no less brilliant than it finds in mechanical arts: and I fully expect to find colour and permanence and many unthought of perfections soon added to those which good photographs already
have. And while the processes of the art are being perfected, the
experience and taste of photographers may also grow; the more
they are masters of their art the better they will know what objects gain most by photography, what lights and what poses are
permanently pleasing, and what treatment and retouching can
be occasionally helpful. The resources of invention in arranging
models can increase indefinitely, and also the tact in catching the
beautiful aspects of cloud, mountain and sea. But when we speak

of coordinating photography with the fine arts, we must beware of confusion. There is no occasion to be niggardly in the use of pleasant words, and since the word art has in some circles a sacramental value, we may gladly use it to describe any ingenious process by which man produces things which by their use or beauty are delightful to him. And, in a genuine sense, the taking and developing of a photograph requires art; and this art, being governed by a desire for beauty and being productive of beautiful things, may well be called a fine art. For fine art is usually said to be distinguished from useful art by having beauty for its chief aim and the love of beauty for its chief inspiration.

But a wide use of words, legitimate if it is inevitable or if it gives anybody pleasure, should not be allowed to blind us to important distinctions in things: and while photography is surely an art and its products are often beautiful, there remains a deep and quite unbridgeable chasm between it and that other kind of art whose essence is not so much to mirror or reproduce the outer aspects of things, however bewitching, as to create in imitation of the processes of Nature, but in different materials, things analogous to the natural. These products of creative art are shadows rather than replicas of reality and present things as they could never have actually existed: men of stone, passions that obey the rules of prosody, heart-throbs that keep time with an orchestra, tragedies that unravel themselves in five acts without irrelevant incidents—in a word, substitutes for reality that transform it into the materially impossible, in order to bring it within the sphere of the persuasive and the divine. In order to touch creative art of this sort, it is not enough to produce beautiful things, else the gardener no less than the photographer would be a creative artist; the gardener also watches his opportunity, training and guiding his natural engine, the plant, to desirable issues. And the gardener, too, is no utilitarian, but exists wholly in the service of beauty. Indeed, if some voluptuary should walk about the earth choosing none but the pleasant places and refusing to lift his eyes on anything but the beautiful, and should studiously keep in his mind's album nothing but images of beautiful things—he would not be a creative artist; his art of opportune perception and enchanted memory would have weakened his energies without producing anything of spiritual value to himself or to the world. And what would have been lacking in that luxurious passivity? Surely the humane reaction, the selective glance that neglects what it despises in order to extricate and remodel what it loves. What constitutes ideal art, then, is the making of something over under the guidance of a human interest. What issues from any process not guided by a human impulse cannot have ideal value, even if that process went on in the *camera obscura* of a passive and indolent brain.

Now a photograph is produced by a machine, just as the images of fancy and memory are reproduced by a machine; both the camera and the brain transform their impressions in many ways, but not as a moral and conscious interest would transform them. The accidental transformations of the image in photography and memory are consequently defects and imperfections, while the intentional transformations of ideal art are beauties. For the function of photographs and of mental images is to revive experience, but the function of creative art is to interpret experience. Creative art must transform the object, in order to tell us something more about it; for an interpretation that merely repeated the identical terms of its text would be a laughable and stupid thing. Yet just this literal repetition makes the success of an art whose function is revival. When you ask a man to explain his words, it is an insult if he merely repeats them; when you ask him to repeat his words, he is a fool if he sets about to explain them. So when I ask a photograph to come to the succour of my weak memory and visual imagination, and to tell me how things look, I do not want that photograph to be retouched or blurred or idealized; and when I ask a poet to tell me what his passions meant, I do not wish him to inform me of the time of day or of the colours of the rainbow. There is one art to focus and revive experience, there is another art to digest and absorb it. The one is an artificial memory, the other a petrified intelligence.

Accordingly it seems to me that a profound misunderstanding lurks in the criticism often made of photography, that it is crude and literal. Its defects are the exact opposite: namely, that as yet it cannot reproduce our visual sensations without subtracting something from their colour and motion, without dropping something of their stimulating and instructive power. When photography becomes perfect, all our visual experience will be revivable at will—and this would be a truly miraculous triumph over mortal limitations, won, as all triumphs are won, by docility to the facts and laws of the real world. To complain of a photograph for being literal and merciless, is like complaining of a good memory that will not suffer you to forget your sins. A good memory is a good thing for a good man, and to admit all the facts is the beginning of salvation. So with the contemplation of Nature and man; a genuine love of mere perception, a clear vision of things as they are, is the necessary condition of artistic power or of critical capacity. Photography is useful to the artist because it helps him to see and to keep seeing, and helpful to every intelligent man because it enables him to see much that from his station in space and time, is naturally invisible. To be accurate and complete is therefore the ideal of photography, as of memory: an ideal which is not the less genuine because it is not absolutely realisable and not the less worthy because, even if it could be realised, it would still leave room for other and higher things. For a virtue of subordinate things, when they are genuine, is to remain subordinate. If memory were perfectly developed it would not prevent us from imagining all sorts of possible and yet unrealised things: on the contrary it would furnish the mind with clearer and more numerous analogies for its invention to follow, and keep its ideals from being childish and irrelevant. So too the prevalence of photography will not tend to kill the impulse to design, but rather stimulate and train it by focussing attention on that natural structure of things by which all beautiful design is inspired.

The same misunderstanding which occasions this reproach of literalness addressed to photography, is the cause also of a mistaken ambition on its part—the ambition to be ideal [a very different thing, I need hardly say, from the ambition to be beautiful]. For good photographs will be beautiful when their object is beautiful and poetical when their object is poetical; but to be ideal they would have to transform the object so as to make it a clearer response to the observer's predetermined interests. The camera cannot have a human bias, it cannot exercise a selective attention or be guided by an imaginative impulse: it will do its honest work in an honest way. Therefore the sentimental photographer is driven to manipulate the model, to try to give it an interesting expression, to make it smile or bend or dress up to resemble something ideal which he has seen upon the stage or in the works of old masters. The art of photography is thus superposed, as it were, on the art of posing, and the new interest which the photograph acquires is the somewhat meretricious interest of the living picture it represents. No, that is a false ambition; and whoever is seriously tempted by it ought to abandon photography altogether, take pen or pencil in hand, and train himself to the production of things not seen by the retina not transferable to a plate, but visible only to the imagination and not to be rendered except by a hand miraculously obedient to the intellect.

Yet, while we may fail to see any genuine affinity between photography and creative art, we need not share that supercilious attitude towards reality and its photographic image, which is affected by some votaries of the imagination. Imagination is a good thing, but it is a substitute for vision which would be better. And while photography can never have the spiritual value, the pathetic and humane meaning of creative art, that real world and that natural beauty which photography reproduces have always been, are now, and ever will be the ultimate object of human interest. The real world is the subject of creative art; it is what the true artist is himself in love with. If you meet a poet who is more interested in his own verses—or in any verses—than in what inspired them; if you meet a painter who cares more for his art than for his perceptions, or a sculptor who delights more in statues than in moving and living forms—set him down without hesitation for a sham. Art is secondary, life and perception are primary; since it is only the fascination exercised over us by real things that can suggest to us the possibility of their ideal perfection: and if we hasten to render this ideal perfection in some artificial medium, and are enraptured even by the dead suggestion of a complete beauty, how much more must we desire that complete beauty itself, as Nature or a better life might some day actually produce it!

It is true that the man of imagination is able, at the present

stage of human development, to give human nature much more
adequate expression than the scientific. . .*

. . . of creative art, we must not think that it excels in potential
dignity that reality which it transmutes into an appearance, in
order to reduce it more easily to a human scale. We should
rather admit creative art as the best mediator between our half-
lighted minds and our half-tamed environment—as a medium
through which these two can communicate in their primitive es-
trangement. Yet, to help us bridge that chasm, we should welcome
any mechanical arts which, like photography, improve and extend
our perceptions, helping us to see and to remember; for by such
means the real world may be made clearer and more familiar to
us—that real world from which all beauty is derived and in which
all beautiful forms, if they could have their way, would be ultimately embodied.

Art and Mr. Santayana

JOHN CROWE RANSOM

I

Among philosophical personalities probably the most urbane
and humanistic since Socrates is Mr. Santayana. I imagine he is
what Emerson might have been if Emerson had had a philosophical instead of a theological background; in other words, if his
Harvard had been the Harvard of today or yesterday. As an

John Crowe Ransom, "Art and Mr. Santayana," *The Virginia Quarterly
Review*, 13 (1937), pp. 420-436. "Art and Mr. Santayana" (Copyright 1937 *The
Virginia Quarterly Review;* renewal copyright © 1965 by John Crowe Ransom)
is reprinted with the permission of Charles Scribner's Sons from *The World's
Body* by John Crowe Ransom.

* The following four pages of the manuscript are missing.

Emerson disturbs the theologians, a Santayana disturbs the philosophers—an admirable function. Each speaks luminously, and that dismays his professional colleagues and drives them to speak primly; and each pours out an incessant gnomic wisdom, so that the colleagues look a little innocent or empty. The likeness goes further: each possesses the technical accomplishment of verse. But here the report is not so favorable. Emerson was too much the theologian to be quite released by poetry, and Mr. Santayana is imprisoned with all his graces in the net of his intellectualism. They do not command the freedom of poets.

And here the parallel stops, for Emerson did not undertake to compete with Hawthorne in another art, but Mr. Santayana has written a big novel, at the moment when his wisdom is ripest. Unfortunately the wisdom, the great shining blocks of it, is a little adventitious for the special purpose of fiction, which on its side happened at the same moment to have reached a stage of enormously subtle proficiency. "The Last Puritan" has distinguished merits, but this is not the novel which will cause the author's secular competitors to cancel their projects and rush off to Academies and Stoas in order to acquire technical philosophy before they write again. It is still they who determine for us what fiction is to be. The flexibility of Mr. Santayana's mind, which is extreme when judged by the standards of philosophical writing, is hardly sufficient for verse and fiction. The philosopher consumes the artist; a very old story. And just as his practice does not quite indicate an understanding of the art-work, neither, I think, does his published theory.

The published theory is scarcely to be found in any one locus, for Mr. Santayana's writings are lavish and various. A good single volume for a quick look at the later and characteristic doctrines is the choice collection of essays, "Obiter Scripta"—an indispensable book for all amateur or general readers with the slightest pretension to knowledge. But I think we had better go further back, to the time when the characteristic doctrines were not yet established, in order to see how and why the Santayana æsthetic had to take its form. As a Harvard professor Mr. Santayana admired Greek philosophers and abhorred German idealists. If one should offer the opinion that the five volumes published in 1905 under the general title, "The Life of Reason," are excellent, without effecting much displacement in the existing body of theory, it would be a misinformation unless one added: But they have an extraordinary literary finish, and the vitality of a discourse that is fertilized by metaphor.

We come to Volume IV of this series, "Reason in Art"; and what is the view taken of the meaning of the arts? It is quite commonplace: they are actions which are useful and expressive at the same time. These two requirements are commented on and illustrated, and we are given to understand that they govern both industrial art, which must not be merely useful, and fine art, which must not be merely expressive. Many a pretty application of this formula can be made by a literary philosopher.

But expressiveness and utility! If the phrase sounds determinate to the uncritical, nevertheless it must be one of the best examples of the worst tradition of philosophical rigmarole. The currency of formulations like it is a disgrace to philosophy, and in particular has doomed æsthetic to remain its most undeveloped branch. This can be said without especially disparaging Mr. Santayana, who has long since thrown the foolish formula away.

Utility may stand, for at least it says something. The utility of a work is objective, and measurable in terms of the satisfactions which man as a biological species exacts of a resistant environment. Economics has appropriated this term perhaps, but the goods with which economics deals are no other than those perfectly arbitrary ones defined by the peculiar human organism. Utility will even stand, I think, with Mr. Santayana's qualifications, as one of the requirements of fine art. We are in the habit of saying that a piece of art must be important, or must have an interest, but the import and the interest are biological too. Mr. Santayana has conceded that it need not be a direct or possessive interest; Kant enforced this point, and we repeat it when we say that the interest is felt in an imaginary rather than an actual situation. The fine arts are all symbolic, and rest on a conscious fiction, or illusion; it is the illusion of reality; "true to life" as we say, or "a preparation for living" as Mr. Santayana says. Schopen-

hauer showed that even music must symbolize life, and otherwise
could not move us as it does; Mr. Santayana shows it too, and is
more explicit than Schopenhauer.

Expressiveness, on the contrary, is a term exquisitely calculated
to conceal thought, if there is really thinking on these premises;
or, what is more likely, to evade thought. Of what is art expressive? Mr. Santayana is thoroughly uncomfortable with the term,
and in using it seems as often as not to be a species of demonologist,
and to think that art expresses certain impish, irrational, and
unproductive impulses, too trifling for him to track down and
name, not ruled by common sense nor aiming at the worth-
while biological values, insisting democratically on their right to
expression, and humored without doing much harm in anomalous exercises called works of art. It is as if he said, Art is a kind
of scientific performance enacted with a great deal of foolishness;
but, not telling us what foolishness is, permitted us to believe the
worst. By this strategy he runs the risk of instructing his readers
to make a savage comment on his own pretty prose and melodi-
ous sonnets, as follows:

We admire the utility of Mr. S.'s philosophical discourses, but it is ob-
structed and indignified by his weakness for rhetoric, and we think we
shall return after all to those philosophers who attend strictly to business. As for his verse, which seems to have niched for itself a secure if
modest corner in the monument of literature, we have looked that up
and found the place where he tells us about a too-aspiring metaphysician:

> Ah, the thin air is cold above the moon!
> I stood and saw you fall, befooled in death,
> As, in your numbéd spirit's fatal swoon,
> You cried you were a god, or were to be;
> I hear with feeble moan your boastful breath
> Bubble from depths of the Icarian sea.

This metaphysician is certainly in a plight, but it is absurd to say he
has flown higher than the moon and fallen into the sea, and what is
ever gained by absurdities, or by false accents and musical accompani-
ments? If this represents a side of Mr. S.'s nature which had to be expressed, he should have had the goodness to be ashamed of it and to
express it in private; most grown men are, and do.

For by the doctrine of expressiveness, in the hands of persons not its enthusiasts, art is disreputable.

But suppose the doctrinaire says that art is expressive not of a contemptible residue of little impulses, disloyal to the practical successes of the organism, but of personality itself, which is imposing, which in fact is the whole organism? The position of art is not much improved. What an odd collocation of terms! Art as utility is dealing with perfectly objective ends, and at the same time as expression is trying to please a perfectly subjective personality. And what is personality? It can only mean: whatever in the organism is responsible for whatever in the work of art is not utility. Personality is mentioned because the doctrinaire is not analytical enough to make out the form that expression takes but can remark sagely that something, probably something big, with about five syllables, is expressing itself. If the utilitarians can point out the objective utility of art, which is indistinguishable from that of science, the personalists might try to point out the objective differentiation which removes art from science. The utility and the residue are equally in the objective record, which is the art-work itself.

Objectively, the works of art make a great show in the detritus of the civilizations; they all but rival the aggregate exhibit of the sciences. The testimony which they furnish is certainly adequate. Yet so little have philosophers done to distinguish the art from the science that intelligent teachers of literature are still addressing astonished pupils in this manner:

Our poem brings to us, then, young gentlemen, a nugget of wisdom, a principle that makes for righteousness and the welfare of humankind. See that you cherish it. But it is only by an abstraction that I have paraphrased it in prose and taken it out of context. The prose statement is the practical or scientific meaning. But the object really before us is the work of art, whole and untranslatable. It is richer than its scientific abstract. In what way richer we cannot exactly say, but if we are spiritually sensitive we can feel it. At best we may say that the artist has fused the bare meaning in his genius and in his personality, and made it glowing and expressive, till it has suffered this sea-change. Such is the magic and the mystery of art.

In the meantime the sceptical scientific population, perpetually on the increase, is rudely remarking that it does not believe in magic, and asking of the apologists of poetry to show what the poet has added to the scientific record except irrelevance and disorder. The apologists presently are obliged in honesty to confess that the scientific or prose value of the poem is often trite and therefore slight, as if in satisfaction of a merely formal requirement, and that the unique or characteristic value of all the poetry everywhere, a sum heroic in magnitude, must depend on other but to them invisible considerations. With which confession in their pockets, it may be predicted that the sceptics with renewed confidence and in even greater numbers will be asking whether there is demonstrably anything in the whole world of human actions except scientific ones, dictated by the animal needs of the organism; and whether any distinction can ever be made between actions except in the respect that they may have different degrees of rigor, or consistency, and therefore may be the more or the less perfect; the so-called sciences more, and the unhappy arts a great deal less.

II

Mr. Santayana evolved and grew, like a good biological organism, and produced doctrines which are original, within the limits which must confine originality at a late stage of philosophy. I shall refer to them so far as they seem to have consequences for æsthetic theory.

He cannot have been happy with his word expressive, and the like words, for the kind of commentary which I have improvised is too easy to have escaped him. He had an objective problem and was falling back upon a vague subjective solution: a bad business for any philosopher, and worse for one who had made it his specialty to point to the healthy metaphysical state of Greeks and to deride subjectivism. In 1923 appeared "Scepticism and Animal Faith," a body blow at the idealists. Animal faith is the new and ingenious weapon. William James had talked about pragmatic truth and the will to believe, so that one might say to an idealist who believed in mind more than in matter that these things were perfectly optional. But Mr. Santayana says no, that belief is compulsive, in mind and in matter alike, being part of the animal function which has to act upon environment. Scepticism is not the mark of the living animal; and unbelief in matter, if it could be genuine, would be far on the road to inaction and death. Idealism, that perverse attitude, could have suggested itself hardly anywhere else than among the romantics of the Northern races. (Idealism as if by the principle of equal and opposite reactions has produced behaviorism, its latest and most precise counterpart, which believes in matter but not in mind; a punishment visited upon the world for the crimes of the Nordic idealists.)

I suppose the new doctrine has no application to æsthetic unless indirectly: it dramatizes more sharply the question whether art is really distinct from science. Is art only another work of animal faith? The form and purpose of its animality are not disclosed. And the truth is that the lover of art, who will "feel" a good deal that he cannot know explicitly, would expect to find its residuary properties quite different from those which interest animals. The Christians need not be brought into the argument, but the Greeks, including even Aristotle, held that man is in part an animal but also in part a god. If in his sciences he has insight into objective nature so far as it is serviceable to an animal, perhaps in his arts he may have a more innocent and indeed a divine insight into nature as it is. But waiving theology entirely, I am sure that many art-lovers have a secret notion which goes like this: Art distinguishes man from the other animals in kind, since they have none of it, while science distinguishes him only in power or efficiency, which means degree. Mr. Santayana had almost behaved too handsomely by animality.

He atoned for it handsomely in the two-volume "Realms of Being," his chief philosophical work, of which "The Realm of Essence" appeared in 1927 and "The Realm of Matter" in 1930. Very properly for this Platonist, essences engaged him first; they are his version of the Platonic ideas.

A refined and even attenuated version, for Plato's have some animal odor on them as compared with the Santayana essences, upon which no animal would think of trying to support life. Yet Plato's ideas, like all the varieties of essence to which his sons have ever become attached, fall short of having the fullness of natural or material existences. Plato punished his animality through being fastidious, in a manner not necessarily aristocratic and indeed rather mean for a Greek: the manner of an animal who has become painfully self-conscious, and who has conceived a powerful preference for his rational or "higher" activities and a distaste for the fortuitous pleasures of sense. This is the ascetic or Puritan pattern of fastidiousness. It is not the only one, for Plato might have decided to embrace what he could not cure and to cultivate even the diffusive senses under the standard which is called taste. Its acquisition is laborious enough to have satisfied the schoolmaster in him. (In England the Cavaliers did not go to school less than the Roundheads but more.) But it would not have produced any Platonic ideas. The world of sense, like real property, may be "improved" in a number of ways, but taste would like to bring it under arts, fashions, rites, and manners, which emphasize those residuary splendors that are of no animal importance. Not electing this sort of discipline, Plato went in for ideas, and created them after the likeness of his preferences: as natural substances dried out, purified, and made fit for disaffected but very rational animals. They claim to be the archetypal forms of all created things, but we know nothing about that; and they claim "really" to constitute the present natural world, but that only means that they might have done so if contingency and confusion had not got into nature. So Plato qualified them as only "real" or "essential" constituents of the world, and we need not waste time objecting; it is a locution against which it would be a great deal of trouble to legislate. But I think I know the briefest and best description of the Platonic ideas: they are *ideals;* moral and religious ones. They have a degree of practicability. They are effective in so far as they can persuade men actually to occupy their minds with rational essences rather than with the whole of the contingent world; and is there not an incorrigible and irreducible Platonic faction in every civilized Western population? It is easy to work with nature as animals must, and then to pretend that we are working with essences, which are so neat and clean.

Mr. Santayana's kind of essence abandons even the rational core of body; yet abandoning so much it is a more honest ghost than the Platonic idea. A body is a locus of properties numerically infinite, while the properties of an essence are numerically finite. But we might arrange essences in a series as including more or fewer properties, and Mr. Santayana's would stand at the end; the poorest excuse for body imaginable, but possibly for that very reason, in their void of animal utility, the noblest essences. They make no pretense to existence, and are not in the least norms or ideals. They are nothing but the pure qualities, each one unique and incomparable. Their realm comprises all the qualities in the world, but it is a grammatical or paper realm. They are the atoms of nature in a quaint qualitative sense, for they are single, when it is well understood that nature, even in its smallest and most empty-looking piece, must offer itself as a vast collocation of qualities. And how have they acquired a realm? I suppose it is very simple. Whenever one comes upon a new quality one takes a picture of it and puts it into a drawer. Perhaps one may return one day and look at the pictures. It would be a harmless pastime, though probably a dull one, not like animal pleasure, not like moral pleasure; and not, one would think, like æsthetic pleasure.

But if the realm of essence is quaint, like a child's collection of colored blocks, it is not so with the realm of matter. Essences are just harmless adjectives, but the forms of matter, the things, are nouns, and in action they are frightful things for an animal to have to deal with, because their activities are unpredictable, and evil more often than good; and they are sadly or comically unsuitable for a scientist, because they cannot be held to strict accountability like the nouns in dictionaries but are possessed of an obscene and malignant fertility for spawning fresh adjectives as long as he has the courage to observe them. Mr. Santayana's account of this realm is a great literary achievement, and should be recommended equally to soft-hearted sentimentalists and hard-headed positivists. The account is more exciting than Milton's picture of Chaos, because nothing should have been expected of Chaos except the chaotic, but in nature we hope to find perfect animal fulfilments and rational processes; for, though we may often have been cheated, we have animal faith.

The animal lives in the realm of matter, which is the natural world, and occupies himself with wresting and worrying his living out of it; and if Mr. Santayana's realm of essence were called to his attention he would find it rather beneath his notice or, as its author might say, above it; but actually he will hardly know nor care if there is such a realm. I come back to the original question, and now it will be in the new terms which Mr. Santayana has furnished: With which is the specific vision of the artist concerned, with essence or with matter?

Mr. Santayana has dallied with essences as if they were to be the fruits of his well-spent life. His long road has led him to this sharp categorical division as if precisely in order that he may justify artists at last; for I cannot find any other occasion for it. But at this stage his admirers, though hoping that he will place the feet of the artists on very firm ground, must feel many ignoble apprehensions lest they suffer the fate of his ambitious metaphysician if it should turn out that he has only essences to give them.

He has only essences. That appears from the papers relating to art which are dated from 1925 on, so far as I can judge from those in the "Obiter Scripta," which are several. In 1925 he is emphasizing ". . . the fact that beauty, as I feel it, transports us altogether into the realm of essence, and that no pleasure, interest, or admiration becomes a sense of beauty unless it does so. Every image, however, if animal faith is suspended in its presence, is an essence seen under the form of eternity."

I may as well remark at once crudely, for it will be already clear that I do not subscribe to this view, that it seems to require us, if we would be artists or follow them, to get out of the world where essences inhere in the living substances, and into the drawer where the little flat images are kept. It does little good to say that in this drawer is a treasure which neither moths can corrupt nor thieves break through and steal, inasmuch as everything here is under the form of eternity. Essences are eternal enough; a similar way of thinking has led Mr. Whitehead to name them eternal objects. To eternize an object is to save it by withdrawing it from circulation; from circulation in the battering and incessant transaction of nature, which is life; but it is a peculiar method of salvation, amounting to death. Mr. Santayana has had a peculiar history as a philosopher. He has censured the idealists for not believing their own natural images, but that is exactly the policy he now recommends to them if they would have æsthetic experience; they are to fly to a realm too thin to pretend to support belief. If we should hold him to his verbal commitments, which might be too harsh a procedure, we would have to say that this is one of the most profound of scepticisms, and that Mr. Santayana himself is a Puritan, and in the last extremity.

A remark about essence as the scientists construe it; for we should keep all these essences straight. Of course they never permit it to receive the modest indefinite article, and this implies that they are under the bondage of animal faith when they handle it. To be scientific is to pursue an exclusive interest effectively, and so the scientists abstract from natural forms what they take to be a nucleus or core of properties, and set this aside as "the essence" of a whole series of forms. They do not put it into an attic drawer but rather into the office files. For these essences are Platonic ideas somewhat vulgarized; that is, more shrewdly selective, and believed in not as broad ideals but as sure things, or specific working formulas. Yet the sum of the scientific interests covers the whole range of animality, and if we should define the world in terms of scientific ideality it might easily wear the look of a perfect Christmas party, where all the drinks and sweets were delicious without painful consequences and all the toys obedient to the mechanics' pleasure; so much it might lack of the austerity of the Platonic vision. At any rate, scientists define "the essential" pattern of an object that interests them, and "the essential" conditions for its production. Both the scientific essences and the Santayana ones are obtained by abstraction, but theirs are for hard animal use, and his are for innocent contemplation; non-animal contemplation, I think we must say.

III

In 1929 Mr. Santayana reports a windfall. Proust, fullest and richest if most laborious of all the novelists, has published an æsthetic doctrine scarcely distinguishable from his. It occurs in the last volume of Proust's great work, the one in which he most broods, I think, upon his preoccupation with the past and the meaning of æsthetic joy. Mr. Santayana writes briefly upon it. I quote from his footnote and with his omissions a passage taken out of Blossom's translation:

The being that was called to life again in me by uniting the present impression with something in the past draws its sustenance only from the essence of things, in that alone does it find its nourishment and delight. . . . Let a sound already heard or an odour caught in bygone years be sensed anew, simultaneously in the present and the past, real without being of the present moment, ideal but not abstract, and immediately the permanent essence of things, usually concealed, is set free and our true self . . . awakes, takes on fresh life as it receives the celestial nourishment brought to it. . . . This contemplation, though part of eternity, was transitory. And yet I felt that the pleasure it had bestowed on me at rare intervals of my life was the only one that was fecund and real. Is not the indication of the unreliability of the others sufficiently evident either in their inability to satisfy us . . . or in the despondency that follows whatever satisfactions they may give? . . . And so I was decided to consecrate myself to this study of the essence of things, to establish its true nature. . . . And if I recapitulated the disappointments in my life, so far as it had been lived, which led me to believe that its real essence must lie somewhere else than in action . . . I came to realize clearly that disappointment in a journey and disappointment in a love affair were not different in themselves but merely the different aspects they assumed in varying situations by our inability to find our real selves in physical enjoyment or material activity.

Commenting on this passage, Mr. Santayana thinks it shows an awkwardness in grasping the essences, which does not affect the value of its testimony:

No wonder that a sensibility so exquisite and so voluminous as that of Proust, filled with endless images and their distant reverberations, could be rescued from distraction only by finding certain repetitions or rhymes in this experience. He was a tireless husbandman of memory, gathering perhaps more poppies than corn; and the very fragility and worthlessness of the weeds collected may have led him to appreciate their presence only when lost, and their harsh scent only when recovered. Thus he required two phenomena to reveal to him one essence, as if essences needed to appear a second time in order to appear at all.

A mind less volatile and less retentive, but more concentrated and loyal, might easily have discerned the eternal essence in any single momentary fact. It might also have felt the scale of values imposed on things by human nature, and might have been carried towards some by an innate love and away from others by a quick repulsion: something which in Proust is remarkably rare. Yet this very inhumanity and innocent openness, this inclination to be led on by endlessly rambling perception, makes his testimony to the reality of essences all the more remarkable. We could not have asked for a more competent or a more unexpected witness to the fact that life as it flows is so much time wasted, and that nothing can ever be recovered or truly possessed save under the form of eternity which is also, as he tells us, the form of art.

From the last sentence of Mr. Santayana's passage we receive the sense of a philosopher seizing on the treasure which is not a treasure, because it comes to him under the hollow form of eternity. And from the last sentence of Proust's passage we receive what? The sense that the artist finds his characteristic pleasure, though it is invidious to say that he finds his "real self," not in animal activity but somewhere else. That is one part of Proust's testimony. The other part is more difficult to translate into intelligible terms: the part which has to do with the special importance of memory in Proust's æsthetic practice. Memory is so unrelated to the doctrine of essence that it is not strange that Proust hardly knows what to do with it, nor that Mr. Santayana in effect has to cancel what he does. I do not know who is so adventurous as to dispute Proust's transcript of actual experience, but it is not to be expected that Proust will have the gift for theorizing it; and if Mr. Santayana has the gift it is hardly to be expected that he will theorize it either, being committed already to fixed theories.

Proust has a repertory of simple images which he employs to invoke the past, and with their assistance he lives and finds his delight in the past. His fiction is about the things past, and it is autobiographical. A psychologist should study these key-images to see of what sort they are; it might lead to an understanding of nostalgia, which is the clear emotional overtone of, I think, more than half of lyric poetry, and perhaps of an even larger fraction of music. Proust mentions here a sound and an odor. A sound is heard which transports him into the past, and he testifies that it is by the help of the past that he fixes upon this sound as an es-

sence and enjoys it. But that seems meaningless; and more important to an understanding of the experience might be the fact,
which I think could be established, that it was no such sound
as, say, the dinner bell; it was not a sound which might lead the
animal in him into an act of retrospective imagination in order
to lick its chops. (It might have been such a sound, but not in the
kind of experience to which Proust refers.) An odor is caught, but
it is that of a flower perhaps, not that of animal sweat, or food.
Nearly any distinct and "unimportant" sound or odor would do;
these senses are specially innocent, in that their images are generally not attended to in the fury of the animal processes. And
once these images start the thing, other images come pouring out
of the past, the past takes form again. The past which they invoke
would seem to be, pending the psychologist's report, *precisely
that past which the man as animal did not attend to.* Memory retained it while he was not attending to it, and memory is available. The automatic memory seems disposed to preserve an innumerable troop of meek and homeless items that the animal
consciousness has rejected; but are they not just the items that
are waiting to be attended to? It is in art, or in the informal indulgence of memory, that we come back and attend to them. For
Proust or for us there are always images accompanying present
experience which are just as innocent as those were, but it is as
hard to attend to them now as it was then, since we are still, presumably, good animals.

The consequence is that what must seem like a disproportion-
ate fraction of art is a fairly literal reading of the memory, and
autobiographical; the artist already has a record of the world
more complete than he can transcribe, and need not take the
trouble to invent a fiction. For that matter, the fiction when it is
invented has to be pieced out of the odd scraps furnished by the
memory. It is by employing the device of systematic memory,
which recovers a past relieved of its animal urgency, or the device
of fiction, which is too hypothetical to engage the inhibitory animal, that the civilized races, who are the mechanized and the
highly scienced, obtain their most solid æsthetic experience. Art
serves them better than nature. And if we often seem to detect in
the childlike aspect of art the trace of something sly, roundabout,
and for theoretical admiration unfortunate, when we have come

from watching the bold front, the almost cynical directness, with which the confident animal moves upon his objectives, that is only another way of saying that art in action is artificial, or indirect. It has to be. It has learned its technique in a hard school.

But I cannot think it credible that Proust's joy should consist, as he and Mr. Santayana believed, in obtaining the simple sound, or odor, and then collapsing into eternity, which is trance, emptied of further consciousness, beside it. The state does not seem likely enough to be even pathological. Freudians have wonderful imaginations, and use them ingeniously to account for a strange phenomenon; the fascination and terror which an apparently simple image may exercise over the morbid; and their answer is that through the mechanism of memory it sets in motion a vast, secret, and terrifying train of imagery, so that the total agent is not simple at all. But for Proust we are told that the image is really simple, and unaccompanied; that this is its whole virtue. If it then can be the cause of so profound an experience as art, we are out of the range of the human economy so far as we have had any understanding of that.

IV

If Mr. Santayana as a free personality in a dull professional world reminds us of Emerson, in the light of his systematic philosophy he is a diffused modern version of Schopenhauer. Both are very well aware of the customary unmannerly ferocity of man as an animal, with Schopenhauer of course grieving more than tolerant Mr. Santayana about that; the animal directing and corrupting the most remote-looking and publicly-esteemed pursuits, like tribal morality, which passes for disinterested action, or science, which passes for the pursuit of pure knowledge; yet kenneled, or put to sleep, or transcended, in at least one free and charming activity, which is æsthetic experience. In art, according to Schopenhauer, we at last have knowledge without desire. It remains only to determine just what this knowledge is about, and there again the two philosophers pronounce similarly. Knowledge of the Platonic ideas, said Schopenhauer, but explained them very mistily; and knowledge of the pure essences, says Mr. Santayana, but they look inadequate.

It cannot be impertinent to refer Mr. Santayana, and those who may have followed or preceded him into the ethereal climate of essences, to that remarkable work of metaphysical description, "The Realm of Matter." The images of art are too crowded, contingent, and energetic to be of much use to scientific animals. But the reason is that they belong to the realm of matter as scientific abstracts do not, and not to the realm of essence as scientific abstracts do. In them the scientific or useful essence finds itself accompanied by an infinite residue, and for scientists this residue is exactly what they have charged: irrelevance and foolishness, which cannot suit the limited aims of animals. But all wealth of circumstance and event is within the realm of matter; Mr. Santayana has precisely distinguished the realms and then has not looked at the right one. From it countless works of art have been equipped with their substance, yet it is undiminished and ready for fresh works. What these works intend is, simply, the widest and most unprejudiced knowledge of nature that is possible. There may not be gods to whom knowledge of this sort is the constant form of their activity, for who knows? But there is man, who is not merely animal, and whose animal preoccupations ought never to have become so binding as to exclude a constant exercise of this free knowledge. Now, in his inevitable decadence, he has fallen apart, and the pursuit of it has become one of the specialized and technical functions of his divided mind.

The Mutability of Æsthetic Categories

GEORGE SANTAYANA

The following observations have been suggested by Mr. Henry Rutgers Marshall's recent book on *The Beautiful*.[1] They are therefore chiefly concerned with æsthetic categories, in which mu-

George Santayana, "The Mutability of Æsthetic Categories," *The Philosophical Review*, 34 (1925), pp. 281-291. Reprinted by permission.

[1] New York, Macmillan and Company, 1924.—pp. x, 328.

tability is doubtless more radical and notorious than in the categories used in other speculations; but the thoughtful reader will not fail to see that the principle is extensible, especially at a time when the categories of physics and psychology, as well as those of logic, are so much in flux as at present.

The Real, Mr. Marshall tells us, may be exhaustively divided into the Beautiful, the Valid or Factual, and the Moral Good. He points out that in the consecrated phrase 'the Good, the True, and the Beautiful' the term 'Good' is ambiguous, since taken broadly it would include the Beautiful and the Useful and, I suppose, even the True, in so far as some true ideas may be useful possessions or may be sources of satisfaction in themselves. If the Good is to be exclusive of the other two categories and complementary to them, it should, according to the author, be limited expressly to the Moral Good, that is to principles of conduct, that approve themselves to the conscience and are held to be decidedly the right principles. The True, in like manner, if it is to be a special category, must not be identified with the Real at large, but limited to the realm of thought, to such opinions as are found to be valid. In respect to the Beautiful, however, Mr. Marshall fears no such ambiguity: it "seems to have but one meaning." Of course he observes that the word is applied to a great variety of objects, and in contradictory ways: yet this by no means implies ambiguity in the concept. On the contrary, he might have urged that two æsthetic judgements could not be contradictory unless the same category were employed in both. If the beauty which one party found in a thing was not at all the same beauty which the other party missed in it, the quarrel would be merely verbal, the paucity and vagueness of words not being able to mark clearly the variety of things and of men's perceptions. Or if the quarrel is more than verbal, it is political and moral, turning on the sort of man and the sort of culture which are desirable; it is not about the æsthetic character of given objects. Two men may see exactly the same characteristics in the Venus de Medicis, yet one may turn his back on it, while the other's mouth waters. It is a moral question what kind of beauty we shall love.

The author himself quotes the opinion that the Greeks never thought of the Beautiful apart from the Good. Indeed I think the Beautiful for them was not an æsthetic category at all, but a moral one: it meant, in the most typical instances, the *honestum,* the noble, excellent, admirable, or rightly constituted. Just so happiness did not signify a state of feeling but the divine favour of an enviable and beautiful fate; so that a man might be happy after his death, in as much as he might still be called blessed. This ancient category of blessedness gives the key to an esoteric notion of heaven which has been fused in the pious mind with the exoteric Jewish notion of a resurrection, and which has gained upon the latter so much that a bodily resurrection has come to seem unnecessary for immortality; yet the esoteric Greek notion of blessedness has never been clearly detached or recovered, the blessed state being conceived not as a moral dignity achieved once for all by living well, but as an endless trance, psychic yet unchanging. Of course this conception in turn has been abandoned in romantic times for the hope of an agitated immortality; whereby the notion of another life has ceased to be a notion of blessedness or of heaven—so shifting are all these categories. Among the Greeks the idea of happiness was æsthetic and that of beauty moral; and this not because the Greeks were confused but because they were civilized. Nor is the Beautiful unambiguous even to modern feeling; as Croce observes, it is a hybrid concept which covers the attractive, the *simpatico,* as well as the expressive, which to his mind is alone the truly æsthetic. But the 'æsthetic,' again, is no single or unequivocal category. Mr. Marshall sometimes uses it as if it were a synonym for the Beautiful: yet in Kant it designated the theory or grammar of all sorts of intuition, without any eulogistic implication; taste he discussed not under the rubric *Aesthetik* but under that of *Urtheilskraft.* That nevertheless it was in his school that the term 'æsthetic' came first to be used in relation to the sense of beauty is a curious indication of the nature of his influence: he became the universal centre of departure, from which everybody moved away. In Croce and other Hegelians the æsthetic, without meaning the Beautiful, implies more than cold intuition or ideation, in that it suggests an element of attainment or expressiveness; for in this school intuition is conceived romantically, as the Titanic but fugitive creation of some secret effort. Such an effort however, even if it existed,

would not help to establish any criterion of taste or any degrees
of beauty; all the creations of intuition, as Croce maintains, will
be equally æsthetic (though of course not equally beautiful) if
intuition or expression is attained at all. Thus for Croce criticism
becomes the gift, or perhaps the illusion, of evoking afresh the intuitions of the artist or the poet. Criticism might then seem to
have no value or function other than that of its subject-matter,
if we did not remember that life, even the life of a literary critic,
is everywhere its own excuse for being.

Æsthetic categories have their surprises even in the prudent
hands of our author, who is led to the unexpected corollary that
the Useful must be a part of the Beautiful. The Useful, he says,
is that which gives satisfaction—very much what the ancients
called the Good; and the Useful exercises an indirect control over
the Moral Good, since conscience will not long continue to rely
on moral principles which are found to lead to permanent trouble and dissatisfaction; and since the Beautiful is defined (as we
shall see presently) to be "that which yields a relatively permanent or stable field of pleasure," the Useful will be a subsidiary
part of the Beautiful; the greatest use of the Useful being, apparently, to establish the Beautiful. Thus, in spite of the alleged
separation of the Beautiful from the Moral Good, even the Moral
Good, since it is controlled by utility, turns out to be subterrane-
ously dependent for its continued authority on the beauties
which the recognition of it will eventually produce. I am not sure
whether the author would admit this, or would consider it an
abandonment of his position; but the point is insignificant compared with another which arises in view of his category of the
Real. The Real is anything in experience which shows stubborn-
ness and constancy, so that it will not down, although it may be
an ideal presence like Duty, but always confronts us, as a hard
fact does, whichever way we may turn; so that we are tempted to
objectify the Real, that is, to believe that it has a substantial existence apart from our imagination.[2] This Real is evidently a

---

[2] Such was not the sense in which I used the word 'objectified' when, thirty
years ago, I called beauty "objectified pleasure." My whole little book *The
Sense of Beauty* was written from a subjective point of view, and nothing was
further from me than a wish to hypostatize either beauty or pleasure. Even

specious or ideal object, a category of the imagination; reality is a dignity imputed to figments of thought only because, and so long as, they persistently haunt the mind and seem indispensable. Here we have a psychological theory of the categories, honestly assuming the transcendental attitude; but like all transcendentalism it ignores its own basis, and its singleness of vision, turned only towards specious objects and their logical architecture, if adhered to persistently, becomes comic. Let objects of thought which are relatively permanent be called real and those relatively fleeting be called unreal: it will then be in the bosom of something even less real than the unreal that all reality will be attributed, since no object of thought can be more unstable than the

---

now, when I speak of the terms actually present in intuition as of so many eternal essences, I expressly deny that any such essence is to be regarded as existing. The terms of thought are universals. The particulars which perhaps exist are sundry passing intuitions of those essences, or else are substances met in action and believed to exist, but not open to intuition. Standing for these dark substances (matter or the energies of living creatures) the sensible universals bandied about in discourse are so many signs or names. I should not now use the phrase 'objectified pleasure,' because I see that a term does not become subjective merely because an intuition of it occurs. Nothing is subjective in experience except experience itself, the passing act of intuition or feeling; the terms distinguished during that experience, such as specific qualities of colour or pleasure, are neither objective nor subjective, but neutral; at most they might be called, so long as attended to, subjective objects, such objects as subjective idealism would admit. On the other hand the objects of animal faith, assumed in action to exist apart from the agent, are past, future, or remote events, not so much objective as substantial, although they may become on occasion the objects of intent or investigation. Pleasure therefore does not need to be objectified in order to be fused into an image to be beautiful: if felt at all, pleasure is already an object of intuition; and the beautiful image is never objective in any other sense. Nevertheless I am far from disowning my old view in its import. I was making an honest effort, with the categories then at my command, to express accurately what happened within me whenever I felt that anything was beautiful. Nor was the phrase 'objectified pleasure' a definition of beauty, a visionary essence utterly indefinable: it was an indication of the conditions and manner in which the momentary apparition of beauty arose and vanished. If I tried now to give such an indication I might perhaps say that beauty was a vital harmony felt and fused into an image under the form of eternity. I add the last five words, which are not strictly requisite, in order to emphasize the fact that beauty, as I feel it, transports us altogether into the realm of essence, and that no pleasure, interest, or admiration becomes a sense of beauty unless it does so. Every image, however, if animal faith is suspended in its presence, is an essence seen under the form of eternity.

act of thinking it; so that reality will be something merely dreamt of and reversible, while the irreversible flux of nature in which all this happens, and which is alone actual, will be nothing at all! This is the same predicament in which, as Mr. Marshall observes, Croce and Bosanquet find themselves when after saying that spirit is the only reality they call the primary form of spirit 'Expression.' Expression of what? Expression for an observer, as by gesture or language, is such a modification of one object that it suggests or seems to be pregnant with quite another sort of thing, perhaps incapable of appearing at all in the same medium, as a visible smile expresses pleasure or amusement, which are invisible things. What then can the primary form of mind express if, as idealists maintain, there is nothing prior to mind? Of course (were such an act not unworthy of idealists) they might wink at us and say that (when they were not idealists) they knew as well as any of us that the primary forms of mind, such as sensation or emotion, express states of the body and its fortunes in the material world; and in the same way, when some image seems beautiful, they surmise that it expresses some subtle harmony in the operations of sense, fancy, and passion in the depths of our animal life. Nor need a consistent idealist abstain from mentioning the body or the material world; he need not abstain from *mentioning* anything; but any conditions or antecedents which he may assign to actual experience must be regarded by him as terms thrown out in the game of thought and merely ideal points of reference for logic. They are ideas which thought creates when it needs them, not genuine antecedents which create thought. Therefore the most playful designations will do for so visionary a phantom as the 'real world,' and Bosanquet (not ordinarily a poet) could say that "nature has in it a life and divinity which it is attempting to reveal" and that "in it mind is all body, and body is all mind." In reality, for Bosanquet and Croce, 'nature,' 'feeling,' 'life,' or any other prior energy which expression might express, is only a postulated ghost, a non-existent frontier of actual experience; and 'expression' for them is merely a hypocritical term, used instead of apparition, in an instinctive effort to disguise the solitude and groundlessness of the spirit, as a consistent idealist would conceive it.

There are, indeed, idealists of a different stripe, Platonic or religious, on whose lips the word 'expression' has a reversed meaning in that the lowest forms of being for a mystic may express or adumbrate the highest; and a worm or a ray of sunlight may, for a Ruskin, express the inexpressible. Such felt expressiveness in the simplest objects or events is what the theologians call anagogical; they may all lead our thoughts upward, becoming symbols or sacraments to the devout mind. This is the opposite of a romantic expressiveness (though many romanticists may have a touch of it); for the romantic heart, dark and pregnant, is nothing if not its own master. In fact, the value which the romanticist finds in life or in beauty is that of a vent for something lower; and although, when he becomes a philosopher, he may deny that such a nether power exists, yet he always looks upon overt appearance as on something forged by his own lurid efforts, as if the very devil had been in him. Reality for him is Will and the passing expressions of Will; not a natural or divine order which it might be his humble happiness to discover and to express, but something whose whole merit is that it expresses *him*. And yet, who or what is he in his own eyes? 'Expression,' on his view, is creation of something that had no prototype by an agent that, until that moment, had no existence. No wonder that every idea, after being inflated by his thought, collapses at once into a husk and a dead form to him, as his spirit hastens on to some fresh embodiment. This which he calls his spirit or Will is something vital but distracted; little as he suspects it, it is matter in him speaking without self-knowledge.

Readers of Mr. Marshall's *Pain, Pleasure, and Æsthetics* will remember his theory concerning the physiological basis of pleasure. Pleasure, he thinks, is never a separable datum but always a quality attaching to a sensation that yields other qualities as well. When a stimulus excites an organ in which surplus energy is stored, the reaction is pleasant. When on the contrary the stimulus puts an excessive strain on the organ, there is discomfort or pain. The secret of a pleasant life might apparently be summed up in the words of Hamlet, "the readiness is all." Now, acute pleasures are naturally evanescent since the potential energy which generates them by its discharge is exhausted in producing them; but moderate pleasures will fade more gradually and when they are numerous and alternate, they will form "a very voluminous mass . . . which will wane so slowly that it will be felt to be stable. We shall then be able to produce a field of relatively stable pleasure."

This statement, vague as it may be on its physiological side, seems a good description of the feeling of health or even of animal happiness. A well-fed organism able to exercise all its powers in turn, and always simmering, as it were, with the memory and expectation of those varied pleasures, is certainly the ideal of young life; even hardship or bereavement might cross such a blue sky without abolishing the steady consciousness of resource and of essential success. But I confess I am not prepared to hear that such a relatively permanent field of pleasure, without more ado, is the sense of *beauty*. "Beauty," the author writes, "is relatively stable, or real, pleasure. Any pleasant element may become part of the field that is relatively stable. We call an object beautiful which seems always to yield pleasure in impression, or contemplative revival." It is to be noted that the word 'object' is here introduced as a matter of course; and the author has previously told us that pleasure can never appear without other qualities appearing as well; so that perhaps we are justified in interpolating that which obviously is requisite to turn such a psychic atmosphere into the glimpse of some particular beauty: namely, a synthesis of distinct terms, an image, and a sense that the glory felt resides in that image or radiates from it. If this flash of instant intuition (something not at all stable) may be taken for granted, I should find myself in hearty agreement with Mr. Marshall in making pleasure the substance of the sense of beauty. The one thing that beauty, as actually revealed, can never be is indifferent: it cannot be divorced from living preference and ineffable charm. The soul must be drawn out by it; an inner commotion and a clear apparition on which the commotion centers are equally essential. On the other hand the suggestion that a thing in order to be beautiful must seem beautiful again and again points, I think, away from the sense of beauty, in the direction of the reasons why given works of art are publicly esteemed, and said to be masterpieces. These reasons may include the fitness

often to produce pleasure; and in popular works, such as sentimental or national songs, this may be an important factor; but
the esteem in which works of art are held by cultivated opinion
depends on all sorts of considerations: date, rarity, typical character, workmanship, significance in the history of art or religion or
sentiment. There are portentous works, like those of Michael
Angelo or Tintoretto, to which every one will assign a high rank
in the history of art; but the interest and wonder which they
arouse may rarely, and only in some persons, pass into a true
glimpse of the beautiful. It is not beauty that collectors or con-
noisseurs look for in the arts. The more a poet or a psychologist
insists on the thrilling and seductive note which to him is the
soul of the beautiful, the less will his theory of beauty be a theory
of art; his sensibility will not help him to understand the arts or
even to enjoy them. The fine arts have to be studied like any
other department of nature; and that study, with much fatigue
and waste of spirit, will yield some pleasures and a larger view of
the world; it will refine a man's taste and enrich it with all sorts
of side-lights, qualifications, and ironies; but I think a lover of
beauty will soon turn his back on concert-halls and museums, and
take to the fields. Yet even the love of nature, and of all the aspects of human life, must be spontaneous if it is to gladden the
heart. Obligatory raptures over sunsets, as over 'art,' are one of
the burdens of the 'cultured home.' In the East and among the
ancients, books being rare and plaster-casts and photographs being unknown, æsthetic enjoyment was something direct and unaffected. Fine houses were conceived like fine gardens—places of
retirement, sheltered or spacious, where one might rest or revel
according to one's mood, and be ministered to by all the arts, dis-
creetly and at first hand. People were not concerned to cultivate
their taste but to live in a grateful environment. This is the spirit
in which a free mind would still choose its possessions. But we
moderns, in all our thoughts and tastes, live among ruins. Our
grand houses are museums; and, as a French writer has said, we
cannot take our ease amid our treasures nor enjoy the present
smothered in crowded relics, but we glide among them like
ghosts, thinking about history, and weighed down with the sense
of the history that is being made in our time.

Mr. Marshall, in deference to current views about art, concedes that artists, when actually at work, do not aim at foregone effects but obey a spontaneous impulse. Invention must be automatic, and I suppose that the first line of a poem, or the new or peculiar characters of any design, must occur to the mind unbidden before the artist, in his capacity of expert workman and critic, can plan his work as a whole and laboriously execute it. But his *art* begins where his inspiration ends. Art is something that can be learned and taught; and in the fine arts, as in all human achievements, that which is most admired, that in which merit is measurable, is precisely this element of success in accomplishing an assignable task. If we still say that the function of the fine arts—*les beaux-arts*—is to create the beautiful, this is only one more illustration of the ambiguity of our æsthetic terms. The beautiful here means the non-useful, the decorative, monumental, luxurious, imitative, surprising, amusing, willful, or grotesque: it by no means implies that such boastful or playful works will give more pleasure or possess more actual beauty than useful or natural objects: but they will attract and hold public attention and if there is any real beauty in them or suggested by them, it will be easier to name and to point to than the thousand intangible beauties which a poet finds in rambling through the world.

An artist or a school of art usually has a technical task set for him in advance, which will test his skill and power, and measure the success of his work. Twice in the history of European painting and sculpture, first in Greece and then at the Renaissance, this task has been to represent things as they look, rendering to the life their structure, perspective, colouring, shadows, movement, and expression. This was a legitimate human ambition, which everybody can sympathise with who is not an æsthetic prig; but it was not a search for a greater beauty. Beauty cannot be searched for; and if a subtler sense for beauty had then been driving men to new types of composition, they might have refined their calligraphy, multiplied the harmonies of design or of sentiment, without becoming more realistic: both decoratively and poetically the archaic arts, as we see today, were the more beautiful. But such was not the ambition, the pride, the fashion of their day. I am far from wishing to imply that those generations of faithful and genial artists had no love for the beautiful: they loved it and fed on it night and day; but they saw it in nature, in the model;

and it was because they loved it so intensely, perhaps so abjectly, in nature that they wished to transfer it to their works with as little loss as possible of its vital power. Hence all those stories, so much derided now by the æstheticians, about masterpieces of deceptive art, speaking likenesses, and painted flies that you tried to brush away with your hand. Such anecdotes report faithfully the boasts of the studio, and the wonder and pleasure—not transmuted into beauty—of the public clapping its hands. Mimicry and ventriloquism give pleasure; much more if the counterfeit presentment is that of something grand and astonishing in itself, something which in nature, if it could be found, would produce thrilling effects. No less legitimate is the technical ambition of many artists today (and equally irrelevant to beauty) when they apply themselves to emphasizing single characteristics or single emotions in violent abstraction, in a sort of tragic caricature. There may be power of sympathy and analysis, there may be a deep pathos in this intensive art, as there was breadth in classic art, and the love of nature in all her splendours. It will be this appeal of the subject-matter, in both cases, that will generally reach the public: only the few will be sensitive to the absolute harmonies in the design, if indeed such harmonies are in it.

That Mr. Marshall's definition of the Beautiful should seem to define health or happiness rather than beauty, I take to be no oversight or accident: his book and his whole attitude to the subject are fundamentally philanthropic. He wishes human life to be enriched for all classes with varied and permanent interests, and he feels how much a greater knowledge and appreciation of the arts, (which may be had almost gratis) might conduce to that end. The people are proud and ambitious; they don't want to miss anything, and they might be inclined to suppress everything which they were condemned to miss. It is therefore the part of kindness as well as prudence to diffuse the love of the arts. The pleasures which are called æsthetic turn out, I think, to be intellectual, historical, and moral in the end and in their chief substance; but this circumstance is nothing against them. It makes for their dignity, as for that of human happiness, that they should be broadly based; and the glints of actual beauty seem all the more living and miraculous when they peep at us from the works of man or of nature in places where no one ever thought of put-

ting them. But as to Mr. Marshall's æsthetic categories, I think
their order might be playfully reversed without any loss of clearness or propriety. We might begin by laying it down that the
Moral Good, if it means moral constraint, is not a good at all, but
a necessary (or sometimes perhaps an unnecessary) evil; while if it
means noble habits become a second nature, the Moral Good is
a part of the Useful, since it is a chief means to that real, or stable, satisfaction which is happiness or the true Good. As to works
of art, it would follow that they too are a part of the Useful, for
much the same reason; but the Beautiful, as actually felt, would
be a part of the Good, being a sublimation of pleasure and an
ingredient in a complete happiness. Finally, although as actually
found the Beautiful would be fleeting, and impossible to attach
securely to any work of nature or art, yet with the health and
liberty of the soul the intuition of beauty would become purer
and more frequent and (in the language of Wordsworth) would
be more deeply interfused with the pleasures of the intellect and
of the affections, so as to form a permanent field of happiness, the
habitual consciousness of a good human life. I do not think that
in so twisting Mr. Marshall's words we should be at all false to
his intentions, so variable are all these categories, themselves
creatures of passing intuition, and so little do they mark any permanent lines of cleavage in the living world.

Santayana and the Fine Arts

WILLARD E. ARNETT

The suggestion that Santayana was unable to approve of the
fine arts, because such approval would have provoked inconsist-
ency in his philosophic thought and system,[1] is perhaps the only
time it has been proposed that he was ever seriously concerned

Willard E. Arnett, "Santayana and the Fine Arts," *Journal of Aesthetics
and Art Criticism*, 16 (1957), pp. 84-95. Reprinted by permission.

[1] Jerome Ashmore, "Santayana's Mistrust of Fine Art," *Journal of Aesthetics
and Art Criticism, 14*, 3 (March 1956), 339-347.

with consistency. Indeed, Santayana has most often been severely criticized for his lack of consistency; and though much of such criticism is either narrowly or mistakenly founded, it seems actually much more just to the spirit of his philosophy than the suggestion that he could, and did, in the interest of consistency, bring ill-founded judgments and mistrust to that area of experience, the arts, which exemplified very clearly to him one of the most positive values of human existence and endeavor.

It is true, of course, that Santayana often used the term "art" in the broadest sense, after the manner of the Greeks' use of "techné," to refer to the application of the methods of reason and achievement of excellence in whatever activities man engages; and certainly tradition and custom, if nothing more common and integral to the various directions of human activity, render this usage a legitimate one. However, this is not at all to say that Santayana consequently ignored the traditional "fine arts" or failed to appreciate their unique values and functions.

It is true also that Santayana could not, and did not, approve of all that claims the name "art," or "fine art," even as he did not approve of all that passes for reason, science, morality, and religion. Indeed, there is a sense in which Santayana mistrusted the claims of all the various areas of experience, and certainly all claims to infallibility and pre-eminence. He was by temperament a sceptic, and sometimes a lofty and uncompromising one. But if he had harsh words to say about artists, and especially the fine arts, it was not fundamentally because he mistrusted their proper and highest functions, but rather because he perceived that the arts are often misused as modes of pretense or hypocrisy and as means of escape rather than as fulfillments of the individual life. The arts, he suggested, like other disciplines may be turned to short-range, self-defeating, and frustrating purposes. Consequently, Santayana's primary distinction is not, as Mr. Ashmore suggests, between rational art and fine art,[2] for rational art includes fine art. He does, however, distinguish between the necessary and optional arts,[3] or between industrial and liberal arts.[4]

[2] *Ibid.,* p. 340.

[3] George Santayana, *Dominations and Powers* (New York: Charles Scribner's Sons, 1951), p. 25.

[4] Santayana, *Reason in Art* (New York: Charles Scribner's Sons, 1905), Chapters II and III.

Santayana's distinctions, and his prevailing attitude toward the
arts, are expressed in the following:

There are two directions in which it seems fitting that rational art
should proceed, on the basis which a limited experience can give it. Art
may come to buttress a particular form of life, or it may come to express
it. All that we call industry, science, business, morality, buttresses our
life; it informs us about our conditions and adjusts us to them; it equips
us for life; it lays out the ground for the game we are to play. This preliminary labour, however, need not be servile. To do it is also to exercise
our faculties; and in that exercise our faculties may grow free,—as the
imagination of Lucretius, in tracing the course of the atoms, dances
and soars most congenially. One extension of art then would be in the
direction of doing artistically, joyfully, sympathetically, whatever we
have to do. . . .
    There is a second form of rational art, that of expressing the ideal
towards which we would move under those improved conditions. For
as we react we manifest an inward principle, expressed in that reaction.
We have a nature that selects its own direction, and the direction in
which practical arts shall transform the world. The outer life is for the
sake of the inner; discipline is for the sake of freedom, and conquest
for the sake of self-possession. This inner life is wonderfully redundant;
there is, namely, very much more in it than a consciousness of those
acts by which the body adjusts itself to its surroundings . . . each sense
has its arbitrary quality, each language its arbitrary euphony and prosody; every game has its creative laws, every soul its own tender reverberations and secret dreams. Life has a margin of play which might
grow broader, if the sustaining nucleus were more firmly established in
the world. To the art of working well a civilized race would add the
art of playing well. To play with nature and make it decorative, to play
with the overtones of life and make them delightful, is a sort of art. It
is the ultimate, the most artistic sort of art, but it will never be practiced
successfully so long as the other sort of art is in a backward state; for if
we do not know our environment, we shall mistake our dreams for a
part of it, and so spoil our science by making it fantastic, and our dreams
by making them obligatory.[5]

Santayana also sometimes referred to this distinction as between
the material and spiritual arts, the economic and liberal arts, and

[5] Santayana, *Three Philosophical Poets: Lucretius, Dante, and Goethe* (Cambridge: Harvard University Press, 1910), pp. 212-214.

the industrial and fine arts. The fine arts, then, are optional,
spiritual, and liberal, as well as rational, insofar as their practice
and productions do not directly affect the material conditions or
duration of man's life, but serve to free his faculties from the
burden of necessary labors and bring with them a delight that is
purely intrinsic and non-instrumental. However, as indicated in
the quote above, their optional, spiritual, and liberal status en-
hances rather than detracts from their value.

Santayana also distinguished rational art from *aestheticism,*
not because aestheticism is a form of art, but because it often
results in a perversion of art. "Aestheticism," said Santayana, "is
a refined sensuality, the gift of finding an immediate joy in the
obvious."[6] The aesthete, he continued, "is essentially an amateur,
a poetic spirit listening rather than composing. But in the modern world, where nobody knows where he belongs, it has occurred
to him to pose as an artist. . . . He would blush to confess himself a mere aesthete coming to be ministered to and not to minister; he wishes to prove that he has a public function, and to justify his existence by doing some work, no matter how bad or
unnecessary."[7] But the aesthete, according to Santayana, perceives only sensuous beauties, and regards this as the very highest
value, thus violating the integral rôle which all interests should
assume in the total pattern of life. For a fanatic about sensuous
beauty, he suggested, is hardly more to be praised than other
fanatics. It is the function of art, Santayana believed, to interpret
and transmute all the vital aspects of life, and not simply to increase and intensify the sensuous joys. The artist must serve the
understanding and intuition as well as the sensibility; he must be
aware of the profundity of human traditions, hopes, and problems. However, "The aesthete armed with his supercilious sensibility and transcendental freedom, intrudes into the workshop
of the arts with his nose in the air; but he remains an amateur in
his craft, plays a game of bluff with the public (a game which for
a time is often successful), but dwindles and soon vanishes from

    6 Santayana, "An Aesthetic Soviet," in *Obiter Scripta; Lectures, Essays and
Reviews,* ed. Justus Buchler and Benjamin Schwartz (New York: Charles
Scribner's Sons, 1936), p. 251.
    7 *Ibid.,* p. 261.

the scene in consequence of his inherent vacuity."[8] Thus, Santayana, contrary to Mr. Ashmore, by no means identifies the fine
artist with the aesthete, and his criticism of aestheticism is in no
respect a criticism of fine art or the appreciation of fine art.

Santayana, however, is not as unsympathetic to the aesthetic
experience as the above, taken out of the context of his total
work, might suggest. In *Interpretations of Poetry and Religion,*
one of his earliest published works, he wrote: "The aesthetic
attitude is not the moral, but it is not for that reason illegitimate.
It gives us refreshment and a foretaste of that perfect adaptation
of things to our faculties and of our faculties to things which,
could it extend to every part of experience, would constitute the
ideal life."[9] And he had already written, in *The Sense of Beauty,*
that "If we attempt to remove from life all its evils, as the popular imagination has done at times, we shall find little but aesthetic pleasure remaining to constitute unalloyed happiness. Even
the knowledge of truth, which the most sober theologians made
the essence of the beatific vision, is an aesthetic delight; for when
truth has no further practical utility, it becomes a landscape.
The delight of it is imaginative and the value of it aesthetic."[10]
Furthermore, the following, from the same work, seems eminently
sufficient to indicate that if Santayana mistrusted the fine arts and
aesthetics as areas of experience, no other element or mode of
human endeavor could provoke an equal estimate of worth: "To
feel beauty," he wrote, "is a better thing than to understand how
we come to feel it, to have imagination and taste, to love the best,
to be carried by the contemplation of nature to a vivid faith in
the ideal, all this is more, a great deal more, than any science can
hope to be."[11] And lest this be considered characteristic only of
the earlier writings of Santayana, it should be observed that much
later he suggested that the moral burden of poetry, which he
for many years considered necessary to the highest poetic art, is
really dispensable, and that there is value enough in "mere grace

[8] *Dominations and Powers,* p. 277.

[9] Santayana, *Interpretations of Poetry and Religion* (New York: Charles
Scribner's Sons, 1900), p. 19.

[10] Santayana, *The Sense of Beauty; Being the Outlines of Aesthetic Theory*
(New York: Charles Scribner's Sons, 1896), p. 29.

[11] *Ibid.,* p. 11.

and feeling and music and cloud-castles and frolic."[12] Certainly
Realms of Being, more than any other of his works, indicates a
profound respect and concern for the spiritual, as opposed to
material values. And "beauty is something spiritual. . . ."[13] Indeed, spiritual values generally are exemplified in aesthetic no
less than in imaginative, intellectual, and emotional experience.
If man would live in the spirit—in contemplation and vision and
in the presence of intrinsic goods—he will turn to the arts or
religions, Santayana suggested, no less frequently than to the
sciences; but even the highest values of religion, he insisted, are
inseparable from the arts which the religions cultivate; and nothing, it seems, is more certain in his philosophy than that science, as
he understands it, insofar as it is not an art, is only a preparation for the life of the spirit—the free life of the mind—as expressed sometimes in perception, sometimes in feeling, sometimes
in contemplation and knowledge, all of which are available in
no small measure in and through the arts.

Turning to the specific issues which, according to Mr. Ashmore, indicate that Santayana mistrusted the fine arts, it is perhaps most surprising to be informed that one of the reasons fine
art was unacceptable to Santayana is the fact that fine art is "a
value of the imagination."[14] Apparently Mr. Ashmore believes
that there is an irreconcilable conflict between the rational and
the imaginative, and concludes that if art is to have a rational
function, as Santayana insists it must, it cannot also be imaginative. Santayana, however, saw no conflict between the rational
and the imaginative faculties, but saw them rather as comple-
ments of each other. Indeed, time and again he pointed out the
indispensable function of the imagination as the source of hypotheses in science and of all rational ideals as expressed in art
and religion. Furthermore, Santayana often expressed his own
preference for the imaginative side of life in no uncertain terms.
In the *Sense of Beauty* he wrote that "unless human nature suffers
an inconceivable change, the chief intellectual and aesthetic

[12] Santayana, *Soliloquies in England and Later Soliloquies* (New York:
Charles Scribner's Sons, 1920), p. 254.

[13] *Reason in Art,* p. 131.

[14] Ashmore, *op. cit.,* pp. 340 and 347.

value of our ideas will always come from the creative action of the imagination."[15] Again, in "A Brief History of My Opinions," he addressed himself directly to the notion that the imagination is bad, and reaffirmed his own conviction that the works of imagination "are good, they alone are good; and the rest—the whole real world—is ashes in the mouth."[16] In the same essay he voiced his general disagreement with William James by noting that James' "pictorial cosmology had the disadvantage of abolishing the human imagination, with all the pathos and poetry of its animal status."[17] In the first volume of his autobiography, *Persons and Places,* he reviewed his prevailing attitude toward life in these terms: "According to my youthful heart, existence was profoundly ugly and wrong. The beautiful remained imaginary. . . . That the real was rotten and only the imaginary at all interesting seemed to me axiomatic. . . . My philosophy has never changed."[18] In his most philosophical work he suggested that the imagination is the faculty which contributes most importantly to all human creativity: "The imagination which eventually runs to fine art or religion is the same faculty which, under a more direct control of external events, yields vulgar perception. . . . Poetic, creative original fancy is not a secondary form of sensibility, but its first and only form."[19] In *Dominations and Powers* he suggested that "Reason is itself a method of imaginative thought."[20] And, finally, in a letter written in 1951, he said: "Fictions, from those involved in sensation to those generated in play and in the liberal arts, seem to me the best of things and signs, when clear and beautiful, of a life being led in harmony with nature."[21]

[15] *The Sense of Beauty,* p. 191.
[16] Santayana, "A Brief History of My Opinions," reprinted in *The Philosophy of Santayana,* ed. Irwin Edman (New York: Charles Scribner's Sons, 1953), p. 5.
[17] *Ibid.,* p. 15.
[18] *Persons and Places; The Background of My Life* (New York: Charles Scribner's Sons, 1944), p. 172.
[19] *Realms of Being; One Volume Edition, with a New Introduction by the Author* (New York: Charles Scribner's Sons, 1942), pp. ix-x.
[20] *Dominations and Powers,* p. 463.
[21] *The Letters of George Santayana,* ed. with an Introduction and Commentary by Daniel Cory (New York: Charles Scribner's Sons, 1955), p. 413.

Whether or not one agrees with this account and estimate of the imagination and its works, there is absolutely nothing in Santayana's explicit statements concerning its worth to substantiate the proposition that he mistrusted the fine arts because they are imaginative. Indeed, the value, not only of art, but of life itself, according to Santayana is actually inseparable from the vistas and values which are imaginative. Of course, he recognized the possible dangers of imagination, and wrote, "If the imagination merely alienates us from reality, without giving us either a model for its correction or a glimpse into its structure, it becomes a refuge of poetic selfishness. Such selfishness is barren."[22] He warned also about the danger of mistaking the imaginary for what is real in a more substantial manner. But he also emphasized that one does not avoid these dangers by denying the existence or worth of the imagination; they are avoided only by recognizing the imagination for what it is.[23]

No less erroneous than the notion that Santayana could not value the arts because they are imaginative is the suggestion that "Santayana's view is veritably an economist's view of art."[24] Again I suspect that this conclusion is based on an inaccurate interpretation of Santayana's metaphysics. Since he was a self-confessed materialist—in the sense that he was convinced that whatever is has its matrix in, and is inseparable from, that "profound fertility and darkness" called matter—it might be concluded by one not a close student of his thought that he could value only material goods. Certainly this seems the only possible foundation for the suggestion. But the essential element of Santayana's thought in this respect was the Aristotelian maxim that everything ideal has a natural (material) basis while everything natural (material) has an ideal development. But Santayana was not at all a materialist in the sense that he sought and prized material existence and wealth above all else. However, he was by no means indifferent to economic security; for he felt that one is free to cultivate the greater values only when the material

[22] *Interpretations of Poetry and Religion,* p. 20.

[23] For a more complete discussion of the relation of the imagination to art and science in Santayana's thought see Willard E. Arnett, *Santayana and the Sense of Beauty* (Bloomington: Indiana University Press, 1955), Ch. III.

[24] Ashmore, *op. cit.,* p. 341.

foundations of life are relatively secure. It seems, indeed, quite clear that Santayana found the pursuit of material things some-what distracting; his books, food, clothing, and shelter were all he craved in the way of material goods. He distinguished between what he called the *natural* and the *spiritual* life, and between natural and spiritual morality. Natural life and morality are valuable primarily for the sake of the spiritual, not because the latter is superior but because it is the completion of the former. Natural morality, then, is concerned with those pursuits and values which are the very basis of animal life; but spiritual moral-ity seeks and develops the positive values of human existence—the expression of the human spirit in science, religion, and art. Without the development of spirituality, Santayana suggested, man's life is very little different from that of the animals. But neither the natural nor spiritual aspects of man's existence are separable from the life of reason, although it is evident that he considered the primary function of reason to be the attainment of security and harmony in the natural and material life; for after all these are the only foundation of all other values. Thus, reason is primarily and most essentially a method by which the urgent practical problems of man are solved and by which his internal life is reconciled with its circumstances. But reason is almost if not altogether vain unless it culminates in aesthetic and spiritual consummations, vistas, and values which are their own justification. Industrial art, then, or "doing artistically, joyfully, sympathetically, whatever we have to do," is really the founda-tion of life, although it is the most congenial foundation im-aginable. But beyond this, "grafted" onto the life of reason (and by no means alien to it but the fulfillment of it) is the free life of the mind, or the spiritual life of contemplation and imagination, exemplified particularly in the fine arts and religions. If fine art is useful, then—and certainly to deny its utility in this liberal sense seemed to Santayana a denial of all worth—it is not useful in any narrow or pragmatic sense. One needs only consider *The Realm of Truth,* and the impatience there with pragmatism, to realize how far Santayana's position is removed from what is commonly understood by thorough-going utilitarian and instru-mental concepts of value. Art at its best—in the fine arts—is useful, not as a means to other goods or values, but as the supreme expression of human aspiration and as the fullest realization of human capabilities. In Santayana's own words, "Art is action which transcending the body makes the world a more congenial stimulus to the soul. All art is therefore useful and practical, and the notable aesthetic value which some works of art possess, for reasons flowing for the most part out of their moral significance, is itself one of the satisfactions which art offers to human nature as a whole."[25]

Consequently, because of equivocation, it is wholly a *non sequitur* to argue from Santayana's defense of the utility of art that his is an economist's view of art. Certainly he perceived and noted that works of art are valued frequently for many of the same reasons that non-artistic objects are valued: rarity, use, the amount as well as the quality of human labor, and social and cultural circumstances are all factors that influence the evaluation (and price) of all human products, including the arts. But Santayana was also keenly aware that none of these is the most poignant or significant appeal of art to sympathetic appreciation, and turned his own attention almost completely to the spiritual aspects of the arts. He wrote, in *The Sense of Beauty,* that "The beautiful does not depend on the useful; it is constituted by the imagination in ignorance and contempt of practical advantage."[26] Even more significantly, so far as the question of his view of art in relation to economics is concerned, he observed in *Dominations and Powers* that "Architecture is a fundamentally economic art and more dominated than any other by its materials, its costs, and its practical uses. Yet its chief masterpieces have been always temples and palaces, triumphal gates and monumental tombs: edifices that a cynic might pronounce scandalously useless."[27] And though Santayana was ever a sceptic, he was much too human, sympathetic, and humble to be a cynic. He was not, perhaps, as indifferent to economic matters as is the stereotyped artist; he recognized the importance and complexity of both economics and man's endeavors in the arts. But he most surely did not in any

[25] *Reason in Art,* p. 15.
[26] *The Sense of Beauty,* p. 158.
[27] *Dominations and Powers,* p. 168.

measure anticipate or serve the notion that art is, except perhaps incidentally, of economic origin, determination, or interest. Of course, he often used the word "economy" in reference to the arts, as well as in regard to science, religion, and philosophy; but he was not referring to an *economy* narrowly conceived or concerned only with material goods; the economy of which the arts are parts is rather the total order or organization of being, the *divine economy,* of both the material and immaterial—an order which would provide a proper and beneficent place for all human needs and interests. To include the fine arts in *human economy,* then, is simply a way of insisting that the fine arts are not the whole of life but must exist harmoniously as parts of a totality where due consideration is given also to science, religion, and the material needs of man. Happiness and civilization are not attained or measured by man's power or dominion or material possessions, but "by the proportion of its energy which is devoted to free and generous pursuits, to the adornment of life and the culture of the imagination. For it is in the spontaneous play of his faculties that man finds himself and his happiness."[28]

It is argued by Mr. Ashmore that Santayana also mistrusted the fine arts because they have no moral commitment.[29] It is true, of course, that Santayana was a moralist, and that he sought moral values, natural or spiritual, in all areas of experience; it is also true that today the proposition that the fine arts are amoral, or non-moral, is widely accepted and defended. However, it is not true that Santayana thought that the fine arts are devoid of moral values or commitments. Indeed, as indicated earlier in this essay, Santayana did not even deny the moral value of aestheticism, although he suggested that the aesthete, because of the limitations of his interest, misses more than he ever finds in the way of moral fulfillment and value. The fact is that for Santayana the moral value of the fine arts is their chief claim to worth; of course, the fine arts contribute little or nothing to natural morality, i.e., to the discovery and propagation of codes or standards of conduct which are designed to enable man to avoid the most serious dangers of living. But in Santayana's view such morality

---

28 *The Sense of Beauty,* p. 23.
29 Ashmore, *op. cit.,* p. 340.

is essentially negative, and all the intrinsic and positive values of experience belong to the spiritual life—and the fine arts are instances of the purest and highest expressions of the spirit. Thus, for Santayana, any good which is not material belongs to the realm of moral values, and any good which does not serve some further end—which does not indicate a danger to be shunned or bring an increase of material benefits—is a spiritual good. The arts, then, are moral goods *par excellence*. Indeed, Santayana affirmed this again and again. In *Reason in Art,* for example, he wrote, "That art is prima facie and itself a good cannot be doubted."[30] And his approval of the fine arts seemed unqualified when he wrote that "a morality organized about the human heart in an ingenuous and sincere fashion would involve every *fine art* and would render the world pervasively beautiful."[31] Or, as Irwin Edman put it, the fundamental import of Santayana's philosophy is that "the combined competence and freedom, in a word, the creativeness of art, would, if incarnate in all the enterprises of men, be the principle of their morality."[32]

So it seems that the only point Mr. Ashmore might have appropriately made in this regard is that although art (as he understands it) cannot be legitimately criticized on moral grounds, Santayana nonetheless insisted that where such criticism is inappropriate, there is no significant art. The important question there, however, is not whether Santayana mistrusted the fine arts because they lack moral commitments (for he was confident of the moral significance and burden of the arts), but whether art is actually independent of the moral, and Santayana's judgments consequently ill-founded. Santayana may, of course, have been mistaken; it may surely be the case that moral judgments are irrelevant so far as works of art are concerned. But it is important, nevertheless, to indicate accurately what Santayana's position was. And Santayana was convinced that insofar as the fine arts contribute to or detract from the pursuit of happiness they must be judged morally. For "Happiness is the only sanction of life; where happiness fails, existence remains a mad and lament-

---

[30] *Reason in Art,* p. 166.
[31] *Reason in Art,* p. 223. Italics not in the original.
[32] Irwin Edman, "Introductory Essay," *The Philosophy of Santayana,* p. xli.

able experiment."[33] The context in which Santayana suggests that moral judgments of art are altogether appropriate and necessary is one which claims that happiness is the greatest good, and that happiness is achieved only when all human interests are harmoniously related, so that no interest or passion frustrates or blights another. "The principle that all institutions should subserve happiness," he wrote, "runs deeper than any cult for art and lays the foundation on which the latter might rest safely."[34] Or with a different emphasis: "To be bewitched is not to be saved; though all the magicians and aesthetes in the world should pronounce it to be so."[35]

The arts, then, according to Santayana, have actually a two-fold relation to the moral. First, and most importantly, the fine arts, as instances of the freest and highest expressions of the spirit, are supreme moral fulfillments of man's nature. But such expressions are not simply formal and empty structures which titillate the senses; they are rather recognitions and celebrations of human puzzlement and aspiration, of hope and despair; art is the comment by which spirit, entangled with the demands of the flesh and plagued by the imperfections of the world, redeems its own life from vanity and reconciles itself to its limitations and sufferings. For Santayana, if art is not moral, it is neither delightful nor meaningful. But, second, the arts are only parts of the totality of life, and whatever they are and do must, therefore, be consistent with the complex of conditions which makes life possible and harmonious. Santayana notes in *Reason in Art,* as he did in the *The Sense of Beauty,* that "We often come upon beauties that need to be sacrificed, as we come upon events and practical necessities without number that are truly regrettable."[36] But the arts, and the aesthetic experience, are not treated more severely than other elements of life. "Every impulse, not the aesthetic mood alone, is innocent and irresponsible in its origin and precious in its own eyes; but every impulse or indulgence, including the aesthetic, is evil in its effect, when it renders harmony impos-

---

[33] *Reason in Common Sense* (New York: Charles Scribner's Sons, 1905), p. 238.

[34] *Reason in Art,* p. 224.

[35] *Reason in Art,* p. 167.

[36] *Reason in Art,* p. 188.

sible in the general tenor of life, or produces in the soul division and ruin."[37] And it is only by means of a rational moral philosophy that one may determine which interests, and beauties, may be wisely indulged. If man's life were not subject to dangers—to hunger, exposure, and unnumbered distractions and conflicts of interest which confuse and hinder the spirit—or if the spirit could achieve perfect freedom, no moral necessities, no negative commandments, would impose themselves on him, and no evils would come to plague the innocence and delight of perception and fancy no matter how random and irresponsible. But in the world as it is, where the spirit is finite and inseparable from the flesh, and the flesh imperfect, "The *fine arts* . . . are vast instruments in the realm of matter, that *seem* to serve the spirit directly, apart from utility or truth; yet even they carry an immense load of impedimenta. All the technical, scientific, historical, social, local and temporal side of art . . . has nothing to say to the spirit about the Good. At best, the ground may thereby be cleared for a free spiritual life, which will begin where those distractions end. I do not mean where they end historically, for they can never end while life in this world continues. I mean where they culminate morally and provisionally and yield their spiritual fruits."[38]

So, according to Santayana, although the arts aspire to be free of moral commitments, to ignore practical consequences and to delight in the pure immediacy of image and sound and idea, life is in fact such that this ideal is both impossible and dangerous to attempt; for it ignores the complex pluralism of human life, and confuses a single good with the total good. It is not at all necessary, however, that art should conform to "a pre-existing rational dogma";[39] indeed, this, too, is dangerous. For the conditions of life, as well as the interests of the spirit, are both various and mutable; but it is necessary, if happiness is valued at all, that one's interest in and devotion to the arts be squared with whatever circumstances in fact prevail. "To criticize art on moral

[37] Santayana, "A General Confession," in *The Philosophy of George Santayana,* ed. Paul Arthur Schilpp (The Library of Living Philosophers, Vol. II [Evanston and Chicago: Northwestern University, 1940]), p. 21.

[38] *Realms of Being,* pp. 805-6. Italics not in original.

[39] Ashmore, *op. cit.,* p. 341.

grounds is to pay it a high compliment by assuming that it aims to be adequate, and is addressed to a comprehensive mind. The only way art could disallow such criticism would be to protest its irresponsible infancy, and admit that it was a more or less amiable blatancy in individuals, and not art at all."[40]

It is suggested, finally, that Santayana mistrusted the fine arts because they are "unnecessary in his conception of the stages of industrial and liberal art," and because they represent "an isolated and irresponsible impulse that would not integrate harmoniously with other impulses in a balanced ideal program for action in living. . . ."[41] Enough has been indicated above in regard to Santayana's ideas of the relation between industrial and liberal art, and of the place of art in the human economy, to render evident the misconceptions on which these statements are based. But there are three additional minor issues raised in Mr. Ashmore's article which demand brief attention.

First, it is said that so far as art is concerned, "Conformity with a rational program rather than exceptional ability" is most important to Santayana.[42] As indicated above, it is surely the case that Santayana regarded the role which the arts play in the total scheme of life more significant than any isolated instances of technical brilliance. However, he also made it clear that insofar as art is judged as art, technical achievements are fundamental. "The specific values of art," he wrote, "are technical values more permanent and definite than the adventitious analogies on which a stray observer usually bases his views. Only a technical education can raise judgments on musical composition above impertinent autobiography." And also, "what painters say about painting and poets about poetry is better than lay opinion."[43] Excellence, in art or in life, Santayana believed, is inseparable from skill, even as the worth of whatever is done cannot be divorced from the manner of performance. Furthermore, he was opposed to the use of any criterion in judgment of works of art which would exclude consideration of some elements in favor of others. "An intelligent

[40] *Reason in Art,* pp. 177-8.
[41] Ashmore, *op. cit.,* p. 347.
[42] *Ibid.,* p. 341.
[43] *Reason in Art,* p. 196.

critic must look *impartially* to beauty, propriety, difficulty, originality, truth, and moral significance in the work he judges."[44]
Santayana saw no conflict between the demand for exceptional
ability, or technical proficiency, and the principle that "in the
criticism of art . . . technical proficiency, and brilliancy of fancy
or execution, cannot avail to establish a great reputation. They
may dazzle for a moment, but they cannot absolve an artist from
the need of having an important subject-matter and a sane humanity."[45] No less than great achievements in science, achievements in art demand great ability; but the pursuit and use of art
and its creations, no less than the pursuit and use of science and
its products, require knowledge, discretion, and a recognition of
other values.

Second, it is said that, according to Santayana, "The creation
of beauty is not a function of the fine artist."[46] This statement
would be accurate enough if it said that the creation of beauty
is not the *only* function of the fine artist. But as it stands the
assertion seriously misrepresents Santayana's attitude toward the
relation of the fine arts to beauty. Although he felt that beauty
is more pervasive in nature than in the arts, and that the arts
have a more profound function than the embodiment of beauty,
Santayana nevertheless insisted that art at its best is inevitably
beautiful. "Aesthetic satisfaction . . . comes to perfect all other
values; they would remain imperfect if beauty did not supervene
upon them, but beauty would be absolutely impossible if they
did not underlie it."[47] Indeed, one of the most obvious instances
of Santayana's use of irony and ridicule is in the essay "Penitent
Art," which is fundamentally an effort to make clear the failure
of any art that forsakes beauty and aims instead at distortion; in
such instances, he suggested, "the poem remains a cry, the story
a dream, the building a glimpse, the portrait a caricature."[48]
Insofar as a work of art is not beautiful, then, it has failed to

44 Santayana, "What is Aesthetics," in *Obiter Scripta*, p. 37. Italics not in
the original.
45 Santayana, *Winds of Doctrine; Studies in Contemporary Opinion* (New
York: Charles Scribner's Sons, 1913 & 1926), p. 39.
46 Jerome Ashmore, *op. cit.*, p. 343.
47 "What is Aesthetics," in *Obiter Scripta*, p. 39.
48 "Penitent Art," *ibid.*, p. 161.

realize fully any other values it may have sought to embody or express. "Maxims in art are pernicious; *beauty is here the only commandment.* And beauty is a free natural gift. When it has appeared, we may perceive that its influence is rational, since it both expresses and fosters a harmony of impressions and impulses in the soul."[49]

Third, it is suggested that because art is "involved with sense and abstraction and therefore . . . unable to possess spirituality,"[50] Santayana could not approve of the arts. It has been emphasized already that Santayana regarded the arts as essentially spiritual. But it is possible, perhaps, to suggest more explicitly the manner in which they are spiritual. The spirit, said Santayana, being limited by its embodiment and by the character of its psyche, is often checked and frustrated in its natural functions; but in such instances the spirit has a resource that is denied other forms of life; that resource is this: "that it may discern and worship many a harmony not vital to its particular psyche, but contained in some other trope, larger or more abstract or otherwise concrete, such as poetry and music and the plastic arts present to the senses. . . ."[51] Or in other words, "In feasting the spirit on . . . its congenial food, the arts liberate it from what is felt as exile or captivity, and allow it for a moment to be itself."[52] Indeed, then, "Art . . . is more spiritual than dogma," and "the spirit is essentially free and always an artist and a poet."[53] Thus, the very core of Santayana's philosophy of art is that "art does not produce curiosities to be collected but spiritual necessaries to be diffused."[54]

Finally, it seems that Mr. Ashmore's thesis, that Santayana mistrusted the fine arts, is defended on the basis of two mistaken interpretations of Santayana's philosophy. First, he interprets Santayana's indictment of aestheticism as an indictment of the fine arts. This, I think, has been shown not to be the case. Of course, it is perhaps not altogether illegitimate by means of a

49 *Reason in Art*, p. 130. Italics not in the original.
50 Ashmore, *op. cit.*, p. 346.
51 *Realms of Being*, p. 734.
52 *Dominations and Powers*, p. 172.
53 *Realms of Being*, p. 726.
54 *Reason in Art*, p. 209.

stipulative definition, to identify the artist with the aesthete and the appreciation of art with aestheticism. But one who does so must also accept the full implications of such identifications. It would be a strange history of the fine arts—especially of literature and architecture, but also of music, painting, sculpture, and the dance—that could be written without reference to the social, political, religious, scientific, and moral facts and concepts which have influenced (and been influenced by) the directions and qualities of the arts. Certainly the aestheticism criticized by Santayana would find this an impossible task. Furthermore, a philosophy of the arts, or of criticism, as some contemporary critics admit, is virtually impossible without a contextual foundation.

Second, Mr. Ashmore misinterprets the relation between the various categories of Santayana's thought; he interprets spirit, reason, imagination, and sense as arranged in a kind of hierarchy. But Santayana made it clear that he intended no such hierarchy, but rather a harmony of these different functions of the human psyche. Certainly spirit, as Santayana conceived it, is not superior to reason ("Spirit is not the whole of life, only a child of the family."[55]), nor is reason superior to imagination, nor imagination to sense; each is only different from the others, and has a different and appropriate function. Neither reason, nor imagination, nor spirit could exist without the senses; and spirit may delight equally in the vistas of sense, reason, or imagination. Of course, and this is Santayana's fundamental point, the life perfected in all these areas is more complex; "and the richer and more complex the organism that attains . . . perfection, the more glorious its perfection will be. . . ."[56] But except for the undeserved felicity of nature, such perfection can be approached only through reason. Reason, then, is not the highest good, but the method by which whatever is valued is rendered as pervasive as possible in life and as secure as the flux of nature will allow. Therefore, "A rational severity in respect to art simply weeds the garden; it expresses a mature aesthetic choice and opens the way to supreme artistic achievements. To keep beauty in its place is to make all things beautiful."[57]

[55] *Realms of Being*, p. 759.
[56] *Dominations and Powers*, p. viii.
[57] *Reason in Art*, p. 190.

POSTSCRIPTUM

Tradition and Practice

GEORGE SANTAYANA

At a moment like this, when some of you stand on the very mountain-top of youth, your traditional education spread out on one side beneath you, on the other the prospect of practical life, and when the rest of us also stand there with you, in thought and by force of sympathy,—it might not be unnatural for some wise man, who had descended long since into the plains, if he were a practical man and something of a reformer, to speak to you in the following manner: "My young friends; you may think you have completed your education; you are mistaken; you are going to begin it. What you have hitherto learned is verbal and, even if true in its way, is not understood by you in its real or human value. The first thing you will have to do is to forget it all, and to learn the alphabet of hard fact, and the arithmetic of practical forces. Your character, if you have acquired a good one, will help you in the world; but your learning and your budding ideas will fade year by year, crowded out by a new wisdom which as yet you know nothing of."

George Santayana, "Tradition and Practice," *The Oberlin Alumni Magazine,* 1 (1904), pp. 4-14; reprinted by permission. Commencement Address at Oberlin College's seventy-first Commencement.

It is in some such way that a man schooled in affairs might perhaps address you; but being nothing but an academic person myself I may be excused if I put the matter somewhat differently. Life after all, is made up of all its periods and the world of all its activities; and youth, too, has its ultimate moments. College is a part of the world, containing in miniature almost all its problems, and the world, if we use it intelligently, is nothing but a second university, another school of friendship, labour, and thought. In this half-hour in which I have the privilege of addressing you, I should like to dwell on this affinity between education and life, between tradition and practice. There is naturally a close connection between receiving something important from society and the past and rendering back something useful to society and to the future. You have heard a thousand times the demand that education should be practical, that traditions should not be insisted on and kept alive artificially, when they have no further function in actual life. You have also heard a thousand times, I am sure, that a man's life should be one of service to the world, that he should measure his own success by the degree in which it enables him to help others. As I repeat these familiar maxims I may seem to be turning a discourse, which presumably ought to be festive, into a class-room lecture or a downright sermon. But perhaps if we put those two commonplaces together we may get a somewhat more speculative idea, one that may well serve to light up the double vista greeting us on this occasion. This idea is that while tradition is only valuable when it is helpful in practice, practice itself is only valuable when it is fertile in tradition—that is, when it helps to create or bring to light something ideal, which can be transmitted from man to man, and from generation to generation.

In the modern world, and especially in America, tradition and practice appear in an anomalous relation. Both exist; both are powerful and complicated; yet they are in a way separated. Tradition flourishes almost unchallenged in the mind, while practice concerns itself chiefly with things material. The historical ground for this anomaly is very clear: if we divide tradition into three great streams—the literary, the religious, and the scientific—only the last, the scientific or economic tradition, which is a short tradition as yet, is native to our society: the other two come to us from alien races and remote periods of history. They were vital elements in civilizations which as a whole are dead; and surviving, as they do, in ours, they have in them something abstract and adventitious; we have to learn them like a foreign tongue. They influence our life, rather than express it; they endure as traditions to which we may give ourselves up more or less heartily; but the more we do so the more we seem to withdraw from practice and suggestions, to the abstract mind and its traditional lore. Here are two most remarkable facts—anomalies if we compare them with what is the case in most nations, and what must be the case with humanity at large—that our literary models are in dead and foreign languages, and that our religion is one to which our ancestors had to be converted, and which we need to be instructed in. Neither tradition is native; neither flows inevitably and of itself from our contact with nature and the spontaneous reflections of our minds. Only the third great stream of tradition—the scientific and economic—has grown up in our race under conditions such as those we still live in; and accordingly this third tradition hardly seems such; it seems rather part and parcel of the constitution of things. But science is a tradition, as government is: and if you or I had to begin a survey of nature for ourselves we should never arrive at a hundredth part of the knowledge needed to invent and construct a steam-engine, or to have our lives insured.

All tradition might conceivably be native in this same way. When a child is born he begins at once to educate his senses; he learns by groping to spell the external world and to attach himself to whatever in it helps to awaken his instincts, and to satisfy them. He explores house and field; he makes experiments in social intercourse, establishing his firm little allegiance and enmities—to parents, playfellows, strangers, and dolls. If we could imagine him growing up quite independently, yet shielded from all dangers as yet too grave for him, he would soon have a poetry, a science, and a morality of his own. Fantastic as these would doubtless be in their form, they would all centre around actual experience and somehow express it: his life, practical and imaginative, would be all of a piece. So poets actually feel the world.

Convention has little power over them, either to impress on them useful things for which they do not care, or to choke off their native insights. It was largely in this way that the Greeks, that childlike and self-taught people, worked out their myths and their science; so that both were beautiful and legitimate, and even true, in so far as experience could as yet avail to control them.

What happens to our children, what happened to ourselves, when we embarked in childhood on this great voyage of discovery? We were led aside—of course, to be instructed—but we were led aside into regions not contiguous to what we could see or appreciate; our souls were transplanted from their native soil and bidden to bear fruits of very singular and alien grafting. I suspect that much of what I have in mind may not have fallen to your lot in the same aggravated form in which it fell to mine. Your teachers have, in many ways, brought education nearer to experience; they have sought in kindergartens and in nature-studies, in manual and economic training, to develop what was present to your senses and lead up without break to activities which were to be yours in future. It is a merit of Protestant Christianity to solicit religion rather than to impose it. It knows how to mould creeds to moral feeling, as this changes its emphasis, and it strives to represent throughout an inner personal impulsion. But suppose that these reforms had not taken place—and at best they are only partial—what would have happened to the child when he went to school and began to absorb tradition? He would have been ushered into hearsay worlds, real perhaps in themselves, but coming to him in the guise of superfluous fictions. These reports may find his imagination more or less receptive; they may entice him, as fairy-tales do, and make him wish he might wake up some fine morning in the world they describe; but I am not sure that it is when they are most welcome that they are most beneficial. Suppose he hears, as I did in my boyhood—and very gladly too—that in this world which he had just begun to spell out and find his place in, there is nothing really important; that to be dissatisfied here is only what is to be expected, for he is a pilgrim and stranger; that the earth is a vale of tears; that close above it, accessible at every turn, there is a supernatural realm, where his true pleasures should live; that there he can have his real friends and his real conversations; that there all his fortunes are mysteriously prepared and will have their miraculous and incalculable issues; so that he begins to walk the earth with a certain incredulity, and to translate its facts, as he meets them, into his own mystical language, reading into them values directly contrary, possibly, to those which they ostensibly have. This new mystical life may offer a congenial fourth dimension for his fancy to spread in; in those supernatural vistas he may discover something kindly and good, a needful refuge from his impotence or loneliness in the real world. But what a struggle in his heart! What an oscillation there must be in his allegiance between this world, in which he cannot well play his part without taking it seriously, and the other world, which he has been drawn into by an incidental tradition! But this is only the beginning of his distraction; another tradition remains behind.

Scarcely, indeed, has he accustomed himself to his double life and learned to speak his two languages together in a way intelligible, at least to himself, when he is led into a third universe. He begins to study the history and literature, perhaps even the philosophy, of Greece and Rome. As most often happens, the boy is merely pestered with what to him is a blind labour, producing a formal sort of knowledge soon happily to be unloaded on an examination paper and forgotten: but if he is quick and imaginative, with some premonitions in him of what a pure humanity might be, he very likely feels attracted to those masterpieces, and falls in love with that civilization, ancient in date, but more than modern, where moral interests are concerned, by its enterprise and freedom. But these classic memories and suggestions cannot be connected in the student's mind either with his own experience or with his religious instruction. Those early heroes are not pictured as doing anything which he himself might do. Those poetic and rhetorical passions do not express his family life, his public duties, nor his private problems and destiny. All is a mere fairyland, a literary tradition about exotic and distant things, surely not uninteresting in themselves, eloquent, very likely, to his speculative mind, but out of all relation to his practical existence.

Such was not the situation out of which those masterpieces

themselves first grew. They were the work of young people, like the American, but people who, unlike the American, had no conscious traditions reaching far behind their youth. They were native products, in every fibre expressions of human nature at first hand. Suppose a copy of Virgil, such as our school-children use, could reach the poet in whatever honourable limbo we may fancy his spirit to inhabit. Would he not be at a loss to understand how things could have come to such a pass among us that we should compel ourselves to study a dead language and to read hundreds of verses none of which can have a native ring in our ears? "Is it possible," he might ask, "that you pretend to form your taste and mind by reading poets in a foreign language? What profit can you find in so artificial an exercise? Is it that you value our religion? No. Rome and the world it conquered perished more than a thousand years ago, and the piety with which I tried to express, in myths which to you have lost all their sanctity, her origin and spirit, is not piety for you: it is archaeology. Have you, then, no poets of your own to recast my patriotism and wisdom, so dressed that you may relish them—for the high passion and dignity of my lines must have been lost with their music? One would think your nations to be without arts: yet if you were wholly barbarous, how could you know the value of culture or go to the extreme pains which so tortured and sterile an education must involve? We Romans, to be sure, used to study Greek; but it was then a living tongue, spoken widely in our own dominions: we had nurses and native masters to teach it to us; we learned to speak it glibly, and found it afterwards useful when we became praetors and proconsuls in the East. Besides, we and the Greeks were kindred peoples, with a similar religion and polity, which in many ways had been developed in Greece more perfectly than in Latium, so that to us Greek literature was something better than native and more truly appealing—it was ideal. But you, to my astonishment, seem to sacrifice for a glimpse of unattainable excellence, and philosophies which you cannot apply to your affairs, whatever comfort, strength, and solid religion a homely education might bring. The Gauls and Germans, the Iberians and Britons of my day, though rude and unhappy, had an honest, patriotic pride which I cannot discover in you.

They despised our traditions, so long as they defied our arms. No one among them, unless he wished to flatter Rome and was at heart a traitor, would have given his sons my poems to read. How comes it that your peoples, who have nothing to fear from our power, are still enslaved by our minds?"

What could we say to Virgil if he spoke to us in this way (as in all seriousness I believe he would) and what apology could we offer for the fact that we still read him? We should have to explain to him the whole riddle of our history: we should have to confess that only our young scientific and economic tradition is the fruit of our own genius: that for high things in literature and religion we still lean upon antiquity, sometimes, as in religion, venturing to adapt that tradition to our needs, and seeking to apply it in practice, sometimes, as in literature, almost abandoning the attempt to continue what we accept from the past, but keeping that past mummified and lifeless, to be the object of a contemplation called philology. And when he protested again at such behavior on our part, and threatened to hurl the word barbarous at us once more, not for our science and machinery, which he would immensely respect, but for our philology and our dependence on dead tradition—we should have to add this further explanation. We do not cling to tradition because it is old; it is not the barbarian's conservatism that makes us worship something conventional apart from ideal uses which it may have had in our own day. No: it is our incapacity so to exhaust and digest experience for ourselves as to rediscover what is eternally true in those traditions, that in them which is still vital in the world. We are in too great haste to understand ourselves, hence we must take for self-expression, and as a substitute for a mastery of experience which we dare not attempt, the self-expression and mastery of ancient, calmer spirits: we must let them still speak for us, because they still speak for us better than we are able to speak for ourselves. Virgil would be less surprised that we puzzle over his pages, if he knew the character of our own literature. Even seen through a veil, his world is clearer and more beautiful than ours. Even disfigured by our pedantic approach to it, his mind seems so majestic, exquisite, and true, that we can find nothing better for a model. His verses, sputtered in a barbarous mouth, are still our standard of excellence: his country's ruins are our best type of greatness: his religion, though not sacred to us as to him, remains the mould of our fancy, without which thought would lose half its symbols and nature half her amenity.

If our traditions, then, are in any way burdensome, if we are obliged to lean on them too much, it is only because we have not learned to draw tradition enough from our own practice. It is because the present yields so little as yet to the spirit, that the spirit looks behind to those heroic nations which knew how to make all things pay tribute to the mind. It was a smaller world, a quieter world, perhaps, that they were able to master: it brought them, for that very reason, more quickly to ultimate things. And for that reason, too, it is not possible for us to profit by their dominion directly. The principle of it we can adopt and reapply: the solution they gave is, in its form, inapplicable to us. Therefore, when we adopt it literally, it is apt to remain in the region of mere words. This, as it seems to me, is the great defect of our traditional education: it is a verbal education. And this is not because the objects with which our literature deals—be it sacred or profane—were themselves empty: no thought is further from my mind than that. The subject matter in both cases was living, it was momentous, it was engrossing; so engrossing, momentous, and living, that it made up, in each case, a whole world, with its own morality and civilization, with its own complete philosophy. But as neither of those worlds is ours, the literatures that express them do not educate us for our own life. They annex something to it; but this something is apt to remain a dead letter, seeing that we should have to transport ourselves out of our age and clime, if we were really to accept it practically and intelligently.

And what happens? We agitate ourselves amid these influences for a few years, while our verbal education is going on; but graduation comes: the real and sunlit world beckons us to begin an education through action. This is the point you have reached today; and many of you, I am sure, without any conscious dissatisfaction with what has gone before, look forward to the change with a high emotion, with the sense of power now for the first time to be really exerted, and real forces now for the first time to be met. You are eager to be done with tradition: it is practice you feel that will free your souls. Such a premonition cannot well be deceptive. It may be frustrated by chance in one or another of you, for in the most brilliant victories many fall by the way; but it can hardly be frustrated on the whole for a race and a generation that feels it distinctly. Much less can it be frustrated in America, where an altogether unprecedented career is open to human effort. This country has had the privilege of beginning with all the advantages of tradition and with none of its trammels. The advantages were a seasoned moral character, a religion free from gross superstition, possessed of the various practical arts and crafts current in Europe, and an almost empty continent in the temperate zone. Under such conditions practice ought to yield fruit quickly, and not to be much misinterpreted by the traditions to which it gives rise. Such traditions have in fact arisen—first in politics, and industry. New and appropriate moulds have been given to political and industrial life which not only secure efficiency but which engross intellect and inspire emotion. American life, every one has heard, has extraordinary intensity; it goes at a great rate. This is not due, I should say, to any particular urgency in the object pursued. Other nations have more pressing motives to bestir themselves than America has: and it is observable that not all the new nations, in either hemisphere, are energetic. This energy can hardly spring either from unusually intolerable conditions which people wish to overcome, nor from unusually important objects which they wish to attain. It springs, I should venture to say, from the harmony which subsists between the task and the spirit, between the mind's vitality and the forms which, in America, political and industrial tradition has taken on. It is sometimes said that the ruling passion in America is the love of money. That seems to me a complete mistake. The ruling passion is the love of *business,* which is something quite different. The lover of money would be jealous of it; he would spend it carefully; he would study to get out of it the most he could. But the lover of business, when he is successful, does not much change his way of living, he does not think out what further advantages he can get out of his success. His joy is in that business itself and in its further operation, in making it greater and better organized and a mightier engine in the general life. The adventitious personal profit in it is the last thing he thinks of, the last thing he is skillful in bringing about; and the same zeal and intensity is applied in managing a college, or a public office, or a naval establishment, as is lavished on private business, for it is not a motive of personal gain that stimulates to such exertions. It is the absorbing, satisfying character of the activities themselves: it is the art, the happiness, the greatness of them. So that in beginning life in such a society, which has developed a native and vital tradition out of its practice, you have good reason to feel that your spirit will be freed, that you will begin to realize a part of what you are living for.

At the same time, these congenial and ideal activities into which you will pass—what is called business, in the widest sense of the word—will still fail to contain all that would be ideal and congenial, it will leave certain powers in you unexercised, powers which in college, perhaps, you once felt you possessed and had begun to exercise. Your business, even if it be the business of teaching or of managing a college, will, as things now stand, look chiefly to material results. The question will be how many buildings you can put up, how many graduates you can turn out, how many books you can publish, and how many athletic victories you can score. To gain material results of this sort is itself an ideal object: without a material basis nothing spiritual can exist, or can reach expression; but the material basis is a basis only, as the body is in personal life, and when that has been rendered vigorous and healthy, the question still remains what further functions you are to give to your soul. There is, as the ancients said, a vegetative soul: it was very profound in them to see that vegetation also is spiritual, and that to perfect material instruments is already to embody an ideal. But the vegetative soul, in man, is only a background and a potentiality: the moral and intellectual functions must be superposed upon it. Will your business life, as you are likely to find it, supply adequately these moral and intellectual functions? Will you never have a pause, as for a Sabbath, and turn a speculative eye upon regions distant and serene? Will you not long sometimes for a holiday in the country, for solitude, for abstraction: thinking in that way to revert to something deeper and higher than your ordinary thoughts? Probably you will: and it is then that at church or in your library or in the woods, you will call back those sacred and remote traditions into which you were initiated in your youth: you will feel the need of them, and sigh, perhaps, for their painted worlds. In that case one thing will be plain: the tradition grounded on your daily practice and embodied there—the scientific, economic, political tradition of our age—will not have sufficed for your daily life. You will need something more, and the question is how you are going to get it.

And at this point, in bringing my discourse to a head, there is one thought I would urge upon you. You will never solve the problem satisfactorily or in a stable manner, you will never contribute to a truly sacred human tradition, so long as you are content to append your higher ideals, like postscripts, to your life. I once had a friend who feeling that there might be something narrow in his profession of glass-blower, thought he would go to Europe, as he expressed it, to pick up culture in the galleries. He went; but I could observe no conspicuous culture sticking to him on his return, and he is now blowing glass without it. Even if he had acquired it, it would have been a private possession, that would have gone with him to his grave. Suppose instead he had staid at home and spent his savings in buying books about glassware, and making experiments in more beautiful and appropriate forms to be given to glasses and bowls; he would have become a really cultivated man, one whose conversation any one would have been glad to listen to, and he would have established a better tradition in his art, one that might have made a difference for generations. Many a man, to take another example, absorbed in business and carrying it on in total abstraction from human feeling, may be most affectionate at home: he makes up to himself there for the inhumanity which he shows to the world. To the world, however, he never makes it up. His affectionate feelings are his self-indulgence, his self-deception: out of his public practice there flows no sweeter or kindlier tradition. It is time, perhaps, that by way of exception some great employer should deny himself a home and a family, as the monks did; that he should live among his workmen, in sight of the factory, so that his humanity might have a chance to spread itself out there, to beautify the places where life is at white heat; and such an employer, when his friends asked him where he lived and what was his family, might point like a sort of a masculine Cornelia to the happier colony about him and say: "These are my children." The principle is the same which the Apostle expresses when he says that whether we eat or drink we should do it for the glory of God: and while a certain alternation and rhythm is necessary in human life, and we must intensify our religion at certain moments, giving it more marked expression on some days and on some occasions than on others, that is merely a physical necessity: it is not the ideal of religion that it should be a thing apart and an escapade, as it were, from existence. Nor is that the ideal of any art; yet there are some people so ill-educated that when they have something to say, say it in the most imperfect and bungling fashion, and then, when their matter is exhausted, put in a rhetorical peroration, by way of showing that they too can be eloquent if they choose. But they prove the opposite, for their mouthings are as little eloquent as their crudities were; since eloquence does not consist in displaying a vocabulary when there is nothing to say. Eloquence is rather the essential rounding out of a thought, as you bring clearly to light the facts and emotions that justify it. You cannot be eloquent unless you are intelligent, and if you seem so, it will be only to those who are unintelligent themselves. Eloquence and art, religion and kindness, do not flourish in water-tight compartments: there needs to be a vital circulation among them if any of them is really to live.

It would therefore be a mere expedient, a sop thrown to Cerberus, if you appended one or more ideal interests to your practical life. In so far as you do so, you merely chill your practice, making it vulgar, unfruitful in liberal traditions, while at the same time you keep your ideality visionary and thin. The remedy, which it will take centuries to make thoroughly efficacious, but which every one may apply in a measure for himself, is simply to deepen practical life, to make it express all its possible affinities, all its latent demands. Were that done, we should find ourselves in unexpected and spontaneous harmony with the traditions which we might seem to have disregarded. For those ancient and alien traditions have survived because they express, each in its language, something which has a meaning at all times, something essentially human. Had our humanity, under its own conditions, found a full expression, it would have repeated unawares those accepted truths. If we then read Virgil, having come round to him in the natural development of our interest for all things human, we should love him for celebrating so loyally things also interesting to us: agriculture, and its cosmic emotions; nationality, with its deep springs and sacred responsibilites. For that is what Virgil is talking about: that is what Virgil is, not a labyrinth of syntax and prosody. In the same way our religious traditions would recover their rights, in the measure in which we found them prophetic of our deepest necessities. All traditions have been founded on practice: in practice the most ideal of them regain their authority, when practice really deals with reality, and faces the world squarely, in the interests of the whole soul. To bring the whole soul to expression is what all civilization is after. We must therefore be patient, for the task is long; but the fields are always white for the harvest, and the yield cannot be insignificant when labourers go forth into the harvest with the high and diligent spirit which we divine in you.

Index